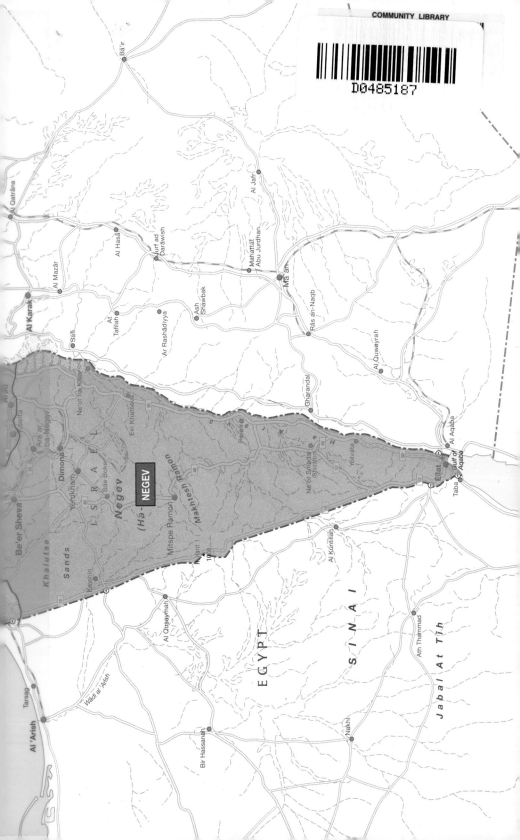

INSIGHT GUIDES
ISRAEL

Contents

THE BEST OF ISRAEL: TOP ATTRACTIONS

From the key sites of Jerusalem's Old City, Bethlehem and Nazareth, rich in history and spiritual significance, to the altogether lighter pleasures of the coast and a Dead Sea mud bath.

△ **Sea of Galilee.** This is really a lake surrounded by a halo of mountains and overlooked from its bountiful shores by towns, villages, and holy places. See page 194.

◁ **Mediterranean coast.** From the ancient ports of Yafo and Akko to Tel Aviv's fashionable seafront and the Mount Carmel hillside, Israel has 200km (125 miles) of golden sun-soaked beaches. See page 205.

△ **Bethlehem.** Picturesque Palestinian hilltop town overlooking the Judean Desert where the Church of the Nativity marks the birthplace of Christ. See page 272.

△ **Nazareth.** Bustling Galilee city and location of the Church of the Annunciation built on the site of Mary and Joseph's home. See page 180.

△ **Red Sea.** Incredible marine life and coral formations make the closest tropical waters to Europe a diver's paradise. See page 309.

△ **Safed.** A Galilee hilltop enclave of bohemian artists and Orthodox Jews overlooking the Meron mountains, where the mystical texts of the Kabbalah were once penned. See page 183.

▽ **Lowest point on Earth.** 400 meters (1,300ft) below sea level, the Dead Sea's excessive salt content enables bathers to float, while its unique mixture of minerals alleviates skin and respiratory problems. See page 281.

△ **Dead Sea Scrolls.** On display at the Israel Museum is the oldest known version of the Old Testament and other ancient scriptures. See page 173.

▽ **Geographical diversity.** The only land link between Africa and Europe/Asia and the continental divide of the Atlantic and Indian Oceans is within Israel's small confines, with deserts to the east, forests to the west, and unique flora and fauna. See page 127.

▽ **Jerusalem's Old City.** Inside the 16th-century walls lie the Church of the Holy Sepulcher, where it is believed Christ was crucified and resurrected, the Dome of the Rock, where Muslims believe Mohammed ascended to heaven, and the Western Wall, the only remaining structure from the Second Temple. Also enjoy the colorful Arab market. See page 137.

THE BEST OF ISRAEL: EDITOR'S CHOICE

The unique sacred attractions of the Land of the Bible, absorbing museums, a dynamic culture, sun-soaked beaches, breathtaking landscapes... here, at a glance, are our recommendations for a memorable vacation.

The Western Wall.

FREE ISRAEL

Holy Sites. The Western Wall and most of the major churches charge no entrance fee. See page 141.

Yad Vashem Holocaust History Museum. This harrowing exhibition of man's inhumanity documents the Nazi era and the extermination of European Jewry. See page 174.

Jewish National and University Library. On the Hebrew University's Givat Ram campus in Jerusalem, see the papers in which Einstein first scratched out his theory of relativity. See page 174.

Baha'i Shrine and Gardens. It costs nothing to tour the gold-domed shrine and the world's longest hillside gardens on Mount Carmel in Haifa, but you must book in advance. See page 219.

The Baha'i Shrine.

BEST BEACHES

Bograshov Beach (Tel Aviv). Enjoys a prime location in the heart of the city – but it gets crowded on Saturdays and public holidays. See page 240.

Sheraton (Separated) Beach (Tel Aviv). This is gender-segregated for religious bathers and for women who don't want to run the risk of being pestered by men. See page 241.

Hof Ha-Carmel (Carmel Beach). Haifa's most popular beach can be found close to the city's southern entrance. See page 216.

Caesarea. Bathe amid the Roman and Crusader ruins. See page 225.

Coral Beach. South of Eilat, snorkelers and divers seek out coral formations. See page 309.

Eyeing up the goods in Jerusalem's Old City.

BEST MARKETS

Jerusalem's Bazaar. Jerusalem's Old City market offers the essence of the Middle East. Enter from either Jaffa or Damascus Gates. See page 138.

Makhane Yehuda. Savor the noise and smells and enjoy the fresh fruit, vegetables, and spices of Jerusalem's leading food market. See page 172.

Carmel Market. Tel Aviv's leading market for food, clothes, and vendors' witty banter. See page 243.

Flea Market. Located in Yafo, this is the country's most popular antiques market. See page 246.

Bedouin Market. Thursday morning in Be'er Sheva is the time to buy a camel, goat, or Bedouin bric-a-brac – or just to watch the spectacle. See page 295.

TOP VIEWS

East Talpiyot Promenade. Spy not only the golden glory of Jerusalem but, in winter, the Jordan Valley too. See page 171.

Azrieli Center. From atop one of the three tallest buildings in Tel Aviv, you can see much of Israel (on a clear day). See page 251.

Mount Carmel. Meander along the Yefe Nof Promenade and enjoy the view of the bay. See page 214.

Masada. The Herodian fortress provides a breathtaking view of the Dead Sea moonscape. See page 285.

Mitspe Ramon Visitors' Center. A splendid view of the massive desert crater with its millennia of geological layers. See page 303.

The Azrieli Center.

BEST WALKS

Jerusalem's Old City. Vehicles cannot negotiate the narrow alleyways anyway. Enter by the Jaffa Gate and turn right in the Arab souk into the Cardo, the ancient Roman thoroughfare. See page 137.

Valley of the Holy Cross. Start from the Monastery of the Holy Cross, head for Jerusalem's Sacher Park, the Knesset, Israel Museum, and Hebrew University. See page 174.

Tel Aviv Promenade. From old Yafo (Jaffa) in the south to Tel Aviv Port in the north, stroll the vibrant seafront. See page 240.

Old Akko. Take in the Crusader walls, fishing port, and Arab market. See page 205.

Mount of the Beatitudes to Ein Tabgha. You don't have to be a practicing Christian to enjoy this delightful stroll down a hillside track to the Sea of Galilee. See page 195.

Tel Aviv promenade and the marina.

Ultra-Orthodox Jews reciting the Tashlich prayer by the Mediterranean, an act of "throwing away" their sins during the days of repentance between Rosh Hashanah and Yom Kippur.

Harvesting olives in the West Bank.

Praying at the Russian Orthodox
Church of Mary Magdalene in
Jerusalem.

Making Yemenite pankcakes in Tzfat.

THE PROMISED LAND

Israel defies indifference; its long history
draws visitors, but the real attraction is
its great diversity of people.

*Crucifixes for sale in
Nazareth.*

Israel is intense. Few locations offer as much per
square kilometer to sustain the spirit, feed the intel-
lect, and stimulate the senses. It is a place where three
continents – Africa, Asia, and Europe – meet, and the
landscape and the people are a fusion of these three continents, a sometimes infuriating mixture of conflict and
harmony. After all, this is the Promised Land to which,
it is said, Moses led the Children of Israel. It is where
Abraham forged his covenant with God, Christ preached
his sermons, and Mohammed ascended to heaven.

You don't have to be a believer to savor all this. The
miracles may be a matter of personal faith, but what
can't be disputed historically is that this is the land of
the Bible, the cradle of monotheism, a geography familiar from childhood religious instruction. The names
resonate in visitors' minds and stimulate their curiosity:
Jerusalem, the Galilee, Bethlehem, Nazareth, Yafo, Jericho, and the River Jordan.

At the site of the Temple you can pray at the one remaining wall the Romans left intact. You can walk along the
Via Dolorosa to the Church of the Holy Sepulcher. You
can visit the El-Aqsa Mosque on the Temple Mount where
the Prophet Mohammed came to pray during his lifetime.
Around the River Jordan you can drink in the atmosphere
of a place where so much history has been made in the
past two millennia – most recently, the emergence of modern Israel, "the
Jewish State" and the focus of much recent conflict.

*Young Israeli at the Druze village
of Daliyat el-Karmel.*

The enduring attraction

The empty stretches and open blue skies of the Arava and Negev Deserts
aside, this is one of the world's most densely packed pieces of real estate.
Israel's population is more than 8 million, while over 4 million Palestinians live in the adjoining Gaza Strip and West Bank. For many visitors,
the enduring attraction of Israel is its people – the inheritors of the rich
tapestry of many invading cultures that have woven their history into
the region.

Contrary to perceived stereotypes, most Israelis are neither right-
wing religious zealots nor left-wing Peace Now activists. Most are

middle of the road, more concerned about the performance of Tel Aviv's stock market, their favorite soccer team, or the Israel Philharmonic Orchestra. One attribute shared by all Israelis, whether they are religious or secular, of European or Afro/Asian origin, right-wing or left-wing, Jew or Arab, is a desire to talk to strangers. In chatting to tourists, Israelis may simply be wanting to practice their English, vent their anger at Israel's perceived misrepresentation in the international media, or, more conventionally, sell something or spend time with a good-looking visitor.

The ruins of Sebastya.

Whatever the motivation, Israelis are undeniably friendly. They can also be incredibly rude and abrasive, though this should be viewed within the context of their candid behavior and tendency to treat even passing strangers like "family." Israelis are known as sabras, after the indigenous prickly-pear fruit, which has a spiky, tough skin but is delicious, soft and juicy inside.

Israelis consider themselves to be part of Europe, although in fact the country, via the Sinai peninsula, forms the only continental land bridge between Asia and Africa.

The European illusion is maintained in the spruce streets of Tel Aviv and Haifa, while because of Israel's geopolitical isolation from the Arab world, the country is permitted to be an associate member of the European Union and a full member of most European institutions, including the UEFA soccer federation and Eurovision. Palestinians get in on the act, too, frequently describing themselves to visitors as European Arabs.

צאתכם לשלום

Go in Peace

رافقتكم السلامة

Sign at the Dead Sea.

However, from the narrow alleyways and markets of Jerusalem's Old City to the stunning desert landscapes of the Dead Sea – at 400 meters (1,300ft) below sea level the lowest point on earth – the cultural and physical landscape is clearly not Europe.

The missing peace

Of course, the major blot on the landscape is the failure of Israelis and Palestinians to reach a lasting peace. Don't be deceived by off-the-cuff angry and chauvinistic comments by each group about the intransigence of the other side. Visitors who engage in more extended conversation with Jews and Arabs will be surprised to discover how much enthusiasm, desire, and goodwill there is toward reaching a compromise, even if it is only because of a lack of stomach for the alternative.

The garrulousness and infectious energy of its people ensure that Israel is seldom boring. The hedonistic visitor seeking sunshine, golden beaches, and nightlife, the nature lover in search of desert vistas and unique flora and fauna, and the historically curious seeking remains from biblical, Roman, or Crusader times will not be disappointed. Most of all, religious visitors will usually come away with their beliefs reinforced, while non-believers have been known to return home with glimmerings of a faith they didn't have when they set out on their journey.

Hiking trail along the Ein Bokek River.

The Dome of the Rock and the Western Wall.

ISRAEL TODAY

Despite divisions between left and right, religious and secular, Ashkenazi and Sephardi, Jews and Arabs, the country's democracy remains robust.

Israel confounds expectations. It is a nation rooted in religion, yet the majority of the Jewish population are brazenly secular, turning to religion only for births, bar mitzvahs, weddings and funerals. There are picturesque bastions of orthodoxy in Jerusalem, in Bnei Brak near Tel Aviv, and elsewhere that are a quaint mixture of medieval Poland and the Middle East, but for the most part long rabbinical beards are rare, many restaurants serve forbidden unkosher foods, the Sabbath is barely observed, and women dress anything but modestly.

It is the army generals rather than the rabbis who have forged the nation's values. Modern Israel is a nation whose military has a peerless reputation for executing the swift, the precise and the dramatically unexpected. Yet the ubiquitous Israeli soldier, rifle slung casually over his shoulder, appears slovenly and unregimented. This informality extends even to the Israel Defense Forces (IDF), but it was these long-haired paratroopers, unshaven officers

A Tel Aviv cyclist wears his heart on his wheel.

Proportional representation acts as a political safety valve, allowing all population groups to be represented in parliament and holding the balance of power between the major blocs, although often granting the small parties disproportionate powers.

and pot-bellied reservists who undertook the Entebbe rescue, bombed the Iraqi nuclear reactor and triumphed in the Six Day War.

Vigorous democracy

Israel's greatest achievements, however, have not been on the battlefield. A nation has been created out of immigrants from more than 80 countries, who shared a religious heritage and a desire to return to their ancestral homeland, but little else – not even a language. In the street you will hear an astonishing Babel of languages: Russian, English, Arabic, Amharic, Hungarian, French, Persian, Spanish, and Yiddish. Hebrew, the language of the Bible, has been resurrected and adapted to everyday life.

Even more surprisingly, parliamentary democracy has flourished – despite the fact that most Israelis originate in countries with no experience of such democracy; despite the frictions between religious and secular, right and left, Arab and Jew; and despite the centrality and power of the army. Even when Prime Minister

Yitzhak Rabin was gunned down in 1995, there was no danger of the sovereignty of the Knesset (Israel's parliament) being overthrown.

If a general seeks political power, he does not plan a coup d'état, as might happen elsewhere in the world, but resigns his commission and enters the political fray. And the chances of success are good: before becoming prime minister Yitzhak Rabin and Ehud Barak were both chiefs of staff in the Israel Defense Forces, while Ariel Sharon was a high-profile general.

Civil rights, freedom of the press, and an independent judiciary further reinforce demo-

grape vines, cotton fields and well-watered lawns. But, come November, the rains begin, and occasional snowfalls can cover inland hills. Flash floods in the desert uproot trees and shift boulders. By spring the countryside is ablaze with flowers and fields are as emerald as Ireland. The land, like its people, is in a state of constant flux and renewal.

In-gathering of the exiles

The essence of this ongoing change is *aliyah*, Hebrew for immigration. Over the past 25 years more than 1 million immigrants have reached

A Passover meal brings families together.

cratic values in a country that takes pride in flouting authority and disobeying regulations.

Organized chaos

So, the eye may initially see Levantine chaos and Mediterranean madness, but beneath the surface is a society that functions effectively. The wars have been won, the desert has bloomed, high-tech industries compete in world markets. From a socialist base, a dynamic capitalist economy has been built with sustained economic growth, enabling Israel to enjoy high living standards.

The diverse landscape and climate complement the heterogeneous nature of the people. The heat of the summer leaves the country parched and brown except for the ripening

GAINS AND LOSSES

The role of Israeli women, like that of their counterparts in the West, has changed in recent decades. They have cut the umbilical cord tying them to their homes but have not escaped entirely from their traditional roles. They are expected both to pursue a career and to raise a family, which many do successfully, but they have lost ground in other areas. On the kibbutzim, women once undertook the same jobs as men, however tough; today they tend to be found in the kitchen and the kindergarten. In the army, women fought as frontline troops for Israel's independence, but today they do not occupy combat positions, although some are now training as pilots.

Israel from the former Soviet Union alone. Over the same period, 60,000 immigrants have come from Ethiopia. This represents 12 percent of Israel's population.

The process has been tackled with relish, though inevitably there are problems. The Russian-speaking newcomers have been assimilated easily into the country's economic life but often remain culturally apart. They are highly secular (over 300,000 of them are not recognized by the rabbinate as Jewish because only their fathers are Jewish, or their Judaism is in doubt) and tend to have right-wing political views. Many

and Romania out of the ashes of the Holocaust; from Iraq, Syria, Yemen, and North Africa escaping Arab anti-Zionism; from Latin America and Turkey fleeing military juntas; from Iran escaping the ayatollahs, and most recently from the Soviet Union and Ethiopia.

There has also always been a steady flow of immigrants from North America, Europe, South Africa, and Australia – immigrants prepared to forgo comfortable lives to rebuild Zion. Golda Meir, prime minister from 1969 to 1974, grew up in America, while former president Chaim Herzog was born in Belfast. There are prejudices

Soviet immigrants arriving in the 1990s.

Tasty bites at the Cordelia Restaurant in Old Yafo.

are highly educated scientists, engineers, musicians, or artists.

The exception to this rule is the Jews who came from the former southern Soviet republics of Uzbekistan and Azerbaijan and the Russian Caucasus. The economic profile of the Bukharian and Mountain Jews has more in common with Ethiopian Jews than their compatriots from European Russia. Like Ethiopian Jews, the older generation struggles to adjust to Israel's high-tech society and is seldom assimilated, but their children try hard to become Israeli and bridge the gap.

Israel is good at blending waves of newcomers into its society. Jews came from Russia before the revolution; from Germany and Austria fleeing the Nazis; from Poland, Hungary,

against newcomers, but immigrants can reach the top despite their awkward Hebrew.

Nurtured by government attempts toward social integration, the cultural mosaic becomes a melting pot. Contemporary Israeli music reflects a fusion between East and West. Strange food combinations include falafel and chips, goulash and couscous, chicken soup and kubbe.

A stable economy

David Ben Gurion built Israel's economy around the powerful Histadrut trade-union movement. Onto this socialist base – which encompassed agricultural production through the kibbutz collectives and moshav cooperatives, much of the health service, and many industrial conglomerates that included the country's largest bank – a dynamic capitalist system has been grafted. In the 1980s, three-digit inflation caused chaos, but starting from 1986 the economic order was restored, with Western levels of inflation and economic growth averaging 6 percent from the early 1990s. However, while Israel's financial system remained robust throughout the global economic crisis that began in 2008, the country's high rate of exports, 46 percent of GDP, meant that the recession began to bite in 2009, although by 2010 the country was again recording 5 percent annual growth.

of the professions, but capitalism rules and the widening gap between rich and poor is surpassed in the West only by the US. '

But Israel must export to survive and big business argues that competitive-edged capitalism is needed to sell goods abroad. In its formative years this was no easy task with polished diamonds, Jaffa oranges and other agricultural produce failing to earn enough foreign currency to support a Western standard of living. Contributions from world Jewry, German compensation for the Holocaust, a limited tourist industry, and, from the 1970s, US government

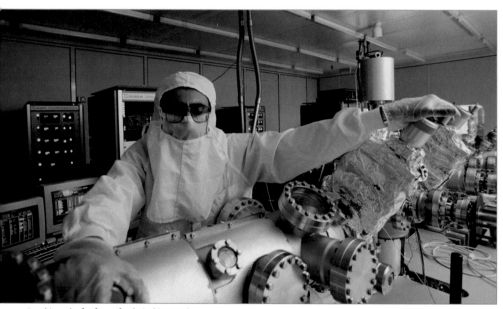

Israel is at the forefront of technical innovation.

The Histadrut was in steady decline for many years selling off almost all its business assets but has revived snice the social justice protests of 2011 with many new service industries unionizing..Union membership today is remarkably universal, from the blue-collar industrial workforce to senior management and members

> In the 1980s, when three-digit inflation raged, Israelis spoke of their "muddled" economy as opposed to the "mixed" economies of Western Europe; yet Israel has shed its socialist economic heritage and become aggressively capitalistic.

EXPORT EXPERTISE

In contrast to polished diamonds, of which Israel exports US$19 billion a year, and where the rough stones must be imported, high-tech goods have high added-value. Israel also continues to export US$1.5 billion worth of agricultural produce a year and a similar amount in its inputs like irrigation equipment. The country also exports nearly US$5 billion a year of natural resources – minerals from the Dead Sea and phosphates from the Negev Desert. About 41 percent of goods are sold to Western Europe, 23 percent to North America and 21 percent to the Far East. Israel has negotiated tariff-free trade deals with the EU and North American nations.

Missiles fired on southern Israel by Hamas and northern Israel by Hizbullah have reduced the inclination of most Israelis to relinquish the mountainous West Bank, which overlooks central Israel.

defense aid enabled the country to balance its books. But, with wars and mass immigration, it was always a struggle.

The picture changed dramatically in the 1990s. The emergence of high-tech in the global econ-

economically dependent on Uncle Sam, Israel would find it difficult to thrive without US diplomatic support, and the country also needs advanced American weaponry (especially with the potential threat of a nuclear Iran).

The elusive quest for peace

The main anxiety caused by dependence on the US concerns peace and territorial compromise. Many Israelis fear that US pressure to hand back more land to the Arabs will leave Israel vulnerable to future attack. The return of the Golan to Syria, for example, which the US has

2011 saw people take to the street in mass protests for social justice.

omy was a godsend for Israel, which was always strong on technological innovation. More than half of the US$67 billion of goods that Israel exports annually are advanced technology systems, military and security systems especially.

Israel also enjoys an income approaching US$3 billion a year from donations by the country's Jewish and Christian supporters. In addition, aid from the United States amounts to nearly US$3 billion a year. This aid began in the 1970s when Israel was perceived as an important ally against the USSR, and was once a vital source of income for Israel. Today, not only has the sum been gradually reduced, it has also become only a small proportion of Israel's national budget. However, although no longer

pressed for, is strongly opposed, even more so since the outbreak of civil war there. Giving up Sinai for peace with Egypt was one thing; it is now a vast, demilitarized desert providing an effective tripwire should Egypt ever want to attack, but the Golan Heights and Mount Hermon tower menacingly over northern Israel.

Peace with the Palestinians poses the greatest challenge. The two sides seem further apart than ever as shown by the fighting in Gaza in 2014, with religious and nationalist extremism growing bilaterally over the past decade. US President Barack Obama seems unable to broker a breakthrough and neither the Israelis nor the Palestinians are yet in the mood for territorial compromise.

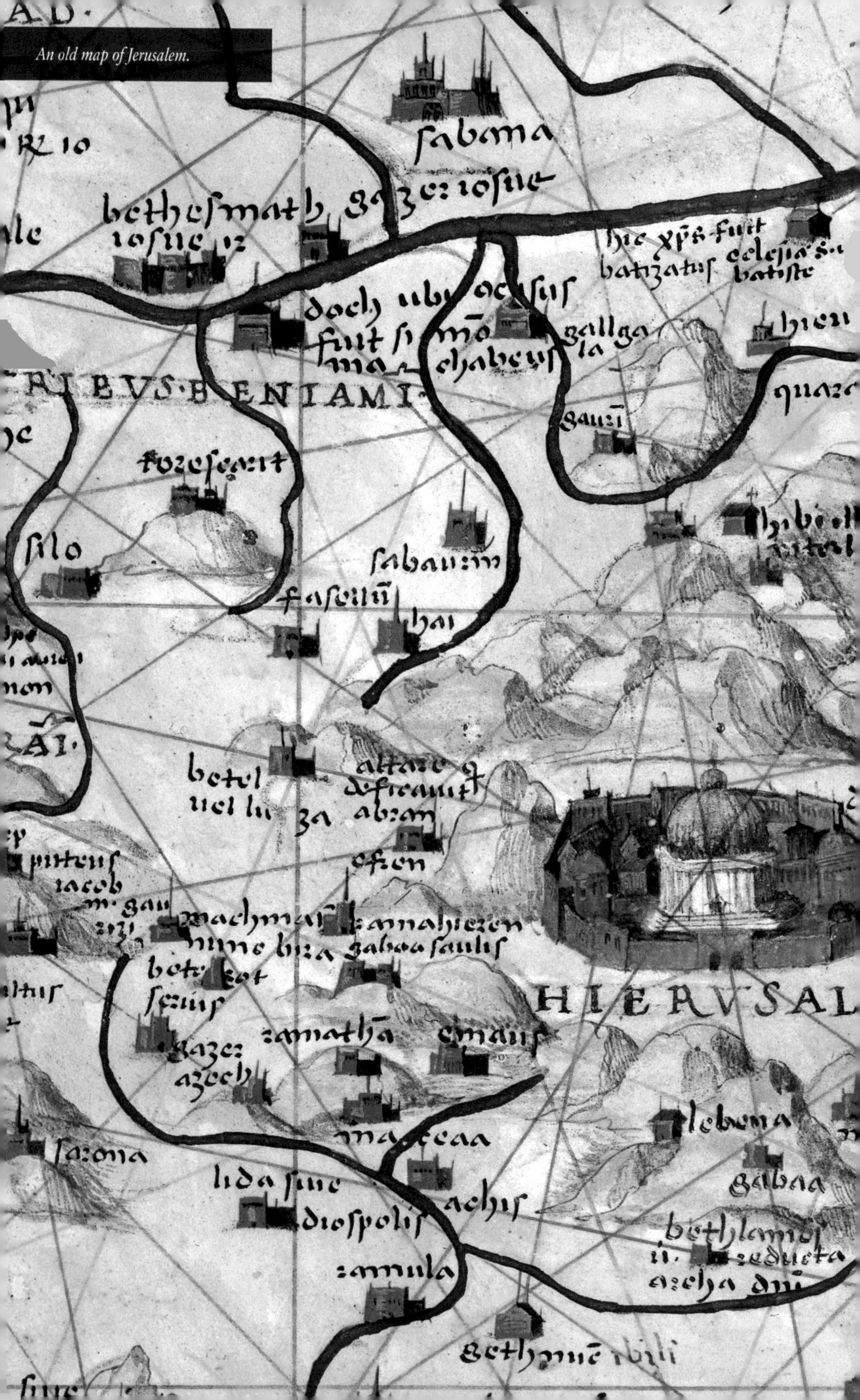

An old map of Jerusalem.

MARE MORTVM SIVE SODOMORVM.

adama

bethagla
genesis so

herodum ii sepultus
est herodum

herodum
ii sepultus
fuit herod
magnus

s. san
ba

bethlia

TRIBV·TV

tecue
s. agaton

iesus

bethlen

pesua
cbion

emma
ommisealfas sionr
s. olias

pastores

s. rachelis
domus iacob

channe
bethiartan

s. rachel

damus
cicodinii

bezach

nechelescos

s. cruz

TRIBVS.
SIMEON

bethsum
humichi
si celech

tapnata

ceila

astaoli

om ii fuerint
pulti machabei

saraa
eleuto
polis

VBVS DAN

moi
mes

DECISIVE DATES

10000 BC–6000 BC
Some of the world's first human settlements are established in the Jordan Valley, Judean Desert, and Mediterranean coast.

3000 BC
Canaanite city kingdoms develop based on Mesopotamia–Egypt trade.

The Biblical period
c.2000 BC
Abraham settles in Be'er Sheva.

c.1280 BC
Moses leads Israelites out of Egypt.

c.1225 BC
Joshua captures Jericho.

c.1000 BC
King David declares that Jerusalem will become his capital.

c.950 BC
King Solomon builds the First Temple.

586 BC
The First Temple is destroyed after the Babylonians conquer Jerusalem and send the Jews into exile.

546 BC
The Jews return to Jerusalem after the Persians defeat the Babylonians.

520 BC
The Second Temple is built.

63 BC
The Romans conquer Judea.

The Dome of the Rock.

37 BC
King Herod assumes the throne, founds Caesarea, and rebuilds the Second Temple.

The Christian era
c. AD 30
The crucifixion of Christ.

66
The Jews revolt against Rome; the Romans recapture Jerusalem after a long siege and destroy the Temple.

132
Bar Kochba's revolt against the Romans fails, and most of the Jews go into exile.

325
Constantine, the Byzantine emperor, converts to Christianity. Palestine is recognized as the Holy Land, and Constantine's mother Helena arrives a year later to identify the sacred sites.

The Muslim conquest
637
Fired by the new religion of Islam, Muslim armies conquer Jerusalem.

691
The Dome of the Rock is built on the Temple Mount.

1009
Fatimids destroy the Church of the Holy Sepulcher.

Crusaders, Mamelukes, and Ottomans
1099
The Crusaders establish the Kingdom of Jerusalem.

1149
The current Church of the Holy Sepulcher is consecrated.

1260
Mamelukes take control of the Holy Land.

1291
The last Crusader stronghold in Akko falls to the Mamelukes.

1492
Many Jews return to the Holy Land after expulsion from Spain.

1516
The Ottoman Turks capture Palestine.

1541
Suleiman the Magnificent completes the construction of Jerusalem's walls.

1799
Napoleon occupies parts of the Holy Land.

The birth of Zionism
1878
The first Zionist settlements are established.

1897
Theodor Herzl convenes the first-ever Zionist Congress in Switzerland.

Yad Vashem Holocaust History Museum.

1917–18
The British capture Palestine and publish the Balfour Declaration favouring "the establishment in Palestine of a national home for the Jewish people."

1925
Large-scale Jewish immigration from Europe.

1945
The full horrors of the Holocaust become known. Survivors emigrate to Palestine but many are imprisoned by the British in Cyprus.

1947
The UN votes for the partition of Palestine into Jewish and Arab states.

The establishment of Israel

1948
David Ben Gurion proclaims the State of Israel and becomes first prime minister.

1950
The Law of Return guarantees the free immigration of world Jewry. The Jordanians formally annex East Jerusalem and the West Bank, and Egypt takes the Gaza Strip.

1956
Israel captures and returns the Sinai following Suez campaign.

1967
Israel captures East Jerusalem, the West Bank, Gaza, the Sinai, and the Golan Heights during the Six Day War.

1973
The Yom Kippur War.

1978
Egyptian President Anwar Sadat visits Jerusalem. An Israel–Egypt peace treaty is signed the following year.

1982
The First Lebanon War expels the PLO leadership from Beirut but leaves Israel mired in Southern Lebanon for nearly 20 years.

1987
The first Intifada begins.

1993
Prime Minister Rabin and PLO chief Yasser Arafat shake hands at the White House.

1995
Rabin is assassinated.

2000
Palestinian leader Yasser Arafat rejects Prime Minister Ehud Barak's offer of most of

War damage in Gaza, 2012.

the West Bank and Gaza and East Jerusalem. The second Intifada begins.

2005
Israel withdraws all Jewish settlements from the Gaza Strip.

2006
Prime Minister Ehud Olmert launches the Second Lebanon War against Hizbullah militants.

2007
The Palestinians are left divided after the West Bank is taken over by Arafat's successor, President Abu Mazen, the head of Fatah, and Hamas stages a military coup in Gaza.

2008
Israel launches a brief war against Hamas in Gaza in an attempt to stop missiles being fired into Israel.

2012
Another brief round of fighting between Israel and Hamas ends in stalemate.

2014
Yet again Israel tries to defeat Hamas with the Gaza rocket threat extended over almost all of Israel. Tension and violence erupts in Jerusalem over the right of Jews to worship at Temple Mount.

Moses as imagined by Joos van Gent (*c.*1435–*c.*1480).

THE DAWN OF CIVILIZATION

The early history of Israel, familiar to many through biblical stories, laid the foundations of Jewish faith and sowed the seeds of future conflict.

The dusty desert sign on the highway down from Jerusalem points northwards to "Jericho – The World's Oldest Known City". At the northern tip of the town is a rather unimpressive series of wooden fortifications. Remarkably, scientists estimate that these fortifications were built 9,000–10,000 years ago.

Evidence suggests that mankind first established farming communities, and the other trappings of civilization as we know it, several thousand years before that. Caves in the Mount Carmel range near Haifa on the Mediterranean coast have yielded jewelry and agricultural implements from 12,000 years ago.

But, as the remains at Jericho indicate, 7000 BC was an important moment in the evolution of Neolithic man. In the 1980s Israeli archeologists discovered a treasure trove of artifacts dating from this period in a cave in the Judean Desert 48km (30 miles) south of Jerusalem. The find, which includes woven fabrics, agricultural tools, decorated human skulls, carved figurines, and painted masks, is on display in the Israel Museum. From these objects, anthropologists concluded that late Stone Age man was far more advanced than had previously been believed.

According to Genesis

Such archeological evidence is anathema to ultra-Orthodox Jewry, which has always insisted that the Creation took place nearly 6,000 years ago. By then, both ancient Egypt to the southwest and Mesopotamia to the northeast had been established as powerful and sophisticated civilizations. Canaanite tribes emerged about 5,000 years ago, founding city-kingdoms based on trade.

About 4,000 years ago, the Book of Genesis relates, Abraham, the son of a wealthy

Abraham and the Angels by Tiepolo (1692–1770).

Mesopotamian merchant family in the city of Ur (today in Iraq), became the first man to recognize a single deity. Rejecting the idolatry of his father, he traveled westward and pitched his tent near Be'er Sheva.

Abraham is today revered as the father of monotheism. But although he believed in one God, he did not keep to just one woman; had he done so, the world might have been a less complicated place. The Arab and Islamic heritage traces its roots to Abraham through his first son, Ishmael, born to his concubine Hagar, while the Judeo-Christian lineage can be traced back to Isaac, Abraham's second son, born to his wife, Sarah.

Sibling rivalry, Genesis tells us, compelled Abraham to cast out Hagar and Ishmael, whose descendants would forever bear enmity to the offspring of Sarah's son Isaac. Even a complete atheist would have to admit that the Bible got that right. The precise location of Abraham's tent is not known – which is probably just as well, for his burial site, the Tomb of the Patriarchs in Hebron, has seen far too many corpses: Jews and Arabs have massacred each other in Hebron throughout history.

The Children of Israel

Of Isaac's twin sons, Esau and Jacob, the latter was also known as Israel (Hebrew for "he

out of bondage, across the Red Sea and through the wilderness. During the Children of Israel's 40 years wandering in the wilderness Moses was given the Torah, including the Ten Commandments, on Mount Sinai. His successor, Joshua, took the Children of Israel back to the Promised Land, scoring his first success in the Battle of Jericho in 1225 BC.

Though the Israelites defeated the indigenous Canaanites and settled on the inland hills, making Hebron their capital, they were unable to conquer the coastal plain where the Philistines in the south and the Phoenicians

Scenes from the Story of Abraham in the dome of St Mark's Basilica, Venice.

struggles"). The name was given to him after a dream in which he fought with a stranger, who is believed to have been God. All told Jacob had 12 sons and one daughter whose descendants are known to us as the Children of Israel.

Jacob's son Joseph prospered in Egypt, where he became a senior advisor to the Pharaoh. He was re-united with his family after a drought compelled them to look for food and shelter in the Land of the Nile. The Book of Exodus relates how successive generations of Pharaohs subsequently enslaved the Children of Israel.

In one of the most enduring of all biblical narratives, Moses, the Israelite, led his people

LAYING THE FOUNDATIONS

It was during Joshua's era that many of the tenets of Judaism were first established. The festival of Passover (Pesach), held in the spring, recalls the Exodus from Egypt, and the miracles that preceded it, while Pentecost (Shavuot) marks the giving of the Torah to Moses on Mount Sinai.

Religious Jews today congregate at the Western (Wailing) Wall for dawn prayers at Pentecost, after spending the night studying the holy book. The Feast of Tabernacles (Succot), which is also known as the Festival of Rejoicing, recalls the 40 years spent in the wilderness and celebrates the joy of returning to the Promised Land.

in the north reigned supreme. The historical importance of these peoples, especially the Phoenicians, who had migrated from Greece, is often overlooked.

The Phoenicians, who settled in the cities of Akko and Tyre in northern Israel and southern Lebanon, are believed to have devised the first alphabet and invented glassmaking. And the Philistines in Ashdod and Ashkelon in the south were skillful metalworkers who were able to manufacture sophisticated weaponry.

The Israelites coexisted with their coastal neighbors, sometimes trading, sometimes fight-

Philistines, though he did win access to the Mediterranean.

Most importantly, in historical retrospect, David conquered a Jebusite hilltop enclave, a fortress settlement that he decided would make an excellent new capital. So he moved his court and administration there from Hebron and called his new capital Jerusalem. The city also helped unite the 12 tribes because it was located on neutral territory.

David's son Solomon became renowned for his wisdom. He consolidated his father's achievements and extended the Israelite

A medieval view of Solomon and Sheba.

ing. Led at first by warrior-judges such as Gideon and Samuel, they felt the need for a king who would strengthen the people by uniting the tribes. Saul was selected, and he set the scene for the golden age that his successor David was to bring about.

The establishment of Jerusalem

David ascended the throne a little over 3,000 years ago. A scholar, poet, and notorious womanizer, he secured his place in history through military prowess and leadership, extending the Israelites' borders to the Red Sea in the south and Syria in the north. But despite his early victory over the mighty Goliath, with a slingshot, he was unable to vanquish the

empire down to the Arabian peninsula and northeastward to the Euphrates. He inherited his father's taste for beautiful women, and sealed strategic alliances by marrying princesses. His exact relationship with the Queen of Sheba remains unclear.

Most significantly, Solomon constructed the resplendent Temple to house the Ark of the Covenant, the focus of Jewish faith that was believed to contain the actual tablets of the Ten Commandments given to Moses on Mount Sinai. A stroll around Jerusalem's Temple Mount today conveys what a vast building it must have been.

Despite his reputed wisdom, Solomon left no strong successor. Soon after his death tribal jealousies resulted in civil war and the secession of the 10 northern tribes who set up their own state, known as Israel in Samaria. The southern state of Judah, based on the tribes of Judah and Benjamin, remained faithful to Solomon's descendants. For two centuries an uneasy coexistence prevailed.

This was the age of the prophets. Isaiah attacked corruption, and Elijah denounced the idolatrous cult of Baal introduced by Israel's King Ahab and his wife Jezebel. In 722 BC Israel fell to the Assyrians, and the people were dispersed. The fate of the "Ten Lost

A 1493 illustration of Jerusalem's destruction under Babylonian rule.

Tribes" is still unknown, and people in every corner of the globe occasionally claim descent from them.

The southern state of Judah survived by accepting Assyrian hegemony, and this status quo endured for 150 years. Its end was foretold by the prophet Jeremiah, who preached gloom and doom and the destruction of Jerusalem.

By the waters of Babylon

Jeremiah's prophecies came true in 586 BC: the Babylonians, led by Nebuchadnezzar, sacked Jerusalem, destroyed the Temple, and transported the elite of Judah to Babylon. In fact, this exile only lasted 40 years, until the Babylonians were defeated by the Persians, whose leader Cyrus the Great allowed all exiled peoples back. The Temple was rebuilt, but the glorious age of Solomon was not recaptured. Judah remained an obscure Persian province for the next two centuries.

The balance of world power moved west to Europe, away from Egypt, Assyria, and Persia. In 333 BC Alexander the Great conquered the region, and Greek rule began. For several centuries the Jews were allowed freedom of worship, but policies gradually became more obtrusive, culminating in the 2nd century BC with the sacrificing of a pig in the Temple and the prohibition of Jewish rituals such as circumcision and the observation of the Sabbath.

Armed resistance led by the Hasmonean family known as the Maccabees saw the Greeks defeated and Jewish control over Jerusalem restored. In 164 BC the Temple was rededicated, a victory celebrated to this day during the festival of Hanukkah.

The Roman Empire

The subsequent century of Jewish sovereignty saw prosperity, as past glories and lands were recaptured. But this taste of freedom was then

> *"By the waters of Babylon we sat down and wept when we remembered Zion." In Psalm 137 an exiled poet wrote the oft-quoted lines.*

lost for 2,000 years. In 63 BC the Romans conquered Judah, which, as Judea, was subject to the decree of the Roman governor of Syria but remained an autonomous province with its own kings. The best known was Herod the Great, who reigned from 37–4 BC, and was given extra territory, expanding his kingdom to include all of Israel and much of today's Jordan. He rebuilt the Temple and constructed grand new cities, such as Caesarea on the coast, which he dedicated to Rome's leader. But Herod and his successors were ruthless despots who even killed their own children in their paranoia over potential conspiracies. Oppressed by Rome and its merciless vassal kings, the Judeans were ripe to be influenced by messianic preachers.

The Crusader Arch at sunset, Caesarea.

The Madonna and Child.

EMPIRES AND EXILES

Successive empires conquered, flourished, then
disappeared, while the Jews were scattered across
the globe without a land of their own.

The son of a Galilean carpenter, Jesus Christ
had a limited impact in his own lifetime, at
least in Jerusalem. Few historical accounts
even mention him, and the best-known contemporary historian, Josephus, devotes only a few
sentences to an obscure Galilee preacher. The
Romans felt threatened enough to execute him,
although in those days of massacres and constant
bloodshed that fate was no great distinction.

But a devoted band of Christ's followers were
convinced that their leader was the messianic
savior the Jews craved. In the following decades
the determination of these disciples was to
change history. Christianity spread north and
east to Armenia and Byzantium, and southward, taking root in Africa, especially in Egypt
and Ethiopia, and subsequently took hold in
Rome and the rest of Europe.

The Jews themselves were unimpressed. For
them Christ remains just one of a string of false
messiahs, distinguished only by the fact that so
many Gentiles accepted his teachings and interpreted them as good reason to persecute the

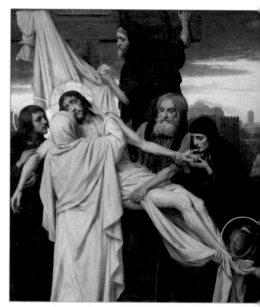

*An extract from Josef Janssens' "Seven Sorrows of the
Virgin" cycle.*

Masada was the most famous of the
fortresses that resisted the Romans. The 10th
Legion conquered the hilltop stronghold in AD
73 but were denied the satisfaction of
capturing its nearly 1,000 inhabitants, who
committed mass suicide.

Jews themselves, who were branded as Christ-
killers. There is no historical evidence that the
Jews conspired in the crucifixion of Christ, but
when Rome subsequently embraced Christianity a convenient scapegoat was needed to draw
attention away from its own culpability. The

claim that the Jews were Christ-killers became
the basis for anti-Semitism down the centuries.

Zealotry and defeat

Not that the Jewish establishment of the time
would have shed a tear at Christ's execution.
The aristocratic Sadducees, who controlled the
priesthood, and the scholarly Pharisees, who
interpreted the law, would have regarded Christ
– those who were aware of his existence – as an
undesirable subversive element.

The Essenes might have been more impressed.
This ascetic cult was in all likelihood a big
influence on Christ's philosophy. As a result,
the Essenes' culture and writings in the Dead

Sea Scrolls (which are displayed in the Israel Museum and include the oldest known version of the Old Testament) are of major interest to Western society.

The Zealots would have been too wrapped up in the nationalist struggle against Roman occupation to pay much attention to a Galilean preacher. Increased Roman oppression, most notably the decision by the Roman emperor Caligula to have his image installed in the Temple, strengthened the Zealots' popularity.

In AD 66 the Jews rebelled. The Romans imported hefty reinforcements and the revolt was slowly crushed: by 69 only Jerusalem and several fortress outposts were holding out, and after a year-long siege Jerusalem was captured. The Romans sacked it, burning the Temple and carrying its sacred contents back to Rome. The city was renamed Aelia Capitolina and all vestiges of Jewish culture were destroyed, except one retaining wall of the Temple, the Western Wall, left standing to remind the Jews of Roman sovereignty.

A failed Jewish uprising against the Romans in 132, led by Simon Bar Kochba, saw most Jews executed, sold into slavery, or exiled, and

An 1847 painting depicts the taking of Jerusalem by the Crusaders, July 15th 1099.

EMPRESS HELENA'S ROLE

After Emperor Constantine the Great embraced Christianity in the 4th century, his mother, Empress Helena, became an enthusiastic convert to the new religion, and played a key role in its dissemination. It is believed that she made a pilgrimage from Byzantium in the 4th century in order to identify the principal sites of Christendom, and to initiate the construction of shrines in these places. These holy sites include the Church of the Nativity in Bethlehem, the Church of the Holy Sepulcher in Jerusalem, and the Church of the Annunciation in Nazareth, all sites that are revered by most branches of Christianity to this day.

this date is often considered as the start of two millennia of exile.

Jewish culture continued to flourish, especially in the Galilee. The Mishna, the Talmudic commentary on the Old Testament, was written by sages in Tiberias in the 2nd and 3rd centuries, while rabbinical scholars in the Mount Meron region near Safed penned the mystical texts that comprise the Kabbalah. But as Christianity took root in the region, after being embraced by Emperor Constantine the Great and the Eastern Roman Empire early in the 4th century, the Jewish presence in the Holy Land dwindled into insignificance. From that point until modern times the glory of Jewish culture was to be accomplished in what became known as the Diaspora.

From Christianity to Islam

It is one of the great ironies that in the Holy Land, where Christ was born, preached, and died, Christians have remained a small minority. By the 5th century they did form a majority, but the Roman Empire was already crumbling. The Persians temporarily conquered the region in the 7th century (before the Byzantines reasserted control), and from 634–7 the Arab followers of Mohammed swept through the region, converting many to Islam. Mohammed's emphasis on the Oneness of God and the need to revive Jewish rituals such as circumci-

Crusaders and infidels

Islamic control of the Holy Land especially irked the Christians of Europe. As a result, during the 11th century the Pope inaugurated a series of Crusades which saw Christianity in possession of virtually the entire Holy Land by the end of the century, with the Kingdom of Jerusalem formally established in 1099 under King Godfrey (who died of illness the following year and was succeeded by his brother Baldwin). The Dome of the Rock was commandeered as the headquarters of the Templars, while the El-Aqsa Mosque was transformed into a church.

sion and dietary laws struck a popular chord.

Islam and the Arab world have coveted the Holy Land ever since. Abraham, the father of the Arab people, is buried in Hebron, while Mohammed is believed to have made a journey on horseback, after his death, to the Temple Mount in Jerusalem from where he ascended to heaven. In 691 Caliph Abd Al-Malik, horrified by the neglect of the Temple Mount, built the Dome of the Rock over the supposed site of Mohammed's ascension. Several decades later the El-Aqsa Mosque was built on the southern section of the Temple Mount. Jerusalem was now sacred to three major religions – Judaism, Christianity, and Islam – attracting pilgrims from all three. But if individuals were content to visit, others wanted not only to come and see but also to conquer.

The ostensible aim of the Crusades was to fight the infidel, but in reality the Crusaders slaughtered far more Christians than non-believers. En route, especially in the Balkans, they laid waste to entire Orthodox Christian communities. In the Holy Land itself, Christian villagers turned out to greet their supposed liberators, only to be put to the sword. Although the Crusaders were sponsored by the Church, many of their number were motivated by imperialist ambitions.

The Crusaders built a network of hilltop fortresses, from Nimrod in the north to Jerusalem in the south, and ruled until 1187, when the Egyptian leader Saladin was victorious at the Horns of Hittim in the Galilee. Slowly the Europeans lost their foothold in the Holy Land. Even Richard the Lionheart, who led the Third

Crusade in 1188, could not turn the tide. Four more Crusades delayed the inevitable, but in 1291 Europe lost St Jean d'Acre (Akko), its last stronghold in the region, to the Mamelukes, who in their turn had defeated Saladin.

Mamelukes and Ottomans

The Mamelukes are the least remembered of the Holy Land's conquerors. For nearly 250 years these slave warriors of the sultans of Egypt, who had been brought from Asia to train as elite soldiers, ruled over the region from Egypt to Syria. Despite its ornate architecture,

Jewish scholars in Jerusalem, early 20th century.

this was an era of decline from which the Middle East has never fully recovered. As Europe flourished and America was discovered, the balance of world power slipped away from the Eastern Mediterranean.

The rise of the Ottoman Turks stopped the rot, at least for a while. The Holy Land, too, regained some luster after the Ottoman conquest in 1516. Suleiman the Magnificent, who ruled from 1520 to 1566, revived the region's economy and built the walls around the Old City of Jerusalem.

However, from the 17th century the Ottoman Empire went into a decline that was to last for 300 years. The Holy Land gradually became a semi-desert, and Jerusalem degenerated into

a crumbling village. The Ottomans, like the Mamelukes before them, ruled Palestine as a province of Syria, further belittling the status of the region in general and Jerusalem in particular. Voltaire, in his philosophical dictionary compiled in the mid-18th century, described the city as a barren wilderness of rocks and dust.

Napoleon's brief conquest of parts of Palestine in 1799 spelled a revival of interest in the Holy Land by the European powers. As the Ottomans weakened, the British and the French vied for hegemony. Offended by the fact that the Christian sites in the Holy Land were dominated by Greeks, Armenians, and Ethiopians, the Catholic, Protestant, and Russian Orthodox Churches were encouraged by their governments to build their own institutions.

In the event, it was the British who wrested control of Palestine from the Ottomans in 1917 during World War I. However, the League of Nations mandate stipulated that the British were to be temporary custodians. Even though significant numbers of Jews had begun returning to their ancestral homeland from the late 19th century onwards, nobody could have predicted that in just three more decades possession of much of Palestine would return to its ancient owners.

In exile

In nearly 2,000 years of exile the Jewish people never forgot Israel. They faced Jerusalem when they prayed and took to heart the sentence from Psalm 137: "If I forget thee, O Jerusalem, let my right hand forget her cunning." But while the Jews never forgot Jerusalem, for years they showed no great inclination to return. Many made pilgrimages to the Holy Land, but there was no significant mass movement to return to Zion.

Over time, the conventional Orthodox belief took root that the return would occur only with the coming of the Messiah. Eventually it was a combination of European enlightenment, nationalism, and anti-Semitism that shook this conviction and promoted the belief that a return to Zion was necessary, both for the physical survival of Jews threatened by extermination and for the perpetuation of Jewish culture corroded by assimilation.

For the most part, the first millennium of exile was unremarkable. Most Jews lived in the Middle East and the Mediterranean basin, where they suffered what was to become a familiar mixture of intolerance and persecution while being patronized for their skills, crafts, and merchant abilities. But if Islam and Orthodox Christianity, centered in Constantinople, had occasional outbursts of anti-Jewish sentiment, these paled into insignificance compared with what the Jews would face in Europe in their second millennium of exile.

Inquisitions and pogroms

By the 11th century large Jewish communities had established themselves in France and Germany. They arrived just in time for the Crusades, and a familiar pattern of massacres was

turned its attention to the non-Spanish, non-Christian infidels in its midst. For a century, under the Inquisition, Jews were either massacred or forced at sword point to convert. Finally, in the 1490s – just as Columbus was discovering the Americas, where the Jews would enjoy a new golden age – they were expelled from Spain. Many stayed, worshipping secretly; others returned to North Africa or settled in the newly emerging Ottoman Empire. Several thousand returned to the Holy Land, settling in Jerusalem and in Safed, which became a center of Jewish scholarship. Some found their

Delegates to the Sixth Zionist Conference in Basle, 1903.

begun, which was to haunt the Jews all the way to Auschwitz. The Church institutionalized the belief that the Jews were satanic Christ-killers, who craved money above all else.

Nevertheless, in the 11th, 12th, and 13th centuries the Jews entered a golden age, especially in Spain, where Jewish aristocrats formed a bridge between the Christian north and Moorish Arab Muslim south. Communal life and autonomous religious institutions flourished in both Spain and Germany, and the Jews even developed their own languages – Ladino and Yiddish – medieval Spanish and German respectively, mixed with Hebrew and written with Hebrew characters.

But as Spain drove the Moorish infidels back into Africa in the 14th and 15th centuries, it

PERNICIOUS PROPAGANDA

The image of Jews as Christ-killers was a pernicious one that was very hard to dispel. Along with it went a number of other superstitions, encouraged by the clerical authorities. One particularly unpleasant myth that persisted into the 20th century was that Jews killed Christian children so that they could use their blood for Passover rituals. The Jews were also blamed for the Black Death, which swept Europe in 1348, and it was widely believed that they poisoned wells to spread the epidemic. Additionally, the fact that Jews were the only money-lenders, when the Church forbade Christians to engage in usury, gave them a reputation for avarice.

way to Holland and subsequently to England, when Oliver Cromwell legalized the community "expelled" in the 13th century.

Germany's Jews fared no better. Hounded by the Church, communities moved to Poland and Russia, establishing *shtetls*, small self-sufficient communities. The Pale of Settlement defined where they could live, excluding them from Russia itself, while pogroms kept them in constant fear. Ironically, the Pale of Settlement in Eastern Europe became a kind of homogenous Jewish state where Yiddish-speaking Jews evolved their distinct ethnic culture.

Zionist visionary Theodor Herzl.

Emancipation and nationalism

The Industrial Revolution and the forces of the Enlightenment transforming Europe also affected Jews. Some turned to messianic cults such as Hassidism, but with nationalism sweeping across Europe many became secularized.

At the same time Europeans started investigating Jewish culture. The discovery that Hebrew was a Semitic language related to Arabic, outside Indo-European linguistic evolution, contributed to the rise of anti-Semitism. Previously the Jews had at least been accepted into the Church, albeit often through forced conversions; now they were set apart racially.

Some Jews were assimilated into middle-class European society. In England, Benjamin

> *Theodor Herzl, the founder of political Zionism, was written off by most Jews as a dreamer. Herzl's response, "If you will it, then it will be," has remained the inspirational credo of Israelis into the 21st century.*

Disraeli's father had the country's future prime minister baptized rather than bar mitzvahed when he was 13. But baptism did not make many Jews of mainland Europe seem European enough. Ultimately, they were still persecuted. The Enlightenment, with its anti-religious liberal emphasis, often worked against the Jews, viewed as religious fundamentalists. Voltaire railed against them, and his anti-religious rationalist writings were developed in the 19th century by a young German Jew, Karl Marx, who rejected his heritage and spoke of a war against capitalists and clerics.

In this era of great change some Jews remembered Jerusalem. British philanthropists such as Moses Montefiore and the Rothschilds set up Jewish communities in Jerusalem and new agricultural villages like Rishon Le-Tsiyon, Zikhron Ya'akov, and Rosh Pina.

Meanwhile, the assassination of Tsar Alexander II in Russia in 1881 was blamed on the Jews and unleashed awesome pogroms. Jews emigrated in their millions to Western Europe and especially to the United States, which from the outset had guaranteed religious freedom in its constitution. And some Jews were persuaded by the philanthropists to settle in the Holy Land.

The birth of Zionism

But it was in France that modern political Zionism was conceived. In the 1890s a young Viennese-Jewish journalist, Theodor Herzl, was sent to Paris to cover the trial of Captain Alfred Dreyfus, the French Jewish officer who was framed as a spy and blamed for his country's defeat in the Franco-Prussian war of 1870. As the trial unraveled, Herzl despaired of the fate of European Jewry. Though an assimilated Jew who knew virtually nothing of his cultural roots, Herzl wrote a book, *Altneuland* (*Old-new Land*), describing the re-establishment of a Jewish commonwealth in ancient Israel.

In 1897 Herzl convened the First Zionist Congress in Basle, establishing the World Zionist Organization, the forerunner of the Israeli government. He lobbied political leaders and courted European royalty, making his only trip to Palestine in 1898 to meet Kaiser Wilhelm II of Germany when the latter visited Jerusalem.

After Herzl's premature death in 1904, the unofficial leadership of the Zionist movement fell to Chaim Weizmann, a Russian-born professor of chemistry at Manchester University. Weizmann won the confidence of the British ruling elite, and after the conquest of Palestine in 1917 that meant everything. Most importantly, he persuaded the British Foreign Secretary, Arthur Balfour, to issue a declaration promising British

more liberal, humane streak. They set up trade unions, rejected the capitalist villages of the Rothschilds, and established their own agricultural collectives, called kibbutzim.

At first the indigenous Palestinians welcomed the Jewish settlers. Their numbers were small, they brought wealth and development, and, while most Palestinians lived on the inland hills, the newcomers were prepared to settle the humid coastal plain. But the Balfour Declaration took the Arabs by surprise and indicated that they had greatly underestimated the Zionist potential.

The British in Palestine during World War I with guns and stores captured from the Turks.

support for a Jewish homeland. This lent the Zionist movement the international legitimacy it desperately needed.

If the likes of Herzl and Weizmann gave the Zionist movement diplomatic access, the foot soldiers in the field were the Jews of Eastern Europe. As Tsarist Russia hurtled towards the revolution, increasing numbers of ideologically motivated Zionist socialists found their way to Palestine. Between 1904 and 1917, some 100,000 came, though fewer than half stayed.

Among them was a lawyer's son named David Ben Gurion, who was to assume the leadership of the *yishuv*, the pre-state Jewish entity. These men, products of pre-revolutionary Russia, were essentially Bolsheviks with a

LOOKING FOR A PEACEFUL LIFE

The *shtetls* of Eastern Europe were small self-sufficient village communities in which Jewish people retained their own culture and way of life. They were portrayed romantically in the musical *Fiddler on the Roof*, based on the Yiddish stories by Sholom Aleichem about Tevya the Milkman, whose faith in God helps him to overcome all the trials and tribulations of life under the Tsars. The rabbi's blessing in *Fiddler on the Roof* – "God bless the Tsar and keep him far away from us" – reflected the antagonism that the Russian rulers had developed towards the Jews, and the Jewish desire to be left undisturbed.

A Henschel portrait of a Palestinian Arab.

PERFIDIOUS ALBION

The Balfour Declaration promised British support
for a Jewish homeland, but Israel soon became
embroiled in international realpolitik.

E ven today, the question is often asked in the Middle East: did the British favor the Arabs or the Jews during the Mandatory period? The probable answer is that they favored neither and that, as elsewhere, they pursued their own interests.

In the aftermath of World War I, Arthur Balfour and David Lloyd George were strong supporters of the Zionist cause because they perceived a Jewish homeland as a potentially friendly outpost of Empire. The notion also appealed to the religious sentiment of British Protestants. But Balfour had underestimated the strength of Arab nationalism, as well as the emerging economic and strategic importance of Middle East oil.

The British government's most hostile opponent of the Balfour Declaration was Edwin Montagu, Secretary of State for India and the only Jew in the cabinet. Like a large section of secular world Jewry, he fiercely opposed Zionism because it cast doubt on his national loyalties. He insisted that Judaism was a religion, not a nationality.

Zionist Dov Ber Borochov and frends in Plonsk, Poland, 1920.

Arab riots

Britain's miscalculation in making the Balfour Declaration soon became apparent. In March 1920 a bloody riot in Jerusalem left more than 200 Jews dead. Widespread Arab violence soon made the British regret the Declaration, and in 1921 Winston Churchill, the Colonial Secretary and previously a fervent Zionist sympathizer, told Chaim Weizmann that 90 percent of the British government was opposed to establishing a Jewish homeland in Palestine.

But the Zionists were better organized than the Arabs and more determined than the British. The Histadrut trade union organization was founded in 1920, while the Haganah, an underground paramilitary body, effectively defended Jewish settlements and became the forerunner of the Israel Defense Forces. Tel Aviv flourished as economic capital of the emerging Jewish entity, and kibbutz agricultural settlements made the local Jewish population self-sufficient in food.

Most vitally, large numbers of Jews began emigrating to Palestine. In the 1920s the Jewish population of Palestine doubled from 85,000 to 170,000. The Arab population numbered about 850,000. These Jewish newcomers included socialists disillusioned by the results of the Russian Revolution, as well as numerous middle-class merchants and professionals from Poland. While David Ben Gurion and his socialist followers became the establishment through the Jewish Agency, a kind of government in waiting, the right-wing nationalist revisionist movement of Vladimir Jabotinsky enjoyed strong support too.

In particular, Jabotinsky and his supporters vehemently opposed Churchill's unilateral decision in 1923 to cede all of Palestine east of the River Jordan, nearly two-thirds of the landmass of Palestine, to Britain's Arabian Hashemite ally Emir Abdullah.

The rise of Nazism

Adolf Hitler's 1933 assumption of power in Germany, together with the rapid economic development of Palestine, attracted even more Jewish immigrants. While most Jews saw Palestine as a safe haven from anti-Semitism, many were now being drawn there for other reasons. Palestine's coastal plain, where most Jewish towns were established, was no longer dominated by sand dunes and swamps. There were bourgeois boulevards lined with large houses, shops and banks, schools, universities, and hospitals.

The Mayor of Tel Aviv showing the city to Lord Balfour in 1925.

POLITICAL MACHINATIONS

Shortly after World War II, Emanuel Shinwell, a Jewish member of Clement Attlee's Labour cabinet in Britain, was proud to identify with the Zionist cause and the establishment of the State of Israel. However, he pointed out that, as Secretary for Energy in His Majesty's Government, he was duty-bound to protect British interests, and that that involved sympathizing with Arab states, whatever his personal feelings. Other British politicians were less candid about where their sympathies lay and about the often unscrupulous choices involved in realpolitik. Of course, the making and breaking of promises is often part and parcel of political life.

By 1939, on the eve of World War II, the Jewish population of Palestine had doubled again, to 350,000. Bitter hostility to Zionism was led by Haj Amin Husseini, the Grand Mufti of Jerusalem, who formed an understanding with Hitler. The region might have been more peaceful had the more moderate King Abdullah of Jordan gained the upper hand.

In an attempt to win Arab support for the impending war with Germany, the British passed a White Paper limiting Jewish immigration to 20,000 a year. So, as the Nazi stranglehold tightened around Europe, with Britain refusing entry visas to Palestine for Jewish refugees trying to escape persecution, there was nowhere for Jewish refugees to flee.

All the same, Ben Gurion and the Jewish Agency insisted that there was no alternative but for Jews to support the British war effort. The revisionists were not so certain. Irgun Zvi Leumi, led by Menachem Begin, agreed to a ceasefire with the British for the duration of the war, but an extremist fringe, Lehi, led by Yitzhak Shamir, continued to attack British targets throughout World War II. Many Jews, however, enlisted in the British Army, which even formed a Jewish brigade – this provided invaluable experience for subsequent battles. Even after the full horror of the concentration camps was known, the British did not relent and issue entry visas, keeping some 73,000 refugees, many of them concentration camp survivors, in detention camps in Cyprus.

The revelation of the Nazi atrocities made the Jews of Palestine all the more determined to achieve independence. The horrors of the Holocaust were no surprise to the Zionists, who had always feared something of the sort but had expected it to be Russian- rather than German-inspired. The prevailing belief was that, had Israel existed at the time, 6 million Jews could have been saved.

Stalin's assistance

Ben Gurion, grasping postwar realities, switched the focus of his lobbying from London to Washington. An intense diplomatic offensive was launched at the newly formed United Nations in New York, and quiet channels were opened to the Soviet Union. The support of Joseph Stalin in the establishment of Israel was to prove crucial. The United States, which voted against the UN-sponsored partition of Palestine in 1946, supported the same resolution a year later. Britain abstained both times. But Stalin, though undoubtedly anti-Semitic, saw a potentially socialist Israel as a Marxist bulwark against the puppet Arab administrations being set up by Britain and France. Consequently he threw his full weight, as well as that of his European satellites, behind the Zionists. He voted for the UN partition plan in November 1948 and even sent arms to help Israel during the War of Independence.

The right-wing Irgun and Lehi denounced Ben Gurion's diplomacy as futile. Their strategy was simple – to bomb the British out of Palestine. British soldiers were killed, Irgun and Lehi members were hanged, and more British soldiers were killed in retaliation. Following the bombing in 1947 of the British administrative HQ at the King David Hotel, which killed 91 people, British public opinion clamored for a withdrawal. After much government deliberation, the pullout was fixed for May 15, 1948.

Although the socialists and revisionists had a violent mutual hatred, it was probably their joint efforts that brought about the establishment of Israel. Ben Gurion's diplomatic success at the United Nations and in gaining the support of both Stalin and the US president, Harry Truman, gave the Jewish state international legitimacy. The revisionists' all-out war against the British forced their withdrawal.

Young David Ben Gurion in Turkish fez.

And so modern Israel arose from the ashes of the Holocaust. Yet it is one of the myths of our time that this is why Israel came into existence, a romantic idea that appeals to a poetic sense of justice: the Jewish people suffered but were compensated with their own state.

This is not the way Israelis see it. They argue that Israel came into being despite the Holocaust, and that had just 1 million of the 6 million who perished reached Israel, the birth of the state would have been easier. They recall that, while Israel enjoyed much international sympathy after the Holocaust, little was done to help. Israel had to work hard to swing the UN vote, and when the British withdrew it was left completely alone to face the Arab world.

Troops inspect the wreckage of the King David Hotel in Jerusalem, shortly after it was bombed by Zionists in 1946.

THE SECOND EXODUS

The birth of the new state was a difficult
one, and in subsequent years political and
economic vision were vital for survival.

A s Israelis danced in the streets following the Declaration of Independence in May 1948, they knew that there would be little to celebrate in the ensuing months. Though vastly outnumbered by the surrounding Arab armies, better organization saw the Israel Defense Forces not only defend Jewish territory but also conquer large areas of the Negev and Western Galilee that had been allocated to Palestine under the UN partition plan.

However, if subsequent Israeli military victories were relatively swift, this first war ground on for nearly a year, costing the new country 6,000 lives, about 1 percent of the Jewish population. Jerusalem saw especially fierce fighting. Under the UN plan the city was meant to enjoy international status, but Jordanian Legionnaires overran the Old City, including the Jewish quarter, while the western, Jewish half of the city was besieged for months. Eventually the city was divided into two, with the Israelis controlling the western half and the Jordanians annexing the eastern section, including the holy sites, as well as the entire West Bank. Egypt helped itself to the Gaza Strip, and Arab Palestine never came into existence.

The first glimpse of the Promised Land.

The fate of the Palestinians

The Israelis have always officially claimed that the Palestinians ran away from their homes in 1948 to escape the fighting, expecting to return after an Arab victory. The Palestinians claim that they were forcibly expelled. Research shows that there is some truth in both versions. About a third of the 500,000 Palestinians living in the region that was to become Israel were coerced into leaving, becoming refugees in surrounding countries; about a third voluntarily fled, and the final third stayed put to become citizens of Israel, which today has an Arab minority of some 20 percent.

THE ARMS INDUSTRY

Ben Gurion had a good eye for young talent, both inside and outside the army. He spotted the creative organizational abilities of a young Polish immigrant called Shimon Peres (who would become prime minister in 1986 and later president) and charged him with the task of developing a defense manufacturing infrastructure. Peres's accomplishments were remarkable, giving Israel a nuclear capability and enabling the country to produce its own tanks and fighter aircraft. Many Israeli weapons, such as the versatile Uzi sub-machine gun, became sought-after export items, and this successful industry boosted Israel's confidence during decades of war.

By the 1960s Israel's Jewish population was split 50–50 between Ashkenazi European Jews and Sephardi Oriental Jews. This cultural divide, accentuated by socio-economic gaps, generated major tensions from the 1970s onward.

Meanwhile, David Ben Gurion set about building his new nation. The architect of such institutions as the Histadrut trade union movement and the Haganah, now renamed the Israel Defense Forces, Ben Gurion was easily able to

Although harsh with his opponents, Ben Gurion knew how to delegate responsibility. After his socialist Mapai Party won 46 seats in the 1949 Knesset elections, he formed a coalition with the Stalinist Mapam Party to the left and religious and liberal groups to the right. Ben Gurion became prime minister and Defense Minister, with Moshe Sharett as his Foreign Minister (and eventually the second prime minister).

Within the army, Ben Gurion advanced the promotion of the daring, one-eyed Moshe Dayan, a notorious womanizer who had sustained his injury while fighting for the British

Thousands of immigrants arrived in Israel in the years following its establishment as a nation.

outflank the world Jewish leader Chaim Weizmann, who also aspired to lead the new nation. Ben Gurion offered Weizmann the post of president, the titular head of state.

At the same time, while allowing the revisionists led by Menachem Begin to participate in Knesset elections, Ben Gurion acted tough, outlawing their paramilitary organizations and blowing up a ship, the *Atalena*, bringing arms for Irgun in June 1948. Menachem Begin and his Herut Party were to remain in the political wilderness for nearly 20 years until, in the run-up to the Six Day War in 1967, Begin was invited by Prime Minister Levi Eshkol to join a national unity government. In elections a decade later, he won outright power.

in Syria. Another man who caught Ben Gurion's attention was the dashing young Yitzhak Rabin, commander of the Harel brigade, who was given a leading role in the armistice agreements negotiated after the War of Independence.

The Law of Return

The most significant new legislation introduced by the Knesset was the Law of Return of 1950, guaranteeing free immigration of world Jewry to Israel. The religious parties wanted to restrict immigration to candidates whose mothers were Jewish, but ended up adopting the same yardstick as the Nuremberg Laws, which had defined anybody with one Jewish grandparent as Jewish.

In the years following the establishment of Israel, waves of immigrants flooded in. Nearly 700,000 arrived between 1948 and 1951, doubling the population. By 1964 another 500,000 had arrived and the population passed 2 million. But the European-born founding fathers were surprised to find that large numbers were arriving not only from Eastern Europe but also from Morocco, Egypt, Yemen, Iraq, and other Arab countries, where entire Jewish communities were expelled in an anti-Zionist backlash.

International orientation

Ben Gurion had planned to pursue a neutral policy in the Cold War. During the War of Independence the USSR was the only country to send arms, though the USA had turned a blind eye to the military aid given to Israel by American Jewry. But, although a Stalinist party shared power in Israel's first government, the country was a parliamentary democracy more akin to the West.

Moreover, Israel needed financial aid, and only the USA could supply that. So in 1949, when Israel took a loan of $100,000 from the USA, a pattern of economic dependence was begun, only to be broken in the 1990s when Israel's high-tech economy emerged. In parallel, Israel's relations with the Soviet Union were strained as Stalin refused to allow free emigration of Soviet Jewry.

However, Israel, in partnership with Britain and France, antagonized both the USA and the Soviet Union in 1956 when it launched the Suez campaign. Following the nationalization of the Suez Canal by Egypt's president, Gamal Abdel Nasser, British and French paratroopers seized the canal, and in less than a week Israeli troops had occupied all Sinai. But the Americans sided with the Egyptians, forcing the British and French to relinquish control of the canal and compelling the Israelis to withdraw from Sinai. Instead of being humiliated, Nasser became a hero.

Economic development

Despite Israel taking in so many impoverished immigrants and illiterate newcomers, plus the cost of remaining on a constant war footing, the economy developed steadily during the 1950s and 1960s. Major national projects were undertaken, including the draining of the Hula Swamp in the Upper Galilee and the building of the national carrier bringing water from the north to the Negev. The arid land was transformed.

Even with its burgeoning population, the country was self-sufficient in food, and a major export industry, especially in citrus fruit, developed. Highways were built, and a health, education, and energy infrastructure was put in place. In this formative stage, the Arab boycott and the unwillingness of overseas investors to put money into a country that might soon be driven into the sea turned out to be an asset, for Israel developed a home-owned industrial infrastructure. The economy was heavily centralized and socialist, but there was scope for entrepreneurs with the patience to unravel bureaucratic red tape.

Draining the Hula swamp, 1953.

In this stage of the country's development, donations from overseas Jewry, especially from North America, were a vital source of capital. In addition, a reparations agreement was concluded with the West German government that compensated hundreds of thousands of survivors, or relatives of victims, for the loss of life, the suffering, and the property lost during the Holocaust. Menachem Begin bitterly opposed this agreement, insisting that no amount of money could atone for the devastation caused by the Nazis.

In 1963, when Levi Eshkol became the third prime minister, Israel was neither wealthy nor a full member of the industrialized world, but was free of the food shortages, disease, and illiteracy that characterized most developing nations.

Celebrating Independence Day in Jerusalem.

COMING OF AGE

Through wars and internal strife Israel has struggled to maturity, while world opinion has fluctuated between praise and blame.

The Arabs have always maintained that Israel instigated the Six Day War in 1967 in order to seize more Palestinian territory. This interpretation of history overlooks the blockade of the Straits of Tiran by the Egyptian president, Gamal Abdel Nasser, which cut off the shipping route to Israel's Red Sea port of Eilat, as well as his boast that he would drive the Jews into the sea.

With hindsight, Nasser's threat was probably bluff, but Israel was not to know. As the Yom Kippur War revealed six years later, Israeli intelligence was poor at the time, and a first strike was crucial for such a tiny country with no strategic depth. So Israel took Nasser's threats at face value and attacked, and the Egyptian air force was destroyed on the ground minutes after the war started. The Golan Heights, from which Syria had been bombarding northern Israel, were captured. Israel also won the Sinai peninsula and Gaza Strip from Egypt, and the West Bank from Jordan. Jerusalem was reunited. Defense Minister Moshe Dayan and Chief of the Army Yitzhak Rabin were hailed as heroes.

Soldiers reach the Western Wall, 1967.

Permanently on the map

Israel was never the same after the Six Day War. It wasn't only that the borders had changed and more than 1 million Palestinians had fallen under Israeli occupation. Perceived worldwide as the underdog in the Middle East conflict, Israel was now viewed as the oppressor. But the West, especially the United States, saw Israel as a potentially strong and reliable ally in the Cold War confrontation with the USSR. Military collaboration strengthened between Israel and the USA, while Britain and France maintained the arms embargo imposed at the start of the Six Day War.

Israel itself was intoxicated by its own success. Prime Minister Levi Eshkol died and was replaced by Golda Meir, who had grown up in the United States and was able to consolidate the US–Israeli romance. The country's new euphoria was not even tempered by a war of attrition from 1967 to 1970, in which Egypt shelled Israeli forces across the Suez Canal, nor by the emergence of the Palestine Liberation Organization (PLO), which carried out bloody terrorist attacks against Israeli targets, including the killing of 11 Israeli athletes during the Munich Olympic Games in 1972.

When Jordan and Egypt annexed the West Bank and Gaza Strip, the PLO had been suppressed and its leader, Yasser Arafat, imprisoned. But after 1967 the PLO was encouraged to spearhead the Arab nations' campaign to regain "the Zionist entity." By 1970 the PLO was so strong that Arafat tried, with Syrian backing, to take over Jordan. In a 10-day bloody war in "Black September", King Hussein quelled the attempted Palestinian coup. Syrian troops who were massed on the border turned back when Israel threatened to intervene to support the Hashemite Kingdom. Arafat and his fighters resettled in Lebanon.

War and peace

The PLO was popularly viewed as a terrorist organization that would eventually go away,

or her successor Yitzhak Rabin, but with Menachem Begin, the implacably right-wing nationalist who won the 1977 election.

The birth of two-party politics

Menachem Begin's success changed the face of Israeli politics, which became a two-party affair, characterized by bitter divisions over the direction of Israeli society. After 29 years in power, Labor lost office because of its failures in the Yom Kippur War. Moreover, Begin's populism appealed both to young Oriental Jews, alienated by the Ashkenazi socialist establishment,

President Sadat is greeted by Prime Minister Begin in 1977.

and Israel considered itself invincible. In 1973, the Yom Kippur War stunned the nation. With a surprise assault, the Egyptians, under President Anwar Sadat, conquered much of Sinai, while the Syrians nearly broke through to the Galilee. Israel recovered, counterattacked, retook the Golan Heights, and even managed to cross the Suez Canal before the Americans, who for the first time became committed allies of Israel by airlifting emergency military supplies to the Middle East, forced a ceasefire.

But the war restored Egyptian pride and was portrayed by Sadat as a great victory. He signed a peace treaty with Israel in 1979 in exchange for the return of the Sinai peninsula. Remarkably, he did not shake hands with Golda Meir,

SUPPORT FROM THE USA

By the late 1970s the United States had come to view Israel as a significant player in its Cold War global strategy, and also a vital support to NATO's vulnerable southeastern flank, which comprised the two bitter enemies Greece and Turkey. This meant that large sums of money – about $1.5 billion a year – were plowed into Israel to pay for arms and to improve the country's military. Another $1.5 billion was given annually to help repay the loans taken out for previous acquisitions and, subsequently, for the expensive redeployment needed after the Sinai withdrawal in 1982. Such close ties with the USA deepened the USSR's hostility towards Israel.

and to Orthodox Jewry, attached to the biblical sites in the West Bank, now called Judea and Samaria.

Yitzhak Rabin had first allowed right-wing Jews to settle Hebron and other West Bank towns in 1975, and in so doing opened a floodgate. Under Begin and his successor, Yitzhak Shamir, tens of thousands of Jews settled the West Bank and the Gaza Strip, and the Palestinians saw the little that was left of their homeland slipping away from them.

All the same, the right-wing Likud, though nationalist in character and reluctant to relinquish land, tended to make pragmatic concessions when pressured by the USA. Begin gave up Sinai after American arm-twisting, and received the Nobel Peace Prize for his pains.

Anti-Zionism

Israel's close identification with the USA made it a target for Soviet Union hostility, and the Communist bloc, Arab and Muslim nations, and the developing world combined to isolate Israel as a pariah nation. The country was depicted as a racist state, with Zionism denounced by a UN resolution as an intrinsically fascist ideology.

The tactic was extremely effective, and even many of Israel's friends in the liberal West distanced themselves from Zionism. Remarkably, this was even before Likud came to power and when there was barely a settler in the West Bank. For Israelis, anti-Zionism was the flip side of anti-Semitism. Persecuted in Europe as Semites, they were now being denounced by the Semitic Arabs as European colonialists.

Ironically, while the Soviet Union was hounding Israel diplomatically and arming Syria, it eased restrictions on Jewish emigration. More than 180,000 Jews reached Israel from the USSR in the 1970s, and an even greater number immigrated to the United States.

Begin won a second election victory in 1981 and the following year turned his attentions on Lebanon. Israel's northern neighbor had been a model of democracy and affluence despite its divisions between Maronite Christians, Druze, Sunni and Shiite Muslims, and Palestinian refugees. But the arrival of the PLO and its fighters in 1970 had disturbed the delicate balance, and the country plunged into civil war in 1975. The PLO used Lebanon as a base for attacks on Israel from sea and land.

Ariel Sharon, the Minister of Defense, convinced Begin that a military incursion into southern Lebanon was required to clear out PLO bases. An invasion was launched in June 1982. Begin, like the rest of the nation, was surprised to learn a short while later that Israeli tanks were rolling through the streets of Beirut. The Americans intervened to prevent the Israel Defense Forces from finishing off Yasser Arafat, who was given safe passage to Tunisia.

In the aftermath of the war, Begin lost his previous vigor. The great orator fell silent and resigned the following year. He felt betrayed,

Israeli bomb attack over west Beirut, 1982.

not only by Sharon but also by his Finance Minister, Yoram Aridor, whose economic policies led to three-digit annual inflation.

The years of power sharing

The 1984 election result was inconclusive, and a rotation pact was agreed, with Labor's Shimon Peres serving as prime minister until 1986, followed by Likud's Yitzhak Shamir for the subsequent two years. Peres withdrew Israeli troops from Lebanon, with the exception of a security belt closest to the Israeli border, and stabilized the economy, reducing the annual rate of inflation from 425 percent to 16 percent.

During the two decades that Israel had occupied the West Bank and Gaza, relations between the Israelis and Palestinians had deteriorated. Immediately after 1967 the Palestinians were infatuated with Israeli liberalism and the economic opportunities that occupation brought. A free press flourished, municipal elections were held, and employment in Israel, although mainly in menial jobs, led to improvements in the Palestinians' standard of living.

But things turned sour, especially after the Likud triumph in the 1970s, as it became clear that Israel was integrating the Palestinian territories into a Greater Israel. Right-wing settlers were becoming more powerful, and the Israeli

Yitzhak Rabin, assassinated in 1995.

government was talking of annexing the biblical Land of Israel.

Palestinian frustration exploded in 1987 with the outbreak of the Intifada, which was characterized by the throwing of rocks and Molotov cocktails at Israeli troops, and by strikes preventing Arab workers from coming to Israel. World opinion strongly sympathized with the Palestinians, and the demographic debate was renewed in Israeli politics, with Labor speaking of territorial concessions. The elections of 1988 saw Likud win the upper hand in a closely fought contest. Shamir continued to lead a national unity government, which broke down in 1990; he then formed a right-wing coalition.

The collapse of the Soviet Union

The unexpected disintegration of the USSR meant that, from 1990 onwards, Russian-speaking Jewry flooded into Israel: over 1 million Russian-speaking immigrants reached Israel in the 1990s. The demise of the Soviet Union saw Israel renew diplomatic relations with the states of Central and Eastern Europe and the former republics of the USSR. Another benefit was that the supply of Russian-made arms to Syria and the PLO dried up.

Before the post-Cold War situation could be digested, Iraq invaded Kuwait, and the Gulf War ensued in 1991. Scud missiles fell on Israel but, under American pressure, the right-wing government did not retaliate, in order not to disrupt the allied coalition, which included Syria.

By November 1991 Israel was sitting round the table with the Palestinians and Syrians at the Madrid Peace Conference. In the wake of these preliminary peace talks, China, India, and much of Asia established full diplomatic relations with Israel for the first time. African countries such as Nigeria renewed ties, and the UN resolution equating Zionism with racism was repealed. But Shamir stalled on progress in the talks, continuing to expand settlements in the West Bank. A confrontation with the United States was averted by Yitzhak Rabin's election victory in 1992.

Peace accords and assassination

Though Rabin had been elected on a dovish platform, Israelis and the wider world were surprised by the secret agreements concluded with the PLO in Oslo. In September 1993 Prime Minister Rabin and PLO Chairman Yasser Arafat shook hands on the White House lawn, and by 1994 Israel had withdrawn from most of the Gaza Strip and all the towns on the West Bank except Hebron. A peace agreement was signed with Jordan, and Morocco and Tunisia opened low-level diplomatic offices in Tel Aviv.

The peace process, combined with the end of the Arab economic boycott, ongoing immigration, and a penchant for developing innovative high-tech products, saw the economy boom. Average annual growth of 6 percent in the early 1990s enabled the standard of living to rise rapidly to Western European levels.

But Rabin's right-wing religious and nationalist opponents were unimpressed by the economic benefits of peace. The opposition to territorial compromise strengthened following a terrorist bombing campaign by the extremist Palestinian Hamas movement. Vociferous anti-government demonstrations took place as the right's supporters took to the streets.

A young law student, Yigal Amir, took matters into his own hands. He stalked Rabin for several months, with a pistol in his pocket. His opportunity came following a peace rally in Tel Aviv in November 1995, when he took advantage of a lapse in security to pump three bullets into Rabin's back from point-blank range.

> *Before his entry to politics, Prime Minister Benjamin Netanyahu was best known as the brother of Jonathan Netanyahu, the army officer killed in Uganda when leading the raid on Entebbe to rescue hostages from a hijacked Air France plane.*

Netanyahu's first administration

Benjamin Netanyahu won the 1996 election because he made a late, pragmatic move to the center: in contravention of traditional Likud

Arial Sharon speaking in 2002.

In the shocked aftermath of the assassination of a widely respected leader, the premiership was assumed by Foreign Minister Shimon Peres. As architect of the Oslo Accords, he had won the Nobel Peace Prize, along with Rabin and Arafat, and he now pushed ahead vigorously with the peace process. However, Syria's President Hafez El-Assad refused to meet him, even though Peres had agreed in principle to return the Golan Heights.

Persuaded by a large lead in the polls, Peres brought forward elections by six months to May 1996. But a lackluster campaign, combined with further terrorist attacks by Hamas and Hizbullah missiles raining down on the Galilee, saw Peres defeated by the narrowest of margins.

policy, he agreed to abide by the Oslo Agreements and to meet Yasser Arafat, and in 1997 he even withdrew from half of Hebron.

If Netanyahu lost allies to the right because of his diplomatic policies vis-à-vis the Palestinians, much of his center-ground support fell away as a result of his domestic incompetence. A polished speaker in both Hebrew and English (he had been raised and educated in the US by his Israeli parents) he began talking hesitantly after receiving the reins of power.

In 1999, Netanyahu faced the Labor Party's new star, Ehud Barak, a former chief of the army whom the late Yitzhak Rabin had groomed as his successor. Barak won on a landslide and a dovish platform, although he had no clear

Knesset majority and needed support from the rightist ultra-Orthodox Shas Party. Relations with the Palestinians improved and the economy boomed as Israel consolidated its position as a global high-tech leader.

Barak gambled everything on a peace summit with the Palestinians at Camp David in the summer of 2000. President Bill Clinton acted as mediator as Barak stunned Israelis by agreeing to relinquish most of the West Bank and Gaza, including much of East Jerusalem and the Old City. To balance the 10 percent of the West Bank that Barak wanted to hang on to, he

that the Palestinian leader was simply unable to bring himself to conclude a final agreement with the old enemy.

Certainly, after the Intifada broke out in 2000, Arafat appeared recharged with a new energy. The nominal reason for the outbreak of hostilities was an insensitive visit by the opposition Likud leader, Ariel Sharon, to the Temple Mount. Rioting broke out across the West Bank – even among Israeli Arabs, 13 of whom were killed by police. The rioting may have been spontaneous, but Arafat's decision several days later to release all Hamas prisoners,

Palestinian child of the Intifada, October 2000.

offered a strip of the Negev Desert alongside Gaza as compensation. But Arafat was playing hard to get. He refused to yield any of the land captured by Israel in 1967 and demanded the right of return of all Palestinians to pre-1967 Israel, which would wipe out the country's Jewish majority. Shas withdrew from the government and Barak soldiered on for several months in the Knesset before calling elections.

Back to the Intifada

The conventional wisdom at the time among proponents of peace was that Arafat's hard line at Camp David was a bargaining posture to squeeze greater concessions from Israel. With hindsight, many Israelis – even on the left – feel

who had been responsible for attacks on Israelis, suggested he had a more extended conflict in mind. In the first stage of hostilities, attacks took place mainly in the West Bank and Gaza against settlers and soldiers. Arafat and Barak carried on talking, but the impetus for peace was buried in bloodshed.

Sharon enters the fray

In the 2001 elections Ariel Sharon, the hardline general, convincingly defeated Barak. Demonized and despised for his role in the Lebanon War of 1982, Sharon was to surprise everybody, most of all his own supporters, by becoming a peacemaker. Between 2001 and 2003 his hard-line policies, including targeted

Former Knesset Speaker Reuben Rivlin was elected president in 2014. This is a titular position that constitutionally parallels the role of the monarch in the UK.

killings of Palestinian leaders, quelled the suicide bombing campaign of the Palestinians. Sharon built a security wall dividing Israel and the West Bank but used the policy to de facto annex more Palestinian land.

After being re-elected in 2003 Sharon stunned the world by announcing that he would unilaterally withdraw all the Jewish settlements in the Gaza Strip, and he achieved what even Rabin had never dared undertake, when Israel abandoned its settlements in Gaza in 2005.

Arafat's death the previous year, combined with the Gaza disengagement, created an opportunity for peace as Sharon and Arafat's elected successor Mahmoud Abbas (Abu Mazen) renewed the peace process. Sharon, who had become a target of hatred for most nationalist orthodox religious Jews, broke with the right-wing Likud and formed his own centrist Kadima Party. But the opportunity was fleeting. Sharon was felled by a massive stroke and, though his deputy Ehud Olmert was elected prime minister in 2006 with a mandate for territorial compromise, the election victory by Hamas (who refuse to recognize Israel's existence) torpedoed any negotiated settlement.

Under Olmert, peace moved further away. In failed attempts to stop the missiles being fired at Israeli civilian towns, brief wars were launched in 2006 and at the end of 2008 against Hizbullah in Lebanon and Hamas in Gaza respectively. The development of Iran's nuclear program became a further cause of anxiety for Israelis. However, what in fact brought down Olmert was not his defense policies but rather a wide range of corruption investigations against him, eventually compelling him to resign. His successor, the Foreign Minister Tzipi Livni, was unable to form a coalition. She called an election, which was won by Netanyahu's right-wing Likud in February 2009.

Although Netanyahu's first spell as prime minister in the 1990s was perceived as a failure, he had been a successful Finance Minister under Sharon and had helped pull Israel out of a recession caused by the second Intifada.

Netanyahu's economic track record attracted voters as Israel faced up to the global economic crisis, while his hawkish views on peace with the Palestinians and Syria, and potential territorial compromise, were also in tune with the electorate's mood. Netanyahu was re-elected in 2013, in part because of the lack of a serious alternative leader. The third Netanyahu administration failed to progress on peace despite pressure from US President Obama and the international community, and also found itself under fire from Israelis disillusioned by the widening gap between rich and poor.

Benjamin Netanyahu at the White House.

YAIR LAPID

The two new political stars who emerged victorious in the 2013 Knesset elections were Yair Lapid whose brand-new centrist Yesh Atid party won 19 Knesset seats (10 percent of the parliament) and Naftali Bennett whose right wing Jewish Home party doubled its tally to 13 seats. Lapid, a handsome journalist and talk-show host who attracted mainstream secular middle class support, became Finance Minister. Bennett, a start-up entrepreneur who had sold his company for over $100 million, extended the popularity of his nationalist orthodox religious party to more mainstream supporters, becoming Minister of Economy (Trade and Industry).

An Ethiopian Jew prays at the Western Wall.

THE PEOPLE OF ISRAEL

This tiny country comprises a highly diverse
mixture of people, many born elsewhere but
all regarding Israel as home.

The only valid generalization to make about Israelis is that there is no such thing as a typical Israeli. The in-gathering of the exiles has brought Jews to Israel from 80 countries, and, beneath their sometimes surly surface, they can behave with Latin American panache, European civility, or overwhelming Middle Eastern hospitality.

Israeli society itself has distinctly different sectors, including black-hatted ultra-Orthodox Jews and more modern Orthodox Jewry, as well as secular European (Ashkenazi) Jews and more traditional Oriental (Sephardi) Jews – in addition to the indigenous, and more rural, Arab population. More than one-fifth of Israel's population of over 8 million belongs to the Arab minority, which is mainly Muslim but also includes Christians and Druze: Israeli Arabs do not include the more than 4.5 million Palestinians of the West Bank and Gaza.

Israel's other minorities include several thousand Circassians, Turkic Muslims from the Southern Russian Caucasian mountains brought to the region in the 1800s to protect Ottoman interests. The Samaritans are an ancient Samarian sect, and the Baha'i religion has its world headquarters in Haifa. The Negev town of Dimona is home to several hundred black Hebrews, and since the 1970s the country has taken in hundreds of Vietnamese boat people, Bosnian Muslim refugees, former pro-Israel Southern Lebanese Christians and most recently thousands of Sudanese refugees. Israel also has an estimated 200,000 foreign workers.

Immigrants from the former Soviet Union now comprise 15 percent of Israeli society, while Ethiopian Jews add diversity to the social landscape. Slick Tel Aviv city businesspeople are increasingly prevalent, but the

Yemenite bride dressed in traditional garb for a Henna Ceremony.

pioneering spirit lives on and rugged, bronzed kibbutznikim can still be found.

An urban emphasis

Kibbutz dwellers aside, Israelis are predominantly urban and suburban creatures. More than half the population lives in the country's three largest cities. Jerusalem has a population of nearly 900,000, more than 2.8 million people live in the Greater Tel Aviv area, and an additional 550,000 in the Haifa Bay conurbation.

Educational institutions and the army have been powerful influences for social assimilation. The Hebrew language enhances social cohesion among diverse Jewish immigrants, although communities may jealously guard their distinct Jewish traditions.

Despite their diversity, native-born Israelis do have much in common and, perhaps because of their diversity, social niceties are rare. Native Israelis are brash, self-confident, and always in a hurry. Yet they can also be considerate, and their openness and curiosity delight the gregarious as much as they intimidate the reticent.

Secular Jewry

For many non-Jews the term "secular Jewry" would seem contradictory. Many Jews, too,

argue that Judaism is a religion and not a nationality and, therefore, Jews can be Orthodox or not Orthodox but never secular. Such semantic discussions overlook the realities of everyday Israeli life. The fact is that most Israeli Jews define themselves as both secular and Jewish.

It is difficult to ascertain who is a secular Jew. By and large, European Jews clearly identify themselves as secular, Orthodox, or ultra-Orthodox, and tend to be more extreme in their allegiances. It was secular Ashkenazi Jews from Europe who were the architects of

Israel has around 200,000 foreign workers.

A young citizen of Tel Aviv.

CREATIVE SOLUTIONS

Where religious rules are concerned it's sometimes hard for outsiders to know where lines are drawn between the acceptable and the unacceptable. Take dietary laws. McDonald's, the multi-national hamburger chain, undertook detailed market research before moving into Israel. Bacon McMuffins were non-starters, because pork of any kind is forbidden, but cheeseburgers were introduced successfully, even though kosher laws prohibit the mixing of meat and milk products. But bread is definitely not permissible during Passover, so McDonald's gets round this by serving cheeseburgers in buns made of potato flour instead of wheat.

the state in the early 1900s. Oriental Jews, who mostly came later, in the 1940s and 1950s, are more traditional. Many non-religious Oriental Jews have assimilated the European contempt for Orthodoxy, but most remain more respectful, even deferential, and are more likely to be contemptuous of secularism as a form of Western imperialism.

The divide between Ashkenazi and Oriental Jewry remains today, although intermarriage is common. Virtually all of the most impoverished Jewish Israelis are Oriental, and this disadvantaged sector of society also tends to have strong religious leanings and is hostile to the secularism of Ashkenazi Jewry. However, most Oriental Jews have made it out of the poor apartment buildings constructed for them when they arrived, and many have prospered. Some members of the current cabinet, including Energy Minister Silvan Shalom and Environment Minister Amir Peretz are Oriental Jews.

Politics and religion

Israel's secular Jews share the liberal, universalist views of their North American and Western European counterparts. Democracy, freedom of expression, and minority rights are the sacred values. Most would not mind if

right-wing Israel-Beitenu Party (supported by Russian-speaking immigrants) are all devoutly anti-clerical, while the centrist Yesh Atid and Hatneuah and right-wing ruling Likud Party led by Prime Minister Benjamin Netanyahu are all predominantly secular. Together these parties control more than 90 of the 120 Knesset seats. Even so, Israel's system of proportional representation and the need for coalition building with the religious parties means that the Orthodox rabbinate can jealously protect its monopoly on issues of personal status, such as marriage, divorce, conversion, and burial.

Dining at an Arab-owned restaurant in Old Yafo.

their daughter wanted to marry a non-Jew but might well be more bothered if she brought home a black-hatted ultra-Orthodox Jew. Though secular Jews firmly hold the reins of political power, there is a belief, backed up by demographic trends that these reins are slipping out of their hands.

Secular Jewry, especially in Jerusalem, feels it is a besieged community, threatened by the much higher birth rate of both the Arab minority and ultra-Orthodox Jewry.

Secular Jewry often complains about the existence of Orthodox religious parties, but the fact is that it is impossible in Israel to separate politics from religion. The left-wing Meretz faction, the left-of-center Labor Party and the

Political expediency has led to an alliance between the essentially anti-religious Likud and religious elements. Likud's reluctance to relinquish the West Bank and Gaza stems from security and nationalistic concerns, while the religious cherish the biblical concept of the Land of Israel. Moreover, Likud traditionally relied on support from the Oriental communities, who incline toward tradition.

Family values

Although many people are surprised by the extent to which Israel's secular majority disregards religious practice, it would be misleading to think that Israelis have no regard at all for religion. On substantive issues such as marriage and burial, opinion polls consistently show the majority of Israelis support the Orthodox monopoly of these rites, though this support is eroding among younger Jews. This has greatly anguished the Reform and Conservative movements, imported to Israel from America, which attempt to adapt Judaism to the modern age, and in particular to integrate women into the synagogue service.

The fact is that secular Israelis have Zionism, which remains an ideology capable of attracting a high level of commitment to the building of the state and is closely linked to conservative

In Jerusalem's Me'a She'arim, home to ultra-Orthodox Jews.

family values. And even the most outwardly secular of Jews still tends to have an inner belief in the essential Jewish values – belief in God and a divine plan. This fills the spiritual vacuum. In the wake of Yitzhak Rabin's assassination, young Israelis found these values helped them to cope with their grief over his death.

Like the post-Christian West, post-Jewish Israel is plagued by crime, violence, drug addiction and inner-city poverty. But, despite a growing divorce rate, family ties remain strong; there is a deep respect for symbols of state, and, on the whole, young people are highly motivated to serve in the army.

Secular Israel is at once both radical and conservative. The long-haired teenager with a ring

through his nose, for example, doesn't usually complain about having a short back and sides and submitting to army discipline at the age of 18. The divisions in Israeli society, though real, are misleading. The assassination of Yitzhak Rabin, a left-of-center secular Ashkenazi, by Yigal Amir, a right-wing religious Jew from a Yemen-born family, seems to epitomize enmities. But this violent deed was an exceptional event. When the chips are down, Israelis have a surprising capacity for joining ranks.

Orthodox and ultra-Orthodox

To a secular Jew the Orthodox and ultra-Orthodox groups have much in common. Both strictly observe the all-encompassing world of Halacha – Jewish Orthodox practice. This means that the men keep their heads covered and pray at least three times a day. Kosher dietary laws are strictly followed, and the Sabbath is a day for absolute abstention from work, including "lighting a spark" – thus prohibiting traveling, cooking, switching on a light, using a phone or computer, and even smoking.

The diverse head coverings of the men often indicate degrees of Orthodoxy. Generally, the larger the *kippa* (skullcap) the more Orthodox the wearer. The *kippot* range from the small knitted variety, worn by the modern Orthodox, to the big knitted ones of the mainstream Orthodox, and the large black skullcaps worn beneath even larger black hats by the ultra-Orthodox. In recent times, young modern Orthodox Jews have tended either to become secular or to take on a more ultra-Orthodox, and usually ultra-nationalist, outlook.

UNDERCOVER ASSIGNMENT

Female visitors to the ultra-Orthodox quarters of Me'a She'arim in Jerusalem and Bnei Brak near Tel Aviv should take seriously the warnings not to wear immodest dress. It isn't just friendly advice, and the dress code is not simply a rather quaint custom; those in violation of the edict may be sworn and spat at, and even stoned. It's one of those occasions when it's wise to put aside one's own feelings about personal choice and resist the desire to make a point to a repressive male-dominated community. Respect the rules and cover up as much as you can while you are in these areas. You will also feel more anonymous and find it easier to explore.

A woman's clothes are a good indication of the Orthodox Jew's lifestyle. A man with a small knitted *kippa* is likely to be accompanied by a woman wearing jeans or other contemporary Western clothing. Women in the large mainstream Orthodox community will wear long dresses, keep their arms covered, and are increasingly wearing wigs or headscarves.

Women in the ultra-Orthodox communities are literally kept under wraps. Not a square inch of flesh is seen other than the face and hands. The ultra-Orthodox woman cannot be in an enclosed room with men other than her immediate relatives. At weddings and parties women will sit in a separate area.

Ultra-Orthodox Jewish society comprises a collection of sects as much medieval Eastern European as biblical in their origins. This is why, on Saturdays (Sabbaths) and holidays, the men wear fur hats more suitable for a Russian winter than a Middle Eastern summer.

Anti-Zionism to ultra-Zionism

Historically all Jews were by definition Orthodox, and three or four centuries ago all of Eastern European Jewry would have followed a moral code similar to that of Me'a She'arim today. Growing secularism in 19th-century Christian Europe compelled Jews to find other outlets of cultural expression, and Zionism emerged as a secular movement. Therefore almost all Orthodox Jews were anti-Zionist to begin with, opposed to the use of Hebrew, the holy tongue, for everyday use and to the notion that a Jewish state could contemplate any degree of separation between synagogue and state.

However, in the 1920s a strong national religious movement emerged, combining the nationalistic values of Zionism with the tenets of Orthodoxy. With its own kibbutzim and workers' movements, it was bolstered by the mass immigration of Oriental Jewry, which had deeper ties with Jewish tradition.

Commanding the political support of about 10 percent of the population, the national religious movement, which historically contained strong elements of liberalism, veered sharply to the right after 1967 when the Gush Emunim settlers' movement sprang from it. Holding the Land of Israel to be sacred, the movement has come to be perceived as the fiercest opponent of territorial compromise.

The national religious movement runs its own schools, distinct from their secular counterparts. Those modern Orthodox Jews who have adopted a more religious lifestyle are called Hardalnikim, literally meaning Haredi national Orthodox.

Ultra-Orthodox Jewry, known in Hebrew as *Haredim*, also has its own education system. These black-clad communities are at best critical of Zionism, at worst still opposed to the Jewish state. Each sect has its own rabbinical leaders, and most of them are based in New York rather than Jerusalem.

An Orthodox Jew at prayer.

The largest *Haredi* sect is the Lubavitchers. Under the late Rabbi Schneerson, revered by his followers as a messianic figure, the Lubavitchers took a pro-Israel hawkish stand supporting continuation of Jewish control of the West Bank. The Satmar, on the other hand, which also has its headquarters in New York, refuses to recognize the government of Israel as the legitimate representative of the Jewish people.

An extreme Jerusalem-based sect called Netorei Karta even supported the PLO when its charter called for the destruction of the Jewish state and frequently sends delegations to Teheran to encourage the anti-Zionism of the Iranian regime. This sect holds that the Zionists are worse than the Nazis, for while the latter sought to destroy the Jews physically, the former are destroying the Jewish people spiritually.

Prayer power

All these sects, even those with pro-Zionist leanings, tend to have contempt for the institutions of modern Israel – the flag, the army, the Supreme Court, etc. Few ultra-Orthodox Jews serve in the army, and those who do will often end up in the Rabbinical Corps, checking that kitchens are kosher. Even the right-wing Lubavitchers argue that praying for the strength of Israel is as important as fighting for it.

As there are no civil marriages in Israel, gays and lesbians cannot marry. But homosexuals who marry overseas can register with the government as a couple and receive related economic rights, as well as being same-sex parents.

pattern of sects, though Israel's European religious establishment did succeed in imposing black hats and suits on many Jews from Yemen and North Africa. But ultimately Sephardi

Ultra-Orthodox Jews gather around their Rabbi's car during a protest against military conscription in 2013.

As a result, secular Jewry dislikes ultra-Orthodox Jewry's lack of patriotism, while the ultra-Orthodox condemn secular Jews' non-religious lifestyle. Orthodox Jewry is caught in the middle, justifying and condemning both sides.

Despite this lack of common ground, secular Israel exercises a certain degree of tolerance, mainly because the ultra-Orthodox parties hold the balance of power between left and right. Moreover, many Jews believe that to harass the ultra-Orthodox communities could leave them open to charges of anti-Semitism.

Oriental Jewry

Religious Jews from Asian and African countries have never fitted neatly into the European

LANGUAGE OF CHANGE

As a result of the huge waves of Russian immigration since 1990, Israel's urban landscape has taken on a decidedly Slavic feel. Cyrillic shop signs abound, vying for space with Hebrew, English and Arabic lettering. Newsstands are bursting with Russian-language publications, and in some suburbs of Tel Aviv and Haifa, Russian is the lingua franca. Russian-speakers have their own state-run radio station, and cable TV brings them all the major television channels from Russia. The newcomers are learning Hebrew as they become assimilated, but it is interesting to see the impact of yet another language on this polyglot nation.

religious leaders, like the late, charismatic former Chief Rabbi Ovadia Yosef, who always wore his Oriental robes, have prevailed. The Shas political party he founded controls nearly 10 percent of Knesset seats. Much of Shas's support comes from traditional rather than Orthodox Oriental Jews, indicating that the divide between observant and non-observant Sephardis is narrower than that between their European counterparts.

About 20 percent of Israeli Jews are Orthodox. This number has remained constant over the past few decades, for, though Orthodox Jewry has a higher birth rate, the overwhelming majority of Jewish immigrants from Russia are secular.

Russian-Speaking Jews

"Let My People Go" was the slogan used by campaign activists pushing for the right of Soviet Jewry to emigrate freely. Nobody believed it would actually happen even in the 1970s, the era of détente when nearly 400,000 Soviet Jews were allowed out, about half of them reaching Israel, the rest heading for the United States.

But as glasnost gained momentum in the late 1980s, the right to emigrate was suddenly granted to Soviet Jewry. For Israel the event was as momentous as the breaching of the Berlin Wall. More than 1 million Russian-speaking Jews reached Israel in the 1990s.

Transforming Israel

During the 1990s, Russian-speaking Jews surpassed Moroccans as Israel's largest immigrant group. Although secular, the Russian-speaking immigrants tend to be right-wing. Their best-known political leaders are the former Soviet refusenik Natan Sharansky and Avigdor Liberman of the far-right Israel-Beteinu Party, who has served as Foreign Minister since 2009. The latest wave of Russian immigrants has a high educational profile. Many are scientists and engineers, musicians and teachers.

Understandably, it took a little while for some of the Russian-speaking newcomers to master Hebrew and become accustomed to the more assertive behavior of Western society, but most have adjusted well, if not fully. After serving an immigrant's apprenticeship sweeping the streets, washing dishes or doing some other kind of menial work, most immigrants managed to find a job in their profession, while their children have merged into mainstream middle class Israel.

These immigrants have changed the demographic balance of Israel. Before their arrival, Israel had a small Oriental Jewish majority. Russian Jewry has tipped the scales back in favor of Ashkenazi Jewry, although 10 percent of these newcomers are Oriental Jews from the ancient communities in Georgia, Azerbaijan, and the Russian Caucasus, as well as Uzbekistan.

Kosher and un-kosher

In the main, Russian-speaking newcomers are Ashkenazi and secular, but about 30 percent of

Jews descended from the communities of the Middle East.

newcomers are not Halachically Jewish. This means that they qualify for Jewish citizenship by virtue of having one Jewish grandparent (as stipulated in the Law of Return of 1950) but do not meet the Orthodox Jewish requirement of having a Jewish mother.

Even those who are fully Jewish had little opportunity to learn about their Jewish heritage while growing up under the Soviet regime. Israel was already a highly secular society before the newcomers arrived, but interestingly these immigrants have failed to make the political impact that their numbers should warrant. At present more than 300,000 Russian-speaking newcomers cannot get married in Israel, which has no civil wedding ceremonies – they must travel abroad, usually preferring Cyprus. But most of these immigrants still adhere to the traditional Soviet belief that taking to the streets to protest is contemptible behavior and, as a result, their voice is not often heard in Israel's robust and demonstrative political culture. Moreover, their political leaders have seen this basic denial of the right to marry as less important than economic and defense issues, and have not rocked the government coalition boat over the matter.

Most of these newcomers are not Zionists who, during the Soviet regime, yearned to

An employee at a Cellcom Israel Ltd retail store.

immigrate to Israel for ideological reasons. The immigrants of the 1970s risked imprisonment in order to leave for the Jewish State. The majority of those who came when the floodgates first opened in 1989 had a profound sense of Jewish identity; they spread their wings and migrated at the first opportunity. But subsequent arrivals have had a less clear agenda, although many are seeking a more secure economic life amid the greater employment opportunities Israel offers. Thousands of these immigrants returned to Russia during the economic boom that preceded the global financial crisis.

The latest wave of immigrants represents nearly 20 percent of the Jewish population.

> *Each year in November/early December, 50 days after Yom Kippur, the Ethiopian Jewish community travels to Jerusalem to celebrate Sigd, when they believe the Jewish people accepted the Torah.*

They and their children are already assimilating Zionist norms of allegiance to the state, service in the army, and fluency in Hebrew. In parallel, they are contributing some of their old culture to their new home, and the influence of their secularism is likely to move large sections of Israeli society even further away from traditional Judaism.

Ethiopians

The dramatic airlifts of Ethiopian Jews from the heart of Africa to the Promised Land in 1984 and 1991 captured the world's imagination. For centuries Ethiopian Jews had cherished the dream that one day they would return to Jerusalem. The dream finally came true, but the reality has not always matched their expectations.

Before arriving in Israel, most Ethiopian Jews had been semi-literate subsistence farmers living in simple villages, usually without electricity or any modern conveniences. Being thrust into a fast-moving, high-tech society has been traumatic, especially for those people who were over 30 when they arrived. For the young, change is of course easier.

Some of Israel's 140,000-strong Ethiopian Jewish community have done well, especially the children of community leaders, but most struggle to keep their feet on the lower rungs of the social ladder. According to Yitzhak Dessie, who became the first Ethiopian-born Israeli lawyer when he qualified in 1998, the essential obstacle confronting Israel's Ethiopian-born community is not discrimination but lack of employment opportunities and their own inability to grasp how Israeli culture functions.

The sense of alienation felt by many Ethiopians has been exacerbated by the reluctance of Israel's rabbinical authorities to recognize their unequivocal Jewishness. Thus they are required to undergo symbolic conversion to Judaism by being immersed in a ritual bath. In addition, the *kessim* (traditional Ethiopian spiritual leaders) are not permitted to officiate at state-recognized marriages.

Positive discrimination

The younger generation (half the community is under 18) have been adept at assimilating Israeli values. The vigor with which they have protested their grievances through demonstrations, the media, and political lobbying bodes well for the future. For its part, the Israeli establishment has allocated major resources for the education of the young generation, though still short of the required amount, and has introduced positive discrimination measures, such as more generous mortgages than those available to other new immigrants.

While institutional racism against the Ethiopians is rare (the most anti-Ethiopian racist sectors in Israeli society are found among the Russian-speaking new immigrants and Oriental Jews), the community sometimes suffers in rather odd ways. For example, the Health Ministry decided that Ethiopians were not suitable blood donors because of a higher incidence of Aids, tuberculosis, and other diseases. Instead of the decision being announced publicly, a secret memo was sent to donation staff asking them to accept Ethiopian blood and then throw it away. The discovery of the policy provoked a storm of protest. An inquiry found that the policy was justified on health and safety grounds but that its underhand method of implementation was inappropriate.

Dramatic rescue

The Ethiopians began reaching Israel by way of the Sudan in the early 1980s, and Operation Moses in 1984 saw 7,000 people airlifted to Israel. Most of them had trekked hundreds of miles across the desert to the Sudanese border, while countless others had died en route. Even more dramatically, during a single 24-hour period in 1991, 14,000 Ethiopians were flown to Israel as part of Operation Solomon. These people had been gathering in Addis Ababa over the course of a year, but had been prevented from leaving by the Marxist regime. The Israeli Air Force succeeded in rescuing them just as the regime was toppled by rebels.

The history and geographical dispersion of Ethiopian Jewry is somewhat unclear, but in modern times most were located in two regions

of Africa. Those who reached Israel in the early 1980s came primarily from Tigre, while the subsequent wave originated principally from Gondar. Although the two groups use the same Amharic alphabet, they speak different Ethiopic languages.

After initially refusing to bring to Israel the Falash Mura, Ethiopian Christians who had converted from Judaism in the 19th century, the government has airlifted some 40,000 to Israel over the past decade, and several thousand more budding immigrants remain in Ethiopia awaiting visas to emigrate.

Prayers at the Church of the Holy Sepulcher, in the Christian Quarter of Jerusalem's Old City.

THE LOST TRIBES RETURN

The origins of the Ethiopian Jews are shrouded in mystery. Known in Ethiopia as *falashas* (invaders), they are believed by some scholars to be remnants of Dan, one of the Ten Lost Tribes. Some claim they are descendants of King Solomon and the Queen of Sheba. Cut off from world Jewry for two millennia, the community has sustained remarkably similar traditions.

There are distinctions, though. For example, the Ethiopians took with them into exile the Five Books of Moses and the stories of the Prophets, but have no knowledge of the Oral Law, which was codified only after the fall of the Second Temple in AD 70.

ISRAELI ARABS

Israel's Arabs occupy an anomalous position, yet
most live harmoniously with their Jewish neighbors
while retaining cultural ties to the Arab world.

N ot all the Arab inhabitants of Palestine
heeded the call of the surrounding states
(and "promptings" from the nascent
Israeli Army) to flee their homes when the State
of Israel was established, despite the promise
that they would be able to return within weeks
once the Jewish State had been snuffed out by
the invading armies. About 150,000 remained,
and numbers have since grown to their present
1.7 million. Half of Israel's Arab population
is urbanized in the towns and villages of the
Galilee. There are large Arab communities in
Nazareth, Haifa, Ramla, Yafo, and Jerusalem.

Of Israel's Arabs 83 percent are Muslim, 9
percent Christian, and 8 percent Druze. All are
faced with the paradox of being at once Arab
and Palestinian, with linguistic, historic, cultural, religious, and familial ties to the Arab
world, and also citizens of a state, which, since
its inception, has been in conflict with that
world. They have managed to walk the tightrope
between their Palestinian nationality and Israeli
citizenship, although in recent years they have
become more assertive and less acquiescent,
with a more militant Islamic and Palestinian
national identity.

The only legal discrimination against the
Arab population is that they are not liable to
military conscription – although they may volunteer – because it is deemed unreasonable to
ask them to fight against their fellow Palestinians. Only the small Druze community is subject to the draft – and that is at its own request.

But exemption from military service has
proved to be a double-edged sword. The army is
the great equalizer, uniting Israelis from wildly
differing backgrounds. Exclusion from it inevitably involves social handicaps. In a more tangible
and unfair form, it renders Israeli Arabs ineligible

In Daliet-el-Carmel, a Druze village near Haifa.

for certain jobs and state benefits and exacerbates
the already disproportionate allocation of government land and economic resources.

The stain of discrimination

The plight of Israel's Arabs was acknowledged
for the first time by the Israeli government in
2003 following a state commission of inquiry
into the killing of 13 Arab demonstrators by
police. The commission not only blamed the
police for over-reacting but spoke of a historical injustice to Israel's Arabs and "the stain of
discrimination."

In spite of this and other disadvantages, the
Arabs of Israel have flourished; the impact of
education and of involvement with Israel's

vigorously open and democratic society have been profound. These days most young Arabs live with their own Western-style nuclear families and are economically independent of their elders. There is still, to be sure, strong attachment to traditional values and customs, but these are tinged with a clear preference for the comforts of the affluent West.

A spiral of radicalism is not inevitable. A new breed of young Arab mayors, leaders, and activists – educated in Israel and at ease with the Israeli system – has emerged at grass-roots level. They are demanding that facilities in their areas

state. Young Druze are conscripted into the Israel Defense Forces (at the community's own request), and many serve in the regular army and border police. Traditionally an assertive people, always ready to defend their interests, they have proved to be first-class soldiers, and large numbers of Druze have been decorated for bravery.

In the Lebanon War of 1982–4, Israel's Druze found themselves in a delicate position when the IDF was aligned with Christian forces in Lebanon fighting the Lebanese Druze. It is a tribute to the strong friendship between the Jews and the Druze that their alliance survived this period.

A Druze woman participates in Isfiya village's annual festival.

Druze woman making bread in the market, Akko.

be brought up to the standard of those of their Jewish neighbors, and their style demonstrates a self-confidence that is at once proudly Arab and unequivocally Israeli.

The increasing Arab clout in the political arena is another significant development. At present there are 10 Arab members of the Knesset out of a total of 120, representing a broad spectrum of opinion.

The Druze community

Although some of the first clashes between the Jewish pioneers in the 1880s and the local residents were with Druze villagers in Metula and other parts of the Galilee, Israel's Druze community has traditionally been loyal to the Israeli

The Druze have been a persecuted minority in the Middle East since they broke away from mainstream Islam in the 11th century, accepting the claims to divinity of the Egyptian Caliph El-Hakim Abu Ali el-Mansur. For this reason they have tended to inhabit inaccessible mountain ranges, where they could hold out against their enemies. Most Druze today live in the Mount Lebanon region of Lebanon and in Jebel Druze in Syria; some 100,000 of them are in the hills of the Galilee and on the Carmel Range in Israel, with a further 30,000 in the Golan Heights. There are records of Druze communities in the Galilee as early as the 13th century, but the first Mount Carmel settlement was established in 1590 when Syrian Druze fled their homes after an abortive revolt against the Turkish sultan.

Druze villages are not very different from Arab villages in the Galilee and the coastal plain, although the elders do not wear black headbands with their *keffiye* headdresses. The religious Druze cultivate impressive moustaches. The women dress in modern clothes, the younger ones in jeans and short-sleeved blouses. Young men are indistinguishable from Israeli Jews.

Few Druze contemplate assimilating into Jewish society, or converting to Islam and assimilating into the local Arab community; virtually

Market shopping in Nazareth.

all are proud of their own identity and culture and do not intermarry with other communities. Some Israeli Druze live in mixed villages, notably Pekiin, where they coexist with their Christian Arab neighbors and some Jewish families who have lived there since Second Temple times.

The Druze were recognized as a separate religious community with their own courts in 1957. Their religion is said to be similar to that of the Ismai'li Muslims. The sheikhs, the religious leaders of the community, guard its secrets, and the ordinary Druze are simply required to observe the basic moral laws prohibiting murder, adultery, and theft.

They have their own interpretations of Jewish, Muslim, and Christian prophets, believing that

their missions were revealed to a select group, the first of whom was Jethro, father-in-law of Moses. One Druze religious festival is an annual pilgrimage to what is believed to be the grave of Jethro, near the Horns of Hittim in the Galilee.

Serving alongside the Druze in the minorities unit of the IDF are the Circassians, about 3,000 of whom live in Israel. They are a Caucasian mountain people, originating in Russia; most of them are fair-haired, with blue or green eyes. Although many of the Russian Circassians are professing Christians, the Middle East branch of this people are Muslims. Almost all the Israeli Circassians live in the village of Kfar Kama, by Lake Kinneret in the Galilee, and in Rehaniya, just north of Safed.

The Bedouin

The Bedouin is the quintessential Arab, the nomad herdsman, dressed in flowing robes, riding his camel across the sands, pitching his tent under the palms before riding on to his next camping site. But like many romantic images, this one, fostered by old Hollywood films, is false – or at least somewhat out of date.

Some 20 percent of Israel's 150,000 Bedouin people live in the Galilee and the coastal plain, in settled villages that are virtually indistinguishable, to an outsider's eye, from other Arab villages. Traditions are stronger in the Negev, and you may still be invited for coffee, reclining on cushions and rugs of black goat's hair, though few Bedouin still live in the traditional manner. Some do still live in tents, and quite a few possess camels and herd sheep and goats, but increasing numbers are moving into permanent

A WOMAN'S PLACE

Israeli laws granting women equal rights have helped to liberalize attitudes toward women in Arab society. The changing aspirations of women (and of their husbands) are reflected in the birth rate – down from an average of 8.5 children per family in 1968 to 4.8 in the late 1990s and 4.2 today – although it is not expected to fall in the foreseeable future to the Jewish average of 3.2 children per family.

In Negev Bedouin society polygamy remains a major problem, with more than 25 percent of adult men having more than one wife, even though this contravenes Israeli civil law.

Bedouin are not conscripted into the Israel Defense Forces, but many of them serve in the army as scouts and trackers, utilizing their traditional skills, and several have reached senior rank.

housing and finding work in construction, industry, the service sector, and transportation.

Life on the land

The Bedouin farm the loess soil extensively, growing mostly barley and wheat but also cucumbers, tomatoes, peppers, vines, and more. For irrigation they use dams, which they have built themselves, as well as former Nabatean structures, which they have carefully restored. They also utilize ancient water cisterns, which they have excavated.

Scores of Bedouin fled from the Negev from 1947 to 1949, around the time of Israel's War of Independence, but later returned. The situation was stabilized in 1953 when a census was conducted, with all those present at the time being accepted as citizens of Israel. Formerly wandering freely between Transjordan, the Judean Desert, the Negev, and Sinai, the Bedouin were forced to recognize the new international realities in the early 1950s. Israel's Bedouin are now confined to an area east of Be'er Sheva extending north as far as the former border with Jordan, and south as far as Dimona. This is only around 10 percent of the area over which they once wandered, but includes some excellent farming land. Today, there is no tribe that does not farm as well as herd its flocks.

The traditional life of the Bedouin shepherds, which involved moving the herds from pasture to pasture, is a thing of the past, and their camps have long been permanent in the Negev. About half the Negev Bedouin live in government recognized settlements. The other half live in unrecognized settlements that lack running water, electricity, and other basic utilities. Their nomadic tradition, and their tendency to live with their dwellings spread out all over the desert, have made it difficult to plan modern villages for them, and they are resisting government attempts to move them into permanent housing in small towns. Instead, their homes are improvised, ramshackle structures usually made of prefabricated metal.

Today, most of the major tribal centers have their own elementary schools, and there are now new high schools at Kuseifa near Arad and elsewhere. Bedouin take education seriously, and because of a lack of educational resources are often compelled to walk more than 16km (10 miles) to school where necessary.

Bedouin arts and crafts still exist, with a flourishing home industry, based on weaving, sewing, and embroidery. These wares are on sale in many places, notably in Thursday's Be'er Sheva market, a popular tourist attraction, and in the arts and crafts center in the village of Lakhiya on Highway 31 northeast of Be'er Sheva.

Bedouin Arab boys.

TRADITIONAL CRAFTS

Traditionally the Druze were successful hill farmers, but with the development of modern agriculture this activity has declined. However, their traditional weaving, carpet-making, basketwork, and other crafts are still flourishing. There are a number of Druze villages with interesting markets selling handicrafts. Daliyat el-Karmel, south of Haifa, is an attractive village, a popular spot for tourists; and the Golan Heights villages of Majdal e-Shams and Mas'ada also specialize in local craftwork. But handicrafts don't keep an entire community employed, and most young Druze these days find work in industry or the flourishing service sector.

THE PALESTINIANS

Nobody pretends that the Israelis and the Palestinians
will ever be best friends, but on both sides there
is a genuine desire to avoid major bloodshed.

Palestinian nationalism was a reaction to
Zionism. As Jews began buying up Arab
land in the early 20th century, so the
indigenous Arab population was compelled
to question its own identity. Historically, that
identity had revolved around the extended
family, the village, the Arab people, and Islam;
but in the modern world of emerging nations,
such an identity was either too parochial or
too broad.

Just as many people – Jews and non-Jews –
originally denied that the Jewish people con-
stituted a nation, so Palestinians found their
legitimacy under fire from both friends and
foes. Many Arabs spoke of pan-Arabism and of
one Arab nation encompassing North Africa and
Asia Minor. Often such talk cloaked the expan-
sionist ambitions of Syria, Jordan, and Egypt.

Irreconcilable aims

For the Jews, of course, the Palestinian national
movement, which denied the right of a Jewish state to exist, could never be reconciled
with Zionist aspirations. Moderate Palestinian
leaders, as well as the Hashemite kings (King
Abdullah and his grandson, King Hussein, and
his son, the reigning King Abdullah), were ame-
nable to coexistence with the Jews. But they
were unable to counter the militant rejection-
ism of Syria and Egypt and of local leaders.

The tragedy of the Palestinian people was the
inability of its leadership to accept the *fait accom-
pli* of a Jewish state. Arab anger is understand-
able, because European anti-Semitism, which
drove Jews back to the Middle East, resulted
in the loss of Palestinian land. But attempts to
drive the Jews into the sea in 1948 and 1967 and
the expulsion of more than a million Jews from
Arab countries saw Israel strengthened.

*Palestinian children in an olive field, at the end of a day of
harvesting.*

The founding of the PLO in 1964 was a crucial
stage in the evolution of the Palestinian national
entity. Even so, Yasser Arafat, its leader from
1965 until his death in 2004, was imprisoned in
Damascus. Since the Muslim conquest, Palestine
had been ruled from Damascus, and the Syrians
saw Palestine – and Lebanon and Jordan – as an
integral part of the modern Syrian nation.

The Six Day War of 1967, and the further
expansion of Israel, saw the PLO come into its
own. It was now in Syria's interest to encourage Arafat to regain Arab lands. Before 1967 the
West Bank was in Jordanian hands, while Gaza
was under Egyptian rule. But if the PLO and its
many factions were puppets designed to restore

Arab sovereignty over as much of Israel as possible, Arafat – and most especially the Palestinians of the West Bank and Gaza – proved to be more independently minded than either Israel or the Arab world had anticipated.

Occupation and acrimony

Israel, after its occupation of the West Bank and Gaza in 1967, enjoyed good relations with its newly conquered Palestinian subjects. Many of the Arabs of the West Bank and Gaza, for their part, were initially beguiled by Israeli liberalism and other Western ways. A free press was

Lebanon, and finally in Tunis, was often viewed as a wealthy Diaspora leader who represented the millions of Palestinians living in Jordan, Syria, Lebanon, Egypt, the Gulf, and elsewhere in the world, but was out of touch with the Palestinians on the frontline of Israeli occupation.

The effects of the Intifada

PLO tactics in the 1970s and 1980s were a mixture of terrorism and diplomacy. Terrorist attacks against civilians in Israel and around the world forced the Palestinian question onto the international agenda. Moreover, Arafat forged powerful

A Palestinian man confronts Israeli soldiers in protest against the construction of the separation barrier in the West Bank.

set up, universities were established, elections were held for the local municipalities, and the economy flourished, boosted by the abundance of labor-intensive jobs in Israel.

Israel presumed that the Arabs of the West Bank and Gaza would prove as malleable as those who had stayed behind in 1948 and taken up Israeli citizenship. But Israeli Arabs were mainly village people, while those of Gaza and the West Bank had a large urban intelligentsia who identified strongly with the Palestinian nationalism espoused by Arafat and the PLO. However, although these Palestinian notables rejected Israeli hegemony, they also felt alienated from the PLO leadership. Arafat, who built his own organizational hierarchy first in Jordan, then in

A WANDERING GOVERNMENT

When given the right to assume Israeli citizenship, the Arabs of East Jerusalem refused the offer, to a man. It took the Israelis, even those on the left, many years to appreciate that Palestinian nationalism was not going to go away. The Palestinians' declared aim is to establish their own government in Jerusalem. After the return of the PLO to the West Bank and Gaza, Palestinian government meetings were held alternately in Gaza City and Ramallah near Jerusalem until the Hamas takeover in 2007. In 2000 Prime Minister Ehud Barak proposed giving much of East Jerusalem to the Palestinians – so the dream is not entirely unrealistic.

alliances with the Soviet bloc and the developing world, which unswervingly supported the Palestinian cause. But, while the PLO succeeded in causing Israel untold political and economic damage and creating a climate of national insecurity, it was unable to achieve its goal of an independent Palestinian state.

The momentum for change came from within the West Bank and Gaza. The Intifada began in December 1987 in the Gaza Strip as a spontaneous uprising against Israeli occupation. Within days it had become an orchestrated campaign against Israeli troops, characterized by

discontinue terrorist tactics. But a brief flirtation with American diplomats in the 1980s ended when Arafat was unable to prevent his own people from launching terrorist attacks against Israel. Nor was the right-wing government in Israel prepared even to contemplate an indirect dialogue with Arafat.

Arafat's stock fell even further after he threw his support behind Iraq's Saddam Hussein after the 1990 invasion of Kuwait. This isolated him from many of his Arab allies and caused the mass expulsion of the affluent Palestinian communities of the Gulf. The collapse of the Soviet

Grilled corn for sale outside Jerusalem's Damascus Gate during the holy fasting month of Ramadan.

the throwing of rocks and occasional Molotov cocktails. The rebellion spread to the West Bank.

A new young Palestinian leadership began to emerge in the West Bank and Gaza. While it didn't discourage stoning the Zionist enemy, it was also prepared to enter into dialogue with Israel. Faisal Husseini, nephew of the arch anti-Zionist Sheikh Haj Amin Husseini, learned to speak fluent Hebrew as a gesture of goodwill.

Arafat jumped on the Intifada bandwagon. But it was the local Palestinian leadership that was calling the tune, while Arafat and his entourage in Tunis looked increasingly remote from the Palestinians in the frontline. Arafat put out diplomatic feelers, letting it be known that he was prepared to recognize Israel and

Union, the PLO's superpower patron, saw Arafat down and, many assumed, out.

Gaza via Madrid and Oslo

But Yasser Arafat proved more resilient and compromising than many gave him credit for. He was allowed to attend the Madrid Peace Conference in 1991 as part of the Jordanian delegation. After the election of the Labor government in Israel in 1992, he seized the olive branch held out by Rabin's dovish advisors, and in less than a year he was shaking hands with the Israeli prime minister on the lawn of the White House in Washington. In 1994 he arrived in triumph in Gaza as Israel withdrew its troops from most of the Gaza Strip.

By 1995 the Palestinian Authority's jurisdiction comprised Gaza and the major West Bank cities, and Arafat's rule was confirmed through democratically held elections.

Until 2000, Arafat forbade terrorist attacks against Israelis – there had been a spate of suicide bombings in 1995 and 1996 and sporadic attacks afterwards – and he had imprisoned Hamas and Islamic Jihad leaders who did not obey his prohibition. But, after the failure of the all of pre-1948 Palestine regained. But Israel hit back hard, and so widespread was the destruction that much of the West Bank resembled a war zone. Daily life became unbearable due to constant raids by IDF soldiers, aerial and artillery bombardment, targeted killings, a virtual siege on towns making movement around the West Bank impossible, and widespread expropriation of land as Israel built a separation wall.

A French-style form of government was introduced with the new post of prime minister beneath Arafat's presidency. Mahmoud Abbas, popularly known as Abu Mazen, was the first to

A Palestinian shepherd tends his flock.

Camp David peace talks in the summer of 2000, a visit by Ariel Sharon, then in opposition, to the Temple Mount sparked the second Intifada.

Unlike the first Intifada, which attracted international support as Palestinians threw rocks at Israeli soldiers, the second Intifada's use of guns and suicide bombers was looked on less sympathetically in the West, especially after the 9/11 terrorist attacks on the US in 2001. Moreover, Arafat was perceived by the international community to have unilaterally pulled out of a viable peace process. But, for the Palestinians, the second Intifada was a War of Independence. During 2002 constant suicide bombings even gave the fleeting illusion that the Zionists might be completely defeated and

THE PALESTINIAN AUTHORITY

If Palestinians had hoped that a more prosperous lifestyle and democratic regime with an independent judiciary and free press would be part of their emerging national entity, they were initially disappointed. Instead, a police state and corrupt administration were established, with Yasser Arafat's cronies diverting overseas aid and Israeli payments into their own overseas bank accounts. The Palestinian in the street felt resentful that life seemed no better in the Palestinian Authority. Many turned to Islam and Hamas. But, when the second Intifada broke out in 2000, this corruption of the 1990s was largely forgotten in the passion of war.

be appointed to the new post. But the veteran PLO leader refused to relinquish any real power. Arafat's death in France in 2004 acted as a catalyst for a ceasefire between the Palestinians and Israelis. The Intifada had anyway been running out of steam and more and more Palestinians had been questioning the point of continued hostilities against Israel. Abu Mazen, the natural successor to Arafat, met with Ariel Sharon, and the two leaders agreed to end the bloodshed. Abu Mazen would prevent suicide bombings and attacks, including the firing of mortar shells into Israel, while Israel would stop its targeted killings.

smuggled into Gaza via tunnels from Egypt. Cat-and-mouse hostilities between Israel and Hamas – the Palestinians firing rockets into Israel, which retaliated with air raids – caused brief Gaza Wars at the end of 2008, in 2012 and 2014 and little progress toward peace subsequently. On the West Bank the status quo held as the economy flourished and hope floundered.

The declaration of Palestinian independence in September 2011 and its recognition by the UN reshuffled, and the Fatah-Hamas accord in 2014 did nothing to change the status-quo stalemate with the Israelis.

Yasser Arafat's "mobile grave" in Ramallah, designed to be moved one day to Jerusalem.

Fatah and Hamas

Abu Mazen was elected president in 2005 with a mandate to pursue peace in the wake of Israel's complete withdrawal from the Gaza Strip and northern West Bank, although he was never able to generate the strength and popularity of Arafat. Tensions between Abu Mazen's Fatah and Hamas erupted in 2007 as Hamas seized control of the Gaza Strip, forcing Fatah officials to flee their homes, while Fatah took over the West Bank. The two-state solution had worked, joked one cynic: the Gaza Strip was run by Muslim fundamentalists and the West Bank by secular Fatah leaders. The international community refused to recognize Hamas control of Gaza, and Israel imposed a naval blockade on the coast with goods and arms

THE COST OF THE INTIFADA

Before the second Intifada, more than 70,000 had daily work permits to enter Israel, and hundreds of thousands more worked and traded illegally. All that stopped in 2000. The World Bank reported a 23 percent drop in the Palestinian GDP over the four years of the Intifada, with unemployment rising from 14 to 37 percent. Nearly half the 3.5 million Palestinians in the West Bank and Gaza lived below the poverty line, and the Palestinians' biggest source of income was an average US$950 million a year in international donor aid. Most of this aid was cut off after Hamas was elected in 2006.

Guest workers

Israel attracts hundreds of thousands of tourists each year, but also has a large number of longer-term guests

Above and beyond its short-term visitors, whether pilgrims drawn by the holy sites or sun-worshippers attracted to the country's beaches, Israel welcomes many guests who linger a while. These include youngsters from around the world wishing to experience Israel in a more profound way, either as a kibbutz volunteer or on an archeological dig, or perhaps studying in a religious institution. Backpackers traveling around the world often stay longer than planned, attracted by the informality and vitality of Israel and the fact that casual work is easy to find, and there is no shortage of cheap, youth hostel-type accommodations.

In fact, the availability of unskilled employment in Israel has attracted workers from around the world. There are an estimated 200,000 foreign workers in the country, half of whom are on legal contracts. This category includes Romanian and Chinese construction workers, Thai agricultural laborers, and Filipino domestic carers.

There are also around 100,000 illegal workers, mainly from West Africa and Latin America, working as house cleaners and factory hands – a number which includes Filipino domestic servants and other formerly legal construction and farm workers whose work visas have expired.

These overseas workers took the place of the many Palestinians who worked in Israel until the outbreak of the first Intifada, compelling Israeli employers to seek alternative sources of labor. The second Intifada from 2000 onward consolidated the position of foreign workers, although the recession of 2002 resulted in sporadic expulsions. In more recent years, tens of thousands of refugees who arrived in Israel from Sudan via Egypt and the Sinai have been able to work in Israel legally. Although they have been given refugee status, they have been refused political asylum.

Flying in the face of Zionism

The abundance of foreign workers in Israel contradicts the Zionist tenet of a Jewish state based on Jewish labor. Many Israelis decry the situation from an intellectual standpoint, but nonetheless are happy for someone else to do the menial work. Like most middle-class parents in the Western world, they would rather their own children became professionals than blue-collar or manual workers.

While most foreign workers come to Israel as individuals and send money home to their families, an increasing number of young migrants are marrying in Israel and building their own "Israeli" families – large neighborhoods in South Tel Aviv have been settled by these migrants, who no longer see themselves as guest workers but long-

The children of guest workers at a Tel Aviv kindergarten.

term residents. The granting of Israeli citizenship to several thousand children born in Israel to these families has incensed many in the country's right-wing circles.

Israel, like all Western countries, is now being faced by the tensions caused by multiculturalism. Yet despite occasional government attempts to expel illegal workers to appease public opinion, the numbers simply seem to rise, with a growing need for workers to fill the jobs Israelis refuse to take. Many yearn for the days when Palestinians took many of these jobs and returned home to their families in the West Bank and Gaza each evening. But with no sign of peace on the horizon, such an elegant solution to Israel's "guest worker" situation seems unlikely.

THE ARMY

Toting sub-machine guns, troops are everywhere:
riding on buses and trains, sitting at sidewalk
cafes, and strolling through shopping malls.

The Israel Defense Forces (IDF) are considered to be one of the world's smartest
armies. A quick glance at the ubiquitous,
scruffy Israeli soldiers slouching around the
streets makes it clear that this reputation is based
on high-tech innovation rather than military
dress code. From satellite surveillance to fighter
jets fitted with the latest computer electronics
capabilities and the world's only anti-tactical bal-
listic missile (the Arrow), Israel's army is streets
ahead of its Arab neighbors.

Dramatic victories such as 1967's Six Day War
have been won, while daring operations such as
the Entebbe raid on Uganda (when hostages were
rescued from a hijacked plane) earned the IDF
widespread admiration. There have also been failures, such as the inability of army intelligence to
anticipate the surprise attack by Egypt and Syria
in the Yom Kippur War in 1973. Most recently the
IDF's image was tarnished by its failure to end
the threat of missiles from Gaza.

An Israeli soldier at target practice.

An independent attitude

Many overseas observers are left initially unimpressed when first encountering the Israeli military, which is like no other army in the world.
Basic training once completed, rules are made
to be broken. Then, officers are never saluted,
orders can be negotiated, and a pink T-shirt
worn as a vest keeps the soldier warm in winter.
Yet the IDF is highly effective, so a soldier's right
to question an officer's orders may be seen as a
strength (though in the heat of battle orders are
usually obeyed). It is said that, rather than do
things "by the book," Israeli soldiers will often
use their heads to adapt to the situation.

Male soldiers fall into several categories. There
are young conscripts aged 18 to 21 doing their
three years' national service, and a small number

of professional soldiers, usually officers, who
carry on afterwards. Then there are the reservists. *Miluim*, Hebrew for reserve duty, involves
men being plucked away from their families
for a month or six weeks a year to serve on the
Lebanese border or the West Bank. Most Israelis
see *miluim* as a burden they would rather evade.
Its unpopularity has a dovish effect, putting
pressure on the government to solve the border
problems that make reserve duty necessary.

However, military service isn't as compulsory
as many believe. About a third of Israeli Jewish
men do not enrol for the army when they are
18. Ultra-Orthodox Jews avoid the draft despite
recent legislation ending study deferments,, and
other youngsters deemed unsuitable because of

delinquent behavior are not called up. Also, any 18-year-old who insists that he does not want to serve will not be drafted: the IDF routinely grants exemptions on the grounds that an 18-year-old is "psychologically" unsuitable for military service. However, in extreme cases conscientious objectors prefer to sit in prison, insisting there is nothing psychologically wrong with them. The number of teenage applicants for combat units is still higher than the places available, so regiments can pick and choose. National service is officially compulsory for Jews, but Muslims and Christians are exempt.

Another radical departure from global military practice is the IDF's long tradition of "purity of arms." This concept stemmed from the classic defense of the German soldier who took part in the Nazi extermination of Jews: "I was only following orders." Deeply enshrined in Israeli culture, therefore, is the notion that a soldier has a right to refuse an immoral order.

Ironically, the IDF's greatest moment – the capture in just six days in 1967 of East Jerusalem, the West Bank, Gaza, the Golan Heights, and the Sinai (returned to Egypt in 1982) – has tarnished the army's image. Hundreds of Israeli soldiers

Female army recruits.

Bedouins, who are renowned for their tracking abilities, serve as volunteers. Druze and Circassians are conscripted, at their own request.

Women at war

Women often fought as frontline soldiers in the struggle for independence, but the IDF confined them to non-combat roles after 1948, despite conscripting women for two years. The Supreme Court ruled in 1995 that the army must accept women for pilots' courses; many have enrolled, and some have qualified. Although the numbers are small, women are increasingly serving in combat units alongside men. Sexism aside, the army is not a bastion of conservatism in Israel. Homosexuals, for example, have always been accepted.

have refused to serve in the West Bank and Gaza on the grounds that the occupation is illegal.

If most of the "conscientious objecting" in the IDF has traditionally come from the left, that all changed in 2004 when the army began implementing withdrawal from Gaza and the northern West Bank. Dozens of religious Israeli soldiers heeded the call of their spiritual rabbinical leaders that an order to expel a Jew from his home in the land of Israel was illegal and refused to fulfil the mission. Like their left-wing comrades before them, they received short prison sentences.

Overall, the IDF remains strong, not only as a military force but as the great melting-pot institution of Israeli society, in which every new recruit has the opportunity to rise through the ranks.

A Torah scroll and its keeper.

RELIGIOUS DIVERSITY

Israel is the Holy Land to followers of three
different religions, who are joined by
members of many alternative sects.

The sheer intensity of religious ardor in this small country is overwhelming: in Jerusalem's Old City, Jews at the Western Wall, Muslims at the El-Aqsa Mosque, and Christians at the Church of the Holy Sepulcher may well be saying their prayers simultaneously, to say nothing of the myriad other synagogues, churches, and mosques in the Old City alone.

Likewise, the diversity of religious experience here is unique. Hassidim wearing 18th-century *kapotas* and *shtreimels* (coats and hats) rub shoulders with robed monks and nuns from every Christian denomination, East and West, while Muslim *imams* in *galabiyah* mingle with secular Israelis and pilgrims to the Holy Land. Many of the holiest biblical sites have hosted synagogues, churches and mosques over the centuries, and even today visitors of one faith may well find themselves paying respects to a chapter of their own history in the house of worship of another.

Muslims perform Eid al-Fitr prayer at Al-Aqsa Mosque in Jerusalem.

The Jewish presence

Jewish spiritual life revolves around the home, house of study (*cheder* for youngsters, *yeshiva* for adolescents and adults), and synagogue – of which the last is the most accessible to the visitor. Jerusalem's hundreds of synagogues range from the humblest *shtible* (several simple rooms) and Sephardi community synagogue to the gargantuan Belzer Center, and the Great Synagogue in Jerusalem's King George Street. Other synagogues worth visiting include the Hechal Shlomo and Yeshurun (both near the Great Synagogue), Italian in Hillel Street and the Hurva in the Old City as well as the 16th century synagogues in mystical Safed.

The Orthodox pray three times a day, but it is on Sabbaths and festivals that the liturgy

is at its most elaborate. The modest Hassidic premises are compensated for by the fervor of the prayers. Such groups exist in Safed, Bnei Brak, and in Jerusalem's northern neighborhoods, although the Me'a She'arim and Geula districts are the most picturesque. Among the warmest and most approachable of the Hassidic groups is the Bratslav, whose Me'a She'arim premises contain the renovated chair of their first and only *rebbe*, Rabbi Nahman, famous for his stories and sayings: "The world is a narrow bridge; the main thing is not to be afraid at all."

Elswhere in Me'a She'arim is Karlin, whose devotees screech their prayers – unlike their

Geula neighbors, Ger, whose tightly knit organization is reflected in their operatic music and self-discipline: "A true Ger Hasid," says one believer, "never looks at his wife." A similar outlook is espoused by Toledot Aharon, whose purity of purpose is matched by their animosity towards political Zionism, which they view as usurping the divine process of redemption. In this they follow the line of Netorei Karta (Guardians of the City), which campaigns for political autonomy. What unites all ultra-Orthodox and Orthodox groups is their opposition to the Conservative and Reform Movements.

The cycle of the Jewish year

The framework of Jewish piety is determined by the lunar-solar cycle (a leap month is added every three years to keep the festivals and seasons synchronized), beginning in September with Rosh Hashana (New Year) and Yom Kippur, the Day of Atonement – a rigorous 25-hour fast. Synagogues are packed; services are long but moving. A controversial custom precedes Yom Kippur: Kaparot, which entails swinging a chicken above the head of the penitent, after which the slaughtered fowl is given to charity. This ceremony can be witnessed in most open market places.

In Jerusalem's ultra-Orthodox Me'a She'arim district.

ULTRA-ORTHODOX OUTREACH

The ultra-Orthodox sect most familiar to worldwide Jewry is the Habad movement, which is famous for its successful outreach programs to secular Jewry. Habad's Israeli headquarters is at Kfar Habad, near Ben Gurion Airport. It was here that the late head of the sect, the revered Rabbi Menachem Mendel Schneerson (1902–94), the Lubavitcher Rebbe, had a redbrick home built identical to his New York mansion, which he planned on making his residence when the Messiah arrived. In the event, Rabbi Schneerson never visited his Israeli home. Some followers expected him to return as the Messiah – a belief condemned by other Orthodox groups.

During Succot (Tabernacles), which combines harvest gathering and prayers for winter rains, celebrants live in temporary tabernacles for seven days to remind the Jewish people of their 40 years in the desert. During the evenings, the pious let down their sidelocks to dance, somersault, and juggle to intoxicating music. The day after Succot is Simchat Torah, when the annual cycle of reading the Torah ends and begins again.

More lights burn during Chanukah, in November/December, when eight-branched candelabra shine in most homes in celebration of the Maccabean victory over the Greeks some 2,300 years ago. The fate of the cruel Persian leader Haman, thwarted in his attempts to kill the entire Jewish community by Queen Esther a couple of centuries earlier, is recorded in the Scroll of Esther and read on Purim (a cheerful, noisy, fancy-dress carnival held in February/March). In March/April, everyone spring-cleans for Pesach (Passover), the annual feast celebrating the Exodus from Egypt, when bread is prohibited. Seven weeks later comes Shavuot (Pentecost), the Feast of Weeks, when thousands congregate at the Western Wall for dawn prayers, having spent the night studying the holy book, the Torah.

Between Passover and Shavuot, the Orthodox invest Independence Day and Jerusalem Unity Day with spiritual significance, creating new festivals. The cycle reaches full circle in summer, with three weeks of mourning for the Temples, culminating in a day-long fast on Tisha B'Av.

Islamic revival

While Israeli Arab and Palestinian society was moving towards secularism a generation ago, Islam has become fashionable once again (this should not be confused with the militant political Islam, which has produced violence and terror). The distinctive voice of the muezzin calling the faithful to prayer five times a day has become more prevalent and alcohol, once casually served up in Muslim-owned restaurants across Israel, is rarely available. Dress codes for women have become more modest – although, in a fascinating visual contradiction, Israeli Arab women will typically cover their hair and every inch of flesh from neck to ankle while wearing the tightest of jeans.

Ramadan is strictly observed, with Muslims fasting from sunrise to sunset, and this can prove extremely difficult when the Holy Month falls during the summer, with the devout unable to drink even a glass of water in the searing summer heat and longer days. Because the Muslim calendar is a lunar calendar of 12 months, Ramadan, like all the Islamic months, rotates backwards in relation to the solar year, with the month of fasting each year falling 11 days earlier in the Gregorian calendar.

Despite the abstention, Ramadan is a time of great festivity. Each evening families meet for an afta banquet-like meal to break the fast, and the final few days of the month constitute Id Al Fitr, a festival of equivalent stature to Christmas or Passover. Otherwise, in keeping with the general Islamic disdain of holidays, there are few other special days in Israel. The Muslim New Year, Al Hijra, is a relatively low-key affair; however, Id Al Adha, the Feast of the Sacrifice which commemorates how Allah enabled Abraham to spare his son, believed to be Ishmael, from sacrifice, is widely celebrated.

The Muslim Sabbath is marked on Friday by attending special Mosque prayers at midday. Tens of thousands of the faithful attend prayers in Jerusalem on Haram esh-Sharif (the Temple Mount of the Jews), sometimes even hundreds of thousands during Ramadan. Generally speaking, the Muslim Sabbath is more akin to the Catholic Sunday in not mandating all commercial activity cease, as with Orthodox Jews and fundamentalist Protestants.

Christians walk along the Via Dolorosa (Way of Suffering) to commemorate the crucifixion and death of Jesus Christ.

Uneasy coexistence

Judaism, Christianity, and Islam live together in the Holy Land in suspicion rather than in harmony. For the most part, Jews and Christians have buried historical differences and fear Islamic militancy (although indigenous Christians are first and foremost Palestinians); the deepest hostilities are reserved for arguments over property and land rather than over tenets of belief and dogma.

Ironically, when they do meet for inter-faith dialogue, Orthodox Jews, Christians and Muslims often discover that they all seek to preserve the same conservative values, values that are under fire in the Western world where secularism prevails.

THE CHRISTIANS

A rich variety of denominations flourishes among
Israel's Christians, the majority of whom are Arabs.

Nowhere in the world is the observant traveler more aware of the fascinating diversity of Christianity than in the Holy Land. On a stroll through Jerusalem's Old City, you might encounter Greek Orthodox or Syrian Orthodox monks, Ethiopian and Coptic clergymen, Armenian priests, Catholic priests, and, without knowing it, clerics and scholars from virtually every Protestant Church.

There is no mystery to the extraordinary variety of Christian congregations in the Holy Land. From the Byzantines (324–636) through the Crusader kingdoms (1099–1291) and 400 years of Ottoman rule (1517–1917) until today, Churches sought to establish – then struggled to retain – a presence in the land where their faith was born.

The result is a rich variety of denominations served by thousands of clergy from almost every nation on earth. The older Churches, such as Greek Orthodox and Russian Orthodox, own many sites in Israel and have sometimes quarreled bitterly over them (the Crimean War (1853–6) was caused by an argument between the Catholics and Greek Orthodox over ownership of part of the Church of the Nativity in Bethlehem). The "younger" Churches – such as the Anglicans, the Church of Scotland, Mormons, Lutherans, the Pentecostals, the Church of Christ, the Baptists, the Brethren, and the Mennonites – also maintain institutions and congregations, as do Seventh Day Adventists and Jehovah's Witnesses. While the indigenous Arab Christians (mainly Orthodox and Catholic) take a strong pro-Palestinian line, many evangelical Protestants of a right-wing Zionist bent have made their home in Israel; belief in the redemption has made them enthusiastic supporters of Zionism (see page 87).

Ethiopian Orthodox Christians.

A time for feasting

Christian groups celebrate some 240 feasts and holy days a year, using two calendars, the Julian and the Gregorian, providing three dates for Christmas: 25 December for Western Christians, 7 January for Greek and other Orthodox churches, Syrians, and Copts, and 19 January for the Armenians, and two sets of Holy Weeks. The highlights of the year for Christian celebrants is Christmas at Bethlehem, where events take place at the Church of the Nativity; and during Easter Week, when there is a re-enactment of Jesus's last days involving walks from the Mount of Olives and along the Via Dolorosa to the Church of the Holy Sepulcher. Here, two ceremonies take place: the Washing of the

Feet on Maundy Thursday, and the Kindling of the Holy Fire – a ceremony in which people have been accidentally burned to death down the centuries – by the Orthodox and Eastern Churches on Holy Saturday. Carrying the cross on Good Friday between the Praetorium and Calvary (Golgotha), along the Via Dolorosa, is repeated weekly by the Franciscans.

Guaranteed freedoms

Israel's founding provoked unease among Christians, who were deeply suspicious of Jewish intentions (the Vatican recognized Israel only in 1994). But Israel's Declaration of Independence pledged to guarantee freedom of religion and protect the holy sites, while Israel's reliance on support from the US has also ensured that Israeli governments protect Christian interests.

The Six Day War of 1967, which left Israel in control of Jerusalem's Old City, revived religious misgivings. Yet the Israeli government has been scrupulous in protecting the Churches' rights and prerogatives.

Evangelical claims

A recent phenomenon that is having an impact on the face of the Holy Land and Christian–Jewish relations is the worldwide growth of Christian evangelical Zionism, which regards Israel as a fulfillment of biblical prophecy. Theological and ecumenical institutions which enable Christians to study in Israel have mushroomed, such as the International Christian Embassy in Jerusalem, and the Mormon University on Mount Scopus. These evangelical, fundamentalist Christians often live permanently in Israel, their views placing them on the extreme right of Israel's political spectrum. They celebrate Tabernacles by marching through Jerusalem in solidarity with Israel and suggest that this was the real time of Christ's birth rather than Christmas – which has pagan origins and has become too commercialized for their taste.

Christian–Jewish reconciliation is not the sole preserve of the new Churches. The Roman Catholic order of the Sisters of Zion, established in Jerusalem in 1855 by French Jewish converts, works towards such understanding. Every year pilgrims visit the order's Ecce Homo Convent next to the Second Station of the Cross on the Via Dolorosa, and many stay to hear the sisters speak of Jesus the Jew and of Judaism as the wellspring of their faith.

Arabic language

The grassroots language of Christianity in Israel is Arabic. The great majority of Israel's 160,000 Christians (including the 20,000 East Jerusalem Christians of East Jerusalem) are Arabs, and their clergy are Arabs.

Christian Arab allegiances in Israel are to the established Patriarchates: Greek Catholic, Greek Orthodox, and Roman Catholic. These divisions are not strong and Catholics will often convert to Orthodoxy and vice versa for marriage with the blessings of both families. There are small communities of Anglicans

Acts of faith in the Church of the Holy Sepulcher.

and Lutherans (both Churches are stronger on the West Bank than in Israel), and despite more than 100 years of missionary work by some 50 organizations, there are fewer than 1,000 local Arab adherents of Evangelical Churches.

Arab Christians, while flourishing economically, have been hesitant about politically pressing issues of Christian concern. The Christian community is a marginal minority, balancing its Christian identity, Arab nationalism, and delicate relations with Muslim neighbors within the context of a Jewish society. Many have emigrated and both Nazareth and Bethlehem have become cities with Muslim majorities.

ECLIPSE OF THE KIBBUTZ

Most of Israel's kibbutzim are no longer run
as socialist settlements, and the government
is even prepared to see them privatized.

The kibbutz, the Israeli version of a socialist collective commune, was considered
one of the great socio-economic experimental successes of the 20th century. Even if
Zionism was unpopular among the left from
1967 onwards, the Israeli farming communes
inspired several generations of revolutionaries,
who cited the communities as living proof that
communism works.

The kibbutz was initially influenced by the
Soviet Union, but in recent years has adopted
the Chinese model of integrating capitalism into
communist values. If the macro-socio-economic
communism of the USSR disappeared because
it simply failed to deliver even the most basic
standard of living, the kibbutz in contrast is a
victim of its own success and growing affluence.

Economic equality is one thing when dividing
up food, clothes, and other fundamentals. But
when a kibbutz is rich, the range of consumer
choices, business decisions, and lifestyles makes
egalitarianism difficult to put into practice. Take
Kibbutz Sdot Yam near Haifa, which owns Cae-
sarstone, a company that manufactures quartz
kitchen countertops worldwide. A share offering on Nasdaq in May 2014 has earned each of
the kibbutz members nearly $2.5 million.

Change of style

This new-found affluence has kept many of
the kibbutzim (plural of kibbutz) very much
alive..Some 106,000 Israelis live on 256 kibbutzim
(the plural of kibbutz) representing 1.3 percent
of the population. This is down from a peak of
125,000 in 1990 (2.5 percent of the population).

The kibbutzim produce 40 percent of the country's agricultural output and export US$6 billion
of industrial goods a year. The vast amount of real
estate that they own has enabled them to open

Life was tough for the pioneers.

shopping malls, gas stations, fast-food outlets,
hotels, country clubs, and much more, and build
homes for sale on the private market.

Kibbutz lifestyles have changed out of all
recognition since 1909 when the first Russian-
born pioneers established the original kibbutz
at Dganya, where the River Jordan flows out
of the Sea of Galilee. Within a decade there
were 40 kibbutzim. These settlements enjoyed
greater prosperity and social cohesion than the
capitalist farms founded by the Rothschilds and
other philanthropists in places like Rishon Le-
Tsiyon and Petakh Tikva.

By the time the State of Israel was established
in 1948 the kibbutz formed the backbone (and
6.5 percent) of Israeli society. Kibbutz members

were looked up to as the social and moral ideal, not least because the kibbutzim had transformed large tracts of arid land into fertile fields. Even more importantly, the kibbutzim, which had been strategically located as pioneering outposts, were created in order to define the borders of the Jewish state.

Most of the Palmach, the elite fighting force of pre-state Israel, were kibbutz members because by definition the kibbutzim attracted people eager to defend the country's borders from the battlefront. These combative traditions have been maintained, and most young

But perhaps the greatest kibbutz invention was drip irrigation, developed by members of Kibbutz Hatzerim in the 1960s. This system uses networks of pipes that drip water onto crops or trees, thus penetrating deeply into the soil and utilising minimal amounts of water. Drip irrigation works on a time clock and can be very simple, but in recent times sophisticated options have been added, such as computer control and fertilizer feeds.

Today Hatzerim's company Netafim has annual sales of US$850 million, and a worldwide presence.

High-tech agriculture has brought the kibbutzim financial gain.

members are still eager to volunteer for prestigious combat units.

From austerity to affluence

The kibbutz initially succeeded because members were motivated to work together, pool very limited resources, and, against the odds, overcome both a hostile environment and the Arab enemy.

It was in a climate of austerity that the kibbutzim laid the foundations for future prosperity. By the effective harnessing of agriculture and technology, the finest fruit and vegetables were grown, bringing premium prices on European markets. Bovine varieties were bred to produce the highest milk yields, as were chickens that laid large numbers of eggs.

THREE DIFFERENT PATHS

There are three kibbutz movements in Israel today: the national religious kibbutz movement combines a communal way of life with Jewish Orthodoxy, while the other two – Meuhad and Artzi – are secular in outlook. The latter two movements split from each other back in 1951, when Meuhad members denounced Stalin as an anti-Semitic dictator while adherents of Artzi remained faithful to the USSR and the party line. The Artzi movement realized that the Soviet experiment was going wrong long before the collapse of the Soviet Union in 1991, but it still leans more toward orthodox socialism than does the Meuhad.

In the 1960s and 1970s austerity was gradually replaced by a more middle-class lifestyle. But a kibbutz member's home remained a modest place, with money channeled into communal projects such as dining halls, sports and educational facilities, and cultural amenities.

Thousands of members left the kibbutzim, lured by the more individualistic lifestyle of the city. Many kibbutz children would choose not to return home after serving in the army. But there were always veteran Israelis or new immigrants eager to take their place as the new pioneers.

Somewhat unfairly, in view of their prominent role in the army, the kibbutznikim were portrayed as traitors rather than patriots, because of their left-leaning political views.

It was also during this period that the kibbutzim got themselves into an economic mess, borrowing large sums from Israeli banks in the 1980s when annual inflation was triple-digit and interest rates high. The economy stabilized but the interest rates remained locked at exorbitantly high percentages.

Many kibbutzim staved off bankruptcy through loan repayment arrangements with bank

A kibbutz in central Israel.

Worker at Kibbutz Ein Gedi, also a botanical garden.

Tarnished image

It is hard to know when the kibbutz stopped being universally admired as a place for selfless pioneers. Perhaps in 1977, when the Labor Party lost the reins of power. The right-wing PM Menachem Begin poured scorn on the kibbutzim, not least because they had traditionally given their support to Labor governments.

Begin described kibbutz members as millionaires who sit around their swimming pools all day. It was an unfair label, but it stuck. Begin was politically exploiting the fact that kibbutzim were almost exclusively Ashkenazi, and, even at its most austere, their lifestyle was considerably more desirable than the poverty suffered by Oriental Jews in the nearby development towns.

and government help. And, although the kibbutzim were forced to give the government some of their land, they retained most of it, to the resentment of the disadvantaged and new immigrants.

Economic evolution

Today the nuclear family has replaced alternative social structures. Kibbutz children were once brought up in communal baby houses by educational professionals, seeing their parents only at certain times of the day, as it was believed they should be part of the community. But these days a child's place is once more with their parents.

Family rather than communal living is being reinforced by the gradual disappearance of the kibbutz dining room. Some 20 percent of kibbutzim have closed their dining rooms and members eat at home; while 80 percent of the remaining kibbutzim have transformed their dining rooms into "pay as you eat" restaurants, open to the public, in which kibbutz members pay lower prices for meals. Some 82 percent of kibbutzim make members pay for all services, including laundry and electricity, while, most significantly, 61 percent of kibbutzim have instituted pay differentials in which members receive salaries related to the work they are performing. There are a handful of austere kibbutzim, such as Tzeelim in the Negev, that remain true to the socialist principles of the past, and the wealthiest kibbutzim, such as Maagan Michael near Haifa and Tzuba near Jerusalem, remain egalitarian, as members are reluctant to relinquish their share of what are in effect highly successful businesses.

An attractive lifestyle

From the point of view of socialist ideology, the kibbutz may not be what it used to be, but it is still a very attractive place to live. It offers a rural lifestyle, guaranteed work in a number of different professions, and comfortable living standards, including a house and garden.

It may be some time until the final nail is hammered into the kibbutz coffin. New legislation allows the kibbutzim to privatize themselves and sell their houses and gardens on the real estate market after buying their land from the government. However, the state and kibbutzim are very far from agreeing the value of the properties, so only a few kibbutzim on the Lebanese border, where real estate is almost worthless, are fully privatized. Meanwhile, the question of whether market forces will ultimately choke out traditional idealism is a matter of fierce debate.

The moshav movement

The privatization of a kibbutz would in fact turn it into a moshav (cooperative settlement). For the Jewish pioneers who wanted a less socialistic form of communal living when the earliest settlements were founded, the moshav offered a more individualistic alternative. Nahalal in the Galilee, the first moshav, was set up in 1921 by a breakaway group of settlers who were disillusioned by the socialist constraints of Dganya, the very first kibbutz. One member of this breakaway group was Shmuel Dayan, the father of Moshe Dayan, who was to become a high-profile Defense Minister and hero of the Six Day War in 1967.

Kibbutz Dan's restaurant serves fresh trout from local tributaries of the Jordan. Kibbutz Mizra, near Nazareth, antagonizes Israel's religious community by rearing pigs and selling pork products.

In the moshav, each family runs its own household and farms its individual plot of land, but machinery and marketing is shared. There are about 400 moshavim in Israel, but most members now work in regular jobs, renting out their land.

Israel Shavuot ceremony at Kibbutz Ein Shemer.

EXPERIENCING A KIBBUTZ

Visitors wishing to sample life on a kibbutz or moshav can either stay at one of the many guesthouses, or volunteer to work for a period of not less than a month. Guesthouses are often in isolated rural areas in the northern Galilee, but a few are within easy reach of Jerusalem and Tel Aviv. They usually offer all the facilities of a comfortable hotel. You can make a booking through the Kibbutz Hotels Chain (tel: 03-560 8118; www.kibbutzhotels.net). Prospective volunteer workers should contact Kibbutz Program Center, 6 Frishman Street/corner Yarkon St, Tel Aviv (tel: 03-524 6154/6; email: kpc@kibbutz volunteers.org.il; www.kibbutzvolunteers.org.il).

MARKETS

Shopping malls offer air-conditioned comfort, but it's the traditional markets that convey the true taste and aroma of the Middle East.

Markets around Israel display a diverse range of goods, from the tempting fresh fruit and vegetables in Jerusalem's Makhane Yehuda and Tel Aviv's Carmel Market to the antique trinkets in Yafo's Flea Market.

However, the market that should on no account be missed is in the Muslim Quarter of Jerusalem's Old City – not so much because anything there is particularly worth buying, but simply because the "souk" provides Western visitors with the ultimate Oriental experience.

This is a bazaar in the classic sense of the word, its narrow alleyways bustling with raw energy, chaotic noise, and the scents of exotic spices. Straight down from the Jaffa Gate along David Street are all the kitsch stalls selling T-shirts, religious icons, and Holy Land paraphernalia. Store owners will invariably ask for well above the value of an item, so visitors should be prepared to bargain. Turn left into Shuk Ha-Basamim, just before the end of David Street, for the heart of the "souk": the spice market. This dark, tightly wound labyrinth is not for claustrophobes, but heaven for those who love the pungent aromas of coffee and spices.

Gastronomes will also enjoy the huge array of pickles, spices, dried fruits, and nuts on offer in Jerusalem's Makhane Yehuda, while the best clothing and food bargains in the land are to be found in Tel Aviv's Carmel Market. Other markets of interest include the one in Akko's Old City and the Druze market in Daliyat el-Karmel, just south of Haifa.

The Muslim Quarter in Jerusalem is where you'll find spices by the shovelful, as well as Turkish delight and blocks of pistachio-incrusted halva.

Fezes and Bedouin accessories on sale in Be'er Sheva on Thursday mornings.

This weekly market with its picturesque setting outside Jerusalem's Damascus Gate throws up a fair few bargains but little quality.

A shopper peruses the knick-knacks for sale in Jafa's flea market.

BE'ER SHEVA'S BEDOUIN MARKET

Thursday is the day to be in Be'er Sheva. Neither the recent removal of the Bedouin market to a location just south of the Central Bus Station, nor the increasing profusion of tourist trinkets, has entirely dulled the ethnic authenticity of the market where Negev nomads come to trade their wares. Although the market is open all day, it's best to get here shortly after dawn to enjoy the full essence of the place as the Bedouin trade camels, goats, and agricultural produce. Carpets, clothes, jewelry, and other arts and crafts are also available.

The highway to the south is strewn with traditional encampments but, due to government land appropriations and financial inducements, most Bedouin are moving to fixed villages – a change increasingly reflected in the character of the market.

A trader at Be'er Sheva market.

n't forget to haggle over the price of religious icons in
usalem – but avoid if you are not really interested or an
n is already cheap.

okahs, prevalent among Middle Eastern Jews and
ditional after a large meal or family get together, are water
es used for smoking fruit-flavored tobaccos.

An ultra-Orthodox Jew follows the reading of the Scroll of Esther during Purim festival prayers.

LANGUAGE AND CULTURE

In just over a century a language has been reborn and a new culture forged from the talents of Israel's diverse population.

Had one to name the single most fundamental contribution made by Israel and the Jewish people to mankind, the immediate answer would be the Old Testament, which, together with the New Testament writings, forms the philosophical and moral web underlying most of Western civilization's values. That book, for all its five millennia or so, remains the most important source and inspiration for much of Israel's cultural creativity.

It is, of course, only one of the strands, but it is the most pervasive. Other distinct strands are the great literary creations of post-Old Testament commentary – the Mishna, the Talmud, and the fashionable mysticism of the Kabbalah – the accumulated wisdom of 2,000 years of Jewish thought.

Israel, like the United States before it, has often been described as a melting pot, as it has struggled with the integration of millions of immigrants from 80 nations, speaking dozens of languages. But a better image would be a

Ultra-Orthodox costumed boys during Purim.

> The lingua franca in the time of Christ was not Hebrew but Aramaic, a closely related Semitic language brought back to the region after the Babylonian exile.

bouillabaisse, the classic Mediterranean fish stew in which all the elements form a homogeneous whole, while each retains its own character, distinct identity, and flavor.

Hebrew: a language reborn

One of the most remarkable facets of the rebirth of the Hebrew nation was the revival of the Hebrew language. Through the 2,000 years of dispersion it had become solely a language of worship and expression of the yearnings for Zion. The *lingua franca* of the Jews in exile became either the language of the country in which they found refuge, or Yiddish, a combination of Hebrew and medieval German; Ladino, Hebrew mixed with Spanish; various forms of Judeo-Arabic such as Mughrabi, a North African blend of Hebrew, Arabic, and French; and Judeo-Persian dialects like Tat in the Caucasian mountain region. The first pioneers who arrived in 19th-century Palestine brought with them their own languages, usually Yiddish or Russian, but they insisted on using Hebrew in conversation in the early agricultural communities, and its re-creation became a cornerstone of Zionist ideology.

The rebirth of Hebrew was virtually the work of one man, the Zionist thinker and leader Eliezer Ben Yehuda. Born in Lithuania in 1858, he immigrated to Palestine in 1881 and saw the revival of the language as an indispensable aspect of the political and cultural rebirth of the Jewish people. With single-minded, almost fanatical determination, he embarked on a lone campaign to restore the Hebrew tongue as a vibrant, living vehicle for everyday expression. When he and his new wife Dvora arrived in Yafo he informed her that they would converse only in Hebrew, and their son Itamar became the first modern

The language in everyday usage.

child with Hebrew as his mother tongue. Ben Yehuda's efforts horrified the Orthodox population of Jerusalem who, when they realized he proposed using the holy tongue to further secular, nationalist, and political causes, pronounced a *herem* (excommunication) against him. To this day, the Ashkenazi ultra-Orthodox Jewish community shun the secular use of Hebrew and the defilement of the holy language, and prefer Yiddish for everyday speech.

The introduction of Hebrew for everyday use was not greeted with universal acclamation even by the non-Orthodox, or the supporting Zionist bodies and organizations abroad. Bitter battles were fought over the language of instruction at the Betsalel School of Art in Jerusalem (founded in 1906) and the Technion in Haifa (founded in 1913). German was the official language of the latter, and it took a strike by faculty and students to compel the supporting institution, the Hilfsverein, to give way. A few years later the language of instruction in all Jewish schools in the country (except for those of the ultra-Orthodox) was established as Hebrew.

Ben Yehuda compiled a dictionary of Hebrew (see box), established an academy, and founded and edited several periodicals. Through these media he coined thousands of new words relating to every aspect of life and every discipline. Not all of them took root; modern Hebrew, the all-purpose language of the country in every field, still borrows words from other languages that sound familiar to non-Hebrew speakers. Ben Yehuda's *sah rahok* ("long-distance speech"), for instance, never displaced "telephone", nor did *makushit* ("something that is tapped upon") take the place of "piano".

The question of slang

Some slang neologisms would undoubtedly make Ben Yehuda turn in his grave and do seriously disturb Hebrew purists: *Tremp* (clearly from "tramp") is the Hebrew for "hitchhiking", a sweatshirt is a *svetcher*, over which you might pull a *sveder* if it gets cold. When your *breks* fail, the garage might find something wrong with your *beck-exel* or, God forbid, with your *front beck-exel*.

Most of these words have Hebrew equivalents, but they have usually been pushed aside in common usage. Yet pure Hebrew words like *machshev* (computer), *tochna* (software), and

---

CROWNING ACHIEVEMENT

The crowning achievement of Ben Yehuda's life was his *Dictionary of Ancient and Modern Hebrew*, completed after his death by his son Ehud and his second wife, Hemda (Dvora's younger sister). This dictionary, and the Academy of the Hebrew Language, which he established in 1890, were the main vehicles through which a new, modern vocabulary was disseminated. Ben Yehuda wrote in the introduction to his dictionary: "In those days it was as if the heavens had suddenly opened, and a clear, incandescent light flashed before my eyes, and a mighty inner voice sounded in my ears: the renascence of Israel on its ancestral soil."

nayad (mobile/cellular phone) have been happily integrated into everyday usage by Israelis.

There's no denying that Hebrew is once more a thriving, and still-evolving, vehicle of daily discourse employed in great works of literature and emails alike.

The written word

If the heartbeat of a nation's culture lies in the written word, then Israel has a problem because, despite the revival of Hebrew, there are no more than 9 million people worldwide (including many Palestinians) who can speak and under-

member of Kibbutz Hulda who now lives in Arad, Oz is heavily influenced by the "return to the soil" labor-Zionist mores espoused by the founding fathers of the kibbutz movement. A literary phenomenon was Ephraim Kishon, Israel's best-known humorist, who died in 2005, a prophet somewhat without honor in his own country although his books have sold millions of copies overseas, especially in Scandinavia and Germany. Many writers who maintain a prolific literary output belong to the "Palmach Generation" (the Palmach was the pre-state elite fighting force drawn from the kibbutzim). Among

Israeli writer, novelist, and journalist Amos Oz.

stand it, and certainly no more than 6 million who can comfortably read it. Hebrew can be considered an arcane, rather exotic language, one where those who choose to write in it must inevitably be faced with the frustrations of writing for a limited audience. But a lively, articulate, and robust body of literature has evolved nevertheless. While the giants of modern Hebrew – Bialik, Tchernikhovsky, Brenner, Agnon (who won the Nobel Prize for Literature in 1966), and others – are still required reading in schools, they are increasingly supplemented by Israeli-born writers whose work can stand comparison with the best of the world's contemporary authors.

One of Israel's best writers (and certainly the best-known abroad) is Amos Oz. A former

them are Haim Guri, Moshe Shamir, S. Yizhar, Benjamin Tammuz, and Hanoch Bar Tov.

Literature has been deeply influenced by the deaths of millions of Jews in the Holocaust. It is that theme which is the all-pervasive *leitmotif* in the writings of Aharon Appelfeld, whose books have been widely translated, and in those of Abba Kovner, "Ka-Tsetnik" (the pseudonym of Benzion Dinur), and many others, all of whom experienced that period themselves.

The center ground in Israeli writing is held today by those who came to literary maturity after the Palmach days and whose vision was tempered through the fires of austerity, of absorption of immigrants, and four wars of survival. Such writers include Yitzhak Ben Ner, Shulamit

Jewish singer Zehava Ben is popular in the Arab world for her covers of traditional Arabic hits such as "Enta Omri", originally sung by legendary Egyptian singer Umm Kulthum.

Hareven, the late Ya'akov Shabtai, Yoram Kaniuk, and others. Among the younger generation of writers there are David Grossman, Meir Shalev, Eshkol Nevo, and Etgar Keret, best known for his very short stories. The late Batya Gur adapted the detective story to the Israeli landscape.

Zubin Mehta, at the helm of the Israel Philharmonic Orchestra.

DANA'S IMPACT

Dana International reflects the clash of cultures which so often characterizes Israeli life. The glamorous pop singer won the 1998 Eurovision Song Contest but is as famous for her sex change operation (she was born Yaron Cohen) and for her numerous platinum-disc releases. The ultra-Orthodox community is not amused, particularly as Dana cannot easily be dismissed as a passing phenomenon appealing only to teenage audiences. Having gained followers in all sorts of unexpected quarters, she has become a symbol of secular resistance to ultra-Orthodox attempts to impose restrictions on Israel's cultural life and media output.

An important phenomenon of the past 15 years or so has been the maturing of a group of writers of Sephardic origin for whom Arabic, rather than Yiddish, was a formative influence. Such writers include A.B. Yehoshua (shortlisted for the first International Booker Prize), Samy Michael, and Amnon Shamosh, whose *Esra Safra and Sons* became a popular television series.

Poetry holds a special place in Israel's literary life, and the great poets of pre-Inquisition Spain such as Yehuda Halevy are still widely read. It has been estimated that 10,000 new poems are published in the country every year. In addition to Bialik and Saul Tchernikovsky, the best-loved poets of past and present include Yehuda Amichai, Dan Pagis, Natan Zach, T. Carmi, Lea Goldeberg, Uri Zvi Greenberg, and Rachel Bluwstein. Emerging contemporary poets like Asher Reich, Arieh Sivan, Ronny Somak, and Moshe Dor make greater use of slang and colloquial Hebrew and less formal use of rhyme.

Music, from classical to jazz

The musical life of Israel is a good example of the country's bipolarity, with its constant influx of immigrant musicians, and outflow of performers who have reached the highest international peaks. Yitzhak Perlman, Pinchas Zuckerman, Shlomo Mintz, Daniel Barenboim: all received their training in Israel and went on to glittering careers on the world's concert platforms. Israel's orchestras, including the Israel Philharmonic, the Jerusalem Symphony, the Beer Sheva Sinfonietta, and many chamber groups, have provided homes for hundreds of players. Their rehearsals are a Babel of Russian, German, Romanian, French, and English – united by a lot of music and a little Hebrew. Reinforced by mass immigration from the former USSR, there are now major orchestras in Rishon LeZion, Haifa, Netanya, Ramat Gan, and Holon.

Israelis are a concert-going people; subscription series to the major orchestras are sold out, and a subscription to the IPO is jealously handed down from parents to children. Zubin Mehta, born in Bombay in 1936 and one of the world's foremost conductors, has led the IPO since 1991, and has done much to involve himself with Israel's struggle for survival. Music-loving tourists have many opportunities to hear well-loved pieces performed by some of the world's greatest talents. Placido Domingo, incidentally, got his first job at the Israel Opera (recently revived as the New Israel Opera), where he spent a year. The standard of choral singing is also very high, especially among the United Kibbutz Choir, the Rinat National Choir, and the Camaran Singers.

Israel hosts a series of international musical events, including the Artur Rubinstein piano competition, the Pablo Casals cello competition, a triennial international harp contest, the Zimriya choirs festival, and annual music festivals in Jerusalem and Abu Ghosh (liturgical), Kibbutz Ein Hashofet, Kibbutz Ein Gev on the shores of the Sea of Galilee, Kibbutz Kfar Blum in the Upper Galilee (chamber music), and the Red Sea Jazz Festival. The Klezmer Festival in Safed has revived the Hasidic Jewish musical tradition.

Classical music is often too Ashkenazi for the taste of many Oriental Jews and Arabs. They have their own musical traditions, and the Israel Andalusian Orchestra reflects the culture of North Africa. But in pop music, East and West are integrated. The best-known songwriters, such as Naomi Shemer, Ehud Manor, and Uzi Hitman (who all died in 2004 and 2005), were Ashkenazi but deeply loved by all Israeli Jews. The late Ofra Haza, who died of Aids, and living artists such as Rita and Gali Atari and bands like Typex, are Oriental but popular among all Israelis.

Dance greats

Israel owes its place in the world of dance to four women. The first was a Russian-trained ballerina, Rina Nikova, who came to Palestine in the 1920s determined to create a local art form incorporating themes from the Bible, Middle East tradition, folk dance, and Russian classical ballet. The second, Sarah Levi-Tanai, harnessed the Yemenite dance tradition, one of the richest and most exotic of the Middle East, into a modern framework, creating the Inbal Dance Theatre, the forerunner of several other successful ethnic groups.

The third, Baroness Bethsabee de Rothschild, founded the Batsheva and Bat Dor dance companies, which remain leading exponents of modern dance in Israel. In recent years the two companies have been joined by the Kibbutz Dance Company and the Israel Ballet, the country's only classical ballet company. The fourth woman was Martha Graham, who was undoubtedly the formative influence on modern dance in Israel. The Israel Ballet was set up by Berta Yampolsky and Hillel Markman.

A company rare in concept and achievement is Kol Demama ("Voice of Silence"), a group composed of deaf and hearing-impaired dancers, whose performances are electrifying. The training method developed by director Moshe Efrati is based on vibrations through the floor transmitted by the dancer's feet. Vertigo, founded in 1992, combines ballet and contemporary dance.

Folk-dance groups abound, and there is no kibbutz or town that doesn't have its own troupe. Outstanding among them is Hora Yerushalayim, a Jerusalem-based group, whose four companies perform at home and overseas. Israelis love to dance, and many festive occasions end up with exuberant *horas, krakoviaks, debkas,*

Ballet flourishes in Israel.

Hassidic dances, and other European and Arab dances that are now part of the heritage. Each summer the Karmiel Dance Festival brings folk troupes to Israel from around the world.

Theatrical roots

Israeli theater owes its origins to the melodramatic tradition exemplified in the first Hebrew theater in the world, Ha-Bimah, founded in Moscow in 1917 (and moved to Palestine in 1931). Since then theater has come a long way in style, presentation, and especially content. Of all the arts in Israel, theater is perhaps the most socially involved, with a new generation of playwrights breaking taboos, tackling controversial topics, and attempting to act as the mirror of society.

Concerns of the past, the Jewish experience in pre-war Europe, the Holocaust, all these still manifest themselves on the Israeli stage, but, increasingly, dramatists are addressing themselves to contemporary issues, problems of daily life in Israel, the Arab-Jewish conflict, alienation between ethnic, religious, and other social groups. A new play by Hanoch Levin, Yehoshua Sobol, or Hillel Mittelpunkt is a major event that will be dissected, analyzed, and discussed as energetically as political events. Hanoch Levin, especially, is a defiant, iconoclastic writer whose works inevitably cause controversy and attract

Street theater in Sheinkin Street, Tel Aviv.

attempted censorship. But his irreverent, nihilistic, often obscene satire makes him Israel's most interesting and original theatrical talent.

Most major repertory theaters – such as the Ha-Bimah, Cameri, Beit Lessin Haifa Municipal Theater, Be'er Sheva Municipal Theater, and Jerusalem Khan – enjoy substantial official support and are very well attended. The language barrier prevents visitors from sharing in the rich offerings, but simultaneous translations are often available. The Arab Theater and Beit Hagefen are Arabic-language companies, while Gesher ('Bridge') produces Russian and Hebrew drama.

The Israel Festival each spring in Jerusalem brings drama companies to Israel from around the world, while the Akko Fringe Festival in

October is Israel's equivalent of the Edinburgh Festival. Haifa holds a Children's Theater Festival each year.

Cinema blossoms

Some Israelis have made it on the international stage, including actors Haim Topol (best known in *Fiddler on the Roof*) and movie moguls Menahem Golan and Yoram Globus, while the best actress award won by Hanna Laszlo at the 2005 Cannes Film Festival for her role in Amos Gitai's movie *Free Zone* showed that Israeli films could compete in the global market-place. *Free Zone* is the story of three women: an Israeli, an American, and a Palestinian traveling in Jordan. Then, 2008 and 2009 each saw an Israeli movie feature in the Oscar nominations for Best Foreign Film (both *Beaufort* and *Waltz with Bashir*, the latter an animated documentary, dealt with Israel's occupation of Lebanon). *Footnote* about the rivalry between father and son who are Talmud scholars, *5 Broken Cameras* about life in the Palestinian Authority, and *The Gatekeepers* about Israel's security services have been more recent Israeli-produced Oscar nominees.

In recent years Israeli TV formats, adapted for international audiences have become a major hit following the success of *Hatufim*, which became the award-winning *Homeland* series. Other international successes based on Israeli formats include: *Rising Star*, *Traffic Light*, *Who's Still Standing*, *In Treatment*, *I Can Do That*, *New York*, *Little Mom*, *Magic Malabi Express*, *The Ran Quadruplets*, and *Mom and Dadz*.

The Jerusalem International Film Festival and Haifa International Film Festival each summer

MOVIES WITH A MESSAGE

Serious filmmaking in Israel began in the early 1920s and 1930s. Most of the output consisted of documentaries, whose main purpose was as a fundraising device aimed at demonstrating the Zionist effort to audiences abroad. These early films, with their images of muscle-rippling pioneers making the desert bloom, against a background of stirring music and an exhortative soundtrack, became known as "Keren Kayemet" films, after the Hebrew name of the Jewish National Fund which sponsored them. Today they seem amateurish, but, like the propaganda films made in post-revolutionary Russia, they are interesting social documents.

are the showcases of the Israeli film industry and non-Hollywood international movies.

Painters and sculptors

Israeli art owes its fundamental quality to a combination of two factors: a classical European tradition brought here by the country's early painters and art teachers, and the influences of the special quality of the light and the natural attributes of the country.

Israeli visual art, possessing its own individual character, has been created in the comparatively short space of time since the establishment of the

(1894–1980), with her line drawings of the Jerusalem hills, have also gained a following.

At the end of the 1970s, following in the steps of the USA and Europe, Israeli art entered the postmodernist era. The work is energetic and forceful, often containing violent images which are, perhaps, part of the reality of war in Israeli life. Currently, Tel Aviv artist David Reeb is among the few whose works have an overtly socio-political theme.

Museums and galleries all over the country cater to the art lover. The main ones are concentrated in two areas: Gordon Street, in central Tel

Art for sale in Safed, a town rich in galleries.

Betsalel School of Art in Jerusalem in 1906. Israeli artists have experimented with all the movements and trends of the contemporary art world, from Cubism to environment and performance art, but few have managed to make the quantum leap from local to universal recognition. Among contemporary artists who have are Ya'akov Agam (his kinetic room at the Centre Pompidou in Paris is a seminal work), Menashe Kadishman, Avigdor Arikha, Mordechai Ardon, and Joseph Zaritsky.

Dany Karavan and Ygael Tumarkin are two sculptors well known abroad whose work can be seen all over Israel. Marcel Janco (1895–1984), founder of the Dadaist movement, Reuven Rubin (1893–1974), painter of lyrical large-scale canvases, and Anna Ticho

Aviv, and Old Yafo. There are others in Jerusalem, Haifa, Ein Hod (an artists' village to the south of Haifa, which staged the Sculpture Biennale in the 1990s), and Safed, a Galilean town full of artists.

Tel Aviv Museum has a large and representative collection of Israeli modern art on permanent display, along with many temporary exhibitions. The Israel Museum, Jerusalem, which has impressive collections of classical, Impressionist, and foreign modern art (as well as a vast collection of archeology, Judaica, and Jewish art and ethnography), rather tended to neglect Israeli art before the 1985 opening of the Ayala Zacks-Abramov Pavilion of Modern Art. This has now become the nation's main repository of contemporary Israeli painting and sculpture.

CUISINE

In diverse Israel, Eastern Mediterranean fare such as falafel, houmous, and mezze salad complement such global staples as pizza and hamburgers.

Jewish and Muslim (kosher and halal) dietary laws are very similar, with both religions prohibiting pork and insisting that animals are prepared for consumption in the same very specific way. There is considerable variety, though, since every Jewish community – whether Ashkenazi, Sephardic, Yemenite, or Russian – has interpreted the culinary requirements of Judaism in its own way.

Most hotels in Israel serve only kosher food and display a sign to this effect. But most restaurants (except in Jerusalem) are not kosher, though often this is because they are open on the Sabbath and therefore not entitled to certification.

Another fundamental tenet of kosher laws is that milk and meat cannot be mixed. So you shouldn't expect to have coffee and a dairy dessert in the same kosher dining room where you can eat a meat dish. Surprisingly, McDonald's in downtown Jerusalem and most of its branches throughout the country are not kosher: you can order a milkshake to wash down your cheeseburger. For the unadventurous, many other fast-food joints have outlets throughout Israel.

The Arab influence

What people traditionally associate with "Jewish food" is actually Eastern European – *matzo* ball soup, *gefilte* fish, *latkes,* and *cholent*. But most Jewish restaurants in Israel are owned by Jews who came from Arab countries, and thus the main food that both Jews and Arabs cook and eat in the country is the kind of fare eaten across the whole of North Africa and the Middle East.

In the Mediterranean tradition this involves a great deal of culinary ingenuity. The best example of this is the chickpea, a humble legume and, on the face of it, an unexciting Middle

Fine dining with a modern flourish.

East staple. But, either fried into small balls and eaten as falafel, together with salad and spices in a pitta bread, or mashed into houmous and mopped up with pitta bread together with olive oil and beans, these make delicious, cheap, filling, and highly nutritious meals. Another popular fast-food dish is *schwarma*. Usually made from turkey, this is carved off the spit and put into pitta bread or *laffa* (a type of bread originating in Iraq), again with a choice of salads and spices. *Borekas,* a Balkan-style pastry filled with cheese, potato, or mushrooms, is another filling fast-food solution.

If you are sitting down to a meal then it is customary to start with *mezze*, a selection of salads eaten with pitta bread. Try houmous, *tahina* (sesame-seed paste), and *tabule* (cracked-wheat salad). Some restaurants in Tel Aviv's Kerem Hatamanim, West Jerusalem's Agripas Street and East Jerusalem's Bab e-Zarha will go overboard with the *mezze*, serving up as many as 20 different

> "Parve" means that a food is neither meat nor dairy. While this includes fruit and vegetables, "parve" usually refers to an artificial milk substitute that can be eaten after meat, for instance "parve" ice cream.

supposedly boneless *gefilte* fish. Authorities can differ: some deem swordfish acceptable, for example, while others don't.

Other dishes worth trying are stuffed dumplings *(kube)*, stuffed peppers, and stuffed vine leaves. The steak restaurants in Agripas in Jerusalem also offer a "Jerusalem mixed grill" stuffed in pitta bread, though this is not for the anatomically squeamish. Indeed, the Jerusalem mixed grill is offered throughout the country.

Jews and Arabs have a sweet tooth, and here visitors can go European or Middle Eastern. Ben Yehuda Street, and elsewhere in West Jeru-

Cordelia Restaurant in Old Jaffa, Tel Aviv.

salads, including pickled cucumbers and olives. It is best to specify which salads you actually want.

The meat, typically beef – *shashlik* kebabs or a steak – can be a bit of a disappointment and relatively expensive. The fish, such as St Peter's fish and Nile perch, can also be an anticlimax. It is generally well seasoned but lacking in body. Often the best option is to fill up on the nutritional salads and forgo the main course altogether. However, the quality of both meat and fish has improved over the past decade.

Kosher laws prohibit the consumption of shellfish and stipulate that fish for cooking must have both fins and tails that can be detached from the skin. Removing bones is also prohibited, hence the popularity of the

salem, as well as Tel Aviv and Haifa's Hadar and Central Carmel, have many Central European-style cafes serving delicious apple strudel. Arab restaurants offer a range of more exotic pastries such as *katayeef*, flavored with vanilla and honey, and *baklawa*, a very rich delicacy with coarsely chopped pistachio nuts, walnuts, or almonds.

Fruit

The range of local fruit and vegetables is best appreciated at Makhane Yehuda market in Jerusalem or Carmel Market in Tel Aviv, where all manner of spices and pickles are also on offer. On a hot summer's day nothing quenches the thirst better than the rich red flesh of the watermelons sold at these colorful markets.

JUDAICA

Jewish arts and crafts experienced a revival with the birth of Zionism, inspiring contemporary artists to give a new twist to old traditions.

A s in ancient times, Jerusalem is the center of Israel's arts and crafts industry, and workers are to be found in their own centrally located quarters. One feature of the arts scene is the accessibility of its artists, enabling collectors to buy directly from the studio shops.

Jewish ritual art, the bulk of Judaica, is divided into two categories: holy vessels, directly associated with the Torah, and ritual utensils, used for tasks in the home and synagogue. While not intrinsically holy, the latter acquire sanctity in the performance of religious duties (*mitzvot*). If a ritual object adds an aesthetic dimension, users have the benefit of fulfilling an additional commandment, *hiddur mitzvah* – in other words, glorification of the commandment.

The rules of creation

Halacha, Jewish law, offers only a few rules for creating specific ritual objects. The Hanuk-

Craftsman at work in the World Heritage Site of Akko.

In most cases, form and decoration followed the fashions of the time and place in which they were produced.

kah lamp is perhaps the most clearly defined. It must have eight separate lights of the same height, and a distinguishable ninth light for kindling the others. They must burn, in a publicly visible spot, for at least 30 minutes past sundown. The rest is left to the artist.

Hanukkah lamps, from the 12th century onwards, have French Gothic windows, Moorish arches, or Italian garlands; wine cups and candlesticks are reminiscent of the Renaissance

and Baroque periods, a single Hebrew letter the only sign that they were used by Jews.

Symbols of the artists' surrounding cultures were given new significance when combined with classic Jewish symbols. Long-standing favorites include (Torah) crowns and double columns invoking the Temple; biblical scenes and signs of the Zodiac; lions of Judah, grape vines and pomegranates, griffins and fish; and, of course, the seven-branched menorah.

Contemporary artists

Israel's contemporary Judaica artists, like their ancestors, favor semi-precious and precious metals, but items can be found in almost every other material, from rare woods, in particular olive wood, to Lucite. Two distinct schools have recently emerged. One is highly traditional, basing its shapes and decorations on patterns from the Baroque period or earlier. Many of these works are imitations or adaptations of well-known museum pieces; others are brought up to date by incorporating the lines of modern Jerusalem or devices such as whimsical moving parts. The second school is strictly, sometimes aggressively, contemporary. Form prevails over function; the artist strives to create artworks, which may be used in ritual.

An informal arts and crafts tour could begin at one of the two non-profit galleries, which offer an instant overview of Israel's craft scene. Neither gallery sells anything but refers visitors directly to its selected artists. At the House of Quality this means going upstairs to the studios where several silversmiths, including veterans Arie Ofir and Menachem Berman, work full-time. At the Alix de Rothschild Crafts Center the director may be on hand for tea and a chat about his latest discoveries.

Nearby, the Courtyard Gallery is the place for fiber-art fans seeking chic handmade baskets, fabrics, and wall hangings. Those who prefer a strictly ethnic look can set off across town to Kuzari, now with its sales outlet in Yoel Salomon Street in the center of the city. It is in the Bukharim Quarter, where local women embroider everything, from tea cosies to Torah covers, in traditional patterns for the Kuzari store.

Khutsot ha-Yoster (Art and Crafts Lane) near Jaffa Gate has top craftspeople like Uri Ramot (ancient glass and beads in modern settings); the Alsbergs (antique coins in custom-made jewelry); and Georges Goldstein (hand-woven tapestries and *tallitot* – prayer shawls). But the lane's greatest distinction is its concentration of outstanding silversmiths. Yaakov Greenvurcel, Zelig Segal, and Emil Shenfeld are ranked among the world's top designers of contemporary Judaica, and Michael Ende is a chief purveyor of the "nouveau antique" school.

Fans of the latter should also visit Yossi's Masters' Workshop (King David Street) and The Brothers Reichman (in Geula). Both offer extraordinary workmanship and classic designs in fine metal. Similar style characterizes the ceremonial pieces by Catriel, a carver of rare woods, in Yohanan MiGush Halava.

Representations of the human figure and face were generally avoided in deference to the Second Commandment ("Thou shall have no graven images"), but they do appear from time to time.

Close to Catriel you will find silversmiths Davidson and Amiel, calligraphic artist Korman, and jeweler Sarah Einstein, who transforms antique Middle Eastern beads into high-fashion jewelry.

Artworks on display in Safed, where there is a fertile art scene.

OTHER ARTS AND CRAFTS

From the artists' quarter in Old Safed to the seaside boutiques in Eilat, on every major city avenue and in the Oriental markets, there's an almost endless array of local handicrafts. In addition to Judaica, Israel is rich with the arts and crafts of other communities. Bedouin goods include special embroidered bags, pillows, tablecloths, and weaving for carpets. These can be found at the Bedouin market in Be'er Sheva on Thursday mornings. Similar Druze handicrafts are on sale in the Carmel village of Daliyat el-Karmel. Distinctive Armenian pottery, which makes a delightful gift, is available on the Via Dolorosa of the Christian Quarter in the Old City.

APPLETONS' JOURNAL

OF LITERATURE ❖ SCIENCE ❖ AND ART

ENTERED, according to Act of Congress, in the year 1871, by D. APPLETON & Co., in the Office of the Librarian of Congress at Washington.

No. 99.—VOL. V.]   SATURDAY, FEBRUARY 18, 1871.   { PRICE TEN CENTS { WITH SUPPLEMEN

THE RECOVERY OF JERUSALEM.*

THIS is the somewhat pretentious title of the narrative of recent English explorations of Jerusalem, by means of excavations conducted by Captain Wilson, of the Royal Engineers, under the auspices and at the expense of the Committee of the Palestine Exploration Fund. Without, perhaps, fulfilling the meaning of the old crusading war-cry, exact knowledge of the scenes and localities in which their first appeared on earth. The explorations have solved many problems, and settled many fierce and protracted controversies. have been sunk and tunnels made in the most secluded and mys parts of the sacred city, and structures brought to light that h

WILSON'S ARCH, DISCOVERED AT JERUSALEM IN 1867.

the "Recovery of Jerusalem," it is undoubtedly a record of researches and discoveries of the highest value, and of the greatest interest to scholars, antiquarians, and, above all, to Christians who desire an

been seen by mortal eyes since the days of Titus, or perhaps of mon.

The beginning of this great work was the Ordnance Surv Jerusalem, made by Captain Wilson, of the English Royal Engi in 1864-'65. Early in the year 1864 the sanitary state of Jeru attracted considerable attention; that city, which the Psalmis described as "beautiful for situation, the joy of the whole earth

---

* The Recovery of Jerusalem. A Narrative of Exploration and Discovery in the City and the Holy Land. By Captain Wilson, R. E., and Captain Warren, R. E. With an Introduction by Arthur Penrhyn Stanley, D. D., Dean of Westminster. D. Appleton & Co.

DIGGING UP THE PAST

Archeology is Israel's national hobby, fascinating all age groups, and tourists and natives alike are encouraged to unearth a rich past.

With more than 20,000 recognized archeological sites in an area of around 21,000 sq km (8,100 sq miles), and finds dating back to 150,000 BC, Israel has several dozen archeological museums in addition to numerous private collections. Yet only a few potential sites have been thoroughly explored; time, money, and manpower have all placed limits on the scope of such exploration.

A gentlemanly hobby

Adherents past and present to what one scholar called the "study of durable rubbish" have been drawn to biblical archeology for a range of reasons: greed, adventure, religion, and scholarship. During the Victorian period it was something of a gentlemanly hobby.

The first known "archeologist" to work in Israel was inspired by religious belief. In AD 325 Empress Helena, the mother of Constantine the Great, the emperor who declared Christianity the official religion of his empire, ordered the removal of a Hadrianic temple to Venus built on a site which she had determined was the hill of Golgotha. Constantine erected the Church of the Holy Sepulcher to commemorate the alleged site of the crucifixion and entombment of Jesus.

During the next 16 centuries the territory changed hands numerous times. Explorers of all religions crossed its borders, armed with

Israeli archaeologist Shai Bar-Tura inspects the burial crypt under the apse of a unique late Byzantine church on February 2nd, 2011.

little more than compasses, picks, shovels, and curiosity. Stories of bribery, untimely deaths, and mystical reunions with long-dead sages and prophets pepper their accounts. Medieval adventurers report that those who dared to enter the burial cavern of the patriarchs and their wives at Hebron were struck blind or senseless or worse. Such tales did not deter others.

Interest in the Holy Land intensified after Napoleon conquered Egypt in 1798 and the Rosetta Stone was subsequently discovered. Scholars, amateurs, and snake-oil salesmen descended on Palestine, then a sparsely populated backwater. Some of these adventurers

In 2005 Unesco declared Israel's three most excavated "tels" (mounds), at Megiddo, Khatsor, and Be'er Sheva, to be World Heritage Sites. Unesco had previously granted such status to the Nabatean settlements of the Negev.

became the victims of archeological fever. For example, when the British Museum rejected as fake certain "ancient" parchments that Moses Wilhelm Shapira had bought from a Bedouin, the amateur archeologist simply disappeared.

In 1911, Captain Montague Parker and his crew of treasure hunters barely escaped with their lives when they were caught excavating under the Dome of the Rock on the Temple Mount. The British mission had been following the hunch of a Swedish clairvoyant who insisted that this was where they would find a cache of objects from King Solomon's temple. Offended Jerusalemites rioted in the streets.

Method in the madness

The foundations of modern archeology as we know it were not laid until the late 19th century, and were marked by the establishment of major academic institutions sponsoring field trips and publication societies. The Palestine Exploration Fund, founded in London in 1865, is the grandfather of these groups, which include such venerable institutions as the American Schools of Oriental Research and the Ecole Biblique et Archéologique Française. The work that Edward Robinson, Claude R. Conder, Sir Flinders Petrie, and other giants carried out during this period continues to cast a long shadow on modern archeology.

It was Petrie who first recognized the importance of stratigraphy – that is, the examination layer by layer of a tel, the artificial mound formed by successive settlements. He was also among the first to recognize the importance of using pottery to date each layer. He realized that, in different periods, particular types of pottery would be associated with particular strata.

Today an eclectic approach to tel excavating prevails. Technological advances enable surveyors to provide archeologists with considerable information before a single shovelful of earth has been removed. Carbon-14 dating has further improved the possibility of fixing an artifact in time. Archeologists can now dig underwater, cross-reference finds on computers and learn more quickly what their colleagues have discovered. They can call on a host of specialists, including paleo-botanists, osteologists, ethnologists, philologists, and biblical exegetes to interpret their finds.

Most importantly, archeologists now emphasize that once a locus – a three-dimensional area

designated for excavation – is dug and artifacts are removed, the site will have been ineluctably altered. By the very nature of their work, they destroy irreplaceable evidence in their search for remnants of the past.

A passion for proof

Archeology is a field whose study bolsters or threatens religious beliefs – as well as pet scholarly theories. It has become a national passion in Israel, representing as it does a method of proving the Jewish people's legitimate right to the Land of Israel – each biblical find conveni-

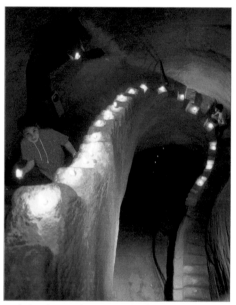

Exploring the Maresha Caves, a relic of Greek quarrying.

ently overlooking two millennia of Arab habitation of the land. Among the most important Jewish discoveries have been Eleazar Sukenik's purchase of the Dead Sea Scrolls, found by a shepherd boy in the Judea Desert in 1947.

Inevitably, digging in Jerusalem is a sensitive matter. The City of David dig just outside the walls of the Old City, near the Dung Gate (and including Warren's Shaft, which 3,000 years ago supplied King David's original Jerusalem with water) are impressive testaments to Jerusalem's founding. However, the digs here and inside the Old City, near the Western Wall, have been plagued by protests from Palestinians on the one hand and ultra-Orthodox Jews on the other hand, who fear that Jewish graves are being despoiled. For their part, Muslim excavations of Solomon's Stables on the Temple Mount have brought Israeli protests that the physical stability of the entire Temple Mount is being threatened.

As a result of all these arguments, in 1982 Unesco added the Old City of Jerusalem to the list of the world's endangered heritage sites.

Bringing history to light

Elsewhere in the country an impressive amount of history has been uncovered from the Roman and Byzantine cities of Caesarea and Bet Shean, settlements of Avdat and Mashit in the Negev, as well as Masada, the mighty fortress overlooking the Dead Sea, which was, a Herodian winter retreat.

Important digs continue to throw up important discoveries. In 2007, King Herod's grave was uncovered by archeologist Ehud Netzer. The grave is within a family mausoleum at Herodion, an impressive hilltop palace in the Judean Desert near Bethlehem. Other discoveries include the Samson mosaics at Huqoq in the Galilee and a statue of Hercules in the Jezreel Valley.

Ruins from the time of Herod the Great at Masada.

with its amphitheaters; and at Tsipori in the north, where there are glorious mosaics to be seen, including the one known as the Mona Lisa of the Galilee in a Roman villa dating back to AD 200.

Tel Megiddo near Mount Carmel contains 26 stratified layers of civilizations and overlooks the Valley of Jezreel, which many believe to be the legendary Armageddon. Further north, in the Upper Galilee, Tel Khatsor has an even larger number of layers, including a Caananite city from the 13th century BC. Tel Be'er Sheva in the south, east of modern-day Be'er Sheva, has remains ranging from 4000 BC to the 16th century.

Also of importance are the Philistine cities of Gath and Ekron in the south and the Nabatean

POPULARIZING THE PAST

The late Yigael Yadin, the son of Eleazer Sukenik, followed in his father's footsteps, and conducted many digs of his own. His books on Masada, Khatsor ha-Glilit, and the Dead Sea Scrolls have dramatized the history of the "people of the book." In addition, much of his work has been popularized by others. Khatsor, a site in northern Israel with an underground water system, is the subject of James Michener's novel *The Source*. And Yadin's dig at Masada – where he discovered a ritual bath and synagogue – became the focus of a TV mini-series focussing on the heroic but futile stand of a handful of Jews against the Roman forces in AD 73.

CONSERVING FOR THE FUTURE

Since the State of Israel was created, forests
have been planted and the land regenerated,
but creeping urbanization remains a threat.

Intrinsic in Zionist ideology was love of the
Land of Israel and the rebirth of its entire
ecosystem. Many admirable things have
been achieved over the past century but, while
it was true that the land had previously been
neglected, all too often the European settlers
tried to create an environment that was too
green, especially in the southern half of the
country, and in many instances deserts have
been transformed into unnecessary forests.

However, the main environmental problem
has been caused by the transplanting of too large
a population into too small an area. As affluence
increases, more and more Israelis are forsaking
their small apartment in an urban high-rise for
a more spacious house and garden. Shopping
malls, high-tech parks, and highways swallow
up the countryside. Industrialization has taken
its toll, and it is said that more than 1,000 Israelis die each year from the consequences of polluted air – more annual deaths than from road
accidents and terrorism combined.

That said, Israel's environment is unlike any
other. The Sinai peninsula, together with Israel
and Jordan, form the only land link between
Africa and Europe/Asia, and the flora and fauna
represent a unique mix of the three continents.
Each spring it is estimated that more than 1 billion birds migrate northward from their breeding grounds in Africa, flying along the Great
Syrian-African Rift Valley. At Israel's more verdant northern border the birds, which include
34 different types of birds of prey, can sense
journey's end.

But Israel has been good to the birds. In the
1980s the US government pressed to build a
$2 billion Voice of America antenna in the
Arava Desert, which would have impeded
the birds' flight path. Under pressure from

A Bedouin of the Negev.

environmentalists the Israeli government said no;
the installation was eventually built in Kuwait.

Preparing for salvation

The Jewish concept of redemption sees not only
people but all God's creations, including animals,
trees, and flowers, being redeemed when the Messiah comes. In the meantime it is man's duty to
tend the environment so that there is something
to redeem. The early Zionists may not have been
"greens" in the modern sense, but they were horrified by the swamp-ridden, barren land that they
found. The region was a desolate backwater of
the crumbling Ottoman Empire and nature had
been ravished. The hand of havoc, it seemed, had
reached into the Garden of Eden.

Lions had disappeared in Crusader times and crocodiles did not survive the 19th century. Few may regret the demise of these predators, but the more widespread introduction of modern firearms was a tragedy for less threatening wildlife. Within a few decades, large numbers of the gazelles and ibex, which had lived here since the days of the prophets, had been ruthlessly killed. A monstrous hunting binge shot several species, such as the wild bear, into extinction. The leopard just survived in the south, though probably no more than a dozen exist.

The local race of ostrich, which so perplexed and incapable of reproduction. Today, Israel's native Madonna lily is a very rare plant.

Loss of vegetation

The big disaster came when the Ottoman Turks built a railway into the Arabian Desert, and the region's forests were leveled. The heavy timbers were used to bridge ravines, middle-sized logs became rail ties, and the smaller pieces were burned as fuel. By the time T. E. Lawrence (Lawrence of Arabia) was attacking the Ottoman trains, Israel had less than 3 percent tree cover. With the loss of vegetation, the soil turned to

Spring flowers bloom among the cacti at Jezreel Valley in the Galilee.

Job, was blasted to nothingness. Israel's native race of Asiatic wild ass, a creature some scholars identify as the animal Jesus rode on Palm Sunday, was annihilated. The spectacular white oryx antelope, the *re'em* of the Hebrew Bible, translated in the King James Version as unicorn, suffered a similar fate. Fortunately, a few specimens were captured for breeding before the last of the wild population was exterminated.

Flora was also destroyed. For centuries Christian pilgrims had scoured the countryside for biblical wildflowers. These were picked, pressed, and sent back to Europe to serve as bookmarks in family Bibles. Generations of Europeans could "consider the lilies" of the Holy Land – but these lilies were lifeless, dried,

HOLDING BACK THE DESERT

Much of the regeneration of the land has been achieved by the Jewish National Fund (JNF), Israel's afforestation agency, which was also responsible for planting the northern hemisphere's most southerly non-equatorial forest, the Yatir Forest, in the northern Negev Desert. The agency is particularly concerned with combating desert encroachment. But, despite its achievements, the JNF comes in for criticism. Some environmental organizations in Israel accuse it of overkill, claiming that it is trying to create European-style forests in places where a semi-arid desert environment should naturally exist. Others accuse it of over-reliance on the Aleppo pine.

dust and was swept out to the desert by the wind. The scant winter rains had no absorbent material to hold them, and water ran quickly to the sea while the wells dried out.

Early Jewish settlers determined to recreate the biblical Land of Israel were confronted by severe problems. The land was exhausted, and could not support either a human population or its own natural processes. The ecological integrity of the land had to be restored.

The 15th day of the Jewish month of Shevat, Tu B'Shvat, is Israeli Arbor Day, celebrated by planting trees in any of the special planting zones in the nation's forests. Israelis plant trees

With the return of trees, soil, and water, agriculture prospered. Israel is one of the very few arid lands that grows enough food to feed itself – and has enough surplus for exports.

With the return of the trees, nature also flourished, and the land began to recover. Life processes dependent upon a good vegetative cover were regenerated. Some are hardly noticed – for example, the sprouting of orenit mushrooms in the Jerusalem forest after the first winter rains, or the growth of colorful mosaics of lichen upon fallen logs. Others are so dramatic that they are impossible to miss, such as the majestic golden eagles, which have returned to the skies.

Migrating cranes gathered in the Hula Valley.

on other days, too – to mark birthdays and weddings, for example. In one forest about 20km (12 miles) west of Jerusalem 6 million trees have been planted as a memorial to Holocaust victims.

Since Israel was founded in 1948, planted forests have grown to cover 2,000 sq km (770 sq miles) – 10 percent of the country's land area. With the return of the trees, winter rains were captured and channeled to the aquifers. Wells again became productive. With the return of the trees, particularly the fast-growing Jerusalem pine (*Pinus halepensis*), soil was regenerated. In many places the pines were cut once the soil was adequate and replaced with apricot, almond, and other fruit and nut trees.

Nature reserves

There are 280 established nature reserves in Israel, covering more than 4,000 sq km (1,540 sq miles) – more than one-fifth of the country's land area. By international standards, the reserves are strictly run. They are maintained in as pristine a state as possible, and visitors are forbidden to pick flowers, to camp, or to picnic. Administered by the Nature Reserves Authority, they serve a variety of functions. Generally, they reflect the need for humanity and nature to coexist. An example can be seen at Banias, a beautiful nature reserve at the foot of Mount Hermon, on Israel's northern border. The name Banias is a corruption of the Greek

"Paneas," and here there are the remains of an ancient Greek temple dedicated to the god of the forests. Other archeological treasures in the area include the remains of the ancient Nimrod Fortress and the Crusader town of Belinas.

The reserve's colorful wild oleander and thick groves of myrtle, plane, and willow trees appeal to the naturalist's eye. It is a haven for a great variety of birds and mammals. The rare stone marten and wild cat live here, and otters splash in the waters that flow down from Mount Hermon.

These waters give a human dimension to this nature reserve, for they are the headwaters of

international effort to "return the animals of the Bible to the land of the Bible." Conservationists have searched the world to find remnants of the species that once inhabited these lands. Some of the discoveries were prosaic: addax antelope were found in a Chicago zoo, and a few Asiatic wild ass came from Copenhagen Zoo.

Deer with false documents

A few of the discoveries have involved some spectacular rescue work. Mesopotamian fallow deer, for example, were spirited out of revolutionary Iran during a howling storm, on false export papers. White oryx – the unicorns

the Jordan River, and much of them eventually enters Israel's national water-carrier system. They flow from taps in Tel Aviv and Haifa, help irrigate the fields of the Galilee, and fill the fish ponds of the Beit She'an Valley.

Many nature reserves are established solely for the preservation of particular natural features: a seasonal pond, a secluded valley where rare flowers blossom, a sunny cliff with good nesting ledges. Some of these reserves are off-limits to human visitors because of their importance to the ecological equilibrium of the region.

One of the most interesting projects is the Khai-Bar program. Khai-Bar is a Hebrew term which simply means "wildlife," but to Israeli conservationists it also identifies an

UNWELCOME IMPROVEMENT

The Hula Nature Reserve in the Upper Galilee is perhaps an example of over-zealous attempts by Israel to "improve" on the existing environment. In the 1950s the Hula Swamp was drained to make way for agriculture. Of the 4,000 hectares (10,000 acres) drained, 80 hectares (200 acres) were left as a nature reserve, the habitat of water buffalo and diverse wildlife. But the farmland beneath the swamp, rich in peat, is becoming less and less fertile, and recently 400 hectares (1,000 acres) were reswamped. This well-intentioned project has been acknowledged as a noble failure, and there are plans to restore the Hula Swamp in the long term.

of the King James Bible – were sourced a few hundred kilometers southeast of the Negev, in the personal zoo of the late Saudi King Faisal. And a flock of ostrich chicks was airlifted out of Ethiopia's Danakil Desert when the Israeli Air Force was sent on a special mission to fetch some new immigrants to Israel.

All the animals, regardless of their origin, are first brought to special reserves set up to rehabilitate them to life in Israel's wild areas. One Khai-Bar reserve is deep in the Negev, about 40km (25 miles) north of Eilat; it specializes in desert animals. Another is on top of Mount Carmel, on the

Israel purifies and recycles 80 percent of its sewage water for use in agriculture, while five major desalination plants on the Mediterranean coast convert sea water into potable water.

is 2,236 meters (7,336 ft); the Dead Sea, at 400 meters (1,300ft) below sea level, is the lowest point on the face of the earth. Broad plains stretch across parts of the Galilee, and fringe the northern Negev with expanses of steppe grasslands.

Ostriches in a nature reserve.

Mediterranean coast near Haifa; its speciality is wildlife of the Mediterranean oak-forest region.

The restoration process is comprehensive and involves years of painstaking work. Indeed, 14 years passed between the acquisition of the Asiatic wild ass from Copenhagen Zoo, and the day when their offspring were judged tough and experienced enough to live freely in the wild. Today they are repopulating remote areas of the Negev and giving birth to wild foals.

Geological diversity

Topography in Israel is a matter of spectacular contrasts. Mount Hermon, on the northern border, towers to a snowcapped 2,814 meters (9,232ft), although the highest peak in Israel

Makhtesh Ramon, a natural crater 40km (25 miles) across, is carved from the central Negev highlands. The north–south range of the Judean mountains forms a continuous ridge, nearly 1,000 meters (3,280ft) high, an hour's drive east of the Mediterranean coast.

The great geographical and topographical diversity is responsible for tremendous biological diversity. There are sub-alpine meadows on the slopes of Mount Hermon, and just 25km (16 miles) south, at the Hula Nature Reserve, there is a lush tropical jungle: the world's northernmost papyrus swamp. Israel is a land of Eurasian oaks and African acacias, Eurasian foxes and wolves, and African Dorcas gazelles and rock hyrax, blending continents, flora, fauna, and geology.

Protecting the coast

Israel's Mediterranean coast is 200km (125 miles) long but overdeveloped – will the Coastline Protection Law turn the tide?

The golden beaches of Israel's Mediterranean coast stretch from the sand dunes dividing Israel from the Palestinian Gaza Strip in the south to Rosh ha-Nikra, a delightful network of underground caves on the coast by the Lebanese border, reached by cable car. About half of the coastline falls under the jurisdiction of Israeli municipalities, which for the most part have lined the seafront with expensive housing developments and hotels.

Even the beaches are not always accessible to the public for free, as local authorities often charge a fee. Elsewhere, marinas have been built in Ashkelon and Ashdod, Tel Aviv and Herzliya, and the deep seaports of Ashdod and Haifa are being greatly expanded, while power stations, military installations, and private developments deny the public access to several kilometers more of the coastline.

The Coastline Protection Law, which was enacted by the Knesset in 2004, is designed to stop this erosion of one of Israel's most important environmental assets. The law dictates that, in those areas where the coast does not belong to a city's municipality, there can be no major construction within 300 meters (980ft) of the beach.

Unique ecosystem

For many "greens" the law is too little too late. The 300-meter limit fails to protect the huge sand dunes that remain just inland from the coast, brought up from the North African deserts by winds and currents over millennia.

Many of the evacuated Jewish settlements in the Gush Katif region of the Gaza strip are being rebuilt in the Nitsanim region north of Ashkelon, the country's last major unspoiled area of these sand dunes and their unique ecosystem. High-rise coastal developments also spoil the view of the sea and block the breezes, which cool the inland regions.

Nor does the law touch on the dire state of Israel's rivers. Although best known for the north–south River Jordan, Israel has several dozen smaller east–west rivers, which flow into the Mediterranean Sea. While the River Jordan provides much of the country's drinking water, a

mouthful of the hopelessly polluted River Yarkon in Tel Aviv or the River Kishon in Haifa could result in a fatal lung infection, although efforts are being made to clean them up. The River Poleg near Netanya is frequently contaminated with sewage. But progress in cleaning rivers means sea turtles have returned to the mouths of the Alexander and Hadera rivers north of Netanya.

One continuing difficulty is that, despite the good intentions of a large proportion of the population, "green" issues are rarely on the political agenda. This isn't because Israelis are indifferent to them, but because questions of war and peace tend to

Bathing along the coast near Caesarea comes with views of Roman ruins, such as this aqueduct.

shoulder other concerns to one side.

Despite the problems, Israel's Mediterranean coastline is still dominated by golden, sun-soaked beaches while the sea itself, with its dangerously deceptive undercurrents, is cleaner than it once was, when particles of oil would stick to bathers' bodies.

The best beaches are at Nitsanim in the south (when it's not being used for pop concerts in the summer), Caesarea in the center of the country, where you can bathe amid the Roman ruins, and at Achziv north of Nahariya.

Other delightful seaside spots, romantically enhanced by their resistance to civilization's concrete onslaught, are the ancient ports and fishing villages at Yafo, near Tel Aviv, and Akko, north of Haifa.

A HIGH-TECH ECONOMY

From internet and mobile phone applications to
medical devices and biotech, Israel's industry
has invested heavily in new technology.

In their book *Startup Nation – the Story of Israel's Economic Miracle* Dan Senor and Saul Singer analyze Israel's innovation and entrepreneurial driven economy. The moniker "Startup Nation" has stuck, reinforcing the reputation that Israel has earned by having more start-ups in absolute terms than any other country after the US.

Israeli high-tech is strong in IT, mobile technologies, semiconductors, defense and security, medical devices, and biomed. The current buzz sectors are big data, cyber security, digital health, and smartphone apps. Each year Israel earns billions of dollars through investments in startups and ultimately their acquisition by major global corporations. One of the best-known startup exits was Waze, a crowdsourcing smartphone app combining GPS and traffic reports, which was sold to Google in 2013 for US$1 billion.

The startup tradition began in the 1990s when young Israeli entrepreneurs took inspiration from Arik Vardi, Sefi Vigiser, Amnon Amir, and Yair Goldfinger. All in their early 20s, they loved the internet but felt frustrated that computers could only find other computers online and could not bring together individuals. They set up Mirabilis, which created peer-to-peer architecture with a central server that provides users with other users' internet addresses. The product they developed was called ICQ and the messaging clones that have since imitated it, such as Microsoft's Messenger, as well as more recent social networking platforms such as Facebook, revolutionized the lifestyle of young people and the way they communicate. In 1998 Mirabilis was sold to America On Line for US$407 million.

The Mirabilis effect was felt far beyond the computer screen. It inspired young high-tech entrepreneurs to dare to transform their dreams into viable business products through their

Winner of the 2011 Nobel Prize in Chemistry, Israeli scientist Daniel Shechtman.

PROTECTING MURDOCH

In the late 1980s Professor Adi Shamir of the Weizmann Institute in Rekhovot persuaded Rupert Murdoch to acquire his encryption system to protect his new Sky TV satellite service. Murdoch's News Data Corp. also set up NDS, headquartered in London but with its development and manufacturing plant in Jerusalem. In a business revolving around code-breakingmany of NDS's senior executives are former Mossad agents. NDS Israel, a global leader in its field, has annual sales of nearly US$1 billion and was acquired in 2012 by Cisco for $5 billion..

own startup companies; it persuaded the business world that there were huge returns to be reaped from investments in high-tech startups; and it emphasized to the international business community that Israel offered unique systems and solutions.

Since then Israel's advanced technology industries have transformed a sluggish economy into a dynamic marketplace attracting billions of dollars in overseas investments. The gleaming glass high-rises sprouting in Tel Aviv and the impressive high-tech industrial parks throughout the country testify to Israel's new-found affluence.

cameras in capsules for medical examinations.

Israeli companies have raised billions of dollars on overseas stock markets. More than 150 Israeli firms are traded on international markets, mainly in New York and London. The country's 100 VC firms have generated more than US$30 billion in investment funds and mobilized more than US$70 billion in high-tech transactions.

High-tech oranges

Israel has always been strong on technology. Even the Jaffa orange and Israel's other agricultural exports have been based on developing new spe-

The not-so-humble orange.

Salt formations of the Dead Sea, whose extracted minerals are big business.

A new business model

Small operations like Mirabilis, which then sells the technology it has developed to a global corporation, have become an industrial sector of their own and created a new business model in Israel. Cisco Systems, Microsoft, HP, Siemens, Broadcom, Qualcomm, Google and, more recently, Facebook and Apple, which opened their first R&D centers outside the US, have acquired dozens of Israeli start-ups between them for billions of dollars. HP acquired Mercury Interactive for US$4.5 billion, and Cisco acquired NDS for $5 billion to name some of the biggest deals. Dozens of innovative developments include the first disk on key brought to market by M-Systems, and Given Imaging's

cies of fruit and vegetables, irrigation techniques, greenhouse technology, pesticides, and fertilizers. The country is the world's largest producer of cut and polished diamonds, selling US$19 billion worth of stones in 2013. Here too software and laser technology have enabled Israeli cutters to come to the fore.

It was military necessity that led the country to develop leading-edge industries. Israel is one of only nine countries with an independent space launch capability and is a global leader in drones, missile technology, electro-optics, lasers, radar and intelligence systems, and homeland defense solutions.

Before the discovery of gas fields in the

Mediterranean, Israel's only natural resources – the bromine, potash, and magnesium in the Dead Sea and phosphates in the Negev – were of little use until the 1980s and 1990s, when scientists developed more efficient ways of extraction and uses for them. More than US$7.5 billion of these minerals are now sold annually.

Typically an Israeli high-tech executive is a graduate of one of the country's universities and an elite combat army unit. Many global firms invest in or acquire an Israeli firm partly in order to have access to a high-tech team capable of fast-tracking a complex project.

Protesting against the gap between rich and poor.

GAS FINDS

Israel, historically reliant on importing all of its energy needs, has had its economy boosted by the discovery of large offshore gas fields. The Leviathan field offshore from Haifa, discovered in 2010, has an estimated 22 trillion cubic feet (TCF; 45 billion cubic meters) of gas and is the largest gas find worldwide over the past decade. The Tamar field discovered in 2009 has 9TCF. More major fields with gas and also oil are expected to be confirmed in the coming years, and Israel will become a net exporter. The US Geological Survey estimates there are 227TCF in the Levant Basin in the economic waters of Israel, Egypt, Lebanon, Cyprus, and Palestine.

Intel's investment

For many years, though it happens less frequently these days, Israel would lose its best minds to the US. One such man was Dr Dov Frohman, who was part of the Intel team, which developed the first computer chip in the 1970s. He returned home and set up Intel Israel in the 1980s, encompassing both an R&D center and semiconductor fab, which today has annual exports of US$5 billion – by far Israel's largest exporter. Motorola, HP, Philips, IBM, GE, Samsung, Apple, Facebook and Microsoft are just some of the multinational corporations that have established Israel manufacturing and development facilities.

Not all Israeli technology has been sold off to the highest international bidder. Some local firms have hung on to their products and generated annual sales of billions of dollars, including Amdocs (telephone billing) and Check Point (IT security).

But by far the largest Israeli company is Teva Pharmaceuticals, the world's biggest manufacturer of generic drugs (pharmaceuticals whose patents have expired), with annual sales of over US$20 billion. Teva is also tapping into Israel's fast-growing biotech sector to develop its own original pharmaceuticals; one such drug – Copaxone, for treating multiple sclerosis – alone has annual sales of US$4 billion.

Israel's financial system remained strong despite the global crisis, and the country recorded 5 percent growth in 2009 and 2010, although by 2013 and 2014 growth had slowed to 3 percent annually.

The gap between rich and poor

Israel's high-tech revolution has not benefited everybody. Alongside greater prosperity, governments have dismantled many aspects of the socialist state, which existed prior to 2000. Although there is high-quality medical care for all citizens, government welfare payments to the unemployed, single parents, large families and the elderly, are very low by Western standards, and the gap between rich and poor in Israel is wider than in any other OECD country except for the US.

According to Israel's National Insurance Institute, 23 percent of Israeli families and 35 percent of children live below the poverty line. For them, faster internet, 3G mobile phones, and satellite technology offer little comfort.

Sport

Historically, sport and Judaism did not mix, and even today ultra-Orthodox Jews reject it and the love of physical prowess as "Hellenistic".

In biblical times the Greek love of physical prowess conflicted with the Jewish moral code, and ancient Greece's attempts to impose its culture throughout the region was resented by the Israelites.

Down the centuries Jews maintained this aversion to sport. Emphasizing the spiritual and intellectual, Judaism rejected the physical world of sport. Secular Zionists, determined to create the new Jew who was a soldier and farmer, saw sport as the ideal means to these ends. Sports movements were established in the early 20th century, tied to political movements – Hapoel (Labor), Betar (Likud), and Maccabi (the defunct Liberal party). Even the Orthodox Jewish community got into sport, founding Elitzur. These sports clubs exist today, and often the political connections have survived – Betar Jerusalem is a bastion of the right and Hapoel Tel Aviv is associated with the left.

Headline events

These clubs encompass amateurs and professionals. Professionally, Israeli sport was slow to take off. The national soccer team reached the World Cup finals for the one and only time in Mexico in 1970. Tragically, the only sporting headline Israel ever made was when Palestinians at the Munich Olympics in 1972 gunned down 11 members of the country's Olympic squad. It was not until the 1992 Olympics in Barcelona that Israel won its first Olympic medals, and the country celebrated its first gold medal in Athens in 2004 when Gal Fridman won the windsurfing competition.

In professional sport Israel benefited from its expulsion from Asian sporting federations in 1973. The country was accepted into the European sporting federations such as UEFA in soccer, and is entitled to compete in such prestigious competitions as the UEFA Champions League. Maccabi Haifa, Hapoel Tel Aviv and Maccabi Tel Aviv have reached the lucrative Group stage, with Haifa even enjoying a 3–0 victory over the mighty Manchester United. Individual players have had successful careers in Europe's top leagues, including Eyal Berkovic, Tal Ben Haim and Yossi Benayoun in England's Premier League, while Avram Grant coached Chelsea to the Champions League final in 2008 and Portsmouth to the FA Cup Final in 2010. Israel hosted Euro 2013, the UEFA Under-21 Soccer Finals.

Israel has most excelled in basketball, with Maccabi Tel Aviv winning its sixth European titles in 2014 while players like Omri Casspi and Gal Mekel have starred in the NBA.. In tennis Israel has had top 20 players in the 1980s (Shlomo Glickstein), 1990s (Amos Mansdorf), and more recently the appropriately named Anna Smashnova and Shahar Peer.

However, with the exception of the occasional World Cup qualifier or Champions League match,

Maccabi Electra Tel Aviv's player Pnini Guy ® during Turkish Airlines Final Four final match in Milan, Italy on May 18, 2014.

there is little to interest the visitor in terms of professional sport. The biggest sporting festival in Israel is the Maccabiah, recognized by the IOC as the Jewish Olympics, when Diaspora Jewish communities compete for medals. The event is held every four years, and the 19th Maccabiah is scheduled for July 2013.

Visitors to Israel will most enjoy the country's participatory water sports, with surfing and windsurfing, water-skiing and swimming in the Mediterranean, the Sea of Galilee, and the Red Sea. Proportionally, the country has the highest number of licensed divers in the world, and diving is the best way to make the acquaintance of the Red Sea's remarkable marine life.

The Tel Aviv skyline as seen from Yafo.

TICKET OFFICE

A swathe of spring flowers in Ashkelon.

Old Yafo.

INTRODUCTION

A detailed guide to the whole of Israel,
with principal sites clearly cross-
referenced by number to the maps.

Strolling along the Dead Sea.

A rriving at Ben Gurion Airport, visitors can choose to
go eastward through the Judean Hills to Jerusalem,
with its history and religion, or westward to Tel
Aviv, Israel's economic capital, a brash place with golden
beaches and a pulsating nightlife, a city looking to its
future rather than its past.

From east to west, Israel (including the Palestinian autonomous zones) is less than 100km (60 miles) at its broadest
points. Tel Aviv is at the heart of the coastal plain, a densely populated,
narrow piece of land stretching from the Gaza Strip in the south to Lebanon in the north, with mild, wet, sunny winters and hot,
humid summers.

The inland hills to the east offer cooler, drier climes.
Jerusalem is perched on a peak 830 meters (2,700ft) high,
and other ancient cities such as the West Bank towns of
Bethlehem and Hebron are also built on hills. Here the hot,
dry summers are tempered by late afternoon breezes, and
in the winter there can even be a dusting of snow. In the
spring, the best time to visit, the hillsides are ablaze with
flowers. The terraced hillsides of olive groves and grape
vines have a biblical charm, but otherwise the landscape
has a Mediterranean familiarity.

The terrain east of Jerusalem is alien and exotic, for the   *Jerusalem's Yafo Road.*
Holy City is a continental divide. The western slopes lead
down through forest and field to the Mediterranean, but to the east the
land dips down dramatically through rugged desert to the Dead Sea
Basin, the lowest point on earth, and the northern stretch of the great
Africa–Syria Rift Valley. The Dead Sea itself is really a lake that nestles
amid a landscape of shimmering mountains and has a high salt content,
which enables bathers to float – a highlight of any trip to Israel.

The 500km (300 miles) from north to south stretch from the snow-
covered peaks of Mount Hermon to the tropical waters of the Red Sea
resort of Eilat – in winter you can actually ski on Mount Hermon in the
morning and go scuba-diving in the Red Sea in the afternoon.

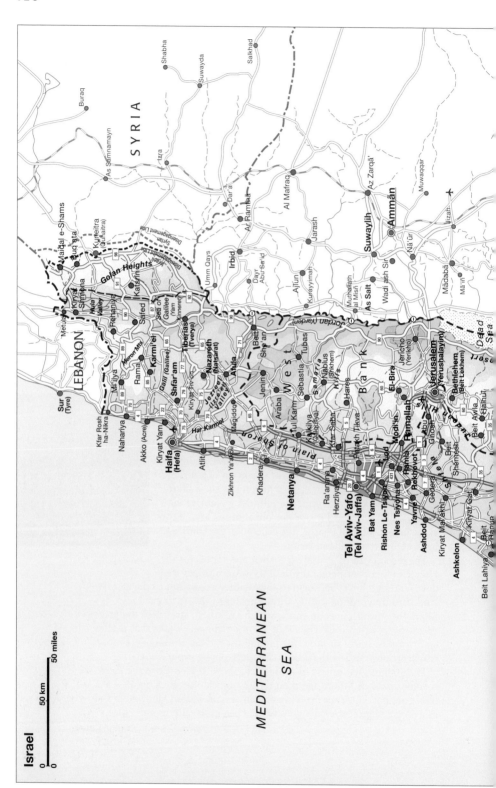

Israel

0
0
50 km
50 miles

MEDITERRANEAN SEA

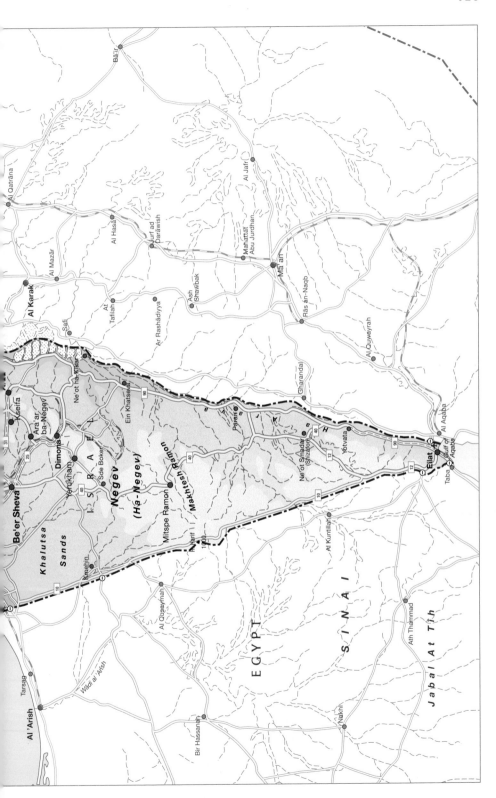

JERUSALEM YESTERDAY AND TODAY

The followers of three major world religions demand a say in the future of the Golden City. To appreciate why, you need to understand its turbulent past.

Main Attractions
Western Wall
Dome of the Rock
Israel Museum

Jerusalem has been called many things: the Golden City, the Holy City, the City of David, the City of Peace. Sadly, it is also a city of strife. To Jews, it is their national and spiritual epicenter: the incarnation of ancient Israel; the place where Abraham went to sacrifice Isaac; the site of David's glory and Solomon's Temple; the eternal capital of the Jewish people. To Christians, it is the city where Jesus spent his last days on earth: the site of the Last Supper, the Crucifixion and Resurrection. To Muslims, it is Al Quds ("The Holy"), the place where Mohammed is said to have ascended to heaven on his steed; indeed, it is Islam's third-holiest city after Mecca and Medina.

From its enduring power as a spiritual symbol, to the quality of the light, Jerusalem is unique. And today, more than 3,000 years after David made the city his capital, Jerusalem still has the ability to stir emotions and fire the imagination like no other city on earth.

Visiting Jerusalem

Still the centerpiece of many a journey to Israel, as it has been throughout the centuries, Jerusalem continues to reward the traveler with its riches. The marketplaces, shrines, ruins, hotels, temples, churches, and mosques are all readily accessible, and the city's tourist board (www.jerusalem.muni.il) is more than willing to provide directions. Yet the soul of the city is more elusive. The rhythm of daily life here is governed by prayer, usually channeled through tightly knit religious communities, and the visitor who merely barters for trinkets in the Old City between hops to famous churches or museums is missing the source and substance of the place.

Also, as the seat of government for the state and a major academic and high-tech center, Jerusalem has an important but shrinking secular profile.

The Shrine of the Book at the Israel Museum.

The Menorah at Heikal Shlomoo.

The classic panorama of the walled city.

Physically, Jerusalem is actually many cities in one, with nearly 900,000 residents. The modern part of the city, spreading out to the west, north, and south, has been a Jewish enclave since its inception in the late 1800s, and from 1948 the capital of the State of Israel. Vast new Jewish neighborhoods have been built in open areas captured in 1967. In many suburbs secular, traditional, and Orthodox Jews live alongside each other. Meanwhile, ultra-Orthodox Jews, with a prolific birth rate, have overflowed from Me'a She'arim in the center to Sanhedria and large new neighborhoods in the north of the city.

Most of Jerusalem east of the old "green line" that divided it from 1948 to 1967 (during which time it was Jordanian) remains Arab, although many neighborhoods have again been cut off from Jewish Jerusalem by the new Security Wall (see page 269). In the center of it all is the Old City, wrapped in its ancient golden walls, containing much of historic Jerusalem and its shrines. It, too, was in Jordanian hands up to 1967.

The Israeli victory in 1967 not only rolled away the wall but also fulfilled the 2,000-year-old Jewish dream of returning to the Western Wall and the Old City. Israel officially annexed the Old City and East Jerusalem in 1967, though the world still looks upon these areas as occupied territory. Ehud Barak, Israel's former prime minister, proposed keeping the Jewish and Armenian Quarters and giving the Christian and Muslim Quarters to the Palestinians.

David's capital

In ancient times it was said that the world had 10 measures of beauty, of which nine belonged to Jerusalem. The city's acclaim (or immodesty) only served to make it attractive to conquerors, and it has been the object of repeated siege and conquest. In part this was due to its strategic situation on a vital trade route, at the crossroads between East and West. Ironically, however, it was later the very holiness of the city that inspired its would-be champions' relentless ferocity.

Jerusalem first crops up in biblical narrative during Abraham's migrations

from Ur to Canaan. Here he was greeted warmly by Melchizedek, King of Salem, "Priest of the most high God." The Israelites were already well-ensconced in the hills of Judea when David captured the city from the Jebusites around 1000 BC. Building an altar for the Ark of the Covenant on the crown of Mount Moriah, he made the city his capital, renaming it Jerusalem "the Dwelling of Peace."

The 35 years under David's rule, and the subsequent 40 under Solomon, brought splendor to the once modest fortress town. The site of David's altar saw the rise of Solomon's magnificent Temple, incorporating the much-sought-after cedar wood from Lebanon, copper from the mines at Timna, and a wide variety of rich metals and carved figures. The city was embellished with the wealth of an expansive empire, its walls reaching in an oblong shape to include David's city on the slopes of Ha-Ofel and down to the pool of Silwan below.

Around 926 BC King Solomon died, and in the absence of his authority the kingdom was split in two by his successors. Jerusalem remained the capital of the southern Kingdom of Judah, as the following centuries saw the city and its kingdom succumb to the expanding control of the Assyrians. In 586 BC Nebuchadnezzar of Babylonia plundered the city, sending its inhabitants into exile. They returned in 539 BC under the policy of the new king, Cyrus the Great of Persia, and set at once to the task of building a Second Temple.

Greeks and Romans

Alexander the Great's conquest of Jerusalem in 332 BC initiated a brief Hellenization of Jewish culture in the city, and then in 198 BC the Seleucids took control. Deprived of religious rights, the Maccabees spearheaded a Jewish uprising, leading to the re-consecration of the destroyed Temple in 165 BC.

Hasmonean rule gave way in 63 BC to Rome, with the conquering armies of the Roman general Pompey. In 40 BC the Roman Senate conferred the rule on Herod the Great and sent him to Judea; during his reign his psychopathic behavior was matched only by his extensive architectural endeavors,

FACT

Alexander the Great exhibited great tolerance for Judaism, and personally encouraged Jews to continue practicing their religion.

TIP

The Model of the Second Temple at the Israel Museum gives an idea of how Jerusalem looked 2,000 years ago (tel: 02-670 8811; see page 173 for opening details; charge).

most notably the Second Temple which, according to the historian Josephus, was built by 10,000 workmen and 1,000 priests. It took eight years to complete the courtyard and another couple of years to finish the Temple itself.

When it was completed, it was widely regarded as one of the wonders of the world. Jerusalem was still a Jewish city under Roman rule when Jesus's crucifixion was ordered by the procurator Pontius Pilate around AD 30.

The increasingly insensitive Roman administration was challenged by the Jewish Revolt of 66, crushed four years later by Titus, who razed Jerusalem and plundered the Second Temple. A second rebellion was instigated by Emperor Hadrian's decree to lay the city out anew on a Roman plan and call it Aelia Capitolina; but the Bar-Kochba revolt of 132 was stamped out, and in 135 Hadrian initiated the reconstruction of the city, banning any Jew from entering its boundaries.

Christianity takes over

The great Christianization of Jerusalem was inaugurated in the 4th century by the Byzantine Emperor Constantine; in the 7th century the city fell to Muslim rule, and in 1099 to the bloody grip of the Crusaders for some 80 years. It once more came into its own under the Ottoman Emperor Suleiman, who rebuilt its walls from 1537 to 1541. After his death, until modern times, it fell into decline.

To this day, Suleiman's walls remain the most impressive monument to the city's multi-layered history. From stone stairways at various points in its span you can mount the restored Ramparts Walk, which follows every circuit but that by the Temple Mount. A "green belt" of lawns surrounds much of the circumference, adding to the view. The seven gates of the city are a source of fascination in themselves (see page 158). Just inside the Jaffa Gate, which serves as the main entrance to the Old City from West Jerusalem, is the famous Citadel, or Tower of David. In reality the structure doesn't have much to do with David; it was built by Herod, who named its three towers after his wife Mariamne, his brother Phaesal, and his friend Hippicus, and was so impressive that Titus let it stand after burning the city. The Mamelukes and later Suleiman reinforced it, adding its minaret.

Exploring the city

For practical purposes, we have divided the rest of the city into three parts. "The Old City" (see page 137) describes the sites within the city walls. "Outside the City Walls" (see page 151) covers the many places of interest just outside the ancient boundaries; and both East and West Jerusalem are discussed in "The New Jerusalem" (see page 163).

Visitors should follow their instincts in exploring this city and take detours to the less obvious sites. No amount of explanation can hope to capture the spirit of this complex place: the patina of gold on the Dome of the Rock, the view from the Mount of Olives at sunset, the shifting moods of its houses and hills, or the bizarre but beautiful echo of interwoven prayers – of all religions – that envelop the city walls.

The Garden of Gethsemane.

Inside the Church of the Holy Sepulcher.

JERUSALEM: THE OLD CITY

A tour of the many sacred shrines, historic houses, and atmospheric markets contained within the ancient walls of the Old City.

Main Attractions

Western Wall
Temple Mount
Dome of the Rock
El-Aqsa Mosque
Via Dolorosa
Church of the Holy Sepulcher

I t's a museum, a bazaar, a collection of sacred shrines. It also happens to be home for tens of thousands of residents crammed within the 4km (2.5-mile) circumference of its old battlements. Its gates never close, night or day, for the hundreds of thousands of overseas visitors who are drawn to the Old City of Jerusalem each year. The Jewish (www.myrova.com), Christian, Armenian, and Muslim Quarters of the Old City each have their own special significance.

Around the Jaffa Gate

The main portal between the Old City and West Jerusalem is the **Jaffa Gate ❶**. The site offers a number of contemporary attractions, which include the **Tower of David Museum of the History of Jerusalem ❷** (Sun–Thur 9am–4pm, in summer until 5pm and 10pm on Sun, Tue, and Thur, Fri and Sat 9am–2pm in summer until 5pm; tel: 02-626 5310; www.towerofdavid.org.il; charge) inside the body of the Citadel, which contains displays describing the tumultuous history of the city, figurines of Jerusalem characters, a 19th-century model of the Old City, and the multi-layered ruins of the structure itself. A multimedia show with a separate entrance describes the various moods of Jerusalem via numerous slide projectors. The walls themselves are the palette for the sound and light

show presented here in a host of different languages (night shows; for times tel: 02-626 5333, or book online www.towerofdavid.org.il; charge).

The Municipal Tourist Information Office is just inside the Jaffa Gate (Sun–Thur 8.30am–3.45pm; Fri 8.30am–12.45pm tel: 02-628 0382). Also opposite the entrance to the museum is the **Christian Information Office** (Mon–Fri 8.30am–5.30pm, Sat 8.30am–12.30pm; tel: 02-627 2692; www.cicts.org). About 150 meters (165yds) in from the Jaffa Gate is the narrow entrance to

Merchandise along the Via Dolorosa.

TIP

Antiquities offered by street urchins are usually genuine. Forgery is unnecessary when so many artifacts are unearthed. But they are hardly museum-quality – and, anyway, such trade is illegal.

the labyrinthine **Bazaar** (El Bazar) **③**. Go straight down into the Arab souk. Aggressively friendly shopkeepers will assault you with all manner of trinkets at "special prices," but take time to distinguish the quality from the trash, because both forms are plentiful. Prices in the stores nearest the Jaffa Gate are generally more expensive, and some shopkeepers even have the *chutzpah* to refuse to haggle. The farther into the market you go, the better the bargains.

It's a wonderful place for bargain hunters. Palestinian pottery and Armenian tiles are attractive, but cheaper varieties have little glazing and will fade. Brass items such as coffee servers and tables should be judged by their weight: too light and it's probably plated tin. Too shiny is also suspect;

a little tarnish suggests authenticity. Sheepskin jackets, gloves, and slippers are popular, but in time these may smell too much like sheep, especially if they get wet. At the end of the alleyway El Bazar, just before a T-junction, a black sign overhead points right to Ha-Kardo. Turn right here and almost immediately you leave the Muslim Quarter and enter the Jewish Quarter.

The Jewish Quarter

Inhabited by Jews as far back as the First Temple Period 3,000 years ago, the Jewish Quarter today is a modern neighborhood housing more than 1,000 families, with numerous synagogues and *yeshivas* (academies for Jewish studies). This thriving little community was rebuilt out of the

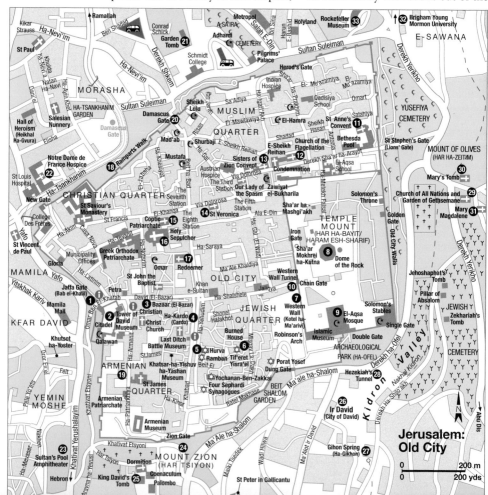

Jerusalem: Old City

0   200 m
0   200 yds

rubble following the reunification of Jerusalem in the 1967 Six Day War. Families who had lived in the quarter prior to their expulsion by the Jordanians in 1948 were the first to move back in. Religious Jews revived many of the old study houses and congregations. Artists, attracted by the picturesque lanes, soon took up residence.

Nowhere is the old-new character of the quarter more evident than in the **Ha-Kardo** (Cardo) ❹. With its modern lamps and smart shopfronts, this submerged pedestrian byway at first looks like a trendy shopping mall incongruously set next to the old bazaar. Ha-Kardo was the north–south axis of the garrison town that the Romans built after they destroyed Jerusalem in AD 70. Subsequently called Aelia Capitolina, the town was laid out geometrically like an army camp, with Ha-Kardo (from the Latin: cardinal, or principal) as its main thoroughfare. In the Byzantine period this colonnaded avenue ran for 180 meters (600ft) to a looming church called the Nea, built by Emperor Justinian in 543 and destroyed in an earthquake in the 8th century. Later the Crusaders used Ha-Kardo as a main market street. After they were expelled by the Muslims, Jerusalem reverted to a backwater and Ha-Kardo was eventually buried beneath 4 meters (13ft) of rubble, to be excavated and brought to life again only in the 1980s.

Signs and diagrams posted along either side of the "new" Ha-Kardo pinpoint the remains of the various civilizations that conducted their daily commerce here. A large excavation reveals the outer wall of the city of the Judean King Hezekiah. At another point, Byzantine Corinthian-style columns have been restored, along with some roofing beams, to illustrate how shops once lined this thoroughfare.

The southern end of Ha-Kardo is open to the sky. Here the big paving stones lie bright in the sunlight, the columns exposed in all their classic beauty. It's also from this point outdoors that visitors can best appreciate the reconciliation of demands for both archeological integrity and neighborhood housing. City planners wanted to build apartments along the route, while archeologists insisted that the

FACT

When the Siebenberg family dug beneath their homes in the Jewish Quarter, they found rare artifacts plus water systems and burial vaults from the First and Second Temple periods. For a personally guided tour, call the Siebenbergs on tel: 02-628 2341; charge.

The Tower of David Museum illuminated for a sound and light show.

EAT

The most popular places to eat are the cafes on David Street, the funky sweet shops along Souk Khan ez-Zeit, and Abu-Shukri's on El-Wad Street, which sells wonderful houmous.

historical heart of the city be exposed. The compromise: apartments standing on stilts above the ancient avenue.

Museums and memorials

Running parallel eastward to Ha-Kardo is **Ha-Yehudim** (Jewish Quarter Road), the site of the **The Last Ditch Battle Museum** (Sun–Thur 10am–5pm, Fri 9am–1pm; tel: 02-628 8141; free), which offers a 15-minute multimedia presentation on the history of the area from the Israelite period to the present. The emphasis is on how the Jewish Quarter was lost to the Arab Legion in Israel's War of Independence in 1948; how it was subsequently regained in the Six Day War of 1967; and how it has since been reconstructed. The museum also has an unusual collection of pictures taken by *Life* magazine photographer John Phillips, both during the battle in 1948, and in 1975 when he returned to find and photograph the survivors.

A few steps away from the museum there is a memorial to the fighters who fell defending the quarter. An electronic map recreates the battle, house by house.

Between the museum and the memorial is the Ashkenazi Court, a synagogue and residential complex established in 1400 by European Jews. The great **Hurva Synagogue** ❺ was burned by angry creditors in 1720 (hence its name, which means ruin). In 1856 it was rebuilt, but in May of 1948 it was blown up by the Jordanians during the War of Independence. The synagogue was again rebuilt in its 19th-century neo-Byzantine style and reopened in 2010. Tel: 02-626 5922 to book tours in advance.

Beneath the Hurva is the **Ramban Synagogue**, built shortly after the noted Bible commentator Rabbi Moses Ben Nahman emigrated from Spain in 1267, and possibly the oldest of the many houses of worship in the Jewish Quarter. Now it is used on a daily basis.

The most enchanting of the venerable houses of worship are on Ha-Kehuna in the complex known as the **Four Sephardi Synagogues**. These synagogues have been lovingly restored to serve both as houses of worship and as a museum documenting their destruction and rebirth. Of interest are the

Praying at the Western Wall.

Italian hand-carved Arks of the Law in the Stambouli and Prophet Elijah Synagogues, and the early 17th-century Yochanan Ben-Zakkai Synagogue, with its cheery folk characters.

A short walk up Or Ha-Khayim, the **Old Yishuv Court Museum** (Mon–Thur 10am–3pm, Fri 10am–1pm; tel: 02-628 4636; charge) illustrates the lifestyles of the Jewish community of the Old City in bygone days when immigrants from a particular village in, say, Poland or Hungary would cluster around one court, sharing many facilities. The grounds incorporate two courts and two synagogues.

At the end of Tif'eret Yisra'el is the most remarkable archeological site in the Jewish Quarter: the **Burned House** ❻ (Sun–Thur 9am–5pm, Fri 9am–1pm; tel: 02-628 7211; charge). This, apparently, was the residence of the priestly Bar-Kathros clan at the time of the Jewish revolt against Rome. Among other clues, ashes from a great conflagration indicate that the house was destroyed when Titus razed the city. The numerous finds displayed within the house include a measuring weight bearing the name Kathros, and, in the kitchen, the skeletal arm of a woman who was apparently struggling to escape the fire.

The Western Wall

The wide stone steps at the end of Tif'eret Yisra'el lead down to the most important site – not only within the quarter, but in all of Jewish civilization. This, of course, is the Kotel ha-Ma'aravi, or the **Western Wall** ❼ (always open; free). Clambering up and down these steps at all hours of the day and night – like so many angels ascending and descending Jacob's ladder – is a stream of worshipers, pilgrims, and tourists. Below and to the left is the Western Wall plaza and the Wall itself.

Above the Wall

The **Temple Mount** (Sat–Thur 7.30–10.30am and 12.30–1.30pm, during Ramadan Sat–Thur 7.30am–10.30am; closed to non-Muslims Fri and Muslim holidays; free) is the biblical Mount Moriah where Abraham nearly sacrificed Isaac, where the First and Second Temples once loomed, and where the

El-Aqsa Mosque.

Inside El-Aqsa Mosque.

Turkish coffee, a legacy of the Ottoman Empire.

Celebrating a bar mitzvah at the Wall.

golden Dome of the Rock and the silvery **El-Aqsa Mosque** now stand. To the right of the Temple Mount is a vast maze of archeological excavations, which lead to the Old City Wall and the Dung Gate.

The Jewish Quarter area was known in Temple times as the Upper City. The plaza below occupies the lower end of what was called the Tyropoeon Valley, the rift that cuts through the entire length of the Old City. Because this was the lowest point in the Old City, rubble and trash have been dumped here over the centuries, filling in much of the space between the upper level and the Temple Mount (and giving the Dung Gate its inglorious name).

Rising to a height of 15 meters (50ft), the Western Wall consists chiefly of massive carved stone blocks from the Herodian era, topped by masonry from the Mameluke and Turkish periods. Contrary to popular belief, it was not a part of the Temple itself, but merely the retaining wall for the western side of the Temple Mount. But because it was the only remnant of the Temple complex to survive the Romans' sack of the city, it has inspired the reverence of Jewish people for 2,000 years. As Jews also gathered here to bemoan the loss of the Temple, the place earned the evocative sobriquet "Wailing Wall."

The tunnel-like enclosure at the northern end of the Wall is the site of continuing excavations. The main arch, named after the 19th-century British explorer Captain Charles Wilson, may have supported a huge pedestrian bridge between the Temple Mount and the Upper City. Below the arch is the deep shaft dug by Wilson's contemporary, Sir Charles Warren. Archeologists have determined that the Wall extends another 15 meters (50ft) below ground level.

The Temple Mount

Mosques and shrines dot the various quarters of the Old City, and most of the gates exhibit Islamic calligraphy; yet the glories of Islamic Jerusalem are on the Temple Mount, which Muslims call **Haram esh-Sharif**, the Venerable Sanctuary (see box for a brief history of the Muslim impact on Jerusalem).

ISLAM'S INFLUENCE

Evidence of an Islamic Jerusalem can be seen throughout all the quarters of the Old City, in their mosques, shrines, and calligraphy. The Muslim impact on Jerusalem came essentially in three stages: the first was shortly after the death of Mohammed, when his successors spread the faith out of Arabia and wrested Jerusalem from the crumbling Byzantine Empire in 638. In this period Caliph Omar built a mosque on the Temple Mount, which was later expanded to the Dome of the Rock, and in the 8th century the El-Aqsa Mosque was constructed nearby.

The second Muslim phase followed the brief Crusader occupation of the Holy Land. The Europeans were defeated by Saladin, and with the recovery of Jerusalem in 1187 the Muslims began a major reconstruction of the city and especially of the mosques. By 1249 the dominant Muslims were the Mamelukes.

But corruption and dissolution marked their regime, and by 1516 the Mamelukes were easy prey for the invading Ottoman Turks. For the next 400 years Jerusalem was ruled from Constantinople. Early in this period (1520–66) Suleiman I built the city ramparts that we see today, and the Damascus Gate. After Suleiman, however, the city simply stagnated until the collapse of the Ottoman Empire in World War I.

Today the Mount is the most disputed portion of this contentious city. The Arab nations are determined that an Islamic flag must fly over the site. In deference to the local Muslim authorities, Israel leaves the administration of Haram esh-Sharif entirely to Muslim officials. Israeli Border Police provide security in the area, but in cooperation with Arab policemen.

Israel's Chief Rabbinate, meanwhile, has banned Jews from visiting the Temple Mount, because somewhere on the hill is the site of the ancient Temple's Holy of Holies, the inner sanctuary which only the High Priest was allowed to enter, and even then only on one day of the year, Yom Kippur. Nevertheless, certain ultra-nationalist Israelis calling themselves the "Temple Faithful" periodically attempt to hold prayer services on the Mount, an act that invariably incenses both the Arab community and other Jews.

Dome of the Rock

The most eye-catching structure on Haram esh-Sharif is the **Dome of the Rock ❽**. The outside of the edifice, which is a shrine and not a mosque, is a fantasia of marble, mosaics and stained glass, painted tiles, and quotations from the Koran, all capped by the gold-plated aluminum dome. Notable, too, are the curved pillars at the top of the steps, from which, according to tradition, scales will be hung on Judgement Day to weigh the souls of mankind.

The inside of the Dome of the Rock focuses on the huge boulder called the **Kubbet es-Sakhra**. This is the sacred rock on which Abraham was said to have prepared the sacrifice of Isaac. It is also the spot on which, during his mystical journey to Jerusalem, Mohammed is said to have mounted his steed and ascended to heaven. Appropriately enough, the heavenly interior of the famous golden dome shines down from above, a truly joyous achievement in gold leaf, mosaic, and stained glass. Beneath the rock, meanwhile, is a crypt where the spirits of the dead are said to gather. Note that non-Muslims are no longer permitted to visit the interiors of the Dome of the Rock or the El-Aqsa Mosque.

TIP

Islam looks upon shoes with disdain, and to sit in any way that shows a Muslim the sole of your shoe is considered the height of rudeness. Shoes must be taken off before entering a mosque, although many mosques do not allow non-Muslims to enter.

The monumental Dome of the Rock.

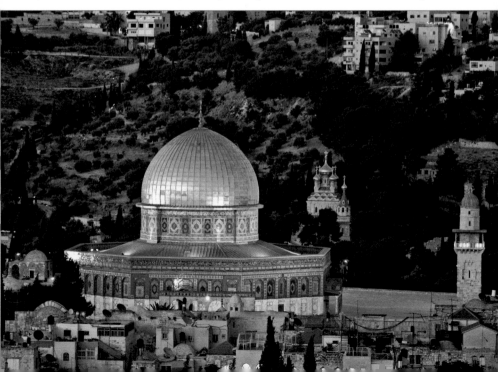

TIP

Tours through the Western Wall Tunnel must be booked in advance. For details, tel: 02-627 1333.

The silver-capped mosque you see at the southern end of the mount is **El-Aqsa** , a vast complex that can accommodate as many as 5,000 worshipers. Serving essentially as a prayer hall, El-Aqsa is more functional in design than the Dome of the Rock. Probably built on the remains of a Byzantine basilica, it also straddles vast underground chambers known as **Solomon's Stables**, where a new mosque has been built recently, and which some fear has undermined the foundations of the El-Aqsa mosque.

El-Aqsa features prominently in the modern history of the region. It was on the doorstep of this mosque in 1951 that a Muslim fanatic murdered Jordan's King Abdullah in sight of his little grandson, who became King Hussein, father of the present King Abdullah. In 1969 a deranged Australian set fire to the building, causing extensive damage and sparking off inflammatory calls throughout the Muslim nations for a *jihad*, or holy war, against Israel.

The **Islamic Museum** adjoining El-Aqsa has interesting exhibits covering centuries of Muslim life in Jerusalem, including lamps, weapons, and ancient Korans. Also noteworthy are the Mount's elaborately carved fountains, intricate wrought-iron gates, the miniature Dome of the Chain and the marble-and-stone *minbar*, or preaching pulpit, outside El-Aqsa.

Although this area can ignite so much political passion throughout the Middle East, it is a tranquil place marked by sunny plazas and quiet gardens where the wind sighs through the trees.

Troublesome tunnel

In front of the Western Wall is the entrance to the controversial **Western Wall Tunnel** . Here archeologists have dug out a 2,000-year-old street leading along the rim of the Temple Mount several hundred meters northward to the Via Dolorosa as it passes through the Muslim Quarter. The Arabs have always feared that the tunneling was a Zionist plot to get under the Temple Mount and blow up the mosques, even though excavations are not actually under Haram esh-Sharif.

The 8th Station of Christ on the Via Dolorosa.

The **Jerusalem Archeological Park** (Sun–Thur 8am–5pm, Fri 8am–2pm; charge www.archpark.org.il) is to the right of the Western Wall. It contains a broad stairway where prophets harangued the crowds on their way to the Temple, the abutment called **Robinson's Arch** (after its 19th-century American discoverer, Dr Edward Robinson), and the remains of palatial buildings and purification baths from Temple times. Seen from the walkway above the excavations, the site is a jigsaw puzzle of incomprehensible stone, but a licensed guide with Bible in hand brings the area to life. New excavations enable the public to see the actual shop-lined street that bordered the surroundings of the Second Temple before it was destroyed in AD 70.

The road to Calvary

Rome likes to think of itself as the center of the Christian world, and St Peter's Basilica is certainly grander than anything Jerusalem has to offer. Yet within the worn walls of Jerusalem are two places that stir the most casual Christian: the Via Dolorosa

and Calvary. These names reside in the consciousness and reverberate in the vocabulary of all Western civilization.

The **Via Dolorosa** begins near St Stephen's Gate (also called the Lions' Gate). In the 1990s the municipality undertook the elaborate and delicate project of repairing the Via Dolorosa, which included the restoration of collapsing buildings and overhead arches along the route, the replacement of the 400-year-old sewage system, and proper demarcation of the Stations of the Cross. When the plaza was cleared of rubble, huge paving stones dating from the Roman period were exposed. These stones, which have been revealed at a few points elsewhere along the route, may very well have been walked on by Jesus and his followers.

Stations of the Cross

Guided tours are recommended, especially as some of the Stations of the Cross are difficult to locate in the maze of the Old City.

Begin at the **St Anne's Convent** ⑪, just inside from St Stephen's Gate (open Mon–Sat; charge), considered to

A street whose name is recognized around the world.

Where the Western Wall meets the Southern Wall.

Detail from carving at the Fourth Station of the Cross.

The venerated Church of the Holy Sepulcher.

be the best-preserved Crusader church in the entire Holy Land. In addition to a crypt designated as Mary's Birthplace, the church compound contains the Bethesda Pool where Jesus performed a miraculous cure.

The **First Station of the Cross**, where Jesus was sentenced, is tucked away on the left inside the courtyard of the Umariyah school, a Muslim boys' institution. The **Second Station**, where Jesus received the Cross, is opposite, on the street outside the **Chapel of Condemnation** and the **Church of the Flagellation** ⑫. It was here that Jesus was scourged and had the crown of thorns placed on his head. The latter church also has a graceful courtyard and quiet garden.

The events associated with the first two stations are believed to have taken place in Herod's **Antonia Fortress**, remains of which are found beneath the churches along the Via Dolorosa. In the nearby **Sisters of Zion Convent** ⑬, for example, is a huge underground chamber called the Lithostrotos (Mon–Sat 8.30am–12.30pm, 2–4.30pm; tel: 02-627 7292;

charge), often said to be the place where Pilate judged Jesus; on the paving stones outside are signs of board games played by Roman soldiers.

Outside is the **Ecce Homo Arch**, which some maintain was constructed by Emperor Hadrian in the 2nd century and which takes its name from Pilate's jeer of "Behold the man." At the end of 1985 the Sisters of Zion dedicated a Roman arch inside the church, which they contend is the Ecce Homo.

Almost all of the subsequent stations on the Via Dolorosa are marked by plaques bearing the appropriate quotations from the Bible, and many are accompanied by a fan-like design in cobblestones on the street.

The **Third Station**, where Jesus fell with the Cross, is commemorated by a column in a wall on Ha-Gai (El Wad), which the Via Dolorosa traverses. Just beyond is the **Fourth Station**, where Jesus encountered Mary. On this site is the **Armenian Catholic Church of Our Lady of the Spasm**, which has a notable Byzantine mosaic in its crypt.

The Via Dolorosa at this point becomes a fairly steep and crowded

commercial lane ascending to the right from Ha-Gai. The **Fifth Station**, just at the juncture of Ha-Gai and the Via Dolorosa, is where Simon the Cyrenian helped Jesus carry the Cross. A bit farther on is the **Sixth Station**, at the **House of St Veronica** ⓮, where Veronica cleansed the face of Jesus with her veil.

At the point where the Via Dolorosa bisects the souk's Khan ez-Zeit bazaar is the **Seventh Station**, where Jesus fell again. This is also believed to be the site of the Gate of Judgement from which Jesus was led out of the city to the place of crucifixion, and where his death sentence was publicly posted.

The Via Dolorosa at this point disappears; buildings cover the rest of the route to the Church of the Holy Sepulcher. But both the church and the last Stations of the Cross are close by. The **Eighth Station** is outside the **Greek Orthodox Chapel of St Charalampos**, constructed on the site where Jesus addressed the women with the words "Weep not for me, but weep for Jerusalem." At the **Coptic Patriarchate** ⓯ compound off the

Khan ez-Zeit bazaar, a pillar marks the **Ninth Station**, where Jesus stumbled for the third time. This is one of the more unusual churches in the city. The monastery is a replica of an African mud-hut village, and the nearby Coptic chapel is located on the roof of the Church of the Holy Sepulcher, within which are located the final Stations of the Cross.

The Holy Sepulcher

Experienced travelers are probably aware that the more venerated a shrine in the mind of the pilgrim, the more disconcerting the reality can be. In the case of the **Church of the Holy Sepulcher** ⓰ (daily, dawn to dusk; www.holysepulchre.custodia.org) both its size and its complexity are rather bewildering. The present church was built by the Crusaders in the 12th century. Much more has been added since the Crusaders left.

Several Christian communities currently share the church, each maintaining its own chapels and altars and conducting services according to its own schedule. Each is responsible

FACT

Protestants doubt that the Church of the Holy Sepulcher is the true site of the Crucifixion and Resurrection. In the 19th century General Gordon identified the Garden Tomb as the possible site of Jesus's burial, and the garden today belongs to the Anglicans (see page 151).

The Christian Friday Procession along the Via Dolorosa.

Sahlab, a sweet, spiced warm drink peddled by vendors outside the Damascus Gate, is a combination of ground orchid root, water, milk, vanilla, and sugar. It tastes especially good in winter and is said to relieve stomach problems.

for the sanctity and maintenance of a scrupulously specified area. Church fathers have battled in the past over such issues as who cleans which steps. With its gloomy interior, its bustle of construction work, its competing chants, and multiple aromas of incense, the Church of the Holy Sepulcher can seem intimidating. Freelance guides cluster about the doorway, offering to show visitors around for an unspecified charge. While some are competent and sincere, many have a routine in English limited to "Here chapel, very holy. There picture, famous, famous."

Despite all this, the church maintains its magnificence. The focal points, of course, are the section built over the hillock where the Crucifixion took place (called Golgotha, from the Hebrew, or Calvary, from the Latin), and the tomb where Jesus was laid. These sites encompass the continuation of the Via Dolorosa and the final Stations of the Cross.

Stairs to the right just inside the door to the church lead up to **Calvary**. The **Tenth Station**, where

A poster over this doorway proclaims that the owner has made the pilgrimage to Mecca.

Jesus was stripped of his garments, is marked by a floor mosaic. The next three stations are located at Latin and Greek altars on this same level and within a few paces of each other. They mark the nailing of Jesus to the Cross, the placing of the Cross, and the removal of Christ's body. The **Fourteenth Station** is below the Holy Sepulcher: the tomb is downstairs under the church's main rotunda. Within the Holy Sepulcher are the Angel's Chapel, the rock that was miraculously rolled away from the tomb entrance, the chapel containing the burial site, and the adjacent tomb of Joseph of Arimathea.

Other notable sites within the church complex include the Catholikon, the Greek cathedral close to the main rotunda, with its stone chalice on the floor marking the center of the world; chapels dedicated to St Helena, to Adam, and to the Raising of the Cross; and tombs of the Crusader Kings of Jerusalem. It is these side chapels and cavern-like tombs that offer contemplative visitors respite from the troops of tour groups that pour through the church. In a chapel beneath the main floor of the church one can sit in relative silence, listening to an Eastern Orthodox mass being chanted in a distant nave, or perhaps watching a solitary monk polishing a candlestick.

Outside the Holy Sepulcher are churches of most denominations. To the right, on the corner of Muristan outside the plaza's left exit (when leaving the Church of the Holy Sepulcher) is the graceful **Lutheran Church of the Redeemer** ⓱. Its tower, the highest point in the Old City (Mon–Sat 9am–5pm; tel: 02-627 6111; charge), offers a magnificent view of the Old City.

The main access to the Christian Quarter is the **New Gate** – so named because it was punched through the Old City walls relatively recently, in 1887. Winding into the city from the gate are Ha-Patriarkhiya Ha-Yevanit

Ha-Notsrim, and Ha-Latinim (Greek Orthodox, Catholic, and Latin Patriarchate roads), all leading to their respective compounds, with churches that often contain interesting libraries and museums.

From the Church of the Holy Sepulcher the main thoroughfare northward leads to the Damascus Gate. From here – as from most of the city gates – there is access to the **Ramparts Walk ⓲** (daily 9am–4pm Fri 9am–2pm; tel: 02-6254403; charge), a walk around the top of the city walls that provides marvelous views. To visit the Old City's remaining quarter – the Armenian Quarter – return via Muristan and David Street to the exit of the bazaar near the Jaffa Gate and then head southward past the Christian Information Center.

The Armenian Quarter

Ha-Patriarkhiya Ha-Armenit is the street leading around the Citadel up from the David Street bazaar. Between the Christian Information Center and the post office stand Christ Church and the Anglican Hospice,

the 19th-century base for many of the British diplomats and clergymen who encouraged the exploration and modernization of Ottoman Jerusalem.

The road passes through a brief tunnel and into the **Armenian Quarter ⓳**, entered on the left through a gate – this is a walled enclave within a walled city. Entrance to the Armenian Quarter is permitted only on Mon–Fri 3–3.30pm, Sat–Sun 2.30–3.15pm. A modest doorway leads to the 12th-century **St James's Cathedral**, one of the most impressive churches in the Old City.

A little farther on is the **Armenian Museum** (Mon–Sat 10am–4pm; charge), a graceful cloister housing a fascinating collection of manuscripts and artifacts. Jerusalem's 2,000 or so Armenians reside in a tight community behind the cathedral-museum complex. As one of the smallest ethnic groups, they have a reputation for keeping to themselves. But in fact they are quite outgoing, proud of being descendants of the first nation to adopt Christianity, usually fluent in English, and most hospitable to visitors.

An Armenian choirboy.

Olive-wood images of Mary and Jesus for sale.

FACT OR MYTH?

Archeologists, as they are wont to do, maintain that neither the Via Dolorosa nor any of the other major sites that we identify today with the Crucifixion correspond to historical reality. But if the Via Dolorosa that we traverse was not walked upon 2,000 years ago, some ancient road is buried underneath the present ground level. Only recently Prof. Shimon Gibson of the Hebrew University of Jerusalem published research claiming that pilgrims trace the steps of Christ in the wrong direction. According to Prof. Gibson, a respected archeologist, the site of Calvary was in fact close to the First Station, while the Church of the Holy Sepulcher stands near the place where Christ began his final journey to the Cross.

Of course, some Protestants have long believed that the site of Calvary was outside of the Old City altogether, at the Garden Tomb. For many Christian pilgrims, being within close proximity of where the Crucifixion and the Resurrection took place, even if the precise location is not certain, is still enough to make a visit to Jerusalem a deeply spiritual and meaningful event.

Pilgrims should not be unduly distressed that today's Via Dolorosa is a commercial street, complete with a Jesus Prison Souvenir shop and a Ninth Station Boutique. Bear in mind that the lane was a bustling city street in the time of Jesus, too.

An Arab shopkeeper.

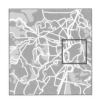

OUTSIDE THE CITY WALLS

Just outside Jerusalem's ramparts are some of
the most revered sites in Christendom and
some extraordinary examples of excavation.

T he sites surrounding the Old City
walls are also redolent with religious significance. In addition,
the streets just outside the Damascus
Gate form the city center of Arab
Jerusalem. The **Damascus Gate ⓴**,
from where you may have begun the
Ramparts Walk (see page 149), is the
grandest entryway to the Old City.
Landscaped in the 1990s, its plaza
offers one of Jerusalem's best forums
for people-watching. The **Roman
Square Museum** (Sat–Thur 9am–5pm,
Fri 9am–1pm; charge) beneath the
gate examines the Roman era of the
city from the lower-level portal of that
period. Also under the Old City walls
close by are **Solomon's Quarries** (Sat–
Thur 9am–5pm, Fri 9am–1pm; charge),
an ancient mine, which tunnels deep
below the alleys to Mount Moriah.

The **East Jerusalem Bus Station**,
just opposite, operates buses to points
in the West Bank, using independent
Arab lines. From alongside the Old
City, East Jerusalem's two main ave-
nues, Derekh Shkem (**Nablus Road**)
and **Salah E-Din**, lead into a cobweb
of traffic.

Several hundred meters to the north
of the Damascus Gate, along Derekh
Shkem, you will come to the **Garden
Tomb ㉑** (Mon–Sat 8am–5.30pm; tel:
02-539 8100; free). Within a landscape
reminiscent of a sumptuous English
garden, this is a dual-chambered cave

that Anglicans and other Protestants
claim could have been the tomb of
Jesus. The Garden Tomb is situated on a
hill which, if viewed from the East Jerusalem Bus Station, suggests to many the
shape of a skull, which is the meaning
of the Hebrew word Golgotha.

A vast necropolis

The whole of East Jerusalem is in fact
something of a vast necropolis, and
is rife with caves and burial crypts.
These include **Jeremiah's Grotto**,
where the prophet supposedly wrote

Main Attractions
Garden Tomb
Mamila Project
Mount Zion
City of David
Mount of Olives
Garden of Gethsemane
Rockefeller Museum

The Garden Tomb.

his Lamentations over Jerusalem, and the **Tomb of Simon the Just**, a Jewish high priest alive in the 3rd century BC. The most awesome chamber is the **Tomb of the Kings** – although it is misnamed, being in fact the tomb of Queen Helena of Mesopotamia, who converted to Judaism in 54 BC.

The hill to the west of the Damascus Gate is dominated by the splendid 19th-century **Notre Dame de France Hospice** ㉒, which is opposite the New Gate. The grandiose, ornate French architecture suggests that pilgrims were not expected to suffer deprivation – and indeed the building now houses a luxury hotel with a *cordon bleu* French restaurant. The building has a fascinating history, too. Badly damaged in the 1948 war, Notre Dame remained abandoned, on the dividing line between Arab and Jewish Jerusalem. When it suffered further damage in the Six Day War, the French Assumptionists decided to cut their losses, and sold the building to the Hebrew University in 1972. The Vatican was livid that such a prime piece of Catholic real estate in the Holy Land had been relinquished.

Rome decided to challenge the sale in Israel's civil courts, claiming that under canon law a Catholic property cannot be sold without Vatican consent. To avoid an awkward trial the Israeli government (which owns the Hebrew University) agreed to sell Notre Dame to the Vatican.

Turning left into Yafo and following the Old City walls, you can see the new Mamila Project to the right. This 19th-century district of workshops and small traders has been transformed into a complex of luxury hotels and apartments with some of the quarter's original buildings, such as the St Vincent orphanage, retained. The main street is a pedestrian shopping mall with outdoor cafes overlooking the Old City and an excellent choice of fashionable stores for gifts and clothing. Midway along the street is the building where Zionist visionary Theodor Herzl slept on his only night in Jerusalem, when he came to meet Kaiser Wilhelm of Prussia. Beyond the Jaffa Gate, at the eastern end of the Mamila shopping mall, is **Khutsot ha-Yoster** (Arts and Crafts

Graceful arches span the Coenaculum.

Lane), which houses the studios and shops of artists and artisans.

Adjoining Khutsot ha-Yoster to the south, down Derekh Khevron, is **Sultan's Pool 23**. This former reservoir has been converted into an amphitheater and, located beneath the walls of the Old City, has to be one of the world's most inspiring venues for outdoor concerts.

On the far side of the Derekh Khevron bridge is the **Valley of Hinnom**. It is hard to realize that these pleasant parklands are believed, in Jewish tradition, to be the scene of child sacrifices in pagan Canaanite times, and therefore synonymous with hell – which is what *Gehenom*, the Hebrew word for Hinnom, means.

Mount Zion

Mount Zion (Har Tsiyon) **24**, overlooking Hinnom, was used as a synonym for Jerusalem and came to symbolize the Jewish yearning to return to the homeland. Indeed, at the end of the 19th century Zionism was adopted as the official name of the national movement of the Jewish

people. In 1948 the Old City fell to Jordan, but Israel retained Mount Zion, where churches and *yeshivas* huddle side by side amid the gardens and wind-bent pines. Mount Zion can be reached by walking along the delightful gardens southward from the Jaffa Gate, or alternatively, for drivers, from the car park outside the Zion Gate.

Within the **Diaspora Yeshiva** (www. diaspora.org.il) complex is the site of **King David's Tomb 25** (Sun–Thur 8am–5pm, Fri 8am–1pm; charge). Archeologists maintain that this is another example of a site not corresponding to historical truth, and most Orthodox Jews doubt its authenticity.

Primary among the Christian sites here is the **Coenaculum** (daily 8am– 5pm; tel: 02-671 3597; free), believed to be the room of the Last Supper (although the Syrian Orthodox St Mark's House on Ararat Street in the Armenian Quarter makes the same claim). Today the Coenaculum is basically an elegant but bare room, empty but for the flow of daylight, and it requires considerable imagination to fill it, as Leonardo did in his classic

TIP

For a magnificent view of the Kidron Valley and Mount of Olives, walk down from the Zion Gate to the Dung Gate and then along the promenade.

The Church of the Dormition on Mount Zion.

fresco. The Coenaculum is located on the second floor of the large, rambling complex that contains David's Tomb.

Turn right outside David's Tomb/ Coenaculum and then head left to the **Church of the Dormition** (Mon–Sat 8am–5pm, Sun 12.30–5.30pm; tel: 02-565 5330; free), a handsome Benedictine edifice commemorating the place where Mary fell into eternal sleep. The church has a noteworthy mosaic floor and crypt, and its basilica is the site for concerts of liturgical and classical music. On the eastern slope of Mount Zion on Malki Tsedek Road is **the Church of Peter in Gallicantu** (Mon–Sat 8am–5pm; tel: 02-673 1739; free), where Jesus was supposedly imprisoned by the high priest Caiaphas.

Farther down the slope on Mount Zion is the **Old Protestant Cemetery**, the resting place of the British subjects who figured in the religious, cultural, archeological, and diplomatic life of 19th- and early 20th-century Jerusalem.

Above the Kidron Valley

The **City of David** ❷⓺ (Sun–Thur 8am– 5pm or 7pm in summer, Fri 8am–2pm or 4pm in summer; toll-free in Israel tel: *6033; www.cityofdavid.org.il; charge) excavations are on the steep hillside outside the **Dung Gate**. This hill is called **Ha-Ofel**, and the archeological dig here has been the scene of violent protests by religious zealots claiming that ancient Jewish graves have been violated. The diggers dispute this but say that the site is too important to leave buried, because the Ophel is where the earliest incarnation of Jerusalem stood: the Jebusite city of more than 3,000 years ago.

Around 1000 BC, King David captured the city and made it his capital. Although his son Solomon was to build the Temple on the high ground above it, the main residential portion of the city itself remained clinging to this slope above the Kidron Valley. It did so because at the foot of the slope is the **Gihon Spring** ❷⓻, at the time Jerusalem's only water supply.

Since the spring was located in a cave on the floor of the valley, Jerusalemites were in danger of being cut off from their water when the city was attacked. But the stunning

The City of David excavations.

engineering project known as **Hezekiah's Tunnel** ㉘ carried out by King Hezekiah about 300 years after King David's time managed to connect the Gihon Spring to the Silwan Pool inside the city some 530 meters (580yds) farther down the valley. The intrepid 19th-century archeologist Charles Warren not only explored the tunnel but also discovered a shaft reaching up through the Ophel to an underground passage from where city residents could come to draw water in buckets. In 1867 Warren had to crawl on his belly through the stream bed to explore the water system. Today visitors can study the schematics in comfort in the **City of David Archeological Gardens**, and then stroll through the illuminated passageway to the top of Warren's shaft to peer at the water rushing below. In the Kidron Valley itself, visitors with candles can tramp along the knee-deep stream in Hezekiah's Tunnel from the Gihon Spring and through the Ophel until they emerge at the Silwan Pool.

The upper end of the Kidron Valley, also known as the Vale of Jehoshaphat, contains several Jerusalem landmarks. The slope off to the northeast is the Mount of Olives, and in the valley itself are the **Tomb of Absalom** and the **Tomb of Zekhariah**. Despite their traditional names, these stately tombs, with their graceful pillars and elaborately carved friezes, are not thought to be the resting places of David's rebellious son or of the prophet. Rather, archeologists believe that they were part of the vast 1st-century necropolis that encircled Jerusalem, and probably served as burial places for wealthy citizens or notables of the Herodian court.

The Mount of Olives

Wherever the historical Golgotha was located, it's agreed that Jesus made his triumphal entry into Jerusalem from the **Mount of Olives**. This hill, with its breathtaking view of the Old City, is mainly a Jewish cemetery dating back to the biblical period and still in use today. Round about the cemetery the Mount of Olives has numerous sites of significance for, in a meeting of faiths, many Jews and Christians believe that the Messiah will lead the

TIP

The walk through Hezekiah's Tunnel is not recommended for those with claustrophobic tendencies. Even the courageous should take a torch with them.

The tomb of Zekhariah, in the Kidron Valley.

Within the church that holds Mary's tomb, where frescoes tell the story of Mary's death and her burial by the apostles.

The Dome of the Ascension.

resurrected from here into Jerusalem via the Old City's Golden Gate, which faces the mount (see box).

The Garden of Gethsemane

At the foot of the Mount is the handsome **Church of All Nations** (open daily; free), noted for its fine Byzantine-style mosaic facade. Also known as the Basilica of the Agony, it was designed by a Franciscan architect, Antonio Barluzzi. Its 12 cupolas represent the 12 nations which contributed toward its construction. Adjoining it is the **Garden of Gethsemane** ㉙ where Jesus was betrayed, or at least, the largest of several gardens identified as Gethsemane. The olive grove here has been verified as being 2,000 years old – although this is not particularly remarkable for olive trees. It has been suggested that it was from one of these trees that Judas hanged himself.

Next to the garden is **Mary's Tomb** ㉚ (daily 6am–5pm; tel: 02-628 4613; free), deep within the earth and illuminated by candles placed by members of the Orthodox Churches. Midway down the stairs to

the 5th-century chapel are niches that are said to hold the remains of Mary's parents, Joachim and Anne, and her husband Joseph.

Among the most notable churches on the way up the Mount, along the narrow side road to the left of the Garden of Gethsemane is the Russian Orthodox **Church of Mary Magdalene** ㉛ (Tue and Thur am only; tel: 02 -628 4371; free). Built by Tsar Alexander III in 1886, it stands on the right and is easily identifiable by its golden onion-domes.

Farther up is the small but entrancing Franciscan **Basilica of Dominus Flevit**, which marks the site where, according to Luke's Gospel, Jesus paused to weep over Jerusalem. Built over Canaanite burial caves and a ruined Crusader church, the lovely tear-shaped chapel was designed by Antonio Barluzzi in 1953. Carrying on up and also on the right is the Church of **Pater Noster** (Mon–Sat; free) a Carmelite convent, with the Lord's Prayer in numerous languages on its interior walls. Here, too, are the ruins of the **Church of the Eleona**, on the site

where Jesus revealed the mysteries to his followers.

You have now reached the ridge of the mountain. On the far side of the mount, with a view of the **Judean Desert** and the red hills of Edom across the Jordan, is the **Bethpage Chapel**, from where the Palm Sunday processions to Jerusalem begin. On the crest of the hill is the **Russian Orthodox Church of the Ascension** (Mon–Sat 8.30am–1pm; tel: 02-628 7704; free), with its landmark bell tower. Nearby, the small octagonal **Dome of the Ascension** (daily; free) marks the traditional site of Jesus's ascent to heaven. Converted to a mosque when the Muslims conquered the city in 1187, the structure is said to have been the architectural model for the Dome of the Rock.

Along the road to the south, which is a cul-de-sac, is the **Seven Arches Hotel** and the classic picture-postcard view of Jerusalem's Old City. This is also the best place for a brief ride on one of the camels, which are always lying in wait with their minders, on the lookout for adventurous tourists.

A Mormon presence

If you backtrack through the Arab village of E-Tur, which straddles the ridge of the Mount of Olives, you will find to the right of the steep hill (Derekh E-Tur) that leads back down to the Old City one of Jerusalem's most aesthetically pleasing new buildings: the **Jerusalem Center for Near Eastern Studies, Brigham Young Mormon University** ❸❷. Students who come to Israel for semester-long courses are warned that they will be sent home if they proselytize. The campus has splendid gardens and an inspiring view of the Old City (tel: 02 626 5666 to book tours).

Going back toward the Old City, on the corner of Sultan Suleiman opposite the walls between St Stephen's Gate and Herod's Gate, you will find the **Rockefeller Museum** ❸❸ (Sun–Mon, Wed–Thur 10am–3pm, Sat 10am–2pm; tel: 02-628 2251; charge). It has a stately octagonal tower, gracious courtyard, and an extensive collection of archeological finds. Still battle-scarred from 1967, it is now part of the Israel Museum.

TIP

From the Dome of the Ascension several paths lead down to the city. Walks here, especially at dawn or sunset, are some of the loveliest experiences that Jerusalem has to offer.

The Church of Pater Noster.

THE MOUNT & TRADITION

Tradition has it that it was through a gate on the site of the Golden Gate that Jesus rode into Jerusalem, just as an earlier Jewish tradition says that this is how the Messiah will enter the city at the End of Days. The gate, however, is tightly sealed. It is said that a Muslim ruler decided to have it bricked up to prevent any Messiah from arriving in Jerusalem and wresting the city from Muslim hands. As to why the Mount of Olives is so bare and rocky: tradition has it that the Romans cut down all the olive trees to build the siege machines used in the destruction of Jerusalem in AD 70 – but that with the Second Coming the trees will flourish again. The reverence for this most sacred of mountains is generally reflected in a spirit of mutual tolerance and understanding.

CITY GATES

The Old City of Jerusalem can only be entered by seven gates, while an eighth, the Golden Gate, is sealed pending the coming of the Messiah.

Jerusalem's gates all have their own story to tell. The Jaffa Gate, known in Arabic as the Hebron Gate, was traditionally the main thoroughfare westward to Jaffa (Yafo). The walls beside it were breached in 1898 so that Kaiser Wilhelm II of Germany could enter on horseback. The Zion Gate, predictably, leads out to Mount Zion, which was inexplicably left outside the city walls. The unfortunately named Dung Gate was the point from which the city's refuse was taken out. St Stephen's Gate is also known as the Lions' Gate and stands opposite the Mount of Olives. The Israeli Army launched a surprise attack here when capturing the Old City from Jordan in 1967. Herod's Gate, sometimes called Flowers Gate, is the least known and offers access to the Muslim Quarter. The Damascus Gate is located opposite the highway that leads north to Nablus (it is called the Nablus Gate in Hebrew). It's the busiest gate, linking Arab East Jerusalem and the Muslim Quarter market. The New Gate, as you would expect, is the most recent. The walls were breached in the late 19th century so that pilgrims from the Hospice of Notre Dame de France opposite would have direct access to the Christian Quarter.

But the Golden Gate is special: set midway along the eastern wall of the Old City, it is blocked up. Through this gate, it is said, the Messiah will enter ancient Jerusalem after crossing a paper bridge from the Mount of Olives.

The main plaza outside the Damascus Gate is always busy: A peddlers sell all kinds of food and beverages, such as sahlab, a sweet drink made from the ground root of wild orchids.

The pockmarked walls around the Zion Gate still bear the scars from the Six Day War.

Mosaic tiles mark the Jaffa Gate.

Evening falls over Jaffa Gate and Jerusalem's city walls.

SULEIMAN'S GIFT TO JERUSALEM

The Old City's walls were constructed by the Ottoman Sultan Suleiman the Magnificent between 1537 and 1541. The walls are 4km (2.5 miles) long, an average of 12 meters (40ft) high and nearly 3 meters (9ft) thick. Along the top of the wall was a patrol path for guards, now open to the public. By 16th-century standards the wall was not especially solid, its main purpose not so much to withstand a concerted attack as to protect Jerusalem's citizens from bandits and predatory creatures. The citadel, the city's main garrison, was incorporated within the walls by the Jaffa Gate, while Mount Zion was inexplicably left outside. Legend has it that Suleiman executed his chief engineer for the omission.

Suleiman supposedly embarked upon the project in the first place because of a recurring nightmare about being chased by a lion. His advisors interpreted the lion as being Jerusalem (the lion of Judah) which had been left naked (without walls) after being conquered by Suleiman's father.

...ims from around the world flock out of the Jaffa Gate.

...ephen's Gate is also known as the Lions' ...e because of the four animals carved into ...tone of the facade.

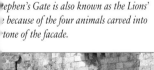

The Golden Gate, facing east, is sealed with stone awaiting the arrival of the Messiah.

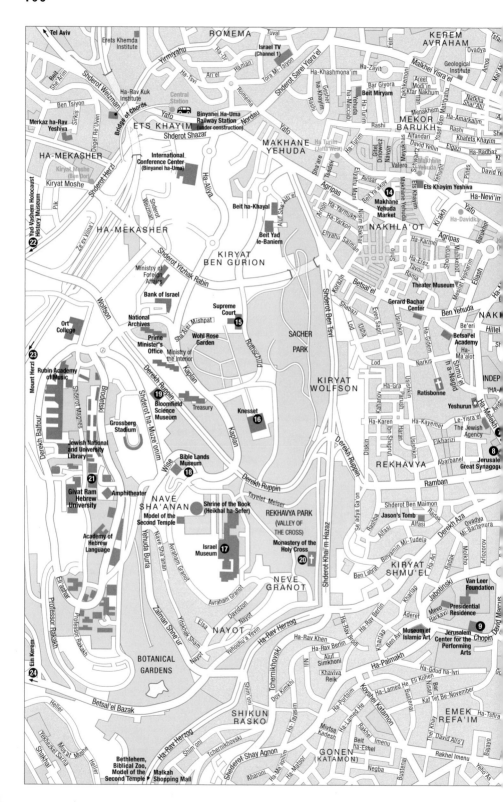

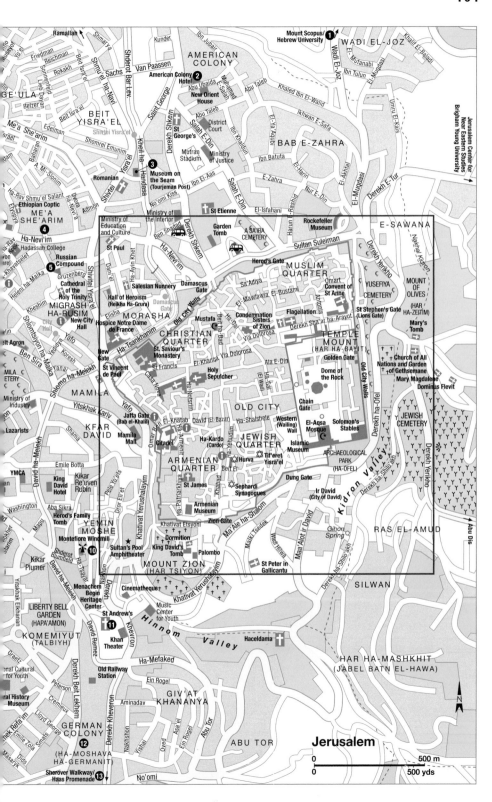

Jerusalem

Malkha shopping mall.

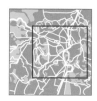
THE NEW JERUSALEM

From Mount Scopus in the east to the somber
Yad Vashem in the west, this chapter explores
the New Jerusalem, its past history and its
present development.

Throughout the ages Jews have wept, sung, and prayed for Jerusalem. Above all, they prayed that one day they might return to their holy city. Yet the Jerusalem that confronted the first waves of Jews who came to start new lives here in the mid-19th century was a dismal contrast to the ideal spiritual capital they had dreamed of for so long. A backwater of the Turkish Ottoman Empire for 400 years, by 1917 the city had been left behind. It was filthy, decrepit and unsanitary, cramped within the confines of its great protective wall.

Even the founder of Zionism, Theodor Herzl, during his 10-day sojourn in Palestine in 1898, noted his disgust with its squalid conditions, writing, "When I remember thee in days to come, O Jerusalem, it will not be with delight. The musty deposits of 2,000 years of inhumanity, intolerance and foulness lie in your reeking alleys. If Jerusalem is ever ours, I would begin by cleaning it up. I would tear down the filthy rat-holes, burn all the non-sacred ruins, and put the bazaars elsewhere. Then, retaining as much of the old architectural style as possible, I would build an airy, comfortable, properly sewered, brand new city around the holy places."

Modern metropolis

Herzl's words proved to be prophetic. The new Jerusalem is much more than airy, comfortable, and properly sewered – it is the fitting capital of the Jewish State that he envisioned. Bold geometric architecture erupts from every hillside; sleek thoroughfares lead into tree-lined boulevards; high-rises tower over church steeples and elegant city parks; and there are bars, theaters, and luxury hotels.

Yet the city that has inspired so much Jewish yearning and Christian and Muslim passion over the centuries is no less reverent because of its modernity; the Christian visitor

Main Attractions
Mount Scopus
Me'a She'arim
Zion Square
Montefiore Windmill
Haas Promenade
Makhane Yehuda Market
Knesset
Israel Museum (including
   Dead Sea Scrolls)
Yad Vashem
Ein Kerem

A Jerusalem girl.

today will be struck by the vast array of churches and hospices of every denomination spread across the streets and hilltops of the city, while for the Muslim pilgrim the resplendent Dome of the Rock and El-Aqsa Mosque are at the heart of their faith. But it is the tremendous blossoming of Jewish spirituality here that has characterized the past century. *Yeshivas*, synagogues, and cultural institutions abound, each place of worship reflecting the specific religious or ethnic coloring of its congregation.

Shabbat is observed scrupulously; from dusk on Friday to Saturday evening most stores and buses cease their service, the streets empty, and a tranquil hush descends on the city, although toward midnight there is a surprisingly boisterous nightlife near Zion Square.

As the capital of the State of Israel, Jerusalem – Yerushalayim in Hebrew – holds a special meaning even for its secular residents, who gripe that the city is far less cosmopolitan and lively than Tel Aviv. The new city is still not exceptionally wealthy or grand (see page 168), and in the past decade has slipped farther behind in terms of the rest of Israel's growing affluence. But many of its structures exude a symbolic significance that outstrips their otherwise modest aesthetic merits.

No event has had more influence on the shape of the city than its unification in the 1967 war. Not only did this clear away the barbed wire and concrete that separated East and West, it also, for a time, took Jerusalem off the frontline of the Arab–Israeli conflict. Since the late 1960s there has been an explosion of development, much of which is attributable to Teddy Kollek, mayor of Jerusalem from 1965 to 1993. He attracted new institutions into the city, conserved Old City landmarks, and presided over the colorful sweeps of new public art as well as the hideous behemoths of rapidly erected housing.

Nearly 900,000 people live in Jerusalem, and the city continues to grow, balancing, with mixed grace, the calls of the past and future. However, since the start of the second Intifada in 2000, the city has been de-facto re-divided,

Hebrew University, on the summit of Mount Scopus.

with large parts of Arab Jerusalem cut off from the city by the Separation Wall (see page 269).

Potent peak

There is no better place to start a tour of the new Jerusalem than **Mount Scopus ❶** Isolated and aloof atop a ridge north of the city, it holds a special place in Jerusalem's history. Its prime importance is as the site of the **Hebrew University**, inaugurated here under the vision of Chaim Weizmann in 1925. It was cut off from the rest of Jewish Jerusalem during the 1948 War of Independence, after a Hadassah Hospital convoy of scientists and staff was massacred in April of that year. Reabsorbed into the city since 1967, the university has enjoyed a spectacular modernization of its campus. Among the most impressive sites here is the classical amphitheater, which hosts concerts and lectures and, when empty, offers an awesome view of the rolling Judean Hills. A new Hadassah Hospital has been built, and other notable monuments include a British cemetery that dates from World War I.

Travel from the university down Churchill Boulevard and left into Aharon Katzir Street. This leads to the wealthy Arab quarter of **Sheikh Jarah**, which includes on its southern fringes along Nablus Road **New Orient House**. This was a Palestinian quasi-government building, but became less important after Faisal Husseini, the Palestinian Minister of Jerusalem Affairs, died in 2001.

On the adjacent street is the **American Colony Hotel ❷** (www.american colony.com), Jerusalem's oldest hotel and a favorite haunt of foreign journalists because of its neutral location on the border between East and West Jerusalem.

Along St George Street and then Kheil ha-Handasa, at the old border, is the **Museum on the Seam ❸**, a former border crossing known as the Tourjeman Post (Sun, Mon, Wed, Thur 10am–5pm, Tue 2pm–9pm Fri 10am–2pm; tel 02-6281278; www.mots. org.il; charge). The museum displays contemporary art that deals with socio-political conflicts between different groups.

The American Colony Hotel, where writers Mark Twain and Herman Melville once stayed.

Religious enclave

A few hundred meters down Shivtei Yisra'el on the right is **Me'a She'arim** ④, where the mood is intense and unworldly. Nearly a third of all Jerusalem citizens are *Haredi*, or ultra-Orthodox, and these neighborhoods reflect the rigorous religious lifestyles of their inhabitants. Me'a She'arim, meaning literally "a hundred gates," is the most famous ultra-Orthodox community. Built in 1875 as a refuge for Hassidic families, the neighborhood has retained much of the intimacy and flavor of a European *shtetl*. The Orthodox Jews who live here speak Yiddish and wear the traditional styles: *peot* (sidecurls), heavy, black garments for the men, and shawls for the women. Signs warn that secular fashions, especially "immodest" female dress, are offensive and not tolerated. These admonitions should be taken seriously: immodestly dressed women are often spat at or even stoned.

Ha-Nevi'im (The Street of the Prophets) runs roughly parallel to the south of Me'a She'arim from behind the Russian Compound to near the

An Orthodox man reads the news in Me'a She'arim.

Damascus Gate, and is one of the main thoroughfares in Jerusalem. This street is famed for its historic architecture and beautiful buildings, whose wonders make a stroll down it an adventure. Where the road meets Shivtei Yisra'el, the Italian Hospital was once home to the Zionist leader Menachem Ussiskin and the author S.Y. Agnon. Today this beautiful building houses the offices of the Ministry of Education.

The **Rothschild Hospital** at the corner of Ha-Rav Kook was built in 1887 and is now occupied by students of Hadassah Hospital, who are undertaking paramedical training.

On the corner of Ethiopians' Street is **Beit Tavor**, built in 1889. Since 1951 it has been home to the Swedish Theological Seminary, and the beautiful courtyard is open to visitors daily. Off the Street of the Prophets lie several religious institutions, including the Ethiopian Coptic Church.

Russians and Prussians

Ha-Nevi'im's western end meets **Jaffa (Yafo) Road** at its mid-point between

he city entrance and Jaffa Gate. The new city's main thoroughfare was paved in 1898 for the visiting German Kaiser, the Prussian Wilhelm II – for whose procession the wall between the Jaffa Gate and the Citadel was rent open. Today Jaffa Road has been pedestrianized and is part of Jerusalem's first tram route. It meanders from the gate to the northern bounds of the city, passing Makhane Yehuda, the Jewish food market, which is a colorful attraction in its own right (see page 172).

Leaving the Old City behind, Jaffa Road passes the new **City Hall** municipal complex and plaza. In the basement of City Hall is a model of central Jerusalem used by architects planning new buildings. The model can be viewed by the public. City Hall also has a **Visitors' Center** at 3 Safra Square (Sun–Thur 9am–4.30pm, Fri 9am–1pm; tel: 02-625 8844).

An alleyway to the north of City Hall leads to the **Russian Compound** ❺, covering several blocks to the right of Jaffa Road. These were purchased by Tsar Alexander II in the wake of the Crimean War as a refuge for thousands of Russian pilgrims who flocked to the city every year, often dirt-poor and under considerable duress from their trip. Started in 1860, this complex marked the first notable presence outside the Old City; most of the buildings, including the handsome green-domed **Cathedral of the Holy Trinity** and the Russian Consulate, were completed by 1864. The compound has been largely bought by the Israeli government, and the buildings now house law courts, a police station, and part of Hadassah Medical School, as well as a plethora of bars, cafes, and restaurants.

The **Hall of Heroism** (Sun–Thur 9am–5pm, Fri 9am–1pm; tel: 02-625 4000; charge) is a small museum at the back of the complex, within what was once a British prison; it is dedicated to the Jewish underground resistance of the Mandate period.

Downtown

On the other side of Jaffa Road are the winding lanes of **Nakhalat Shiva,** Jerusalem's second-oldest residential suburb, now delightfully renovated. Founded by Joseph Rivlin in the early

Me'a She'arim's central street.

FACT

Anna Ticho (1894–1981), who moved to Jerusalem in 1912 from the Czech city of Brno, became one of Israel's most popular artists. "Her eyes can see real landscapes," said Dr Haim Gamzu, a former director of the Tel Aviv Museum, "but they can also penetrate into the soul of the landscape."

The new Jerusalem Light Rail.

1860s, the enclave had grown to hold some 50 families by the end of that decade. Now Rivlin and Salomon Streets, which have been pedestrianized, cross the old neighborhood and, despite their narrow alleyways, house many of the city's favorite restaurants and bars as well as much of its nightlife and upscale Judaica stores. At the end of Nakhalat Shiva, next to the car park, artisans sell their wares during the summer months.

At the hub of it all is **Kikar Tsiyon** (**Zion Square**) ❻, always crowded, always crazy. It was named for the Zion Cinema, now long gone, and was a rallying spot for young Zionists in the 1930s. Zion Square is still a popular venue both for young Israelis to meet up and for occasional political demonstrations.

A block up Ha-Rav Kook, on the north side of Jaffa Road and down an alleyway to the left, is an unexpected little nook, **Beit Ticho**. In the early 20th century it was the home and office of the Jerusalem landscape artist Anna Ticho (see margin) and her husband Avraham, an eminent ophthalmologist.

The childless couple bequeathed their home to the Israel Museum, and the house contains its original furnishings, paintings by Anna, and Avraham's books and Hannukah menorahs. The lobby and the large garden contain a popular restaurant.

Ben Yehuda, the five-block-long pedestrian avenue that begins at Zion Square was once the place where everyone came to see (and be seen), to drink (though drunkenness is rare), sip cappuccino, sample pastries, and simply mingle with friends and strangers. Musicians, young couples, and would-be prophets are always out in force. The street is still popular, but the new **Mamila Mall** and Emek Refa'im in the German Colony have both become more trendy for cafe connoisseurs.

Marking the city's main north–south axis is **Ha-Melekh George** (**King George V Street**) ❼, which cuts across Ben Yehuda at the top of the street. The contrast between old and new is most vivid at the plaza in front of the City Tower, where the preserved doorway facade of an earlier building stands oblivious to its new

JERUSALEM LIGHT RAIL

The Jerusalem Light Rail is a tram system stretching 14km (8.5 miles) from Pisgat Ze'ev in northern Jerusalem via the city center to Yad Vashem in the southwest. The light rail has transformed the city center, with the length of Jaffa Road becoming pedestrianized (except for the trams) and traffic also barred from many side streets. The rail system began operating in August 2011 and the line is currently being extended from Yad Vashem to Hadassah Hospital in Ein Kerem. More than 4,000 trees have been planted along the route, and the centerpiece is the Bridge of Chords designed by world-famous Spanish architect Santiago Calatrava, which carries trains over the western entrance to the city.

surroundings. Hillel, leading back down toward the Old City (parallel to Ben Yehuda on the south), is the site of the lovely, ornate **Italian Synagogue and Museum** (Sun, Tue, Wed 10am–5pm, Mon closed , Thur noon–9pm – Fri 10am–1pm; tel: 02-624 1610; www.jija.org; charge). It was transported here from Conegliano Veneto, near Venice, in 1952 and dates originally from 1719.

The **Beit Agron**, or press building, is farther down, opposite the park and an ancient reservoir, **Mamila Pool**. In the basement of Beit Agron is the Time Elevator, a simulated ride through the city's history in a converted cinema.

The Jerusalem Artists' House on the western side of King George (corner of Betsalel and Shmuel Ha'Nagid) is again the home of Jerusalem's premier arts college, founded in 1906 and moved in the 1990s to Mount Scopus; the college returned to the city center in 2008. The delightful building houses art exhibits and is a popular eatery.

Religion dominates Ha-Melekh George farther to the south. The **Yeshurun Synagogue** across from the park is followed, farther down the block, by the **Jerusalem Great Synagogue ❽**. The 18th-century ark covering the Torah scrolls was brought here from Padua, in Italy. Next door is the seat of the chief Rabbinate of Israel, **Heikhal Shlomo**.

King David Street

At the end of Ha-Melekh George, turn left down Gershon Agron, which rims the final edge of Independence Park, a pleasant expanse of green in the center of the city. This avenue leads down to the formidably named Taxation Square, now dominated by newly built luxury hotels, the David's Citadel (tel: 02-621 1111) and the Waldorf Astoria (tel; 02-542 3333). The latter was opened in 2014 but preserves the facade of the once sumptuous Palace Hotel built nearly 100 years ago, but pushed out of business when the King David Hotel opened for business. Before you is the Mamila Mall.

Turn right into David ha-Melekh (**King David Street**), which hosts two of Jerusalem's most celebrated

TIP

A good time to visit the Jerusalem Center for the Performing Arts is in May during the Israel Festival, when there are visiting artists from overseas and outdoor performances in the plaza in front of the theater complex.

Mamila Mall.

The YMCA building.

The Montefiore Windmill, in the Yemin Moshe neighborhood.

edifices. The **YMCA**, built in 1928–33, was the work of Shreve, Lamb & Harmon, who were simultaneously designing the Empire State Building. Its 36-meter (120ft) tower offers an outstanding view of Jerusalem and its environs, and its symmetrical rotundas reflect an elegant harmony with modern Middle Eastern form.

The **King David Hotel** (tel: 02-620 8888), opposite, was built with old-world grandeur by Egyptian Jews in 1930. It was a British base of command in the Mandate period, and the building's entire right wing was destroyed in a raid by the Jewish underground in 1946. It is customary for visiting heads of state to stay at the King David.

Below the King David, an airy park holds the cavern of **Herod's Family Tomb**, where the stormy monarch buried his wife Mariamne and two of his sons after murdering them in a paranoid rage.

The **Jerusalem Center for the Performing Arts** ❾ can be reached by going up Jabotinski and turning left into Marcus. This attractive neighborhood, known as Talbiyah, contains the city's most expensive houses. The arts complex includes four theaters and auditoriums (www.jerusalem-theatre.co.il); it is also a delightful place if you just want to sit around, and to have a meal or a cup of coffee.

Along Chopin, at the junction of Ha-Palmakh, is the **Museum of Islamic Art** (Sun–Thur 10am–3pm, Tue until 7pm, Fri 10am–2pm Sat 10am–4pm; tel: 02-566 1291; www.islamicart.co.il; charge). The museum has a delightful collection of clocks and watches, which were stolen in 1983 and only returned in 2006 after the burglar confessed to the crime on his deathbed. The **Presidential Residence**, home of the titular head of state, can be found to the right at the start of Jabotinski.

The Montefiore Windmill

Opposite the bottom end of Jabotinski is Shderot Blumfield, which leads to the **Montefiore Windmill** ❿, a conspicuous landmark built by the British philanthropist Sir Moses Montefiore in the 1860s. It now houses a modest museum (Sun–Thur 9am–4pm, Fri 9am–1pm; free). There is another windmill behind the Jerusalem Great Synagogue, but the Montefiore Windmill, which stands above the oldest Jewish neighborhood outside the Old City, is the better known.

Until the 19th century the Old City walls served as the city limits for Jerusalem's Jews; outside, robbers posed a threat. Opposite the Old City, between the Jaffa Gate and Mount Zion, the first Jewish suburb to penetrate this barrier remains in situ. Wishfully called **Mishkenot Sh'Ananim** (Dwellings of Tranquility), the long, block-like structure (on the steps beneath the windmill) was built in 1860 by Sir Moses Montefiore with the bequest of Judah Touro, a New Orleans Jew.

During the next four years Montefiore bought an adjoining plot of land and expanded the quarter, calling it **Yemin Moshe**. In the wake of the 1967 war Yemin Moshe was revitalized

as an artists' colony, and today its serene walkways and stone houses command some of the highest prices of any neighborhood in the city. Montefiore built the windmill at the edge of the quarter to provide flour for the settlement, and in 1948 it served as an important Israeli observation post.

As you head south, with the **Liberty Bell Garden** (Hapa'amon) on the right, the modern city opens onto the old. Embedded on the side of the **Valley of Hinnom** like a rugged gem, the **Cinematheque** on Derekh Khevron is a popular landmark. Its theaters show foreign and alternative movies, including first screenings at July's annual Jerusalem International Film Festival.

Opposite the Cinematheque is the **Menachem Begin Heritage Center** (Sun–Mon, Wed, Thur 9am–4.30pm, Tue 9am–7pm, Fri 9am–12.30pm; tel: 02-565 2020; free, but tours must be booked in advance www.begincenter.org.il). This includes a museum dedicated to the life of the former prime minister and Nobel Prize winner.

Above the heritage center, the Scottish **St Andrew's Church** ⑪ has a well-regarded hospice, and a memorial to the Scottish King Robert Bruce who, on his death in 1329, requested that his heart be taken to Jerusalem (unfortunately it was waylaid en route, in Spain, and never made it). Around the corner, the **Khan Theater's** atmospheric archways are the venue for drama, folk music, and jazz performers.

The train station opposite dates from 1892, but the daily service was discontinued many years ago. The former station – **Hatahana** – has been reopened as a popular major leisure complex with cafes and restaurants, an Israel Railways museum and even a strip of beach in the landlocked city, which has angered the ultra-orthodox community because it encourages women to desecrate the city by wearing bikinis. From Hatahana the former railway tracks have been transformed into a delightful park leading all the way down to the new station at the

Malkah shopping mall, from where trains now run to Tel Aviv. The complex immediately south of the train station has some of the city's most popular restaurants, bars, and nightclubs.

The German Colony

Stretching due southwest from Hinnom is an area of tree-lined boulevards and homes. The area immediately east, called the **German Colony** ⑫, was founded in 1873 by German Templars and still has a subtly European air. The central street is Emek Refa'im, a fashionable boulevard of restaurants, and cafes, leading down to the large Arab-style houses of Baq'a and the Talpiyot industrial zone, a less salubrious mix of discount stores, wedding halls, and nightclubs.

To the east is one of the city's most delightful spots. Turn left from Emek Refa'im into Pierre Koenig and left again into Yehuda and continue straight into Daniel Yanovsky to reach the **Sherover Walkway** and **Haas Promenade** (East Talpiyot) ⑬. Linking up the Arab village of Abu Tor with the Jewish neighborhood of East

FACT

Jerusalem has acquired dozens of names over its 3,000 years of history. In the Bible, it is variously referred to as Moriah (Genesis 22:2), Jebus (Judges 19:10), Zion (II Samuel 5:8), Ariel, Lion of God (Isaiah 29:1), and Neveh Tzedek (Jeremiah 31:22).

The view from Haas Promenade.

TIP

The train to Tel Aviv from the new Malkha station takes 75 minutes compared to 45 minutes by bus, but the hillside views make the railway a more worthwhile experience. There is also a station at the Biblical Zoo.

Talpiyot, these parklands offer a splendid view of the Old City and, when the summer heat haze dissipates, a breathtaking panorama of the Judean Desert. The promenade ends at Government House, now the HQ of the United Nations' regional operations. This is also known as the **Hill of the Evil Counsel**, where Judas Iscariot is said to have received his 30 pieces of silver.

A little south, Kibbutz Ramat Rakhel also offers an inspiring view of the desert, and nearby to the south is the monastery of Mar Elias (see page 277).

To the west is the sprawling suburb of Gilo, which overlooks Malkha. Adjacent to **Teddy Soccer Stadium**, home to Beitar Jerusalem, one of Israel's leading teams, is the **Malkha Shopping Mall** (Kanyon) and the new train station. With air conditioning in the summer and heating in the winter, the shopping mall can be a pleasant place to find gifts, entertain the children, and eat a meal.

Kolitz Street, east of the shopping mall, leads to the **Biblical Zoo**, also known as the Tisch Family Zoological Gardens (Sun–Thur 9am–7pm, Fri 9am–4.30pm, Sat 10am–6pm; tel: 02-675 0111; www.jerusalemzoo.org.il; charge). The zoo is attractively landscaped into the hillside and contains animals mentioned in the Bible.

The government area

The various institutions of government can be found near the western entrance to the city. But to feel the political pulse of the country, journalists often wander through the colorful **Makhane Yehuda Market**  which straddles Yafo (Jaffa) and Agripas streets to the east of the Central Bus Station and the west of Zion Square. The vendors, who offer a tempting array of fresh fruit and vegetables and other foodstuffs, tend to lean to the right in their readily available opinions.

To the west of the Central Bus Station at the western end of Yafo Street is the recently erected Bridge of Chords. This is an impressive harp-like structure designed by the world-famous architect Santiago Calatrava, for the Jerusalem Light Rail (see page 168).. Calatrava was no doubt flattered to

View of the Old City from Haas Promenade.

design a bridge for the entrance to Jerusalem, but his awe-inspiring design seems awkwardly out of place in a shabby neighborhood.

High on the hill above **Sacher Park**, the largest in the city, which is opposite the end of Agripas and Bezalel Streets, is the **Supreme Court** 15 (tours in English Sun–Thur at noon; tel: 02-675 9612; charge). Completed in 1992, this impressive edifice uses light, shade, and glass to great effect. The Supreme Court justices comprise the highest court in the land and have the power to interpret Knesset (parliamentary) legislation. Opposite is the Cinema City entertainment complex, with stores, cafés, and restaurants.

Just to the south, past the Bank of Israel and the Prime Minister's Office, is the nation's Parliament Building, the **Knesset** 16 (Mon–Wed during debates, Sun and Thur 8.30am–2pm for guided tours, which must be booked in advance, passport required; tel: 02-675 3337; www.knesset.gov.il; charge). This is the symbol of Israel's democratic system. Be sure you take the tour of the interior, which includes

a tapestry designed by Marc Chagall. The **Wohl Rose Garden** above is sweetest in spring and late autumn.

The **Israel Museum** 17 (Sat–Mon, Wed–Thur 10am–5pm, Tue 4–9pm, Fri 10am–2pm; tel: 02-670 8811; www. imj.org.il; charge) is reached from the Knesset along Kaplan to Derekh Ruppin, and is Israel's national museum and a leading showcase for the country's art, archeology, and Judaica. Its most famous exhibit is the Shrine of the Book which displays the **Dead Sea Scrolls**. These scraps of tattered parchment represent the oldest known copy of the Old Testament.

There is a **Model of the Second Temple** in the Israel Museum compound. This impressive 1:50 scale model of Jerusalem in AD 66 conveys just how vast the Second Temple complex must have been. (See page 157.)

Opposite are two more museums. The **Bible Lands Museum** 18 (Sun–Thur 9.30am–5.30pm, Wed 9.30am–9.30pm, Fri-Sat 10am–2pm; tel: 02-561 1066; www.blmj.org; charge) in Avraham Granot displays artifacts dating from biblical times. Along

Bust of Hadrian in the Israel Museum.

The model of the Second Temple at the Israel Museum.

TIP

Yad Vashem is so busy that the car park is usually full. An alternative is to take the shuttle bus from the Mount Herzl car park.

Remembering at Yad Vashem.

Ruppin to the northwest is the hands-on **Bloomfield Science Museum** ⑲ (Mon–Thur 10am–6pm, Fri 10am–2pm, Sat 10am–4pm; tel: 02-654 4888; www.mada.org.il; charge), imaginative and popular with children.

Beneath the Israel Museum is the Valley of the Holy Cross, a biblical landscape of olive trees dominated by the **Monastery of the Holy Cross** ⑳ (Mon–Sat 9.30am–5pm, Fri 9.30am–1.30pm; charge). Here, it is believed, grew the tree (planted by Abraham's nephew Lot after he was saved from Sodom's destruction) from which the wood was taken for the cross on which Christ was crucified. The Crusader-style monastery was built in the 7th century and belonged to the Georgian Orthodox Church until the 19th century when (for lack of funds to maintain it) it was handed to the Greek Orthodox Church.

To the west of the Valley of the Cross are the **Botanical Gardens**, a small but pleasing garden of international flora, set by a lake. They are part of the **Hebrew University's Givat Ram Campus** ㉑, established after 1948 when Mount Scopus was cut off. The campus includes the science faculties of the university as well as the **Jewish National and University Library** (Sun–Thur 9am–7pm, Fri 9am–1pm; www.jnul.huji.ac.il; free), one of the largest libraries in the world. It counts among its treasures the actual papers on which Albert Einstein worked out his theory of relativity.

Yad Vashem and Mount Herzl

Remembrance is a key theme of modern Judaism, and Jerusalem has no shortage of memorials. The two most potent of these lie side by side on the western ridge of the city, powerful testimony to the two events that altered the course of 20th century Jewish history: the Holocaust and the creation of the State of Israel. You can reach them by returning along Ruppin and Wolfson and turning left into Shderot Herzl.

The **Yad Vashem Holocaust History Museum** ㉒ (Sun–Wed 9am–5pm, Thu 9am–8pm, Fri 9am–2pm; tel: 02-644 3802; www.yadvashem.org.il; free) is a striking memorial to the 6

million Jews massacred by the Nazis. Daring in its design, the museum is housed in a linear, triangular structure (which some compare to a Toblerone container) stretching for 160 meters (525ft) beneath a hillside (see box).

The complex also includes a central chamber, **Ohel Yizkor**, or the **Hall of Remembrance**, which sits on a base of rounded boulders. Inside, an eternal flame flickers amid blocks of black basalt rock engraved with the names of 21 death camps. Most visitors spend between one and three hours in the complex.

Mount Herzl ㉓ honors the Viennese journalist Theodor Herzl, who founded the Zionist movement between 1897 and 1904. His remains were transported to Jerusalem in 1949, and his simple black granite tomb marks the summit of the mount. Also buried in the cemetery here are Vladimir Jabotinksy and other Zionist visionaries, joined most recently by the late prime minister Yitzhak Rabin, assassinated in 1995. On the northern slope of the ridge lie the graves of Israeli soldiers who died defending the state. The **Herzl Museum** (Sun–Thur 9am–5pm, Fri 9am–1pm; charge) stands guard at the entrance to the mount.

Biblical retreat

Ein Kerem ㉔, the small picturesque biblical village nestling in a valley to the west of the city proper, beneath Yad Vashem, is as timeless as the hills and well worth a whole afternoon to itself. It is rich in religious history. The most renowned sites include the **Franciscan Church of the Visitation**, designed in 1956 by the architect Antonio Barluzzi, on the spot where the Virgin Mary visited Elizabeth, John the Baptist's mother; and the central **Spring of the Vineyard** (also known as Mary's Fountain), which gave the town its name. At the **Church of St John**, mosaics and a grotto mark the traditional birthplace of the Baptist.

The **Hadassah Hospital** complex, above the village, is internationally known for Marc Chagall's stained-glass windows, depicting the 12 tribes of Israel.

At the Yad Vashem Holocaust History Museum.

YAD VASHEM

The idea of establishing a Holocaust memorial in Palestine was first proposed in 1942, and the Holocaust Martyrs' and Heroes' Remembrance Authority, which runs it, was finally established in 1963. Today its archive holds 62 million pages of documents and 260,000 photographs, its library has more than 90,000 titles, and the International School for Holocaust Studies has more than 100 educators on its staff. The old Jewish tradition of *Vehigadeta Lebincha* ("And you will tell your children") is much in evidence.

A major expansion and refurbishment of the complex culminated in 2005 with the dedication of a new Holocaust History Museum, three times the size of the old one. The new Yad Vashem uses the latest multimedia means to recount the horrifying story of Jewish massacres from 1933 to 1945, and includes the world's largest collection of Holocaust art, comprising 10,000 works, many of them on carefully preserved thin scraps of paper.

Only the apex of the museum is above ground, forming a skylight. The gray concrete walls intensify the harshness of the structure, which gashes brutally through the Jerusalem hillside. The effect is powerful and, as the museum puts it: "Every visitor leaves Yad Vashem with a personal impression of an event that has universal dimensions."

Lotem Valley in springtime.

THE GALILEE AND THE GOLAN

This tour takes in the Christian landmarks of Nazareth, mystic Safed of the Kabbalah, the Roman baths of Tiberias, and the forbidding heights of the Golan.

A white-robed Druze puffing away on his pipe in a mountain-top village; a bikini-clad bather soaking in sulphuric springs at a Roman bathhouse: these are the stark contrasts typical of Israel's dynamically diverse north – the Galilee and the Golan.

Extending from the lush Jezreel Valley to the borders of Lebanon and Syria, this relatively compact region, at one moment a desolate expanse of bare rock, can suddenly explode into a blaze of unusual blood-red buttercups and purple irises. Here Christians can retrace the steps of Jesus, while Jews can reflect on the place that produced their greatest mystics.

Lying on the main artery that linked the ancient empires, the Galilee has been a battleground for Egyptian Pharaohs, biblical kings, Romans and Jews, Christians and Muslims, Britain and Turkey.

Jewish pioneers established the country's first kibbutzim here. In subsequent decades the kibbutzim have mushroomed to cover much of this region, where tribes of Bedouin still live and Arab and Druze villages lie nestled in the hills. A circular tour of the entire Galilee and Golan covers less than 400km (250 miles) – a day's leisurely drive – but even over the course of a one-month tour the visitor would get only a passing appreciation of this region's incredible history,

sacred sites, diverse inhabitants, and breathtaking landscapes.

The valley

Highway 65 from the center of the country suddenly dips into the **Jezreel** (**Izre'el**) **Valley**, which, stretching from the Samarian foothills in the south to the slopes of the Galilee in the north, holds the title of Israel's largest valley. Because of its strategic location on the ancient Via Maris route, the list of great battles that have scoured this seemingly tranquil stretch is a long and

Main Attractions

Tel Megiddo
Nazareth
Safed
Tel Hazor
Hula Valley
Mount Hermon
Sea of Galilee
Capernaum
Tiberias
Beit She'an

Church of the Seven Apostles at Capernaum.

colorful one. However, the greatest battle of all has yet to be fought here. It is the one that the Book of Revelation says will pit the forces of good against the forces of evil for the final battle of mankind at Armageddon.

The site referred to is **Tel Megiddo** (Mount Megiddo) ❶ (daily 8am–4pm, until 5pm Apr–Sept; tel: 04-659 0316; charge), a 4,000-year-old city in the center of the valley. Turn left at Megiddo Junction onto Highway 66 and the Mount is 2km (1.3 miles) to the north.

Even the first written mention of Megiddo – in Egyptian hieroglyphics – describes how war was waged on the city by a mighty Pharaoh some 3,500 years ago. Since then many a great figure has met his downfall on this ancient battleground. It is said of the Israelite King Josiah, who was defeated at the hands of the Egyptians around 600 BC: "And his servants carried him in a chariot dead from Megiddo" (I Kings 10:26). In World War I the British fought a critical battle against the Turks at Megiddo Pass, with the victorious British general walking away with the title Lord Allenby of Megiddo.

In the heap of ruins that make up the *tel* (mound) of Megiddo, archeologists have uncovered 20 cities. At the visitors' center a miniature model of the site gives definition to what the untrained eye could see as just a pile of stones, breathing life into what is actually a 4,000-year-old Canaanite temple, King Solomon's stables (built for 500 horses), and an underground water system built by King Ahab 2,800 years ago to protect the city's water in times of siege. Steps and lighting enable easier exploration of the 120-meter (390ft) tunnel, and of the almost 60-meter (200ft) high shaft, which was once the system's well.

Beit She'arim

Head north along Highway 66 through the pleasant but unremarkable countryside of the Jezreel Valley and turn right at Hatishbi Junction onto Route 722 and right again several kilometers later onto 75. You will soon reach **Beit She'arim** ❷ (daily 8am–4pm, until 5pm Apr–Sept; tel: 04-983 1643; charge). This is Israel's version of a necropolis and was the most important burial place in the Jewish world during the Talmudic

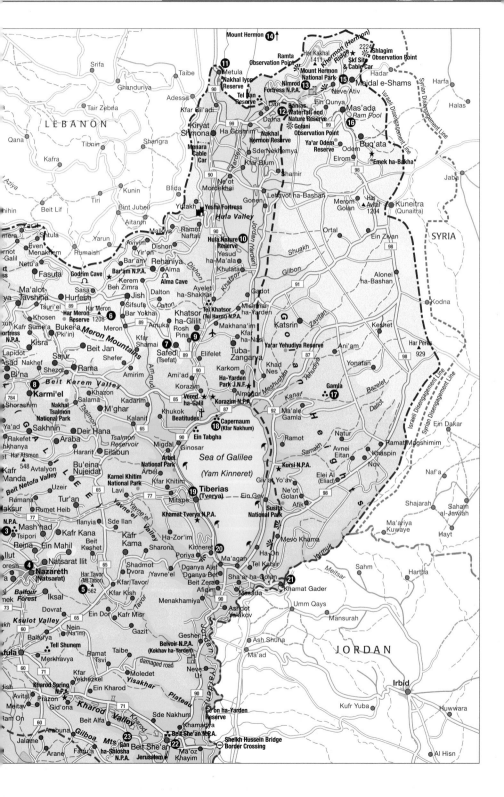

period. The limestone hills have been hollowed out to form a series of catacombs. Inside the labyrinths, vaulted chambers are lined with hundreds of sarcophagi of marble or stone (depending on the social rank of the deceased). Each of the coffins – often elaborately engraved – weighs nearly 5 tonnes. When the Romans forbade the Jews to settle in Jerusalem, the center of Jewish national and spiritual life moved to Beit She'arim, and this 2nd-century burial ground became a chosen spot not only for local residents but also for Jews everywhere.

It's worth climbing the hill for a good view of the Jezreel Valley and the Carmel mountain range. On the hilltop is a bronze statue of Alexander Zeid, who discovered the necropolis in the 1920s.

Back along Route 75, right on 77 and right again along 79 is **Tsipori** ❸ (daily 8am–4pm, until 5pm Apr–Sept; tel: 04-656 8272; charge), known to the Greeks as Sepphoris. Reflecting this settlement's long history are a 4,500-seat Roman ampitheater, a beautifully preserved 2nd-century mosaic

of a woman dubbed "the Mona Lisa of the Galilee," and a Crusader fortress.

Cradle of Christianity

Further along Highway 79 is **Nazareth** ❹ (www.nazareth.muni.il), a strange blend of the timeless and the topical, the sacred town where Jesus Christ spent much of his life and which is today a bustling city of more than 80,000, Israel's largest Israeli Arab city. "Can anything good come out of Nazareth?" (John 1: 46). This rhetorical question might seem puzzling today, particularly to millions of Christians for whom Nazareth is equated with Christianity itself. But when it was posed two millennia ago, the only feature that distinguished this village in the lower Galilee was its obscurity.

Since then, the quaint village where Jesus grew up has become one of the world's best-known towns. Today, of almost two dozen churches commemorating Nazareth's most esteemed resident, the grandest of all is the monumental **Basilica of the Annunciation** (Mon–Sat 8am–6pm, until 5pm in winter, Sun 2–5pm; tel: 04-657 2401;

Crucifixes for sale in the market in Nazareth, a town synonymous with Christianity.

free). The largest church in the Middle East, it was completed only in 1969, but it encompasses the remains of previous Byzantine churches. It marks the spot where the Angel Gabriel is said to have informed the Virgin Mary that God had chosen her to bear His son. The event has been given an international flavor, and is depicted inside in a series of elaborate murals, each from a different country. In one, Mary appears kimono-clad and with East Asian features; in another, she's wearing a turban and bright African garb. Not to be outdone, the Americans have produced a highly modernistic Cubist version of the Virgin.

In the basement of the **Church of St Joseph** (next to the basilica) is a cavern reputed to have been the carpentry workshop of Joseph, Jesus's earthly father.

Some of the simpler churches, however, capture an air of intimacy and sanctity that the colossal Basilica lacks. This is especially so in the **Greek Orthodox Church of St Gabriel**, nearly a kilometer further north at the end of Maria Road. Upon entering the

small, dark shrine you hear nothing but the faint rush of water. Lapping up against the sides of the old well inside the church is the same underground spring that provided Nazareth with its water 2,000 years ago. Another very atmospheric church is the tiny Catholic one, which was previously a synagogue. At one time believed to be the actual building attended by Jesus, it is now thought to have been built on the same site, probably in the 2nd century AD.

Eight kilometers (5 miles) north of Nazareth on Highway 754, nestled among pomegranate and olive groves, is the Arab village of **Kafr Kana**. Shortly after being baptized, Jesus attended the wedding of a poor family in this town. Here, says St John's Gospel, he used his miraculous powers for the first time, making the meager pitchers of water overflow with wine. Two small churches in the village commemorate the feat.

Har Tavor (Mount Tabor) **⑤** rises to the east of Nazareth and south of Kafr Kana, but it is necessary to travel around almost four sides of a square – best east along 77 then south on 65

FACT

Safed's **Israel Bible Museum** exhibits 300 visual scenes of the Bible by the artist Phillip Ratner. The **Kabbalah Museum** explains kabbalah teachings. Mila Rozenfeld's **Doll Museum** (Eshtam Building) has a collection of costumed dolls. **Beit Hameiri** is a historical museum documenting Safed's Jewish community.

Nazareth, the country's biggest Israeli Arab city.

Traditional themes get a contemporary look from an artist in Safed.

Praying for Selichot (request for forgiveness) at the tomb of Rabbi Yehuda Bar Ilai, on the eve of Yom Kippur.

– to reach this huge hump of a hill. Mount Tabor offers an overview of the whole Jezreel Valley – a patchwork of gold and green farmland. This strangely symmetrical hill dominates much of the valley. It was here that the biblical prophetess Deborah was said to have led an army of 10,000 Israelites to defeat their idol-worshiping enemies. Two churches commemorate the transfiguration of Christ, which is also said to have taken place here.

When his sermons began to provoke the Jews, Jesus took three of his disciples and ascended Mount Tabor. There, the Gospels say, "He was transfigured before them – his face shone like the sun and his garments became white as light." The Franciscan **Basilica of the Transfiguration** commemorates the event, which Christians believe was a foreshadowing of his resurrection.

Atmospheric Safed

About 30km (18 miles) due north of Mount Tabor are the highest peaks in the Galilee. Many people believe that they exude an inexplicable air of something eternal that makes them seem even higher than they are. Travel north along 65, west along 85, and northeast on 866 to the Meron mountains. To reach the highest peak, **Har Meron ⑥** – at 1,208 meters (3,955ft), the highest summit in pre-1967 Israel – you have to continue on Highway 89 for 11km (7 miles) and turn south onto the mountain road. When not marred by the summer heat haze, the sweeping view from the Mediterranean to Mount Hermon is exceptional. These mountains are filled with the mystery of the tombs of the rabbis who composed the Kabbalah, the now fashionable great Jewish mystical texts that have enchanted the likes of pop singer Madonna.

At the base of the mountain, back on Highway 89, in **Meron** village, is the tomb of Shimon Bar-Yochai, the revered rabbi who drew Jews to the region in the first place. On the feast of Lag Ba'Omer in May you can still see tens of thousands of his devout followers gather outside the synagogues of nearby Safed and make their way in a joyous procession to his grave at the foot of Mount Meron.

SAFED

The Shulchan Aroch, otherwise known as the basic set of daily rituals for Jews, was compiled in Safed. But the real focus of Safed's sages was not the mundane but the mystical. Many had been drawn to the city in the first place because of its proximity to the tomb of Rabbi Shimon Bar-Yochai, the 2nd-century sage who is believed to have written the core of the Kabbalah, Judaism's foremost mystical text.

The efforts of Safed's wise men to narrow the gap between heaven and earth left not only great scholarly work and poignant poetry but also a legacy of legends about their mysterious powers. At one synagogue (Abohav) an earthquake destroyed the entire building but left unscathed the one wall facing Jerusalem.

Immediately southeast of Meron is **Safed ❼** (www.safed.co.il). This attractive hilltop town can be reached by heading southeast along 89. Sheltered by the highest peaks in the Galilee, Safed seems also to be sheltered from time itself. Its narrow, cobblestoned streets wind their way through stone archways and overlook the domed rooftops of 16th-century houses. Devout men, clad in black, congregate in medieval synagogues, the echo of their chants filling the streets. A modern area of Safed, with some 34,000 residents, has sprung up around the original city core.

When the Spanish Inquisition sent thousands of Jews fleeing, many ended up in Safed, bringing with them the skills and scholarship of the golden age they had left behind in Spain. The rabbinical scholars of Safed were so prolific that in 1563 the city was prompted to set up the first printing press in the Middle East (or, in fact, in all of Asia).

Every synagogue here is wrapped in its own comparable set of legends (see box), which the *shamash* (deacon) is usually delighted to share. Not all the synagogues are medieval, many of the original ones having been destroyed and replaced by more modern structures, but the spirit of the old still lingers in these few lanes off Kikar Meginim.

The special atmosphere that permeates Safed has captured the imagination of dozens of artists who have made it their home. Like the rest of the Old City, the artists' quarter of Safed remains untouched. "Nothing has been added for the benefit of the tourist," is the claim. Nothing has to be. Winding your way through the labyrinth of lanes, you'll find more than 50 studios and galleries as well as a general art gallery and a museum of printing. Another highlight in Safed is the Klezmer Hasidic Musical Festival each August.

Towering above the center of Safed, littered with Crusader ruins, is **Citadel Hill**, an excellent lookout point, taking in a panorama that extends from the slopes of Lebanon to the Sea of Galilee.

Havens in the hills

The wide open spaces of the Western Galilee (west of Safed) act as a haven,

TIP

Almost all the historical, archeological, and natural sites around the country – there are a dozen mentioned in this chapter alone – are run by the Israel Parks Authority. Entrance to each site costs about US$9 per person. But a US$45 green card gives access to all 65 sites around the country. www.parks.org.il; tel: *3639 from within Israel.

Safed's old city is full of art galleries and shops.

attracting various idealists seeking to carve their own small utopias on its slopes. So, in addition to the more common settlements like kibbutzim, Bedouin encampments, and Arab, Druze, and Circassian villages, you'll find a community of transcendental meditationists at **Hararit** who have found their nirvana on these secluded slopes. There is also a colony of vegetarians at **Amirim** who have set up an organic farm as well as running guesthouses and restaurants where visitors can indulge in gourmet vegetarian meals. The villagers of **Harduf** also eat only organically grown foods, while **Klil**'s residents will only utilize energy that is generated by the sun or wind. **Shorashim** is billed as a pluralistic, egalitarian community belonging to the conservative synagogue movement.

To be sure, even the mainstream Jewish inhabitants of this region tend to lead a lifestyle governed by environmental if not religious concerns. Many have left the crowded center of the country to seek a higher quality of life and fresher air. There are many high-tech opportunities in the region, and the commute to Haifa is only 30 minutes.

Karmi'el ❽ has burgeoned into the largest town in the Western Galilee. It was established in 1964, and its population of 52,000 includes native-born Israelis as well as Jewish immigrants from 34 countries (including many Americans and, recently, Ethiopians and Russians). Clean, pretty, and prosperous, Karmi'el is considered a model development town. Near its center, against a backdrop of desolate mountains, is a series of larger-than-life sculptures depicting the history of Israel's Jewish people. Each July Karmi'el hosts an International Folk Dance Festival.

Karmi'el is set in the **Beit Kerem Valley**, the dividing line between what is considered the Upper Galilee (to the north), with peaks jutting up to almost 1,200 meters (4,000ft), and the Lower Galilee (to the south), a much gentler expanse of rolling hills, none of which exceeds 600 meters (2,000ft). This area west of Safed has not been included in the formal route of this tour, but the landscape is spectacular and many of the aforementioned "offbeat" villages offer accommodations.

The Galilee panhandle

Descending eastward from Safed on Highway 89 is the land extending north of the Sea of Galilee, which gradually narrows into what is known as the finger of the Galilee in Hebrew or the Galilee panhandle in English with Metula at its tip. This is particularly pretty countryside. The east opens up into the sprawling Hula Valley, beyond which hover the Golan Heights. Towering over the valley to the west are the **Naphtali mountains**, beyond which loom the even higher mountains of Lebanon. These picturesque peaks were in the past a source of frequent Katyusha rocket attacks on the Israeli towns below.

Apart from the beauty it offers, the road to Metula is an odyssey through the making of modern Israel. The

Looking out over the Sea of Galilee.

first stop on this trek is **Rosh Pina** ❾. On the rock-strewn barren terrain they found here over a century ago, pioneers fleeing pogroms in Eastern Europe set up the first Jewish settlement to be founded in the Galilee since Roman times. They called it Rosh Pina, meaning "the cornerstone", a name which came from the passage in Psalm 118: "The stone which the builders rejected has become the cornerstone." The original 30 families who settled here were part of the first wave of Jewish immigration that began in the 1880s.

Rosh Pina, a quaint town of about 1,000, has maintained something of its original rural character. Cobblestoned streets line the old section of the town, and 19th-century houses, being gentrified, still stand.

Continuing northward toward Metula on Highway 90, the next stop after several kilometers takes you off the road of modern history, exposing instead the far more ancient foundations of the country. **Khatsor ha-Glilit (Tel Hazor)** (daily 8am–4pm, until 5pm Apr–Sept; tel: 04-693 7290; charge) is one of the oldest archeological sites in Israel – and by far the largest. With its 23 layers of civilization spanning 3,000 years, it was the inspiration for *The Source*, James Michener's 1965 novel.

The Hula Valley

This is the region of the **Hula Valley**, a stretch of lush land dotted with farming villages and little fish ponds that would seem like a mirage to someone who had stood on the same spot 60 years ago. Then you would have seen 4,000 hectares (10,000 acres) of malaria-infested swamp land – home to snakes, water buffalo, and wild boar.

The draining of the valley was one of the most monumental tasks undertaken by the State of Israel in its early days. It took six years. By 1957 the lake had been emptied, leaving a verdant valley in its place, but now part of the region has been re-swamped, as excessive peat in the ground is impeding agriculture. You can get an idea of what the area was like before the drainage by visiting the 80 hectares (200 acres) of swampland that have been set aside as the **Hula Nature Reserve** ❿

TIP

The fee to Tel Hazor includes free entrance to the museum at **Kibbutz Ayelet ha-Shakhar**, and visitors are encouraged to stop off at the museum first in order to understand the excavations better. The kibbutz also runs a popular guesthouse.

Common Cranes at Hula Valley Nature Reserve.

(Sat–Thur 8am–4pm, Fri 8am–3pm; tel: 04-693 7069; charge). Three kilometers (2 miles) after Yesod Ha-Ma'ale Junction, turn right into the reserve. A further 4km (2.4 miles) to the north is the Agamon Hula Nature Park, where you can undertake an 8-km (5-mile) hike around the re-swamped Hula (Sat–Thu 8am–4pm, Fri 8am–3pm; tel: 04-681 7137; charge). Golf carts can be hired. This is a great place to see the millions of birds migrating between Eurasia and Africa along the rift valley. There is also a museum devoted to the natural history of the region at **Kibbutz Khulata**, known as the Dubrovin Farm, just to the south; it recreates living conditions in the late 19th century. There is a guesthouse in the northern part of the valley at **Kfar Blum**, a kibbutz founded by English immigrants. From just south of Kiryat Shmona on Highway 90, the Manara Cable Car travels 750 meters (2,460ft) up into the Naftali Hills and offers a splendid panorama of the Hula Valley (daily 9.30am–4.30pm; tel: 04-690 5830).

The landscape of the Lower Galilee.

The nearby town of **Kiryat Shmona** began life as a series of corrugated iron huts known as *ma'abarot* (essentially refugee camps). Situated close to the border, it has been for years the target of rocket attacks and terrorist infiltrations from the Lebanese mountains that overlook it, and the town was devastated by hundreds of missiles during the Second Lebanon War in 2006. Today the town is quiet, with a population of 25,000, but it has little of interest to tourists.

The road to Metula

When the end of World War I left Palestine's status unclear, Arab gangs attacked the Jews in this most northern region, forcing them out of their settlements. The settlers at **Tel Khai** and **Kfar Gil'adi**, north of Kiryat Shmona, though outnumbered, held out under siege for months until their leader, Joseph Trumpeldor, was shot and killed. The incident prompted the Jews to improve their self-defense and triggered the formation of the Haganah, predecessor of the Israel Defense Forces.

The building from which the settlers defended themselves is now a museum devoted to the Haganah.

Nearby is a memorial to Trumpeldor and seven fellow fighters, including two women, who died in the attack. Thousands of Israeli youths converge on the Tel Khai site on the anniversary of Trumpeldor's death. There is also a youth hostel here and a guesthouse at neighboring Kfar Gil'adi, today a flourishing kibbutz.

Just before Metula, in the **Iyon Stream Reserve** (daily 8am–4pm, until 5pm Apr–Sept; Fri 8am–3pm; tel: 04-695 1519; charge), is a picturesque waterfall that flows impressively in the winter months (Oct–May) but is completely dry the rest of the year. This is due to a longstanding arrangement by which Israel permits Lebanese farmers to divert the water for agricultural use.

Until the Golan was captured from Syria in 1967, **Metula** ⓫ (www.metulla.muni.il), Israel's most northern point, surrounded on three sides by Lebanese land, was the target of frequent rocket attacks. Founded in 1896 by Baron Edmund de Rothschild, who purchased land from local Druze for the same wave of Russian immigrants that had settled in Rosh Pina, it was

for two decades the only settlement in the area. Even today, the nearest major shopping center is 10km (6 miles) away in Kiryat Shmona. But one attraction is the **Canada Center**, the country's only Olympic-size ice rink.

Apart from the fresh mountain air, abundant apple orchards (much of the country's supply comes from here) and charming *pensions*, what draws tourists to this secluded town of 600 inhabitants is its now famous border with Lebanon. Since Israel withdrew from Lebanon in 2000, there is no daily stream of Lebanese workers coming to Israel each day, but the "Good Fence" border offers Israelis an opportunity to stare into the troubled territory of their northern neighbor.

The source of the River Jordan

Return to Kiryat Shmona and travel east on Highway 99. Some 10km (6 miles) east of Kiryat Shmona, on the edge of the Golan Heights (and what used to be the Syrian border), is the archeological site of **Tel Dan** (daily 8am–4pm, until 5pm Apr–Sept; tel:

FACT

Kibbutzim aren't what they used to be. In 2013, Kibbutz Ma'anit, near Hadera, raised US$65 million on the US NASDAQ market for its lipid based nutritional products.

Neat rows of crops near Kiryat Shmona.

Banias Waterfall.

04-695 1579; charge). Situated at the northern tip of Israel, it was founded in biblical times by members of the tribe of Dan, after quarrels with the Philistines forced them to leave the southern coast. It is also notorious as one of two cities where Jeroboam permitted idolatrous worship of the golden calf.

Today the site includes various Israelite ruins, a Roman fountain and a triple-arched Canaanite gateway. In the summer, volunteers help to excavate this active and scenic *tel*, where the source waters for the Jordan River emerge in attractive bubbling brooks. The museum at **Kibbutz Dan** nearby has descriptions of the geology of the region and the reclamation of the Hula Valley below. The kibbutz also runs a very popular restaurant, the **Dag on the Dan**, specializing in fresh trout from the nearby streams.

The **Dan River** provides the greatest single source of the Jordan River – in fact, "Jordan" is a contraction of the Hebrew *Yored Dan* (descending from Dan), and that's precisely what this biblical river does. For its 264km (165-mile) length, the Jordan flows from the snowy peak of **Mount Hermon** to the catchment basin of the Dead Sea, 400 meters (1,300ft) below sea level, and the lowest point on the face of the earth.

The Golan

Several kilometers further east, the **Banias Waterfall** ⑫ is among the most popular natural attractions in the country – and has been for thousands of years. "Banias" is a corruption of the Greek *Panaeas*, and in a cave near the spring are the remains of an ancient temple built in honor of Pan, the Greek god of the forests.

Roman and old Crusader ruins may also be visited at **Banias**, which is in the **Hermon Stream National Park** (daily 8am–4pm, until 5pm Apr–Sept; tel: 04-690 2577; charge), but the real attractions are the waterfalls, including the country's largest, and some inviting pools.

Before 1967, Banias was located in Syrian territory. Thus you are now officially on the fiercely contested Golan Heights. **The Golan** (www.golan.org.il) is a sombre massif doomed by history and bloodied by almost ceaseless war. It

is a great block of dark gray rock lifted high above the Upper Jordan Valley, and those who possess it have the power to rain misery upon their neighbors.

The Golan is a mighty fortress created by the hand of nature. During the Tertiary Age, geological folding lifted its hard basalt stone from the crust of the earth. Today it is a sloped plateau, rising in the north to heights greater than a full kilometer above sea level. It stretches 67km (42 miles) from north to south and 25km (15 miles) from east to west.

Israel annexed the Golan in 1981 and there are currently 25,000 Jewish settlers in the region. Talk of territorial compromise has dissipated since the start of the Syrian civil war in 2011.

Historic redoubt

The Golan has been disputed throughout history (see box). Archeological evidence indicates a substantial Jewish population until the time of the Crusades; for the next eight centuries, the area was practically desolate.

At the end of the 19th century the Ottoman Turks tried to repopulate the Golan with non-Jewish settlers, to serve as a buffer against invasion from the south. Among those who put down roots here were some Druze, Circassians fleeing the Russian invasion of the Caucasus mountains in 1878, and Turkomans who migrated from Central Asia. A village of Nusseiris (North Syrian Alawites) was also established here.

After World War I, when British troops under General Edmund Allenby drove the Ottomans off the Golan, the region was included in the British Mandate of Palestine, but in the San Remo Conference of 1923 it was traded off to the French sphere of influence. From 1948 to 1967 the Syrians used the Golan Heights as a forward base of operations against Israel. Jewish villages in the Hula Valley were shelled by Syrian artillery mounted here. Syria continued to install fortifications in the Golan throughout the 1960s, converting the region into a military zone.

War finally broke out on June 6, 1967, with Syrian army attacks on Kibbutz Dan, Ashmura, and She'ar Yashuv. The attack was blunted the following

FACT

Many of the ancient buildings in northern Israel are built from black volcanic basalt rock taken from the Golan Heights.

Qumran, from the Dead Sea.

THE GOLAN IN ANTIQUITY

The Golan stands out as having been disputed throughout history. In antiquity it was the greatest natural barrier traversed by the Via Maris, the "Sea Highway" that led from Egypt and the coastal plain across the Galilee and the Golan to the kingdom of Mesopotamia. The Golan was allocated to the tribe of Manasseh during the biblical era, but was frequently lost and recaptured over the centuries. Under Roman rule, Jewish settlement in the Golan increased, and a few generations later, during the Jewish Revolt against Rome (AD66), many of the descendants of those settlers met cruel deaths during the epic battle for the fortress of Gamla (see page 193). The mountain range changed hands frequently during the following centuries.

FACT

The Golan Druze still have strong ties with Syria. Many young people study at universities in Syria and marriages are often arranged, usually between young Syrian Druze women and Golan men. The economic opportunities are greater on the Golan.

Take in the wildlife of the Golan Heights.

day, and on June 9 Israeli troops counterattacked. Within 48 hours all Syrian units on the Golan had either retreated or surrendered.

From war to peace

Only six inhabited villages, with a total population of 6,400 people, remained on the Golan at the time of the Israeli victory. These included five Druze communities and one Shiite village at Ghajar. Today these villages house more than 25,000 inhabitants, who live peacefully within Israel but have refused to take Israeli citizenship and "pragmatically" speak publicly in support of Syria for fear that they may one day find themselves looking to Damascus as their capital.

Within weeks of the 1967 conquest, members of Israeli kibbutzim began establishing communities in the unpopulated hills, the first of these being Merom Golan. During the following years the region was transformed as orchards were planted with apples, pears, peaches, almonds, plums, and cherries, and vineyards were established.

Syria attacked again on October 6, 1973, the Jewish Day of Atonement. The next day Syrian troops occupied nearly half the Golan. Israel responded on October 8 in what was to become the greatest tank battle in history. Within a week Syria had lost some 1,200 of an estimated 1,500 Soviet-built tanks. By 24 October, Israeli units were within sight of Damascus when the United Nations called for peace, and Israel complied. A dangerous legacy of minefields remains.

Now for more than four decades peace has prevailed. Indeed, this has been Israel's quietest border despite several incidents initiated by rebels since the start of the Syrian civil war. President Hafez el Assad and subsequently his son Bashir, have scrupulously adhered to the armistice agreement signed with Israel in 1975. As a result, domestic tourism to this region, which remains delightfully cool in the summer months, has flourished, although it remains rarely visited by overseas tourists. Ample but unexceptional bed-and-breakfast accommodations have sprung up on most of the region's settlements.

Most Israelis see the Golan as a vital buffer zone between them and Syria, an enormous bunker filling its ancient role of blocking invasion. But visitors who do come usually tour the old Syrian fortifications that dot the area. The **Nimrod Fortress** ⓭ (daily 8am–4pm, until 5pm Apr–Sept; tel: 04-694 9277; charge) on the northern Golan – turn left onto Highway 989 from 99 – is one such example. From this 13th-century Syrian fortress, constructed to defend the waters of Banias below, one gains a spectacular view of the Northern Galilee and the Naphtali Hills beyond, and it is easy to understand the strategic reasons for its construction.

Mount Hermon

Towering above the north end of the Golan is **Mount Hermon** ⓮ (2,814 meters/9,232ft), with several ranges radiating from it. It occupies an area roughly 40 by 20km (25 by 12 miles) and is divided between Lebanon, Syria, Israel, and several demilitarized zones under UN jurisdiction. About 20 percent of this area is under Israeli control, including the southeast ridge

Ketef ha-Hermon (the Hermon Shoulder), whose highest point rises to 2,236 meters (7,336ft).

The higher areas of Mount Hermon are snow-covered through most of the year, and each winter brings snow to all elevations over 1,200 meters (3,900ft). Israeli ski enthusiasts have opened a modest ski resort on these slopes, with a chair-lift and an equipment rental shop for skis, boots, poles, and toboggans. The slopes are often compared to those found in New England – not particularly lofty, but nevertheless a challenge and a pleasure to ski. The ski resort (8am–4pm generally Jan–Apr, depending on snowfall; tel: 1-599—550-560; www.hermonski.com) can be reached by continuing along Highway 989 and turning north onto 98 in the outskirts of Majdal e-Shams. Even when there is no snow to enjoy there is a mountain sled and bike park.

Nature on Mount Hermon is of particular interest to Israelis because it's the only sub-alpine habitat in the country. Several birds, such as the rock nuthatch and the redstart, are at the southernmost extremity of their range

FACT

In the winter the adventurous sort will sometimes ski on the Hermon in the morning and drive down to Eilat to go scuba-diving on the same day.

Ski lifts on Mount Hermon.

here, while others, such as the Hermon horned lark, are found nowhere else.

Many dolinas are scattered around Mount Hermon. These are cavities in the surface of the rock formed by karstic action on the mountain's limestone. In the winter the dolinas fill with snow, and they are the last areas to melt in the spring, thus supporting lush green vegetation long after the rest of the slope has dried out under the intense sun.

Druze villages

At the foot of Mount Hermon is **Majdal e-Shams** ⓰, the largest of the Druze villages on the Golan, which is located at the junction of Highways 989 and 98. The town has good restaurants and souvenir shops, and is popular with tourists.

The Druze village of **Mas'ada,** 8km (5 miles) to the south along 98, overlooks the **Ram Pool** ⓰, a fascinating geological phenomenon. This is one of only two extinct volcanos in the world which over time has evolved into a small lake (the other is in Kenya).

A popular tourist pastime in the spring and summer on the Golan is visiting farms that allow you to pick (weigh and pay for) your own fruit such as cherries, blackberries, and raspberries, which are expensive delicacies in Israel. Among other places, this can be done at Elrom, 7km (4 miles) south of Mas'ada.

Katsrin, 20km (13 miles) southwest along Highway 91, is the modern "capital" of the Golan and the region's only municipal center. Established in 1977, it is designed in the shape of a butterfly and is home to the **Golan Archeological Museum** (Sun–Thur 9am–4pm, Fri 9am–1pm, Sat 10am–1pm; tel: 04-696 9634; charge) which exhibits artifacts from the ancient settlement of Katsrin.

With a population of 7,000, **Katsrin** is the home of Golan Wineries, one of the country's largest winemakers, which in the 1980s revolutionized the country's wine industry, previously known for cheap sweet red wine used for religious purposes. For Israelis, Golan is synonymous with good wine and, assisted by Californian experts, it sells US$40 million worth of quality wines a year, including US$8 million

Olive oil factory on the Golan Heights.

GRIFFONS OF GAMLA

The ruins of Gamla are clustered on a steep ridge, and, if you tour the area between late winter and summer, there is a very good chance of seeing magnificent griffon vultures. You don't have to be an ornithologist to appreciate these impressive creatures, with their 2-meter (7ft) wingspan. Moreover, because the vultures' nests are just below the hilltop lookout, visitors are given the unusual treat of seeing the birds from above.

There are an estimated 40–45 pairs of vultures here, which makes it the largest flock in the Middle East, and major efforts are made to protect them and help them breed. They are officially listed as a "vulnerable" species, one step above "endangered." The site also commands a fabulous view of the Sea of Galilee.

in exports. Dozens of other smaller Israeli wineries have taken their inspiration from the Golan venture.

You can visit the Golan winery in Katsrin (Sun–Thur 8.30am–5.30pm, Fri 8.30am–1.30pm; tel: 04-696 8435; www.golanwines.co.il; free entry and free samples). Teetotallers will prefer the tour of the nearby Mei Eden mineral water factory, also free with free samples (Sun–Thur 9am–4pm; book the tour in advance).

Gamla

Another often-visited site on the Golan is **Gamla** ⑰ (daily 8am–4pm, until 5pm Apr–Sept; tel: 04-682 2282; charge). Travel south from Katsrin on 9088, and go left and right onto 808. Gamla was the "Masada of the north," a fortified town of the south-central Golan which, in AD 66, was the focus of one of the early battles in the Jewish revolt against Rome. Initially, the rebels put Vespasian and three full Roman legions to shame. The overconfident Roman leader threw his troops against the Jewish bastion, only to have them humbled by a much smaller and less professional Jewish force. Recovering, the embarrassed Romans besieged the Jewish town in one of the most bitter battles of the war. Vespasian vowed that no mercy would be shown.

The Romans gradually pushed the Jews to the precipice above which this mountain-top city was built, and, when Roman victory appeared imminent, many defenders committed suicide rather than surrender. Four thousand Jews were killed in battle; another 5,000 either committed suicide or were slaughtered by the Romans after Gamla had fallen to them.

"The sole survivors were two women," historian Flavius Josephus wrote. "They survived because when the town fell they eluded the fury of the Romans, who spared not even babes in arms, but seized all they found and flung them from the citadel."

The site was reduced to rubble by the Romans and then lost to history for precisely 1,902 years. In 1968, Gamla was rediscovered during a systematic Israeli survey of the region. Today it is possible for visitors to stroll through

Overlooking the Sea of Galilee.

FACT

Vered Hagalil Guest Farm (between Tiberias and Rosh Pina; tel: 04-6935785; www.vered hagalil.com) was created by Yehuda Avni, who emigrated from Chicago to Israel in the late 1940s, and his Jerusalem-born wife, Yonah. They transformed barren land into a leisure complex.

The city of Tiberias, on the shores of the Sea of Gallilee.

the ancient streets of this community and inspect the remains of many ancient houses, and even a synagogue, all of which were constructed out of the Golan's somber black basalt stone.

Among the fields to the east of Gamla it is possible to find several prehistoric dolmens. These are Stone Age structures, which look like crude tables, with a large, flat stone bridging several supporting stones. They are generally considered to be burial monuments, and most are dated to about 4000 BC. Dolmens are found at several other sites around the Golan and the Galilee.

Jewel of the Galilee

Glowing like an emerald, its tranquil surface framed in a purplish-brown halo of mountains, the **Sea of Galilee** (Yam Kinneret) is probably the most breathtaking lake in the country. At 21km (13 miles) long and 11km (7 miles) wide, with a depth of no more than 45 meters (150ft), it may not be enormous by global standards, but it has, through some romantically inspired hyperbole, come to be known as a "sea" (the Sea of Galilee, the Sea of

Tiberias, and the Sea of Ginossar are its most popular names). In Hebrew it is called Yam Kinneret because it is shaped like a *kinnor*, a harp.

Not surprisingly, these bountiful shores have been inhabited for millennia, with the earliest evidence of habitation dating back 5,000 years to a cult of moon-worshipers that sprouted in the south. Some 3,000 years later the same lake witnessed the birth and spread of Christianity on its shores, while high up on the cliffs above, Jewish rebels sought refuge from Roman soldiers. The dramas of the past, however, have since faded into the idyllic landscape. Today it is new water sports, not new religions that are hatched on these azure shores

Around the lake

Descend Highway 869 to the lake and travel anticlockwise along 92 and then 87 to Capernaum. It was in the numerous fishing villages around the Sea of Galilee that Jesus found his first followers. The village of **Capernaum** ⓲ on the northern tip of the lake, became his second home. Here he is

said to have preached more sermons and performed more miracles than anywhere else.

It was a metropolis of sorts in its heyday, and at least five of the disciples came from here (it is after one of them, a simple fisherman named Peter, that the Galilee's most renowned fish gets its name). Today the site houses the elaborate remains of a 2nd-century synagogue – said to be built over the original one where Jesus used to preach. There is also a recently completed church, shaped like a ship, on what was believed to be the house of St Peter, a Franciscan monastery, and the colorful red domed roofs of the Greek Orthodox Church of the Seven Apostles.

In the neighboring town of **Ein Tabgha**, Jesus is said to have multiplied five loaves and two fishes into enough food to feed the 5,000 hungry people who had come to hear him speak. The modern **Church of the Multiplication** (daily 8.30am–5pm) was constructed over the colorful mosaic floor of a Byzantine shrine in 1982. Next to it stands the Church of Peter's Primacy.

It was standing on a hilltop overlooking the Sea of Galilee that Jesus proclaimed to the masses that had gathered below: "Blessed are the meek, for they shall inherit the earth." This well-known line from the Sermon on the Mount is immortalized by the majestic **Church and Monastery of the Beatitudes** (daily 8am–5pm; free). An octagonal church, it is set in well-maintained gardens, belongs to the Franciscan order and was built in the 1930s. Beneath the Church on Highway 90 (turning left at the Korazim Junction) is **Domus Galilaeae** (Mon-Sat 9am–12, 3pm–4.30pm; tel: 04-680 9100; www.domusgalilaeae.org), a resplendent 21st century monastery overlooking the Sea of Galilee. It was built a decade ago to fulfil the vision of Pope John Paul II to stress the Hebrew roots of Christianity.

Moving back south along Highway 90, you will first come to the towering cliffs of **Arbel**. Today a rock climbers' haven, during Roman times they served as a hideout for Bar Kochba and his Jewish rebels.

Nearby is **Ginosar**, an especially beautiful kibbutz with a luxurious

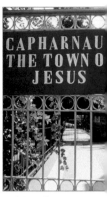

A claim to fame.

Restored remains of the synagogue at Caspernaum.

guesthouse. Ask some of the residents about the perfectly intact 2,000-year-old boat recently uncovered on the shores of the kibbutz.

Tiberias, a lakeside resort

The capital of the lake, **Tiberias** (Tverya) , has become known for its "fun in the sun" spirit. A sprawling city of 50,000, halfway down the west coast, it is one of the country's most popular resorts. On its new boardwalk, lined with seafood restaurants, you can dig into delicious St Peter's fish while enjoying a stunning view of the lake. On the marina you can have your pick of water-skiing or windsurfing, or go for a dip at one of the beaches along the outskirts of the city. During summer you'll need to dunk yourself in the water one way or another.

With all the distractions available in this popular playground, it's easy to forget that Tiberias is considered one of the four holy Jewish cities. To remind you, there are the tombs of several famous Jewish sages buried here, including the 12th-century philosopher Moses Maimonides and the

self-taught scholar Rabbi Akiva, who was killed by the Romans after the Bar-Kochba uprising.

When it was founded by Herod Antipas around AD 20, Tiberias failed to attract devout Jews because it was thought to be built over an ancient Jewish cemetery and so considered impure. But eventually economic incentives, as well as a symbolic "purification" of the city by a well-respected rabbi, cleared the way for settlement. During the 2nd and 3rd centuries it reached its zenith. With a population of 40,000, it became the focus of Jewish academic life. It was at Tiberias that scholars codified the sounds of the Hebrew script and wrote the Mishnah, the great commentary on the Bible.

By the eve of the Arab conquest of 636, Tiberias had become the most important Christian center outside Jerusalem. A 12th-century battle between Muslims and Crusaders destroyed the city, and, after being resettled, it was again reduced to rubble in 1837, this time by an earthquake. The repeated destruction of

The Jordan Valley at the south end of the Sea of Gallilee.

the city has, unfortunately, left only sparse remnants of its vibrant past. A few remains of Crusader towers dot the shoreline, and an 18th-century mosque is crammed in between ice-cream stands in the main square.

For historians and hedonists alike, Tiberias's main drawing-card is the **hot springs** on the main road, less than a kilometer south of Tiberias city center. There are many hypotheses about what caused this natural wonder. In fact, the same cataclysmic convulsions that millions of years ago carved the Jordan Rift also created these 17 springs that gush from a depth of 2,000 meters (6,500ft) to spew up hot streams of mineral-rich water. The therapeutic properties of the springs have been exploited for centuries.

Spa treatments

Opposite is the **Rimonim Mineral Tiberias Hotel**, which manages the hot springs and offers a range of treatments, from whirlpools to electro-hydrotherapy, that are reputed to cure everything from skin ailments to respiratory problems and, some claim, sterility. In the winter, a soak in these mineral-rich waters can be a soothing respite from the damp Galilee air.

You can see the original baths the Romans built in a fascinating little **museum** (Sun–Thur 10am–noon, 3–5pm; charge), in the **National Archeological Park** across the street. Also within this national monument, which is the site of the ancient city of Khamat, archeologists have uncovered a 2nd-century mosaic synagogue floor – undoubtedly the most exquisite ruins you'll find in Tiberias. Maimonides tomb on Ben Zakai Street, just south of the hotel district, is a popular site for Jewish pilgrims.

Just outside the city, 4km (2.5 miles) to the west along Highway 77, are the **Horns of Hittim** (Karnei Khitim), where in 1187 the Muslim forces of Saladin defeated the Crusaders in the decisive battle that brought an end to the Crusader Kingdom.

Baptism in the Jordan

Shortly after Jesus left Nazareth at the age of 30, he met John the Baptist preaching near the waters of the

TIP

Many kibbutzim, such as Sedot Nehemia, rent out inner tire tubes, on which you can float down the River Jordan – an extremely relaxing experience.

Jordan. In the river that the Bible so often describes as a boundary – and, more figuratively, as a point of transition – Jesus was baptized. Once thus cleansed, he set out on his mission. One tradition holds that the baptism took place at the point where the Sea of Galilee merges with the Jordan River near what is today Kibbutz Kinneret, 12km (7 miles) south of Tiberias on Highway 90.

The **Yardenit Baptismal Site** (Sat–Thur 8am–5pm, Fri 8am–4pm; tel: 04-675 9111; www.yardenit.com; charge) has been established just outside the kibbutz in order to accommodate the many pilgrims who still converge on the spot. There is also a rival "Site of the Baptism" further south, near Jericho.

Around the point where the lake merges with the Jordan River in the south are three kibbutzim: **Dganya Alef**, **Dganya Bet**, and **Kinneret**, ⑳ which were the first kibbutzim in the country. From the ranks of their members sprang many of Israel's legendary leaders. At the entrance to Dganya Alef is a Syrian tank, stopped in its tracks in

the 1948 War of Independence. Kinneret's cemetery, on the lakeside by Kinneret Junction, is the burial place for leading Israeli artists and is a marvelous place for tranquil contemplation but the beaches around the lake are expensive and often crowded and dirty.

Several settlements have guesthouses and camping facilities, including **Moshav Ramot**; **Kibbutz Ein Gev**, site of a gala music festival every spring; **Kibbutz Ha'On**, which had an ostrich farm before they became popular in other parts of the world; and **Kibbutz Ma'agan**. Also on the east coast is the Golan Beach and its water wonderland, the Luna Gal. At **Beit Zera**, on the southern tip of the lake, are the ruins of an ancient moon-worshiping cult.

Ancient baths dating from the Roman period are found on the southern Golan at **Khamat Gader** ㉑ (Sat–Wed 8.30am–5pm, Thu–Fri 8.30am–10.30pm; tel: *6393; www.hamat-gader.com; charge), near the Yarmuk River, and reached traveling eastward on Highway 98. Set in a secluded

Beit She'an's Roman theater.

mountain nature reserve and with Israel's only naturally flowing hot mineral springs, Khamat Gader is the country's most popular commercial tourist attraction. The site's renovated Roman baths and a range of other attractions, including treatments and massages, a water park, a crocodile farm and other animal exhibits, as well as restaurants, draw 500,000 visitors a year. Khamat Gader was established in the 2nd century AD by the Roman Empire's 10th Legion. The spa soon became recognized as the second-most beautiful baths in the empire, after Baiae in Italy, and was known internationally as the Three Graces – symbolizing charm, youth, and beauty. The baths were badly damaged by an earthquake in the 7th century and eventually abandoned in the 9th. The site also has an exclusive hotel and spa.

Beit She'an

Back along 98 and south on 90 for 30km (19 miles) is the ancient *tel* of **Beit She'an** ㉒, reflecting 6,000 years of civilization and billing itself as Israel's Pompeii. Near it in the Beit She'an National Park (daily 8am–4pm, until 5pm Apr–Sept; tel: 04-658 7189; charge) sits Israel's best-preserved Roman theatre, which once seated 8,000; and there is an archeological museum featuring a Byzantine mosaic floor. Beit She'an was once a member of the Roman Decapolis, meaning that it was one of the 10 most important cities in the Eastern Mediterranean. Other structures here include a colonnaded street, on the east side of which is a ruined temple that collapsed in an earthquake in the 8th century. Excavations have revealed 18 superimposed cities, so those in search of archeological intrigue should not miss Beit She'an.

The modern town, however, is a rather dull little place with little to offer. If you're thinking of going to Jordan, there is a Japanese-funded crossing here called the **Jordan River Crossing**, opened in 1999 and sometimes known as the **Sheikh Hussein Bridge**. It is 90 meters (nearly 300ft) long.

Easily accessible from the highway north of Beit She'an are the impressive ruins of the 12th-century Crusader

The Zodiac mosaic at Kibbutz Beit Alfa.

Khamat Gader hot springs and resort.

fortress of **Belvoir** (daily 8am–4pm, until 5pm Apr–Sept; tel: 04-658 1766; charge). Perched on the highest hill in the region, it offers an extensive view of the valleys below and of neighboring Jordan.

The Jordan Rift

South of Beit She'an and east of the Gilboa mountain range is one of the lowest points in Israel: the **Jordan Rift**. Encompassing the Jordan Valley and the Beit She'an Valley, it is part of the same 6,500km (4,000-mile) rift that stretches from Syria to Africa and is responsible for the lowest point on earth – the Dead Sea. Even here, at 120 meters (390ft) below sea level (it gets to 390 meters/1,280ft further south), it's like a kiln baking under an unrelenting sun during the summer. By way of comparison, Death Valley, California, the lowest point in the United States, is only 87 meters (285ft) below sea level. But nourished by the Jordan River, the Yarmuk River, and a network of underground springs (including the Spring of Kharod), this remains a lush region, bursting with

Uncover millennia of civilization at Beit She'an.

bananas, dates, and other fruit. It is home to some of Israel's most prosperous kibbutzim.

A water system not quite as historic as Megiddo's but impressive in its own way can be found at **Gan ha-Shlosha** (The Garden of Three) ㉓ (daily 8am–4pm, until 5pm Apr–Sept; tel: 04-658 6219; charge), west along 6667 from Bet She'an. Modern developers have managed to recreate a tiny piece of Eden in this stunning park. It is also known as Sachne, meaning "warm" in Arabic, because of the warm waters of **Ein Kharod** (The Spring of Kharod) that bubble up from under the earth to fill a huge natural swimming pool.

The Spring of Kharod actually starts at the foot of the Gilboa mountains, just southeast of Afula, and flows all the way to the Jordan, but for most of the way the warm waters are underground and diverted for use in local settlements. The only other spot where they surface is at Gid'ona, where the Israelite warrior Gideon supposedly assembled his forces 3,000 years ago, and which in more recent times served as the training spot for the forces of the Palmach, the elite fighting unit of the Jews before the State of Israel was created.

About a mile west of Gan ha-Shlosha is **Kibbutz Beit Alfa** (daily 8am–4pm, until 5pm Apr–Sept; tel: 04-653 2004; charge), where you'll find the country's best-preserved ancient synagogue floor. Discovered when kibbutz members were digging an irrigation channel, the 6th-century floor consists of a striking Zodiac mosaic and a representation of the sacrifice of Isaac.

Overlooking the length of the Jezreel Valley are the **Gilboa mountains**. Here King Saul met his untimely end at the hands of the Philistines, causing David to curse the spot forever: "Ye mountains of Gilboa, let there be no dew, nor rain upon you, neither fields of choice fruit" (II Samuel 20: 21–3). Return to Afula and travel eastward on 65 to Megiddo.

Israeli wine

Over the past two decades, Israeli wine has become something to take seriously.

Quality wines have taken their place on the nation's table, pushing aside the sweet red wines that were once produced for religious benedictions. The once poor condition of Israeli wine was not helped by vineyards being initially planted along the humid coastal plain. In recent decades, Israel's wineries have found that viticulture is an art best practiced in the cooler, drier inland hills of the Golan Heights and Galilee, the Judean Hills, and the Negev highlands.

The establishment of state-of-the-art wineries and importing know-how and the finest vine stock from France, California, and Australia has seen the local industry bloom. Most of all, the enthusiasm of a new generation of wine growers, and an ever-increasing, discriminating, and affluent local market have enabled over 200 companies, most of them boutique wineries, and another 100 small family winemaking farms, to make their mark on the local scene. Israeli wines have also developed an international reputation, winning prizes in overseas competitions. Some US$35 million worth of Israeli wine is exported annually and is available mainly in locations with large Jewish communities.

Winemaking is as ancient as the Old Testament. The grape was one of the seven biblical species and the Kiddush sanctification and drinking of wine during Sabbath and holiday meals has been a pillar of Judaism down the centuries.

The largest Israeli winery is Carmel Wines, established in 1882 by French Jewish philanthropist Baron Edmond de Rothschild. The Golan Heights winery founded in 1983 set new standards by introducing California know-how, while Israel's other major winery, Barkan, traces its history back to 1899, although the modern winery was built in 1988. These big three control 80 percent of Israel's domestic market.

Before the 1980s wine revolution, the most popular grapes cultivated were Emerald Riesling, Semillon, and Colombard for whites, and Petite Syrah, Grenache, and Carignan for red and rosés. When wine-growing shifted to the hills, new varieties were introduced such as Chardonnay, Muscat, and Sauvignon Blanc for whites and Cabernet Sauvignon, Merlot, Pinot Noir, and Zinfandel for reds and rosés to name but a few.

The proliferation of vineyards has transformed the Israeli countryside with the rich green rows of vineyards etched across hillsides in the otherwise dusty summer landscapes.

Experiencing the wine trails

Traveling or trekking for the more adventurous across wine trails has become a popular Israeli pastime and there are potential routes in five regions, which include history, archeology, and breathtaking landscapes: the Galilee and the Golan, the Carmel region, Central Israel, the Judean Hills, and Negev.

Suggested wine routes for tourists include the Judean Hills west of Jerusalem – travel along Road 38 south of Beit Shemesh through the Haela Valley, where David, it is believed, slew Goliath. There are eight wineries in close proximity to the highway: from north to south on the west side at Mony, Tzora, Teperburg, and Agur, and on the east side at Katalav, Ella Valley, and two Hans Sternbach Vineyards. www.mil-media.co.il/wine/winejerusalem.htm.

In the Galilee, travel north of Tsefat along Road 89 to the Yashfe Wineries, and then along Road 886 to the Dalton, Miles, and Rimon Wineries, while further north along Road 889 is the Galil Mountain Winery. www.mil-media.co.il/wine/winegalil.htm.

A proliferation of vineyards has transformed the Israeli landscape.

THE CRADLE OF THREE RELIGIONS

For pilgrims the Holy Land bears witness to the truth of the Bible, while the more cynical see tourism turning it into a religious Disneyland.

From the historical point of view there can be no dispute. This is where Abraham first spoke of monotheism, the place to which Moses led the Children of Israel, and where Solomon built his Temple. During the Roman period Christ preached in the Galilee and was crucified in Jerusalem. Five centuries later Mohammed prayed in Jerusalem, and Muslims believe that after his death he came to Jerusalem on horseback before ascending to heaven. For believers of all three religions the sites associated with these events are sacred. For non-believers there is still a historical and archeological fascination with the shrines.

Jews consider Hebron, Jerusalem, Tiberias, and Safed to be holy cities. In Hebron the Tomb of the Patriarchs – Abraham and family – is located at the Cave of Machpelah. In Jerusalem the Western Wall, the one remaining structure from the Temple complex, is considered the holiest shrine. Tiberias was where the oral law section of the Talmud was compiled.

The principal Christian sites are the Church of the Nativity in Bethlehem, where Christ was born, the Church of the Annunciation in Nazareth, where his family lived, and the Church of the Holy Sepulcher in Jerusalem, where he was crucified and rose again.

Muslims revere the Tomb of the Patriarchs in Hebron, as Abraham was also the father of the Arab people, and the Temple Mount where the El-Aqsa Mosque and the Dome of the Rock are holy sites, both associated with Mohammed.

Praying at the Western Wall.

The Sanctuary of Abraham complex, or Ibrahimi Mosque, in Hebron.

Muslims at prayer during a Friday of Ramadan outside the enclosure of the Cave of Machpelah (Cave of the Patriarchs).

Nazareth's monumental Basilica of the Annuciation.

The Church of the Holy Sepulcher, in the Christian Quarter of Jerusalem's Old City.

THE VIA DOLOROSA

Unlike the other Christian shrines in the Holy Land, which date back to Byzantine times, the traditional route of the Via Dolorosa was only established in the late Middle Ages. Since then Christians have re-enacted Christ's last journey, bearing a cross through the narrow, winding streets of Jerusalem's Old City. Every Friday Franciscan friars lead a procession along the Via Dolorosa from the Church of the Flagellation. These processions are especially colorful and intense on Good Friday.

There are 14 Stations of the Cross, the last five inside the Church of the Holy Sepulcher, where it is believed Christ was crucified, buried and resurrected. The Catholic and Orthodox Churches do not doubt the authenticity of the Via Dolorosa and the Holy Sepulcher, but some Protestants suggest that Calvary was at the Garden Tomb site, near the Damascus Gate.

...ing history to life – part of the scenery at Kings City, indoor biblical theme park in Ellat.

Ethiopian Christian pilgrims carrying a cross on the Via Dolorosa on Good Friday, commemorating the path Jesus traveled on the day of his crucifixion.

In Akko's old town.

THE NORTH COAST

Wander into the past in ancient Akko, then return to the present along the delightful north coast, with such pleasures as water sports, as well as grottoes and stunning views.

The stretch of Mediterranean coast between Haifa and the Lebanese border has excellent beaches and much more, including the ancient port city of Akko, the Persian gardens and tomb of the former Bahai leader Mirza Hussein Ali, and the Crusader fortress of Monfort. The coast stretches up to the delightful underground grottos at Rosh ha-Nikra on the Lebanese border, which are reached by cable car from the cliffs.

Akko ㉔ (www.akko.org.il) is probably the most atmospheric place in Israel. Battered over the centuries by successive invaders, it holds its own against the flow of time and tourism. The old sea wall, built by the Crusaders, overlooks the the Mediterranean and Haifa Bay, while Gothic archways and minarets mingle within the city. The ancient stone piers still give port to fishermen; the markets and cafés still overflow with friendly service and mysterious faces.

Chosen as the key port of the Crusader Kingdom by Baldwin I in 1104, and successfully defended against Simon Maccabeus and Napoleon Bonaparte, Akko has left behind the glorious fury of its past. Yet if it is a backwater, it is a dramatic one, as richly eloquent as any in the Holy Land.

Crusader capital

Akko is among the world's oldest known seaports. It was already a major population center when the Phoenicians dominated the northern coast. Its ancient industries include glassware (Roman historian Pliny credits Akko with discovering the art of glassmaking) and purple dyes – extracted from the *Purpura*, a sea-snail that gave the color its name. Around 333 BC, Alexander the Great passed through the then-flourishing Greek colony; Julius Caesar came 300 years later, in the process laying the stones of the first paved road in Roman Judea – from Akko to Antioch.

Main Attractions

Akko
Nahariya
Akhziv
Monfort
Rosh ha-Nikra

Repairing fishing nets in Akko port.

TIP

If you are in Akko during the Succot/Tabernacles Festival, don't miss the Fringe Theater Festival, Israel's equivalent of Scotland's Edinburgh Fringe. A major theme in much of the drama is the Jewish–Arab coexistence that the city exemplifies.

Shopping for loofahs in Akko's souk.

The Arabs held the city from AD 636 to 1104, fortifying and rebuilding much of it, yet Akko only hit its zenith during the Crusader era. The First Crusade was launched with the capture of Jerusalem in 1099. Five years later Akko fell, and the Crusaders, and the city developed into a major trading center by Genoese merchants, and renamed St Jean d'Acre, it became the principal port on the eastern Mediterranean rim.

Many of the most powerful and colorful Crusader orders – the Knights Templar, the Teutonic Order, the Order of St Lazarus, and the Hospitaller Order of St John – established centers here. In 1187 Saladin defeated the Europeans at the Horns of Hittim, and many Crusader cities fell into Saracen hands. Led by Philip Augustus of Spain and Richard the Lionheart of England, the knights of the Third Crusade recaptured Akko, and made it the capital of their kingdom in 1192. The remains left from the ensuing century of Crusader rule testify that this was the city's finest hour, before it fell once more into obscurity.

In the mid-1700s the port was revived by the Bedouin Sheikh Dahar el-Omar, followed by Akko's most notorious prime builder, the Ottoman Pasha Ahmad, known as "el-Jazzar"(the butcher) on account of his penchant for cruelty. His architectural legacies include Akko's best-known landmarks. In 1799, aided by British warships, el-Jazzar accomplished what much of Europe could not: he defeated Napoleon in a two-month siege. Turkish rule and the advent of the steamship ended Akko's importance as a port, and the town regained prominence only in the last years of the British Mandate, when its prison held hundreds of Jewish freedom fighters, including the Zionist leader Ze'ev Jabotinsky, and was the scene of a remarkable jailbreak in 1947. Since independence the city has retained its maritime character, and today it holds close to 54,000 residents, both Jews and Arabs. In 2001, Unesco declared Old Akko a World Heritage Site.

Entering Old Akko

To enter the Old City from the New follow the coastal strip or the parallel

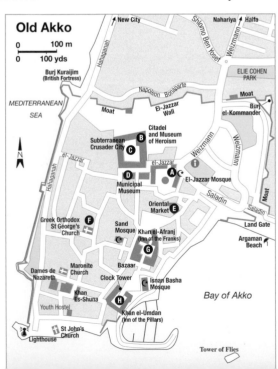

Old Akko

0   100 m
0   100 yds

Burj Kuraijim
(British Fortress)

MEDITERRANEAN
SEA

New City

Nahariya / Halfa

Shlomo Ben Yosef

Weizmann

ELIE COHEN PARK

Napoleon Bonaparte

Moat

Moat

El-Jazzar Wall

Burj el-Kommander

Citadel and Museum of Heroism   **B**

Subterranean Crusader City   **C**

Weizmann

Weizmann

el-Jazzar

el-Jazzar

D

A

El-Jazzar Mosque

Municipal Museum

Saladin

Moat

Saladin

Oriental Market   **E**

Greek Orthodox St George's Church   **F**

Sand Mosque

Khan el-Afranj (Inn of the Franks)

G

Land Gate

Argaman Beach

Bazaar

Dames de Nazareth

Maronite Church

Clock Tower

Isnan Basha Mosque

Khan Es-Shuna

H

Bay of Akko

Youth Hostel

Khan el-Umdan (Inn of the Pillars)

St John's Church

Lighthouse

Tower of Flies

Weizmann Street, where the **Visitors' Center** (daily 8.30am–5pm, until 6pm in summer; tel: 04-995 6706) stands in the Enchanted Park on your left before you enter the Old City. It's a good idea to stop off here, because considerable savings can be made by purchasing multiple-entrance tickets for the Old City's major sights. The center also shows movies about Akko, and exhibits archeological finds from the city.

Go into Old Akko through the dry moat and city walls, built by the Crusaders and later refortified. You can climb the wall here, and visit the northeastern command post, the Burj el-Kommandar, with a strategic view and a restored promenade, which continues on to Land Gate, at the bay.

As you enter the city, the first prominent structure is the elegant **el-Jazzar Mosque** ⒶA (dawn to dusk; charge), built in 1781–2 by "the butcher" and now the site of his tomb and that of his adopted son, Suleiman. Ringed with domed arcades and swaying palms, the mosque is considered the finest in Israel, and serves as a spiritual center for Israel's Muslim community. Except for a shrine containing a single hair from the beard of the prophet Mohammed, the interior is as stark as it is magnificent.

On the right-hand side of Weizmann Street, dominating the old city skyline, is the towering **Citadel and Museum of Heroism** ⒷB (Sat–Thur 9.30am–5pm, Fri 9.30am–noon; charge). Built by el-Jazzar on Crusader ruins, the fortress has been used variously as an arsenal and a barracks and, since Turkish times, as a prison. This was the center for the incarceration and execution of Jewish underground fighters during the British Mandate, and exhibits in the museum document this unsettling period.

Abutting the Citadel is the most interesting site of all, the dank and dramatic **Subterranean Crusader City** ⒸC (Sat–Thur 9am–4.30pm, Fri 9am–12.30pm; charge). While not excavated in their entirety, the halls of the sprawling complex contain such unusual historical testimony as carved fleur-de-lis insignia. Now reclaimed, the halls are the venue for the October **Akko Fringe Theater Festival**, part of the Succot Festival, which brings together the best

TIP

For information, maps, and tours when traveling to inaccessible spots such as Monfort Fortress, contact the Society for the Protection of Nature, tel: 02-623 2936 (Jerusalem), 03-638 8653 (Tel Aviv), or 04-866 4136 (Haifa).

St John's Crypt, a venue for theater in the Crusader City.

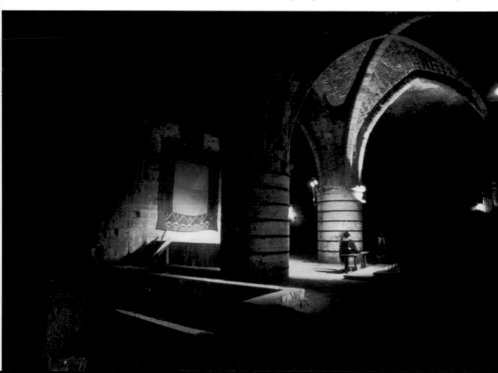

of Israel's experimental and alternative drama companies.

Turn into a small lane into a restored Turkish bathhouse, which is now the **Municipal Museum ❷** (same hours as Crusader City; tickets valid for both). The museum contains exhibits on archeology, Islamic culture, folklore, and weaponry.

Deeper into the maze-like streets of Akko is the Sand Mosque, which is off the **Souk**, the fascinating **Oriental Market ❸**. Further in is the **Greek Orthodox St George's Church ❻**, dedicated to two British officers who fell at Akko in 1799 and 1840. Of special interest are the *khans* (inns) that grace the portside area. These include the imposing **Khan el-Afranj** (Inn of the Franks) **❼**, near the **Bazaar**, and the unequalled **Khan el-Umdan** (Inn of the Pillars) **❽**. The lower storeys of the latter were used as stables and its upper ones as lodgings. Its geometric courtyard is memorable, and the clock tower (minus its clock) offers a glimmering view of the port.

Beneath the tower, wander by the fishing port and up along the sea wall, which houses one or two lovely cafes among its layered arches. The youth hostel is here, and, further on, the lighthouse; and from this corner you can take in the sunset view of the sea wall heading north to the new city, the old stone houses huddled in its tired embrace.

North to the border

Arching north from Akko along the coast on Highway 4 lies the final architectural gift from el-Jazzar, the austere spine of the **Turkish Aqueduct**, which once ran 15km (9 miles) to the spring at **Kabri**, now a picnic and camping site.

Just north of Akko, the **Baha'i Tomb and Gardens** (daily 9am–4pm) mark the burial site and villa of Mirza Hussein Ali, an early leader of the Baha'i faith, known also as Baha'u'llah (Glory to God). Surrounding the tomb is a lovely formal Persian garden. To the north is Kibbutz Lohamei HaGeta'ot, which has museums dedicated to the Warsaw Ghetto fighters and the children who perished in the Holocaust (Sun–Thu 9am–4pm, Sat 10am–5pm).

Further north, is **Nahariya ㉕**, a

At the entrance to the grottoes.

resort community founded in 1934 by German Jews. Its most noticeable landmark is the quiet stream, the Ga'aton, which flows down the center of the main street.

From here continue northward along Highway 4. **Akhziv National Park** ㉖, 5km (3 miles) north of Nahariya along Highway 4 (daily 8am–5pm, until 7pm July–Aug; tel: 04-982 3263; charge) is a rocky coast and beach with bays, lagoons, deep natural seawater pools, and man-made seawater pools, shallow enough for children to splash in. Also here are the remnants of an ancient settlement and extensive, grassy lawns.

Several kilometers further north turn inland along Route 899 where, at the Shlomi junction, lies an intriguing natural formation. The **Rainbow Arch** was formed when a section of the cliff edge dissolved, leaving a large, almost perfect arch. From the roadside the marked footpath is a gentle uphill stroll to the arch and panoramic view.

Some 15km (9 miles) east of the coast along Highway 899, atop a steep ridge, and accessible only by footpaths, lies **Monfort Fortress** ㉗ (daily 8am–4pm, until 5pm Apr–Sept; tel: 04-985 6004; charge), the most important of a string of Crusader forts, now set in the Yehiam Fortress National Park.

Rosh ha-Nikra

On the way back to the coast, along the final few kilometers to the Lebanese frontier, there towers the rocky border point of **Rosh ha-Nikra** ㉘, Israel's northernmost coastal limit. The view from the chalk-white cliffs set off against the crashing azure waves is entrancing, but it is Rosh ha-Nikra's **grottoes**, formed by millennia of erosion, that are the prime attraction. A cable car operates year-round (daily 8.30am–4pm, until midnight mid-July–mid-Aug; tel: 04-985 7108; www.rosh-hanikra.com; charge) takes you down over the pounding tide, and there is also a footpath.

Atop the cliff, the southernmost edge of the range known as the **Ladder of Tyre** offers a view over the now walled-up railway tunnel that once led to Lebanon. On a clear day, looking south, one can just make out **Haifa port** (see page 211).

The cable-car ride to the Rosh ha-Nikra grottoes may only take a couple of minutes, but is touted as being the steepest in the world.

The old port of Akko.

The Baha'i Temple.

HAIFA

Haifa is a busy working port where Jews and Arabs live in relative harmony. The domed Baha'i shrine and resplendent gardens are the most prominent landmarks.

In 1750 the Bedouin Sheikh Dahar el-Omar destroyed a squalid coastal village because its inhabitants neglected to pay homage. The town lay in ruins for eight years, until, having made his point, the sheikh rebuilt it and improved its natural harbor. **Haifa** ㉙ grew from that unpropitious beginning, and has since evolved into a bustling port city and maritime center.

Today Haifa (www.haifa.muni.il) is Israel's third-largest city, one of the centers of the nation's renowned high-technology industries. From its original cradle on the narrow coastal strip between the Mediterranean and the Carmel range, Haifa has marched up Mount Carmel, settling itself lazily among the gentle slopes. The city is built on three levels, rising from its original location along the waterfront. The second level, in the Carmel foothills, is Hadar Ha-Karmel, the central business district and the oldest residential area. The newest neighborhoods have climbed all the way to the crests of the peak, and cling to its sides, connected by a network of excellent roads. At the very apex is the **Carmel Center**, where some of the city's most attractive homes and exclusive hotels and shops are located. Seeing the glorious views of the bay and azure Mediterranean, it is no surprise that

the affluent have built their lives at the mountain's summit. In addition, however, an ugly urban sprawl of industrial chimneys and apartment blocks spreads northward to Akko. Haifa itself has a population of more than 300,000, while over 600,000 people live in the metropolitan area.

Historic port

Haifa had been known since the 2nd century as a safe haven for passing ships, situated as it was along one of the Mediterranean's oldest sea lanes.

Main Attractions

Carmel Center
Carmelite Monastery
Seafront and Port
German Colony
Baha'i Gardens and Temple
Hadar
Carmelit

Looking down over the German Colony.

But at the time of its premature destruction in the mid-18th century it was little more than an assemblage of huts, with fewer than 250 inhabitants. Reborn, it thrived, and by 1890 some 8,000 people lived within its limits. Yet it took a combination of railroads, war, and the need for deeper seawater ports to catapult the city into significance in the 20th century.

The causes were interlinked: under the impending pressures of war, the Ottoman Turks built the Hejaz Railroad connecting Haifa to Damascus in the north, while the British started the Sinai Military Railroad, which was later to link Haifa to Qantara on the Suez Canal. At the end of the war, when the British controlled Palestine under a League of Nations mandate, they gradually modernized Haifa's port, rejecting Akko's waters as too shallow for the bigger ships of the age.

With a steady increase in maritime traffic, and a continuing stream of immigrants, the population reached 25,000 by 1918. By 1923 it had more than doubled, and by 1931 doubled

Viewpoint over Haifa.

again to exceed 100,000. After Israel's independence in 1948 further development of the port became essential. Israel's land borders were sealed, and Haifa's port became the Jewish state's only opening to the world.

From blue collar to high-tech

Today the port, monitored by a centralized computer system, bristles with massive electronically operated cargo-handling equipment and berths the world's seagoing mammoths. It was Israel's premier maritime center, but it has now been overtaken by Ashdod. But Haifa has also become a versatile industrial center. Known affectionately as the "Red City" because of its longstanding identification with the nation's labor movement, it was for many years essentially a blue-collar city, though with the advent of high-tech industries fewer and fewer people perform manual work.

At the northern edge of the city an industrial zone accommodates an extensive petrochemical industry, oil

refineries, and many small manufacturing units. At the southern end is a large high-tech park, home to companies like Intel, Apple, IBM, Google and Qualcomm.

Despite its industrial base, Haifa is a highly cultured city with a large number of museums, a theater company, and two universities – Haifa University and the Technion, Israel Institute of Technology. The latter is the country's oldest university and one of the world's leading science and technology universities. Many of Israel's foremost high-tech entrepreneurs are Technion graduates, and two of the university's professors were awarded the Nobel Prize for Chemistry in 2004 for describing the way cells destroy unwanted proteins, and another in 2011 for the discovery of quasicrystals.

Arab communities

A Saturday bus service is unusual in Israel. The fact that it happens in Haifa reflects the formative influence of its Arab citizens on the city's social patterns. There has always

been a significant Arab presence in Haifa, and Jews and Arabs here have a long history of mutual give-and-take. Israeli Arabs constitute about 10 percent of Haifa's population, and the city attracts thousands more every day from the surrounding villages. Although there are some mixed areas, most Arabs have remained in their own neighborhoods, in many cases in the same places where their families have lived for generations.

There are two distinctive Arab communities in Haifa. **Wadi Nisnas** is one of the area's oldest neighborhoods, adjacent to Hadar, near Beit Ha-Gefen, Haifa's Arab-Jewish community center. With its buildings of massive sandstone blocks, window grilles, and arched doorways, its prevalence of Arabic and Middle Eastern music, and the range of exotic food and clothing for sale, Wadi Nisnas is a graphic reminder that Haifa stands with one foot firmly planted in the Levant.

In sharp contrast to Wadi Nisnas, **Kababir**, perched high on a ridge overlooking the Mediterranean, is

TIP

Haifa is well served by Israel Railways. The main line from Tel Aviv stops at Hof ha-Karmel at the southern entrance to the city, then at Bat Galim, the city center, and carries on through the northern suburbs to Akko and Nahariya.

The cable car to Carmel Heights.

an Arab neighborhood of sumptuous dwellings and lush gardens. Established as an independent village in 1830, the community opted for annexation to Haifa when the State of Israel was established in 1948, anticipating the benefits of schools, health services, water and sewage systems. The majority of residents are Ahmdya Muslims, a small Islamic sect distinct from the larger Shiite and Sunni groups in Wadi Nisnas. Although fully integrated into the Haifa municipality, Kababir is administered locally by a committee of six elders elected annually by the men of the community. A new mosque, completed in 1984, is the only one of its kind in the Middle East.

The Carmel slope

The **Carmel Center** (Ha-Karmel) **Ⓐ** is where most of Haifa's hotels are located. Here, atop towering Mount Carmel, panoramic scenes of the city, sea, and mountains burst into view at every turn. Shops line Shderot ha-Nasi along with sidewalk cafes and restaurants specializing in kosher,

Chinese, Italian, and Middle Eastern foods.

Atop the crest of Mount Carmel, reached by traveling south along Shderot ha-Nasi, looms the contemporary features of the **University of Haifa**, its distinctive tower thrusting resolutely against the sky. Founded in 1972, the university serves the entire northern district, and has branches in some of the more remote areas. The 25-floor **Eshkol Tower**, designed by the Brazilian architect Oscar Niemeyer, offers an unparalleled view of northern Israel, which makes the 5km (3-mile) journey here from the Carmel Center well worthwhile.

Tucked within the mountainous folds of upper Haifa are a number of hidden treasures. On the slope near the promenade of the Carmel Center is the **Mane-Katz Museum Ⓑ** (Sun–Mon, Wed–Thur 10am–4pm, Tue 2–6pm, Fri 10am–1pm, Sat 10am–2pm; tel: 04-838 3482; free) is housed in the building where the Jewish-French Expressionist lived and worked in his later years. Besides his paintings and sculptures,

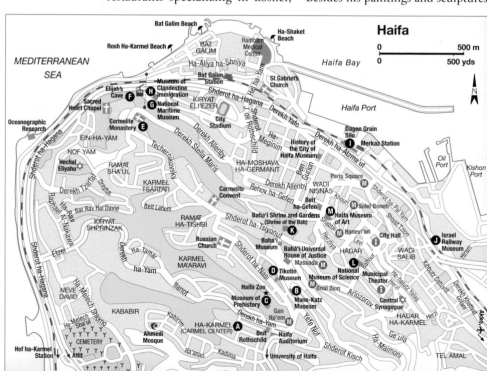

the display also includes his personal collection of Judaica and antique furniture. A short distance away is the Edenic Mothers' Garden, the biggest of Haifa's parks – and there are nearly 400 of them. Among curving paths, flowers, and picnicking families is the **Museum of Prehistory and Haifa Zoo**  (Sun–Thur 8am–3pm, Fri 8am–1pm, Sat 10am–2pm; tel: 04-837 1833; charge), displaying finds of the Carmel area, which way back in prehistory was home to Neanderthal Man. The zoo is pleasant and well maintained.

Israel's only museum of Japanese art, the **Tikotin Museum** **D** (Sun–Mon, Wed–Thur 10am–5pm, Tue 4–8pm, Fri 10am–1pm, Sat 10am–4pm; tel: 04-838 3554; charge), is back in the heart of the Carmel Center, at 89 Shderot ha-Nasi.

Going down the slope for several kilometers, along Shderot ha-Nasi and then turning left down Techernikovsky, you reach that part of the city known as **French Carmel**, an expensive but cosy residential district.

The Carmelite Monastery

At the end of this area, Mount Carmel levels off into a promontory, and this is the site of the **Carmelite Monastery** **E** (daily 6am–1.30pm, 3–6pm; tel: 04-833 7758), the world center of the Carmelite Order. Situated at the end of the mountain, along Stella Maris Road, the church commands one of the most spectacular views of the city. The site was selected in the 12th century by a small band of Crusaders who settled there to devote themselves to asceticism, solitude and prayer. The order, which grew from that beginning, was officially founded by St Brocard in the 13th century. The church was built in the 18th century, over a grotto associated in the Jewish and Christian traditions with the prophet Elijah and his disciple Elisha. The interior dome depicts events in their lives, and a small museum displays local archeological discoveries.

Elijah's Cave **F** (Sun–Thur 8am–5pm; free) can be reached by a footpath from the monastery. The prophet is said to have rested and meditated

This eagle statue is one of a pair perched on pillars flanking the gate leading into the Baha'i Gardens.

Elaborate ceiling at the Carmelite Monastery.

A spot of German architecture sits on the hillside.

here in the 9th century BC, before his momentous encounter with the Baalists on one of the peaks of the Carmel range. After leaving the cave, he is said to have climbed to the top of Mount Carmel, where an altar had been erected by the worshipers of Baal and other Phoenician deities. Elijah challenged their priests to light a flame under a sacrifice by means of their religious powers.

According to tradition, the pagan priests failed; Elijah called upon the Lord and the flames were instantly ignited. Ahab, the Jewish king who had angered the Lord by worshiping Baal, was witness to the event. Rejecting paganism, he ordered the massacre at the Kishon River of all the Baalists. The event is recorded in detail in I Kings 18:17–46. Some Christians believe the cave to have sheltered the Holy Family on the way back from Egypt, and know it also as the **Grotto of the Madonna**.

The surprisingly attractive Dagon Grain Silo.

Along the seafront

Opposite the monastery itself, a sinuous platform marks the upper terminal of Haifa's cable-car system (daily 10am–5.30pm, Fri 10am–1.45pm; tel: 04-833 5970). The system ferries passengers from the Carmel Heights down to the seaside Bat Galim Promenade. Haifa has some glorious beaches, and because of the shape of Israel's coastline, Bat Galim Beach is the only one in the country facing north, making it the best for surfing.

It is an easy walk to the **National Maritime Museum** ⓖ (Sun–Wed 10.30am–4pm, Thur 4–7pm, Fri 10.30am–1pm, Sat 10.30am–3pm; tel: 04-853 6622; charge) and the **Museum of Clandestine Immigration** ⓗ (Sun–Thur 8.30am–4pm, Fri 8.30am–noon; tel: 04-853 6249; charge). The immigration museum contains the tiny ship in which Jewish immigrants sought to evade the British Mandatory government's blockade in the years before the State of Israel was declared.

Adjacent to the port area, a 3km (2-mile) bus or taxi ride northward along the coast, is the **Dagon Grain Silo** ⓘ, probably one of the only architecturally pleasing silos in the world. Besides its commercial use

HAIFA MUSEUMS

In Hadar, the level above the waterfront (use the Carmelit subway), the original edifice of the country's preeminent Institute of Technology, the **Technion**, has been preserved as an architectural landmark and is now the home of the exciting hands-on **National Museum of Science** (Sun–Mon, Wed–Thur 9am–4pm, Tue 9am–7.30pm, Fri 10am–2pm, Sat 10am–6pm; tel: 04-862 8111; charge). The magnificent old building, constructed in 1924, was designed by Alexander Baerwald, combining European lines with an eastern dome, crenellated roofs, and intricate mosaics. The Technion recently expanded into a large new campus in the Neve Shannon neighborhood; free tours are offered daily.

Beit Dagon (Palmer Square; tel: 04-866 4221; guided tours Sun–Fri 10.30am) explains how grains of wheat have been cared for from ancient times.

The **Israel Oil Industry Museum** (2 Tuvia St; Sun–Thur 8.30am–3.30pm; tel: 04-865 4237) is not concerned with the Middle East's "black gold" but instead illustrates the production processes of edible oils, yesterday and today.

The **Israel Electric Corporation Visitors Center** (Salman Road, Shemen Beach; Sun–Thur 8am–3pm; tel: 04-864 6176; free, but book in advance) is for those who have always wanted to visit a power station.

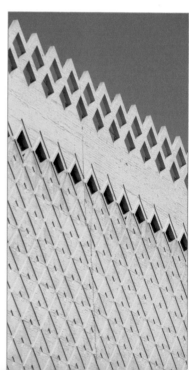

for receiving and storing grain from ships anchored in the port, the silo houses a **museum** (guided tours Sun–Fri 10.30am; tel: 04-866 4221; free) devoted to the history of bread- and beer-making. An assortment of old implements is displayed with explanatory photographs, murals, and mosaics, and there is a working model of the silo's own mechanized system.

Hugging the waterfront, the **Israel Railway Museum** ❿ (Sun–Thur 8am–4pm; tel: 04-856 4293; charge), opposite 40 Khativat Golani Street, is several kilometers farther south. Housed in an attractive old Ottoman building, it pays tribute to the importance of the railway in Haifa's history. Steam engines that hauled freight from the hinterlands to the port are preserved, along with luxury passenger cars, ornate sleeping cars, and wood-paneled dining cars. Visitors are encouraged to climb aboard and try out the accommodation.

The German Colony

Several streets inland from the port is the **German Colony**, one of the most attractive parts of Haifa, which can be reached along Derekh Allenby from the National Maritime Museum, or by descending Shederot ha-Tsiyonut from Shderot ha-Nasi. Built in 1868 by the German Templars, this area has become gentrified in recent years with delightful old houses and gardens. At 11 Ben Gurion Avenue is the History of the City of Haifa Museum (Mon–Wed 10am–4pm, Thu 4–7pm, Fri 10am–1pm; charge; tel: 04-851 2030). The beauty of the German Colony has been further accentuated by the recently completed **Baha'i Gardens** ⓚ, rising majestically up the hill, with the gold-domed Baha'i Shrine at their peak.

Hadar

The **Haifa National Museum of Science** ⓛ (see box) is housed in the heart of Hadar on Balfour Street, in the original 1920s building of the Technion, Israel Institute of Technology. The exhibits are child-friendly and fun for adults and children alike. The new **Haifa Museum of Art** ⓜ (Mon–Wed 10.30am–4pm,

FACT

The 31,000-seat Sammy Ofer Stadium, opened in 2014 at the southern edge of the city, is the home of Maccabi Haifa, one of Israel's top football teams.

Elijah's Cave, below the Carmelite Monastery.

A day trip away from Haifa in the Carmel Winery, in Zikhron Ya'akov.

Dining out in the German Colony.

Thur 4–7pm, Fri 10.30am–1pm, Sat 10.30am–3pm; charge; tel: 04-852 3255) at the southern edge of Hadar, on Shabtai Levy Street, is crammed with displays. Comfortable viewing from good vantage points isn't always possible, but the variety and quality of the collections make a visit worth the effort. Special exhibitions are occasionally held. Work by contemporary Israeli artists is exhibited at the Chagall Artists' House, established in 1964 at 24 Hazionut Boulevard (Sun–Thur 9am–1pm, 4–7pm, Sat 10am–1pm; tel 04-852 2355; free). Marc Chagall (1887–1985) visited Israel eight times, and his work can be found in the Knesset and in the Hadassah Medical School in Jerusalem.

Carmel Tunnels

Opened in 2010, the Carmel Tunnels serve as a city bypass from the southern entrance of the city, running 6.5km (4 miles) under the mountain due west to the Checkpost Interchange. In the rush hour a 60-minute journey has now been reduced to five minutes. The tunnel breaks in the middle, enabling vehicles to exit to Neve Shanan on Mount Carmel. This is a toll tunnel costing NIS 7.50 for each section – thus NIS 14.90 for the full 6.5 kilometers. Unlike Israel's other toll roads, payment is by cash at toll booths, except for those vehicles that register in advance and thus pay automatically using license plate recognition technology.

Israel's only subway

One block up the hill from the *falafel* stands of He-halutz is the Hadar entrance to the **Carmelit**, Israel's only subway. While most visitors are accustomed to subways, the Carmelit is one of a kind. Its tunnel, hacked through the interior rock of the mountain, operates on the same principle as San Francisco's cable cars: one train hurtling down from the Carmel Center at the top of the mountain hauls the other train up the steep incline from sea level. Even the cars are designed at an angle. From top to bottom, the trip takes seven minutes.

The Baha'i Complex

The world's longest hillside gardens are to be found in Haifa's Baha'i Complex, home to the headquarters of the Baha'i religion.

Dominating the Mount Carmel hillside in Haifa, the Baha'i Complex includes the world's longest hillside gardens, as well as the golden-domed Baha'i Shrine and the palatial Seat of the Universal House of Justice (Baha'i World Headquarters).

The centerpiece of the hillside garden, midway down on terrace number 10 (of 19), is the gold-domed Shrine of the Bab. Completed in 1953, the building contains the tomb of Siyyad Ali Mohammed – the Bab – a Muslim in Persia who proclaimed the coming of a "Promised One" in 1844. He was executed for heresy in 1850, and his disciples brought his remains to Haifa in 1909.

Baha'ism and the Haifa link

Haifa became the center of Baha'i activity because the man that the Baha'is believe was the "Promised One" – Mirza Hussein Ali, Baha'u'llah – was exiled from Persia and settled in what was then Palestine under the Ottoman Turkish Empire. He is buried near Akko where he died in 1892. Baha'u'llah's son, Abbas Effendi, instructed believers to purchase large tracts of Mount Carmel overlooking Haifa Bay, which Baha'u'llah had foreseen as the world headquarters of the Baha'i faith.

The Baha'i religion emerged from Muslim society (though the Baha'is hate to be called a Muslim sect, which they are not). The Baha'u'llah transformed the religion into a universal one; he taught that he himself and the Bab were the latest of nine manifestations of God after Abraham, Moses, Christ, Mohammed, Krishna, Buddha, and Zoroaster. Some 2 million of the world's estimated 5 million Baha'is live in India; other concentrations are in Iran, where they are a persecuted group, and the US.

Few Baha'is live in Israel, but some 700 volunteers from abroad serve in the Baha'i World Center, the spiritual and administrative center of Baha'ism. The Baha'is do not engage in any missionary activity in Israel.

In addition to the Shrine of the Bab and the Seat of the Universal House of Justice – the faith's international governing body – two administrative buildings are being constructed.

Extending from the summit of Mount Carmel, this unique hillside terraced garden, completed in 2001, spreads out spectacularly along the northwestern slope of the mountain. The hillside garden has a classically European ambience. The terraces are lined with stone balustrades, fountains, and stone eagles. Black iron gates give access to the trees, bushes, flowerbeds, and neatly manicured, bright-green lawns. But the garden's crowning glory is its breathtaking panoramic view of Haifa Bay and the Mediterranean Sea stretching serenely to the horizon.

Amram Mitzna, the former Labor Party leader who was mayor of Haifa when the gardens were first opened, said: "We have been incredibly lucky. Not many cities get a park like this for free."

Indeed, the Shrine of the Bab and the Baha'i Gardens are open to the public for free. The inner gardens are open daily 9am–noon, the outer gardens daily from 9am–5pm. There is an English tour every day at noon except Wednesdays. First come first serve: www.ganbahai.org.il. Remember to dress modestly. Tours start from the top: from the bottom in the German Colony opposite Beit ha-Gefen, and at 61 Yefe Nof, finishing midway at Zionism Avenue near the Golden Shrine..

The Baha'i Gardens, with the Shrine of the Bab at their center.

Fishermen near Gaza City.

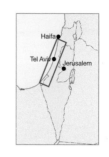
CENTRAL AND SOUTH COAST

Crusader ruins, pioneer settlements, and citrus groves line the coast, but for most people the sand and the surf are the major attractions.

The Mediterranean coast means many things to Israelis. It is, first and foremost, the spine of the country, in terms of population as well as geography. The coastal plain is the site of the country's most luxurious hotels and some of its most important ruins. It is a prime transportation corridor and the location of the fertile Sharon Plain, the source of Israel's citrus industry.

For the average Israeli the Mediterranean coast means one thing: recreation. From April to October thousands of bronzed sabras flock in droves to the sands, to bake in the sun, play paddleball along the water's edge, swim, wade, run, sail, tan, and then watch everyone else do the same. While many of the best-known beaches are a kaleidoscope of human activity in the summer, there are lesser-known ones, which offer fewer facilities but equally pleasant access to sun and sand. It is not unusual to take a dip against a backdrop of an ancient aqueduct, or the looming silhouette of a power plant.

From the environs of Caesarea in the north to Ashkelon in the south, Israel's central and south coast is citrus country – the fertile Sharon Plain. However, Israel's growing population means that the orange groves are being transformed into housing estates, industrial zones, and shopping centers. Yet the citrus crop was never

indigenous to the area, and well into the 19th century the central coast was a miasma of malarial swamps. By the turn of the century, however, the development of pumps, which could raise the buried groundwater to the soil surface, and the importing from Australia of eucalyptus trees, which soak up surplus moisture, harnessed the land to the needs of its pioneer settlers, who set about draining the marshes and cultivating new orchards.

Today, citrus is Israel's most valuable agricultural export. The varieties under

Main Attractions
Mount Carmel National Park
Zikhron Ya'akov
Caesarea
Netanya
Herzliya
Rishon Le-Tsiyon
Ashdod
Ashkelon
Yad Mordekhai

Planting a seedling at a coastal kibbutz.

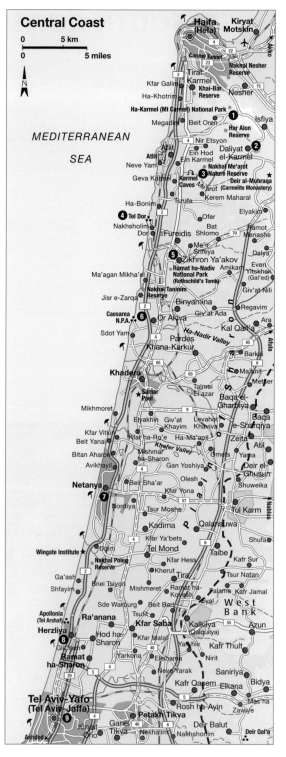

Central Coast

0   5 km

0   5 miles

cultivation run the spectrum, with the sweet "Jaffa" oranges and their kin dominating along the coast, grapefruit mainly thriving in the thicker, river-washed soil farther inland, and lemons flourishing on the hills. The citrus harvest is from November to April, and this is when the fruits are at their most intoxicating, swinging ripely off their evergreen branches, their fragrance wafting out over the road to the sea.

The Carmel range

The Carmel range takes its name from the words Kerem-El, meaning "Vineyard of God." It runs for about 25km (16 miles) along the coast, rising to some 500 meters (1,650ft) and falling steeply to the Mediterranean. Today it contains **Mount Carmel National Park ❶** (daily 24hrs; tel: 04-822 8983; charge per car, extra charge for overnight camping), located south of Haifa University on Highway 672 but also accessible from Road 70 west from the Elyakim Interchange, and from Road 4 east from the Oren Junction. This is Israel's largest national forest preserve, lush with hilly woodlands, well-marked hiking trails, picnic facilities, and breathtaking vistas. Almost one-tenth of the 8,500-hectare (21,000-acre) park is a nature preserve where deer and gazelle roam freely.

An extra fee is charged for entering the **Khai Bar Nature Reserve** (daily 8am–3pm; tel: 04-832 0648; charge), where rare fallow deer from Iran, previously extinct in this region, have been reintroduced.

Just beyond the park, to the south on 672, tucked among the slopes and valleys of the Carmel range, are the Druze villages of **Daliyat el-Karmel ❷** and **Isfiya**. Surrounded by tawny precipices plunging to verdant valleys carpeted with tangled foliage, the villages are easily accessible by car or bus. The marketplaces offer traditional handicrafts and pleasant cafes where Turkish coffee and succulent pastries can be enjoyed under the trees. The **Carmelite Monastery** at **Muhraqa**, nearby, stands over the site where Elijah defeated the Baalists.

Winding down the mountainside on Highway 721, the road arcs through the gorges of a severe, astonishingly attractive landscape: the region is known as **Little Switzerland**. Kibbutz Beit Oren, tucked between the pines here, operates a guesthouse. At the crest of the ridge lies the ultimate view of the Carmel coast.

Just to the south, on the right-hand side of the road is the **Nakhal Me'arot Nature Reserve** ❸ (daily 8am–4pm, until 5pm Apr–Sept; tel: 04-984 1750; charge). Declared a UNESCO World Heritage Site, there is evidence here of human settlement dating back 1 million years, with stone carvings and and shell-necklaces from as long as 12,000 years ago.

Turn left at Highway 4 and left again onto 7111 to reach Ein Hod (also called En Hod). Ensconced amid gnarled olive trees and Moorish arches, the artists' colony of **Ein Hod** was conceived in 1953 as a rugged oasis of creativity, and today provides living and working space for some 200 artisans.

The gallery and restaurant in the town center warmly welcome company.

The Carmel coast

Down on the coast you will find the imposing Crusader fortress of **Atlit**, perched wearily on the rocks above the Mediterranean. At present the ruins are off-limits to the general public, as this is a military zone.

Slightly farther south, past Ha-Bonim Beach and the moshav of the same name, you come to one of Israel's most active ongoing archeological sites: **Tel Dor** ❹. The excavations have as yet only unearthed a fraction of this sprawling ancient city, but the ruins on display, including Canaanite, Israelite, and Hellenistic finds, indicate a vast metropolis of tens of thousands of inhabitants. Archeology aside, this is a site of enormous natural beauty, the lagoons and water washing against the cliffs complementing the rolling hills of Mount Carmel inland.

Abutting the *tel* just to the south is the lovely beach of **Nakhsholim** (Breakers), and there is a kibbutz of the same name with a roomy guesthouse and a friendly

Israel is a nation of coffee lovers.

The studio of Marcel Janco in Ein Hod.

Allow at least half a day for a visit to Caesara.

Zikhron Ya'akov.

atmosphere. In the grounds is an illuminating **Glass Factory Museum** (Sun–Thur 9am–2pm, Fri 9am–1pm, closed Sat ; tel: 04-639 0950; book in advance), housed in a turn-of-the-century building that was once a glass factory. The museum holds a selection of treasures culled from underwater excavations, and their exhibits range from Phoenician catapult balls to relics dating from Napoleon's naval misadventures off this shore in 1799.

Along the length of this coast, rows of vegetables sheathed in white plastic dot the roadsides, often under the stately presence of towering cypress or eucalyptus trees. Toward evening, when the hues in the sky drift into violet, lilac, and pale orange, the landscape looks as if it has been painted by Claude Monet.

Take a turning inland just after Nakhsholim on 7011, and after a short distance south on 4, passing the tranquil Arab town of Fureidis (Paradise), you reach the town of **Zikhron Ya'akov ❺**, which was established in 1882 in memory of James (Jacob) Rothschild, the father of the great benefactor of Israel's first settlers, Baron Edmond (Benjamin) de Rothschild.

The **Aaronson House and Museum** (Sun–Thur 8.30am–3pm, Fri 8.30am–1pm; tel: 04-639 0120; charge), just off the main street (Hameyasdim Street), details the lives of Aaron and Sarah Aaronson. Aaron was a botanist who, in the early 1900s, isolated durable strains of wheat for cultivation in Palestine. He and his sister are enshrined in legend because of their role in organizing the pro-British "Nili" spy ring during resistance to the oppressive Turkish regime. Caught by the Turks, and afraid she would give away information, Sarah shot herself in her home in 1917.

Rothschild's Tomb

A minute's drive to the south on 652 is **Rothschild's Tomb**, built in the 1950s to house the remains of the Parisian banker and his wife Adelaide. Situated amid a fragrant garden (Yad ha-Nadiv) of date trees, sage, roses, and other flowers, this sensuously designed landscape opens up to a magnificent panorama of the Upper Sharon, while

a concrete map indicates the locations of the settlements made possible by Rothschild (whose generosity lingers today in the bar-room phrase "put it on the Baron's account"). The tomb itself is contemporary and tasteful; the site, all told, is one of the most significant in Israel.

Heading south toward Caesarea on Highway 4, one immediately enters the area of the excellent birdwatching country of the **Kabara Marshes**, where some of the first Zionist settlements were established in the early 20th century. The Crocodile River bears testimony to the once intimidating nature of the terrain, but the last crocodile here died in the early 20th century. You can view the birds and the river on the coast just south of Ma'agan Mikha'el, in the Nakhal Taninim Reserve.

Crusaders at their best

Although its greatest historical importance was as a Roman colony, it is to the Crusader ruins at **Caesarea** ❻ (daily 8am–4pm, until 6pm Mar–Sept; tel: 04-626 7080; charge) that tourists flock by the busload today, and these ruins are as impressive as any in Israel. It takes a good half-day just to take in the site, while the visual impact of Crusader arches, crumbling walls, and smashed Roman pillars is constantly disarming, and attests to the layered history of habitation here. Despite being one of Israel's most lauded archeological sites, Caesarea is difficult to reach via public transportation, which means that individual tourists must either rent a car, stay overnight nearby, or join a tour. Note that Caesarea cannot be reached from the coastal motorway (Highway 2), but only by Highway 4 farther inland.

While settlements in the region date back as far as Phoenician times, the history of the city only really began with the Romans in 22 BC, when the royal master-builder Herod the Great founded it, naming it in honor of the emperor Augustus. Around the year 6 BC it was designated the official residence of the governors of Judea, and for 500 years Caesarea was the capital of Roman administration in Palestine. At the time of Jesus, Pontius Pilate lived here, and St Paul was imprisoned here for two years before being sent to Rome from this port.

The great Jewish Revolt in AD 66 began in Caesarea, and in the struggle that followed the city's prisons saw the torture and execution of many captive Jewish zealots. In AD 70 the Roman general Vespasian was crowned emperor here. With the Bar Kochba uprising, many more notable Jews met their deaths here, among them the great sage and spiritual leader Rabbi Akiva, in 135. (The rabbi is commemorated in the nearby community of Or Akiva.)

During the period of Pax Romana, the city was a center of Hellenistic and, later, Christian culture. The Crusaders, under Baldwin I, captured the city in 1101, and during the next 200 years Caesarea changed hands with confusing frequency. King Baldwin believed it held the Holy Grail, from which Jesus sipped at the Last Supper, but the massive fortifications that so commend it

Beautiful Crusader vaulting at Caesarea.

today were only added after 1254, with the reconquest of the city by Louis IX. Muslim forces captured the city in 1265 (and again in 1291), and Caesarea never regained its importance, being pillaged over the centuries by successive rulers.

The contemporary visitor to Caesarea enters the **Crusader City** through a vaulted gatehouse, after passing over a bridge across a wide moat. The walls around the city, which slope down precipitously from an imposing height, are perhaps the most awe-inspiring monument here; walking the breadth of this imposing redoubt, imaginative tourists can easily picture the spectacle of hand-to-hand combat that took place here time and again. Inside the city are numerous ruins of Crusaders' homes and streets. Along the waterfront, Roman pillars used as foundation stones by the Crusaders jut out among the waves.

Outside the entrance to the Crusader City, a Byzantine Street of Statues represents the city that preceded the Crusaders, its headless figures pondering the passing of their power. Some 500 meters (550yds) south of the city walls

Graceful ruins by the sea.

is the restored **Roman Amphitheater** (hours as for the Crusader ruins). This arena witnessed mass executions in Roman times. More recently it has hosted popular summer concerts.

The handsome aqueducts stretching north from the city once conducted fresh spring water; today they provide shade for lounging bathers on Caesarea's wonderful beaches. Inland from the ruins is one of the few golf courses in Israel, in the grounds of the elegant and pricey **Dan Caesarea Hotel**.

Cities of wealth and taste

The region just north of Netanya is the **Valley of Khefer,** and although it isn't really a valley, the area gets a mention in the Old Testament. This marshy plain is linked to the efforts of the pioneers of the 1930s, whose sweat and foresight revitalized the land. Kfar Vitkin was among the first of these new settlements, and today it is among the country's largest moshavim (collective farming settlements).

The only remarkable thing about the city of **Khadera**, just south of Caesarea, is its huge power station on

the coast – you can't help noticing the chimneys – which supplies 60 percent of the country's electricity. However, the electricity company can take credit for cleaning up the River Khadera and planting an attractive parkland along its banks, south of the power station.

About 10km (6 miles) south of Khadera is **Mikhmoret** Beach, beautiful and seldom crowded. Here you can find sandy coves to nestle in and extraordinary sunsets from atop the cliffs; if you are lucky, you might stumble across the local population of large sea turtles.

Several kilometers farther south lies **Netanya** ❼ (www.netanya.muni. il), the capital city of the Sharon region. Founded as a citrus colony in 1929, Netanya has blossomed. It has an attractive beach and promenade including a striking glass elevator down to the beach just south of the city center to help the infirm negotiate the high cliffs. Netanya has a population of 215,000 and a galaxy of budget-priced hotels clustered along King David and Machnes Streets, by the beachfront. The Tourist Information Office (Sun–Thur 9am–5pm; tel: 09-882 7286) is in Independence Square (Kikar Ha'atzmaut) at the end of Herzl Street just before the seafront.

Heading south from Netanya, you pass over the Nahal Poleg (Poleg River), at one time set in an unpleasant morass, now tamed as the **Nakhal Poleg Nature Reserve**, which is to the east. Close by stands the Wingate Institute, Israel's premier center for sports and physical training instruction. It is named after Charles Orde Wingate, a British general who served in Palestine from 1936 to 1939, and who helped instruct the Jewish police force in defensive fighting techniques. The Wingate Institute is best known worldwide for its sports medicine expertise, and the "Wingate Test" is a routine procedure for discovering an athlete's capacity for anaerobic breathing.

The high life

The city of **Herzliya** ❽ (pop. 100,000) is home to many of Israel's wealthiest citizens. It is a favorite with diplomats and ambassadors, and with business executives, who are only too happy to take advantage of the stylish beaches

Netanya's long seashore and many beaches have created a holiday industry.

DIAMOND CITY

Netanya, known as Diamond City, is the center of Israel's highly profitable diamond industry, the country's second-most important export after high-tech electronics. The dealing is all done in the high-rise office towers in Ramat Gan near Tel Aviv, but much of the cutting and polishing is performed in Netanya.

Inaugurated by immigrants from Belgium and the Netherlands in the early years of the state, the business has grown to the extent that, since 1974, Israel has held the title of the world's number one exporter of polished diamonds (the raw stones being imported from Asia and Africa). To give an idea of the scale of the industry, Israel exported US$19 billion worth of diamonds in 2013.

TIP

Only swim on beaches where lifeguards are on duty. The Eastern Mediterranean has a deceptively strong undercurrent, and each year around 120 people, many of them tourists, drown in Israel. Avoid the Mediterranean in late June and early July when the sea is full of jellyfish.

Herzliya's beach.

and company, and whose villas stud the slopes above the shore amid such ritzy five-star hotels as the Sharon, Accadia, Daniel, and recently-opened Ritz-Carlton. To the west of Highway 2 is the most expensive part of the city, Herzliya Pituach, between the high-tech park (which also has many of Israel's finest restaurants) and the coast.

On the seafront road a kilometer north of Herzliya is Tel Arshaf in the Apollonia National Park (daily 8am–4pm, Apr–Sep until 5pm; charge). On this site are the ruins of an ancient Hellinistic city and a Crusader fortress. On the southern edge of Herzliya seafront is the city's marina, the largest in the country, which also has a large upscale shopping mall.

South of Tel Aviv

From Herzliya, the best way to bypass **Tel Aviv ❾** (see page 235) and reach the southern coastline is to drive through the very heart of the city. The Ayalon Highway (Road 20), together with a major suburban railway line, runs north–south parallel to the sea through the city center, beneath the

high-rise office towers, and on to the southern suburbs of Holon-Bat Yam before reaching **Rishon Le-Tsiyon ❿**. This city, whose name means "First in Zion," was founded in 1882 by Polish and Russian Zionists.

Rishon Le-Tsiyon has the first synagogue built in Israel in modern times (1885), the first kindergarten to teach in Hebrew, and the first Hebrew cultural center, where the national anthem *Ha-Tikva* (The Hope) was composed and sung for the first time. Rishon Le-Tsiyon has expanded enormously in the past 20 years, eating up the sand dunes between the west of Highway 4 and the coast. The city now has a population of 250,000, although it is considered a suburb of Tel Aviv rather than an independent entity. Turn west on 441 to reach Rishon's industrial zone, which has the country's largest shopping malls, a cinema city, and amusement park (**Superland**).

Yavne Yam, the ancient port of Yavne, and the swimming beach of **Palmakhim**, said to offer Israel's finest surfing, as well as being the site where

Judas Maccabeus gained a victory over Greek forces in the 2nd century BC, are just south of Rishon, reached along Highway 4311 off Highway 4. This is where the Sorek River flows into the sea. The Palmakhim air base several kilometers inland is Israel's space launch site, and every few years bathers are surprised by a rocket heading for the stars.

Yavne

As you continue south along Highway 4, the next place of note is **Yavne** ⑪, a town that proffers a rich history. The legend goes that in AD 70, when the fall of Jerusalem seemed imminent in the war against Rome, the renowned Rabbi Yohanon Ben Zakkai appeared before the Roman general Vespasian to request permission to found an academy here, predicting that one day the general would become emperor. The prophecy came true shortly afterward, and the request was granted. Whether or not the legend is true, Yavne did become the site of a great academy, and is known as the site where the Mishna, the great commentary on the Bible, which adapted Judaism to a modern framework, was started.

The *tel* of Yavne today consists of a lone Mameluke tower, built on Crusader ruins on top of a ridge. Today, Yavne is notable as the site of a small atomic research reactor, Israel's first, built in 1960 by architect Philip Johnson.

Philistine cities

Still on the coast, some 10km (6 miles) south, is **Ashdod** ⑫ with its concrete skyline. Its Philistine history now long behind it, Ashdod is a burgeoning man-made harbor, Israel's most important deep-water port, and, if not much of a gift to tourism, a striking example of commercial success.

Re-founded only in 1957, Ashdod grew in five decades to a city of more than 240,000 people, and is bursting at its seams with rugged vitality. Its populace includes a mix of North African and Russian-speaking immigrants. From Memorial Hill, just below the lighthouse, there is a clear view of the port, with great ships lined up to carry away exports such as potash and phosphates.

Outside the city, to the southeast,

The Mameluke tower at Yavne.

At Ashkelon, these Roman pillars used in the city walls were retrieved from the sea.

Red wine and Matzo crackers, a substitute for bread during Passover.

lies the grave of the ancient metropolis, **Tel Ashdod**. The site is quite literally a *tel* (mound), as little remains other than a hillock and the scattered sherds of Philistine pottery.

On the coastal highway 7km (4 miles) south of Ashdod is the access road (3631) to **Nitsanim**, one of the country's finest strips of beach. Just inland from the beach are freshwater pools. The only access to the beach is by car, and there is a US$15 charge for parking.

Ashkelon, an ancient trading post

One of the world's oldest cities, **Ashkelon** , some 40km (25 miles) south (population 132,000), has retained far more of its Philistine heritage. Situated on a crest of dunes above the sea, Ashkelon is an amalgam of industrial plants, contemporary apartment towers, and lovely beaches. But it is the archeological park that makes it special, and thoughtful preservation has ensured that the area is rewarding for visitors.

The multi-layered ruins of this strategic harbor city attest to the diversity of the people who have lived here over the centuries. Lying along the famous Via Maris, the roadway linking Egypt and Syria, the city was a trading center from its earliest days, its exports including wine, grain, and a variety of local onion which is now known as a scallion, after its place of origin. In the early 12th century BC the town was conquered by the Philistines, in their sweep of the southern coast, and in the following years it grew to become one of the five great Philistine cities – the others being Ashdod, Gaza, Gath, and Ekron.

The next two centuries witnessed bitter rivalry between the Philistines and the Israelites, and although the Jews never took the city it filtered into Jewish history through the story of Samson, whose exploits included his victory with the jawbone of an ass, the episode in which he set fire to the Philistine fields by tying torches to foxes' tails, and his famed ill-fated romance with Delilah.

When King Saul died at the hands of the Philistines, it prompted David's oft-quoted lament: "Tell it not in Gath, publish it not in the streets of

ISRAEL'S FIRST WINERY

In 1887 Baron Edmond de Rothschild, in one of his first acts as Israel's benefactor, established vineyards in Rishon Le-Tsiyon. He imported shoots of grape vines from Beaujolais, Burgundy, and Bordeaux, and the vineyards flourished, producing mainly sweet wines for Jewish ceremonial occasions. After years of Rothschild ownership, the company became a cooperative in 1957, and today the Carmel Oriental Vineyards produce a wide variety of wines in all price brackets. Most of their vineyards are in the Galilee, the Golan, and the Judean Hills near Jerusalem, where the cooler climate is better for quality wines. For the small fee charged, it is well worth a visit to the 19th-century winery in Rishon at 25 Hacarmel Street, just off Herzl Street near the municipal building, now with recently refurbished wine cellars and tasting rooms. Book in advance (tel: 03-948 8888).

One of Israel's largest wineries is the Barkan Winery at Kibbutz Hulda near Rekhovot, where tours and tastings can also be booked (tel: 08-944 7790). Carmel offer tours of their winery in Zichron Ya'akov, south of Haifa (tel: 04-639 1788), and there are many more wineries both there and in the neighboring town of Binyamina. Try Tishby at 33 Hameyasdim in the main street of Zichron (tel: 04-638 8635), and Binyamina Wineries in Binyamina (tel: 04-610 7535). Another option is the Recanati Winery in Emek Hefer (tel: 04-622 2288).

Ashkelon, lest the daughters of the Philistines rejoice, lest the daughters of the uncircumcised triumph" (II Samuel 1:20). Three centuries later Ashkelon was still a Philistine stronghold, provoking the wrath of the prophet Zephaniah, who, in one of the final books of the Old Testament, proclaims, "For Gaza shall be forsaken, and Ashkelon a desolation: they shall drive out Ashdod at the noonday, and Ekron shall be rooted up" (Zeph. 2: 4).

Eventually, of course, they all were. Taken in the ensuing centuries by Assyrians, Babylonians, and others, Ashkelon once more experienced growth in the years of Greek and Roman rule. Herod the Great was supposedly born here, and contributed greatly to the city. Ashkelon fell to the Arabs in the 7th century, and briefly to the Crusaders in 1153, and, in the process, was pillaged of its monuments and stones. In 1270 the city was destroyed completely by the Sultan Baibars.

Today, most of the city's antiquities are encompassed within the **National Park** (daily 8am–10pm; tel: 08-673 6444; charge). Here, near the seafront, one can ramble by the ruins of Herodian colonnades and ancient synagogues, along a Roman avenue presided over by the headless statue of Nike, goddess of victory, in a long-abandoned Roman amphitheater. The site is surrounded by a grass-covered Crusader wall, while, on the beach below, fallen pillars rest forlornly against the pressing of the tides.

Modern Ashkelon

The modern city includes distinct residential areas: **Midgal**, a former Arab town, to the east; **Afridar**, a newer suburb, along the shore, founded in 1955 by Jews from South Africa; and new neighborhoods linking the two, built in the 1990s to house new immigrants from the former Soviet Union. Afridar, distinguished by its tall, fenestrated clock tower, is the pleasant downtown area where one can find the commercial center and two preserved Roman sarcophagi.

There are a number of hotels here, including Holiday Inn, Leonardo, West Boutique, and Dan Gardens, as well as many bed-and-breakfast places near

TIP

Yachtsmen and women sailing into Israel can berth at marinas in (north to south) Akko, Haifa, Herzliyah, Tel Aviv, Yafo, Ashdod, Ashkelon, and Eilat.

Ruins at the harbor city of Ashkelon.

FACT

Dagon, the name of one of Ashkelon's hotels, is Hebrew for mermaid.

the seafront. The beaches are fine for bathing, and enjoy such biblical names as Samson Beach, Delilah Beach, Bar Kochba Beach, etc. Other notable sights include the Roman-era **Painted Tomb**, and, in Barnea to the north, the remains of a Byzantine church and 5th-century mosaic.

The end of the road

Ten kilometers (6 miles) farther south along Highway 4 lies the kibbutz of **Yad Mordekhai** ⓮. Named after Mordekhai Anilewitz, who died leading the Jews in their uprising against the Nazis in the Warsaw Ghetto in 1943, the kibbutz was founded that same year by Polish immigrants, and played a pivotal role during the Israeli War of Independence. Attacked by the Egyptian Army as it made its advance north in May 1948, the settlement managed to hold out against vastly superior Egyptian forces for six days, thereby allowing Tel Aviv to muster adequate defense.

Several structures at the kibbutz commemorate the heroic episode; the morbid but effective battlefield reconstruction includes cut-out figures of the advancing Egyptian soldiers, and a taped narration describes events.

Close by, the imposing **museum** (daily 8am–5pm; tel: 08-772 0529; charge) houses displays about the fighting and the four kibbutzim that stood together here, and a memorial to the Polish-Jewish community that was annihilated during the Holocaust. On a ridge nearby are the graves of those who fell defending the young settlement.

Overlooking today's community, the statue of Anilewitz stands in defiant pose, grenade in hand, while behind him rests the fallen water tower, its rutted surface preserved in commemoration of all it withstood. The overall effect of Yad Mordekhai is unquestionably sobering rather than joyful, yet it does provide a potent insight into the mentality of this small nation, which has time and again been besieged by hostile forces.

Four kilometers (2.5 miles) farther south is the **Erez Checkpoint**, the northern frontier crossing to the Gaza Strip, the scene of many bloody encounters between Palestinians and the Israeli Army.

Sculpture celebrating farming at Kibbutz Yad Mordekhai.

Gaza

This hotly contested, densely populated strip of land saw all of its Jewish settlements removed in 2005, yet peace remains elusive.

Gaza ⓫ is the symbol of Palestinian resistance to Israel, with 1.9 million residents living in a narrow strip only 6km wide and 45km long (4 by 28 miles). Israel removed all its settlements from the Strip in 2005 but rather than becoming a platform for peace, hostility to Israel escalated after an armed takeover by Hamas from the Palestinian Authority in 2007. Three short wars have been fought at the end of 2008, 2012 and most recently in 2014, with Israeli retaliating strongly in response to rocket attacks by Hamas on Israel and a sophisticated systems of tunnels leading into Israel for guerrilla attacks.

Gaza begins at the Shikma River in the north and extends to the Egyptian border at Rafah. Gaza was once a part of the seafaring Philistine federation; it was here that the illustrious Samson met the beguiling Delilah, who turned out to be his nemesis.

According to Arab tradition, Samson is buried under the site of the Great Mosque, a structure built by the Crusaders in 1150 and transformed into a mosque by the Mamelukes. Since Samson's time, Gaza has hosted (not always willingly) Muslims, Crusaders, Ottoman Turks, the British, and even Napoleon's soldiers. In 1948 Egyptian soldiers were perched on this gateway to Palestine, and Egypt retained control after Israel's independence.

About a fifth of the 800,000 Palestinian Arabs displaced by the 1948 fighting ended up in Gaza. Egypt's President Gamal Abdel Nasser organized the first fedayeen (underground fighters) and encouraged guerrilla warfare against Israel. Israel responded in 1956 with the Sinai Campaign, during which it briefly occupied the Sinai peninsula and the Gaza Strip. In the Six Day War of 1967, Israel seized the territory from Egypt again.

The 1987 Intifada

In Palestinian circles, Gaza was always seen as being led by the more prosperous and better-educated West Bank population. But surprisingly the Gazans took their place in the frontline of Palestine's confrontation with Israel by initiating the 1987 Intifada, and it was to Gaza that Yasser Arafat returned triumphantly in 1994.

Before traveling to Gaza, it is important to keep abreast of political events and to heed security measures. There is little to see in the way of tourist sights, but the street life is an attraction. The city centers are busy with merchants selling a variety of wares: cotton clothing (the word "gauze" comes from Gaza), terracotta pottery (a specialty), wicker furniture, and mounds of camel-hair carpets.

The coastline has some excellent beaches and, if peace and stability are ever achieved, these golden sands could provide the basis for an important tourist industry. The sandy land here is fertile, too, and agriculture thrives, especially citrus.

Hamas has remained defiant in its refusal to recognize Israel's right to exist even after the 2014 war, which saw over 2,000 Gazans killed. However, with the involvement of the Palestinian Authority, the international community, and wealthy Gulf Arab states to support civilian rather than military development, there has been some movement towards lifting Israel's blockade and rebuilding the Gaza Strip. With a well-educated, hard working population, the potential for the economic development of Gaza could yet be realized.

Surveying the damage in Gaza following the 2014 conflict.

TEL AVIV

This detailed tour of Israel's capital of style finds a biblical flavor in Old Yafo, and round-the-clock pulsating energy in the rest of the city.

T**el Aviv ❾** encapsulates the essence of modern Israel (www.tel-aviv.gov.il). If Jerusalem represents past yearning down the centuries by Jews longing to return to their biblical roots, and the promise of future redemption when the Messiah comes, then Tel Aviv is emphatically about the present. Tel Aviv is about the pursuit of material gain and pleasure. It is a city of high-rise office towers, shopping centers, golden beaches, upmarket restaurants, nightclubs, and – most of all – boundless, bustling infectious energy. Tel Aviv is hedonistic while Jerusalem is holy. Tel Aviv is sexy while Jerusalem is sacred.

Tel Aviv is Israel's commercial capital, while Jerusalem is the country's political capital. Even so, the international community does not recognize Jerusalem's primacy and chooses to place its embassies in Tel Aviv; the two cities vie for the title of cultural capital. Tel Aviv's mayor, Ron Huldai, likes to tell visitors that his city spends far more on culture than Jerusalem, and to be sure, if culture is defined as music and dance, drama and art, then Tel Aviv takes the title of Israel's cultural capital.

Despite their differences, Tel Aviv and Jerusalem live side by side separated by just a 50-minute drive, complementing each other rather than clashing.

Modern towers in Tel Aviv.

Old and new

Tel Aviv may be a city of the present, but it has a fascinating history. Over 100 years ago the sand dunes north of Yafo (Jaffa) were transformed into a middle-class garden suburb. The founders named the city Tel Aviv after something old and something new. *Tel* means an archeological mound, while *Aviv* is Hebrew for spring.

Of course, Tel Aviv as we refer to it today is not truly 100 years old. In 1950 the modern Tel Aviv municipality was formed to include Jaffa just to

Main Attractions

Jewish Diaspora museum
River Yarkon and Port
Seafront Promenade
Carmel Market
Neve Tsedek
Yafo
Rothschild Boulevard
Sheinkin
Dizengoff
Yitzhak Rabin Square

Tel Aviv-Yafo

0 _____ 500 m
0 _____ 500 yds

N

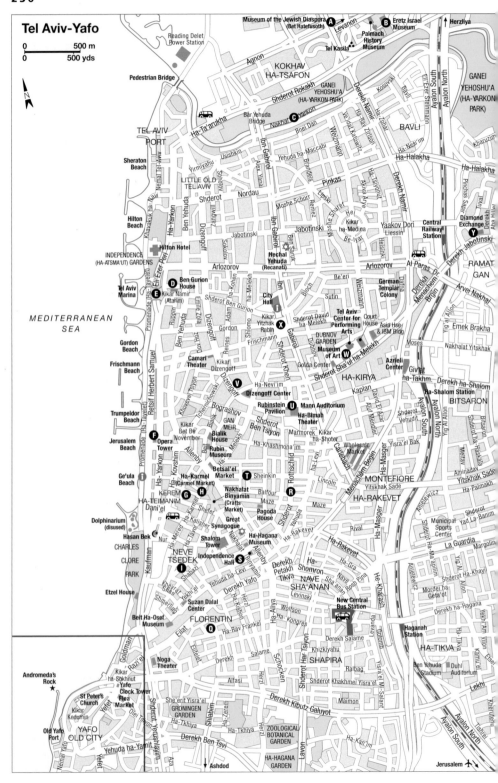

Museum of the Jewish Diaspora (Bet Hatefusoth) **A**
Levanon
Reading Delet
Power Station
B Eretz Israel Museum
Herzliya
Palmach History Museum
Tel Kasila

Pedestrian Bridge

Agnon

KOKHAV HA-TSAFON

GANEI YEHOSHU'A (HA-YARKON PARK)

Shderot Rokakh
Derekh Namir
Kosovski
Bavli
 Eli'Ezer Steinmann
Avalon South
Avalon North

GANEI YEHOSHU'A (HA-YARKON PARK)

Bar Yehuda Bridge
Nakhal Yarkon **C**
Ha-Ta'arukha
Bnei Dan

TEL AVIV PORT

Usishkin
Ibn Gabirol
Yehuda ha-Maccabi
Weizmann
Via dat Katowitz
Ha-Rav Zirlson

BAVLI

Ha-Nesi'im
Kharuzim

Sheraton Beach
Yirmiyahu
Alex. Yanai
Brandeis
Akiva Arye

Ha-Halakha
Ha-Halakha
Ha-Tsiyonut
Derekh Namir

LITTLE OLD TEL AVIV
Nordau
Shderot
Moshe Schorr
Remez
Pinkas
Lipski
Pinchas Sapir

Hilton Beach
Ben Yehuda
Dizengoff
Zangvil
Jabotinski
Ben Sarouk
Hei
Moshe Sharet
Kikar ha-Medina
Yaakov Dori
Central Railway Station
Diamond Exchange

Hilton Hotel
Hechal Yehuda (Recanati)
Be-Iyar

INDEPENDENCE (HA-ATSMA'UT) GARDENS
Arlozorov
Arlozorov
Al Paras. D.
RAMAT GAN

Ben Gurion House **D**
Be'eri
German Templar Colony
Derekh Menachem Begin
Arvei Nakhal

Tel Aviv Marina **E**
Kikar Namir (Atarim)
Shderot Ben Gurion
City Hall
Sutin
Weizmann

MEDITERRANEAN SEA

Kikar Yitzhak Rubin **X**
Shderot David ha-Melekh
Tel Aviv Center for Performing Arts
Court House
Asia Hse & IBM Bldg
Emek Brakha

Gordon Beach
Gordon
Frischmann
Dubnov
DUBNOV GARDEN
Museum of Art **W**
Moses
Nakhalat Yitskhak

Frischmann Beach
Camari Theater
Kikar Dizengoff
Golda Center
Azrieli Center
Givat
HA-KIRYA
Shderot Sha'ul ha-Melekh

Trumpeldor Beach
Dizengoff Center **V**
Ha-Nevi'im
Kaplan
Ha-Shalom Station
BITSARON

Bograshov
Rubinstein Pavilion **U**
Mann Auditorium
David El Azar
Ayalon South
Ayalon North

Jerusalem Beach
Opera Tower **F**
GAN MEIR
Bialik House
Ha-Bima Theater
Marmorek
Kikar ha-Shoter

Ge'ula Beach **G**
Rubin Museum
Betsal'el Market
Ha-Khashmona'im
Wholesale Market
Yisra'el Bak
Mettay

Ha-Karmel (Carmel Market) **T**
Sheinkin
Rothschild
Lincoln
MONTEFIORE
Yitshak Sade
Aminadav
Yitskhak Sade

KEREM HA-TEIMANIM
Dani'el **G** **H**
Nakhalat Binyamin (Crafts Market)
Balfour
Maze
HA-RAKEVET
Ha-Masger

Dolphinarium (disused)
Great Synagogue
Pagoda House
Ha-Rakevet
Rival
Municipal Sports Center
La Guardia

Hasan Bek
Shalom Tower
Ha-Hagana Museum
CHARLES CLORE PARK
Independence Hall **S**
Derekh Petakh Tikva
Ha-Shomron
Rosh Pina
New Central Bus Station

NEVE TSEDEK **I**
Shabazi
Yekhi'el
Derekh Yafo
NAVE SHA'ANAN
Levinski
Wolfson
Haganah Station

Etzel House
Suzan Dalal Center
Herzl
Ha-Aliya
Ha-Kongres
HA-TIKVA

Beit Ha-Oset Museum
FLORENTIN **Q**
Eilat
Ha-Rav Frankel
Derekh Salame
Khizkiyahu
Ben Yehuda
Duhl

Andromeda's Rock
Noga Theater
Kikar ha-Sokhnut
Salame
Schocken
SHAPIRA
Ralbag
Stadium
Auditorium

St Peter's Church
Yafo Clock Tower
Flea Market
She'erit Yisra'el
GRONINGEN GARDEN
Alfasi
Shderot Khakhmei Yisra'el
Maimon

Old Yafo Port
YAFO OLD CITY
Ha-Tkhiya
Derekh Ben Tsvi
ZOOLOGICAL BOTANICAL GARDEN
Derekh Kibutz Galuyot

Yehuda ha-Yamit
Ashdod
HA-HAGANA GARDEN
Lavon
Jerusalem ✈

the south. Jaffa, where Jonah set sail on his ill-fated voyage, is one of the world's oldest ports, with a history stretching back centuries, even before biblical times. The Neve Tsedek neighborhood, which links Jaffa to Tel Aviv, was established in 1887.

The original city of Tel Aviv around the impressive Rothschild Boulevard's western end had (and still has) large townhouses and spacious thoroughfares. Tel Aviv quickly expanded as Jews left overcrowded Jaffa and immigrants from fashionable cities in Central and Eastern Europe fleeing anti-Semitic prejudice heard that there was now a modern Hebrew city with 20th-century utilities. Tel Aviv rapidly spread northward and eastward. The 1930s were good years for the city as German immigrants fleeing Nazi persecution brought prosperity, culture, and know-how. They introduced Bauhaus architecture, which characterizes early Tel Aviv, and earned it the name of the White City.

The early 1940s were prosperous times too. And, with World War II not reaching Palestine, the global hostilities actually boosted the economy, as the British used Palestine as a strategic military and economic base. However, the news seeping through from Nazi-occupied Europe, and the German advance on Egypt meant that few Tel Avivians could enjoy their affluence.

It was in Tel Aviv that David Ben Gurion proclaimed independence in 1948, and the city soon fell on hard times. Austerity did not suit Tel Aviv's sense of style and panache, and tens of thousands of immigrants from Arab countries were settled in hastily constructed suburbs to the south. To this day, Tel Avivis refer to *tzafonim* (northerners) and *daromim* (southerners). The former are middle-class, liberal Ashkenazim, the latter working-class Sephardim. But in recent decades the differences have become blurred. Many Sephardim have made it to the affluent fleshpots of north Tel Aviv, while many of the residents of south

Tel Aviv are new immigrant Ashkenazim from the former Soviet Union, migrants, and refugees.

Through to the 1980s, Tel Aviv never recovered the sense of style and international prominence that it felt it deserved. At best it had a shabby charm accentuated by those glorious beaches. It was often compared to Latin American cities – a comparison that irked its residents, who aspired to European elegance and American dynamism.

Until the high-tech boom of the 1990s Tel Aviv was a city still searching for its true identity. High-tech fitted in nicely with the city's image of itself: young, dynamic, leading-edge, innovative, and "cool." It also brought in the billions of dollars any city needs to look and be attractive. Even today, cosmopolitan Tel Aviv is still a provincial city – more like Minneapolis or Manchester than London or New York. But don't say that to its residents – they might be offended.

Greater Tel Aviv

Tel Aviv's population today is a surprisingly small 500,000. But this figure

FACT

Tel Aviv was also the name given to the Hebrew translation of Theodor Herzl's book *Altneuland* (Old-new Land), in which he conceived of the Jewish State.

Ayalon freeway.

אילון דרום
Ayalon South
20 20 20

In front of the Carlton and Marina Hotels is Tel Aviv's large seawater swimming pool. Aerobic exercise sessions are held on the beach in the summer, and a roller-skating rink operates in the evening near the pool.

is deceptive, and here, once again, Jerusalem has stolen Tel Aviv's clothes as the country's largest city. The Israeli government has steadfastly refused to amalgamate Tel Aviv with its surrounding suburbs because it would then overtake Jerusalem in size. In fact, visitors are not aware that they have left Tel Aviv to enter Ramat Gan or Givatayim to the east, or Holon and Bat Yam to the south. When Israelis talk of Gush Dan (the Dan block – this region belonged to the tribe of Dan in biblical times) – or Greater Tel Aviv, they refer to a metropolitan area encompassing over 3 million citizens. And that doesn't include Netanya 30km (19 miles) to the north and Ashdod 40km (25 miles) to the south, each cities of 200,000. Jerusalem is only 60km (37 miles) to the east, and it is not uncommon for people to commute from the holy city to Tel Aviv and vice versa.

Orientation

The most important streets to get to know are the six major north–south axes running parallel to the coastline.

Ha-Yarkon runs along the coast itself, with Allenby/Ben Yehuda and Dizengoff running close alongside, slightly inland. Ibn Gabriol, a kilometer inland, is where City Hall is located. The next two north–south roads are more for transportation in and out of the city – Derekh Petakh Tikvah becomes Derekh Namir and the road to Haifa, while the Ayalon Highway is Tel Aviv's main urban freeway or motorway, transporting vehicles in and out of the city. The railway runs in between the carriageways of the Ayalon Highway.

There are no west–east roads in the center of the city that will take you directly through from the seafront to the Ayalon Highway. If traveling by car, try Derekh Kibutz Galuyot in the far south, Arlozorov in the north (one-way east to west), Pinkas/Nordau or Shderot Rokakh.

Tel Aviv University

In the far north of the city, salubrious suburbs surround Tel Aviv University campus (www.tau.ac.il). On the eastern side of the neatly manicured lawns of the campus, the country's

Boating on the Yarkon.

largest university is the **Museum of the Jewish Diaspora** (**Bet Hatefusoth**)  (Sun–Tue 10am–4pm, Wed–Thur 10am–7pm, Fri 9am–1pm; tel: 03-745 7808; www.bh.org.il; charge). When it was founded in 1979, it was, in concept and methodology, a radical departure from the accepted notion of a museum, for, apart from a few exhibits, Bet Hatefusoth contains no preserved artifacts. Its principal aim is reconstruction.

The body of the main exhibit is handled thematically, focusing on general themes of Jewish life in the Diaspora: family life, community, religion, culture, and the return to Zion. Its striking displays include a collection of beautifully intricate models of synagogue buildings from across the globe. A memorial column in the central atrium commemorates Jewish martyrdom through the ages. (Note that a completely revamped core exhibition is scheduled to replace the existing exhibition in 2017.)

An audiovisual depiction of the migrations of Jews is presented in the hall known as the **Chronosphere**.

Four video study areas enable visitors to view documentary films selected from a catalogue, while a computer system allows them to trace their own lineage. Special exhibitions highlight topics related to Jewish communities around the world.

Nearby in **Ramat Aviv** – cross to the western side of the campus and then go south and west along Levanon – is the sprawling **Eretz Israel Museum**  (Sun–Wed 10am–4pm, Thur 10am–8pm, Fri–Sat 10am–2pm; tel: 03-641 5244; www.eretzmuseum.org.il; charge). The museum is the region's most comprehensive storehouse of archeological, anthropological, and historical findings. Its spiritual backbone is **Tel Kasila**, an excavation site in which 12 distinct layers of civilization have been uncovered, its finds including an ancient Philistine temple and Hebrew inscriptions from 800 BC. The complex consists of 11 pavilions, including exhibits of glassware, ceramics, copper, coins, folklore and ethnography, and a planetarium.

Next door to the Eretz Israel Museum, immediately to the west, is

TIP

Tel Aviv has two tourist information offices. 2 Marzuk St. (Jaffa Clock Tower) Sun–Thur 9.30am–5.30pm Fri 9am–4pm Sat (summer) 10am–4pm. 46 Herbert Samuel St, corner Geula St (on the seafront). Sun–Thur 9.30am–5.30pm, Fri 9.30am–1pm (tel: 03-516 6188). The tourist police are also located in this office (tel: 03-516 5382).

The city skyline as viewed from Jaffa.

the **Palmach History Museum** (book in advance Sun–Thur, tel: 03-643 6393), which tells the story of Israel's fight for independence, using actors and theatrical sets.

River Yarkon and Tel Aviv port

Defining the northernmost limit of the city proper, rather than the municipal entity, is the River **Yarkon** , which once marked the border between the tribes of Dan and Ephraim. Today the river is lined with rambling **parkland** and serves to accommodate scullers who row along it in the cooler hours of the day. Near the river's western rim can be seen the dome and chimneys of the Reading Power Station, while the greenery of the city's exhibition grounds marks the river's eastern limit. Despite efforts to clean up the river, swimming is strictly prohibited, due to pollution.

To the south of the Yarkon River is the trendy quarter known as **Little Old Tel Aviv,** where three of the city's major north–south roads begin: Ha-Yarkon, Ben Yehuda, and Dizengoff.

Druze woman making pitta bread, Carmel Market.

There is a large number of cafes, restaurants, and bars in this quarter – and Tel Aviv's disused port has now been rejuvenated in a project often compared to London's Covent Garden or San Francisco's Fisherman's Wharf. Tel Aviv Port itself as a working dock and harbor only had a relatively brief existence. It was opened in 1936 as a Jewish-owned port to compete with the British-run port in nearby Jaffa, which was frequently strikebound by Arab stevedores protesting against the allegedly pro-Zionist policies of the Mandate authorities. The port was closed down in 1965 because its relatively shallow waters could not harbor the large vessels shipping goods to and from Israel.

There is a wide range of restaurants, cafes, and bars in the Tel Aviv Port complex, as well as fashionable retail outlets. Even if you don't want to eat out or party, Tel Aviv Port, linked by a seafront promenade to the city in the south, makes an ideal destination for an evening stroll, with the sea breezes tempering the city's spring and summer humidity.

To the south of the port stretches **Independence Gardens**, a strip of green offering a stirring view of the Mediterranean from its cliffs. Alternatively, there is a path on the promenade below. Independence Gardens hides among its shrubbery various archeological finds, and in the evening it is a gay pick-up point.

Just inland, in Ben Gurion Boulevard, after the Tel Aviv Hilton, is **Ben Gurion House**  (Mon 8am–5pm, Sun, Tue–Thur 8am–3pm, Fri 8am–1pm Sat 11am–2pm; tel: 03-522 1010; www.bg-house.org; charge). This was the home of Israel's first prime minister and is today a public museum housing the personal mementoes of David Ben Gurion.

Hotels and best beaches

The seaside promenade is dotted with cafes, restaurants, ice-cream parlors, and the like, all offering free sea air and costly refreshments. On summer nights the promenade is clogged with people strolling, cycling, running, and in cars, maneuvering for some sea breeze after the day's oppressive heat.

The **marina** rents out sailing and motorboats, and equipment for windsurfing, sea-surfing, water-skiing, diving, and other water sports.

You can't help noticing – but should avoid – **Kikar Namir** (still known locally by its former name, **Kikar Atarim**) **E**, a concrete monstrosity squatting over the marina. This open-air mall offers concrete mushroom sunshades, tourist items, and a chance to lose one's way. Its cafes, pizzerias, and restaurants, tolerable in the sunlight, turn seedy at night.

The city's main hotel district lies along the coast here. From the north of the city to the south, the coastline is dominated by an imposing row of hotels lined up like dominoes, including (among others) the Hilton, north of Arlozorov, and the Carlton, Sheraton, and Dan. The **Opera Tower F** to the south of the hotels is a distinctive building that houses apartments, restaurants, shops, jewelry stores, and a movie theater.

Each hotel has its own beach strip (the beaches are all public) with showers, easy chairs, and refreshment facilities. Marking the end of the hotel line to the south, across from the Dan Panorama and David Intercontinental, is the **Dolphinarium**, a white elephant, now unused, obscuring the magnificent view of Old Yafo from Tel Aviv's coast.

Where east meets west

Just inland, several blocks south of the Opera Tower, is the **Kerem ha-Teimanim** (Yemenite Quarter) **G**, its exotic winding streets a jolt back in time, preserving the look and feel of the Yemenite community that settled here a century ago. Here, in Arab-style stone houses, is the best place to sample the spicy, pungent Yemenite cuisine: Pundak Shaul, Zion, Pninat Hakerem, and Maganda are among the best Yemenite restaurants in the country. Like the Yemenite Quarter, Tel Aviv's marketplaces are an inseparable part of the Levant. The biggest

Keyrings in Carmel Market.

Architecture

A high concentration of buildings in the Bauhaus style, many now slickly restored, have earned Tel Aviv the title of World Heritage Site

Tel Aviv has been named a Unesco World Heritage Site because of its unique collection of International Style (Bauhaus) buildings. The city has more than 1,500 such buildings, by far the largest number of any location worldwide, with most of them to be found on Rothschild Boulevard and the roads to the north.

Beneath Tel Aviv's high-tech glass towers, it's hard for the visitor to pick out the Bauhaus buildings. The understated cubic style is often hidden behind trees, and in many instances urban grime. But many of the buildings have been restored to their former glory, and property developers are rehabilitating many more, usually adding on expensive penthouses, which are carefully designed (with close municipal supervision and encouragement) to enhance the entire structure. These additions are incentivized as part of a comprehensive plan to make entire buildings better prepared to withstand potential earthquakes.

Bauhaus style.

The original architects may not have approved. Bauhaus appealed to the early Zionists because of its minimalist, ascetic, and socialistic style.

Until the emergence of Bauhaus in the 1920s, Tel Aviv buildings had an eclectic style with Oriental and European designs alongside each other and sometimes incorporated in the same building. Bauhaus architecture itself, which had developed in Germany after World War I, was simple. In the wake of new engineering developments, architects at the Bauhaus school were asked to forget everything they had been taught. For example, walls could now be built around steel frames and no longer had to support the building. There was also a social aspect to the architecture, which appealed to socialists, as the new style was able to provide less expensive homes for the less affluent, while using less land.

Eventually Hitler threw the Bauhaus school out of his country because it was un-German. It became known as the International Style, and the fact is that architects around the world, like Le Corbusier in Paris, had been developing similar ideas.

Birth of the White City

Many of the architects who left Germany were Jews who found their way to Tel Aviv and influenced the design of the city. Old postcards and pictures from the 1930s show Rothschild Boulevard in its full glory and also reveal why the first Hebrew city was once called the White City. Unfortunately, with urban grime taking a toll on white walls, the White City soon lost its luster. Many of the buildings are being restored in their original gleaming white. Number 71 Rothschild is one such example. That building's strip passages between apartments on the upper floors are typical of the straight lines, rectangles, and cubes that make up the International Style design.

Engel Street, a delightful mews off Rothschild to the east, which is made up entirely of Bauhaus buildings, and Dizengoff Circle are both excellent places to appreciate the full cumulative effect of Bauhaus architecture. Property developers and homeowners wishing comprehensively to renovate a building are entitled to loans and grants from the municipality, but they must restore all features, including reopening enclosed balconies. Indeed, much work needs to be done, with dozens of the Bauhaus buildings still looking like neglected slums.

Visit the Bauhaus Center at 99 Dizengoff Street for an exhibition about the history of Bauhaus (Sun–Thur 10am–7.30pm, Fri 10am–2.30pm, Sat noon–7.30pm). There are two-hour English tours of Bauhaus in Tel Aviv every Fri at 10am for $17.

and best known of these is the **Carmel Market (Ha-Karmel)** ⑩, stretching along from Kerem ha-Teimanim to Allenby. Always crowded with shoppers and hagglers, the market is a medley of colors, smells, and sounds. A large variety of exotic fruits, vegetables, and herbs can be found here, as well as clothes, shoes, pickled foods, and pitta bread, all at bargain prices.

To the left of the entrance to the Carmel Market on Allenby Street is a pedestrianized street called **Nakhalat Binyamin**. Here, on Tuesdays and Fridays, arts and crafts traders bring their wares to parade and sell. A great place for present-shopping, as the artisans combine jewelry with juggling, cactus plants with camel bags, and woodcarvings with wonderful art. On these days, and throughout the week, the street-side cafes are crowded.

Between the Yemenite Quarter and Neve Tsedek, on the fast road to Yafo, is the **Hasan Bek Mosque**, contrasting sharply with the contemporary high-rise near it. Built in 1916 by Yafo's Turkish-Arab governor, the mosque was intended to block the development of Tel Aviv toward the sea. During the War of Independence the mosque served as an outpost for Arab snipers. In 1992 it was sold by its local Muslim owners to a Tel Aviv businessman who planned to open a nightclub there. After protests of outrage from the Arab world the mosque was bought by the Egyptian government, which has refurbished both the exterior and interior.

Neve Tsedek

Inland from the Dan Panorama Hotel is the city's oldest quarter, **Neve Tsedek** ❶ (not counting Yafo). It was founded in 1887 as a suburb of Yafo, and is a picturesque maze of narrow streets flanked by low-built Arab-style houses. At the time the quarter was considered a luxury suburb, despite the crowded housing and less than sanitary conditions. In recent years the quarter's quaint old dwellings have

taken the fancy of artists and well-to-do families, who have restored them and replanted the inner courtyards.

The **Neve Tsedek Theater**, otherwise known as the Suzan Dalal Center, and specializing in avant-garde drama, opened in the building of the city's first girls' school, incidentally also the first all-Hebrew school in Israel. The building is home to the **Batsheva Dance Company** and the **Inbal Dance Company**. With the theater's opening in a magnificent plaza dotted with orange trees, several colorful galleries, restaurants, and nightclubs popped up, lending a new vitality to the century-old streets. Also in Neve Tsedek, the former Yafo train station (now called Hatahana) has been converted into an attractive cafe, shopping, and exhibition center.

Yafo

Neve Tsedek stretches southward to Yafo, the place where it all began. It is said that, when God got fed up with his creatures, he brought the Great Flood on the world to wipe the slate clean and start afresh. After the flood

Stone head in Yafo.

The neighborhood of Neve Tsedek.

subsided and Noah's Ark landed on Mount Ararat, Noah's youngest son, Japheth, found a pleasant hill overlooking a bay and settled down, naming the site "Yafo" (Hebrew for beautiful). One of the world's oldest cities, Yafo has retained its biblical flavor, spiced by centuries of historical events and myths. The famous Cedars of Lebanon to be used by King Solomon in building the Temple in Jerusalem were shipped to Yafo – even then an important Mediterranean trading port. The miracle of raising Tabitha from the dead was performed by the Apostle Peter when he stayed at the Yafo house of Simon the Tanner (Acts 9:36–42).

Some 3,400 years ago Yafo was conquered by the Egyptians. Subsequently Alexander the Great, Herod, Richard the Lionheart, Napoleon, and the Turks (among others) all passed through, alternately destroying and building. The British took over from the Ottomans at the end of World War I, and Yafo returned to Israel during the War of Independence in 1948.

Jewish residence was resumed in Yafo long before that, in 1820, when a Jewish traveler from Constantinople settled here. Soon after came a large number of settlers, mainly North African merchants and craftsmen, who merged with the local Arab community. By the time of Israel's independence the city had close to 100,000 residents, more than 30,000 of them Jewish. Modern Yafo has retained its Eastern flavor, and today holds a colorful medley of immigrants from North African and Central European countries, as well as a community of more than 20,000 Arabs.

Old Yafo today

Old Yafo was reconstructed and renovated in 1963, with cobbled paths and winding alleys twisting through the massive stone fortifications surrounding the city. Today it sports an artists' colony, art galleries, craft shops, tourist shops, seafood restaurants, and nightclubs.

Old Yafo begins at the **Clock Tower** ❶ on Yefet, built in 1906 by the Turks and facing the local police station. The tower's stained-glass windows each portray a different chapter

Doorway to a Greek Orthodox church in Old Yafo.

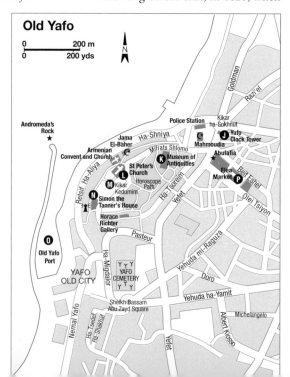

in Yafo's history. Walk past the police station and, on your right, an entrance leads to the **Mahmoudia Mosque**, built in 1812 and named after Yafo's Turkish governor.

Turning right from Yefet onto Mifrats Shlomo, toward the renovated section of Old Yafo, one passes the **Yafo Museum of Antiquities**  (Sun–Thur 9am–1pm, Tue also 4–7pm, Sat 10am–2pm; charge), where archeological exhibits from many years of excavations trace the city's development. Erected in the 18th century, the building was the Turkish governor's headquarters and local prison. Later it won acclaim throughout the Middle East as the soap factory of the Greek Orthodox Damiani family. The sidewalk opposite the museum offers one of the best views of Tel Aviv's beaches and coastline.

The Franciscan **St Peter's Church** is farther along, situated on one side of Kikar Kedumim. The **St Louis Monastery** in the courtyard was named after the French king who arrived at the head of a Crusade and stayed here in 1147. The monastery

later served as a hostel for pilgrims to Jerusalem and was known in the 17th century as "The Europeans' House." Napoleon also relaxed here after conquering Yafo.

A little way north and toward the sea is the minaret of the **Jama El-Baher Mosque**, located next door to the first Jewish house in Yafo, built in 1820. The **Armenian Convent** and church here mark the site of a 17th-century pilgrims' inn. A magnificent renovated Turkish mansion behind the museum, once a Turkish bathhouse, has been converted into a wedding hall and restaurant, **El-Hamam**.

At the top of the hill, past the Pisgah Park, **Horoscope Path** begins to wind its way through the Yafo wall. It goes all the way to the lighthouse at the wall's southern entrance, on the corner of Shimon Haburski. At the center of the renovated section is a square called **Kikar Kedumim**, in which the Yafo excavations present a reconstruction of the city's multi-faceted history; this is also one of Tel Aviv's most popular evening spots. Down an alleyway to the right is **Simon**

The limestone Clock Tower was built at the beginning of the 20th century to commemorate the silver anniversary of Sultan Abd el-Hamid II.

Playing up the Napoleon connection in Old Yafo.

TIP

Tourists staying in Tel Aviv are entitled to free English-language guided walking tours. For details, phone the Tel Aviv Municipality's tourism department 03-5166188, www.visit-tel-aviv.com/free-walking-tours for details or ask at the Tourist Information offices.

the **Tanner's House** (daily 8am–7pm; charge), where, in addition to performing miracles, Peter is believed to have received divine instruction to preach to non-Jews.

On the southern side of the wall, along Pasteur, a modern structure rather spoils the beauty of the ancient walls. This is a shopping area, which has a number of restaurants and cafes. Farther along Pasteur Street is the Horace Richter Gallery.

From here you can descend to the port and its delightful fish restaurants. The **Old Yafo Port**, recently renovated, is still the home port of the local fishermen, who haul in their catch every dawn. Their booty end up in the cauldrons of the town's many restaurants, three of which are located right in the old port, overlooking the pier and bobbing boats.

Looking seaward one can make out a cluster of rocks, the largest of which is said to be Andromeda's. But recent renovation of the pier, which included the bombing of some of the formation, nearly blew the rock out of existence. For the rest, time seems to have stood

still. Primitive ovens still churn out an infinite variety of Oriental spiced pitta breads, and the ancient streets hum with assertive shopkeepers, pastry vendors, and meandering passers-by.

Back on Yefet, turn left and walk down the hill, crossing the road. Just before the traffic lights on the right is **Abulafia**, Yafo's first pitta-bread establishment (dating back to the 1880s). It reputedly does its briskest business on Passover and Yom Kippur, when droves of bread-craving Israelis queue outside. The area is especially lively after dark, when Tel Aviv's night-owls descend on Yafo.

Yafo's famous **Flea Market** lies in the next complex of alleys just east of here. It specializes in antiques, copperware ("antique" specimens made while you watch), jewelry, and second-hand junk. It isn't open on Saturdays.

To the northeast of Yafo lies **Florentin**, an ugly, ramshackle neighborhood, which is nevertheless considered Tel Aviv's trendiest and most bohemian quarter, with a flourishing nightlife, often compared to New York's Meatpacking District and London's Hoxton. East of Florentin is the new Central Bus Station, a vast complex of shops, offices, and eateries. Other than stopping to grab a quick, great-value *falafel* with as much salad as you want, it is advisable to board your bus as quickly as possible. (The area to the north, where the old bus station is, is the rather seedy but colorful home of Israel's foreign workers and African refugees.) The Central Bus Station now has an overhead walkway leading across the Ayalon Highway to the Haganah railway station.

Financial district

Immediately north and west of the Bus Station is the city's financial district. The streets are overlooked by the **Shalom Tower**, on Herzl, for many years the tallest building in Israel.. The Shalom Tower soars 35 floors – and 140 meters (460ft) – above the city, an austere white rectangle. Its main

A Rothschild Boulevard character.

significance lies in its location. Here stood one of the first buildings to be erected in Tel Aviv – the Herzliya Gymnasium (High School). Built in 1910 on the first thoroughfare, the school was a symbol of pioneering and became the cultural and economic nucleus of the town. It was torn down in 1959. All that remains of it is a huge fresco on the wall of the center, created by artist Nahum Gutman.

Today, **Rothschild Boulevard ®** (an appropriate name) at its western end forms the heart of Israel's financial district. Built in 1910 over a dried riverbed, the boulevard was once Tel Aviv's most elegant address. It's elegant once more, its central promenade dotted with trees, benches, and refreshment kiosks as well as a cycle path, and its buildings embrace a jumble of styles. The house at number 13, in the Betsal'el style (named after the Betsal'el Art School in Jerusalem), combines European and Oriental design.

The public museum, **Independence Hall ❺**, is at number 16, the former residence of the city's first mayor, Meir Dizengoff. The Declaration of Independence was signed here on May 15, 1948, and it was also the first home of the Knesset (parliament) until it moved to the Opera Tower building on the beach, then to Jerusalem. The second and third floors comprise the **Bible Museum** (Sun–Fri 9am–1pm, Sat 10am–2pm; charge).

Across the road is the **Israel Defense Forces** (Ha-Hagana) **Museum** (Sun–Thur 9am–4pm; tel: 03-560 8264; charge), located in the former residence of Haganah commander Eliahu Golumb. Here, and dotted around the city, are square brown signs that refer to the original use of the buildings. Before Israel's independence the resistance forces fought underground from these positions, against both the British and the Arabs. The IDF (Israel Defense Forces) headquarters is still located in Tel Aviv at the Kirya, originally a German Templar settlement, turned into their headquarters by the British, before being taken over by IDF. This explains what Saddam Hussein was aiming for when his forces fired Iraqi missiles at Tel Aviv in the 1991 Gulf War.

FACT

The large abstract sculpture in Ha-Bimah Square is the work of Menashe Kadishman.

Rothschild Boulevard, a sought-after address.

Bialik House, with its Islamic-influenced interior.

Musicians from the Breslav Center entertain on Sheinkin Street.

Breuer House at number 46 was built in 1922; it has tiny decorative balconies, a pagoda-like wooden roof, a minaret, and a large enclosed garden. On the verge of demolition in 1948, it was saved when the Soviet ambassador requested it for his headquarters. It served as the Soviet Embassy until 1953, when diplomatic relations with the USSR were severed. Renovated in the 1990s, it now houses Sotheby's Israel offices.

Typical Bauhaus-style buildings may be seen at numbers 89, 91, and 140, and on nearby Engel, recently converted into a pedestrian mall.

Sheinkin ❼, which stretches eastward off Rothschild farther along, is the bastion of Israel's trendy, leftist, and secular community, although the ultra-Orthodox Lubavitchers (Habad) have their Tel Aviv headquarters in Sheinkin too. Sheinkin is the local equivalent of New York's Greenwich Village or London's Notting Hill. Stretching from Allenby all the way east to Yehuda ha-Levi, it is a street that has it all. Don't bring a car on Friday, when it is virtually closed to traffic to allow shoppers to buy wallpaper, furniture, or home appliances, to discover a second-hand fake-fur coat, bind a book, buy eggs in a shop selling only farm-fresh produce, have their hair done, or simply sit sipping coffee or alcohol on one of the street's many cafes.

Sheinkin is renowned for its leading fashion designs, and for hip Tel Avivians who can be seen flaunting their stylish outfits. At the western end of Sheinkin is the Betsal'el Market (adjoining westwards to the Carmel Market), reputed to have the best *falafels* in Israel, as well as the usual discount quality fashion items and bric-a-brac.

A walk on Bialik

Farther north along Allenby, **Bialik** is another pleasant street dating from the city's early days. At number 14 is the **Rubin Museum** (Mon, Wed–Thur 10am–3pm, Tue 10am–8pm, Fri 10am–3pm, Sat 11am–2pm; tel: 03-525 5961; www.rubinmuseum.org.il; charge), the former residence of Israeli artist Reuven Rubin. A short walk from here is **Bialik House** (same hours as Rubin

House; tel: 03-525 4350), once the home of Israel's national poet, Haim Nahman Bialik. Built in 1925, it has a little tower and dome, a prominent pink balcony, and arched columns, like those of the Doge's Palace in Venice.

The post-1948 city

To the east of this neighborhood, at the northern end of Rothschild and the eastern extremity of Dizengoff, is Tel Aviv's premier cultural complex, including the **Ha-Bimah Theater**, the **Mann Auditorium**, and the **Rubinstein Pavilion** . During the Russian Revolution a group of young Russian-Jewish actors formed a collective and dreamed of a Hebrew theater. The dream came true in Tel Aviv, dozens of years later. The Ha-Bimah Theater (ha-Bimah means "the stage" in Hebrew), built in the square of the same name, originally had creaking wooden chairs and lousy acoustics: today it has two theaters (one seating 1,000 and a smaller one with seats for 300), revolving stages, and simultaneous translation into several languages during the high season.

Just next to the theater is the **Mann Auditorium**, the home of the Israel Philharmonic Orchestra. Tickets here are highly prized and hard to get. The third building in this complex is the **Rubinstein Pavilion** (Mon, Wed Sat 10am–6pm, Tue, Thur 10am–9pm, Fri 10am–2pm, closed Sun; tel: 03-528 7196; charge), a branch of the Tel Aviv Museum, which specializes in modern art exhibitions. The little park in the middle of the complex hides the chic brass-and-chrome **Apropos Café.**

Dizengoff's cafes

This arts complex is at the start of **Dizengoff** , once the city's most fashionable thoroughfare and although less grand today, still one of Tel Aviv's principal streets. Cafe-going is a major part of any self-respecting Tel Avivian's way of life. Some people go to cafes for their first coffee of the day; others conduct business meetings or entertain guests; retired people spend their mornings over cappuccinos and croissants. On a sunny day you may get the impression that the entire city is on holiday, sipping coffee at sidewalk cafes.

FACT

The fountain in the center of Dizengoff Circle was designed by a leading Israeli artist, Yaakov Agam. The same Agam style adorns the side of the Dan Hotel on Ha-Yarkon.

There are good cycling tracks along the seafront.

CITY CYCLING

Cycling is the best and potentially cheapest way of seeing the city. Tel Aviv has some 120km (75 miles) of cycle tracks and a municipal renting system called Tel-O-Fun, with some 150 cycle stations around the city. Bicycles can be rented by credit card for about US$1.50 per hour rising to $45 for just 4.5 hours. An access fee of $5 must first be paid for registering on the website. The first 30 minutes are free, so by using the green bikes for less than 30 minutes, returning them to any of the stations and waiting for 10 minutes before re-hiring, there is no charge. The best cycle lanes are along the seafront promenade and through the Yarkon Park along the banks of the river. Tel Aviv is flat, but take plenty of water during the humid summer. For queries tel: *6070, www.tel-o-fun.co.il, for maps of cycle lanes and stations.

The three towers of the Azrieli Center.

Café-going is a Tel Aviv hobby.

Much of Israeli cafe activity still takes place along Dizengoff, although Sheinkin is more trendy, and pedestrianized Nakhalat Binyamin a more convenient cafe location. Young, upbeat, and action-packed, this street is a constant parade of beautiful people, window-shoppers, tourists, actors, models and in-vogue pop stars, vagabonds, soldiers, and businesspeople. A seat in a Dizengoff cafe is an excellent vantage point from which to observe the human panorama.

At no time is Dizengoff more glamorous or crowded than on Friday afternoons, when groups of Tel Avivians congregate to unwind with friends from the long working week, try to chat up girls, catch up on gossip, and learn of the night's best parties.

A block north of the Ha-Bimah complex is the **Dizengoff Center**, a modern multilevel shopping complex offering everything from offbeat pets to Oriental carpets, complete with cinemas, restaurants, sports shops, and banks. Those who like to combine sightseeing with food can then eat their way along this end of Dizengoff,

which is crowded with snack bars and restaurants, offering everything from fruit juice, pizza, and hamburgers to Hungarian *blintzes* and *schwarma*.

The raised piazza with the sculpture-fountain spouting in its center is **Kikar Dizengoff**. Originally a traffic roundabout, the pedestrian level has since been lifted above the street, creating a peculiar urban hub but allowing the free flow of people above and traffic below.

The next street to cut across Dizengoff is Gordon. Works of the great masters, such as Picasso and Chagall, are displayed here beside paintings by leading Israeli artists such as Agam, Gutman, and Kadishman. Although these works are displayed in galleries, which are essentially stores, it is the Tel Aviv custom to walk in, around, and out of these stores along Gordon and adjoining streets like Dov Hoz, as if in a museum.

More arts off Ibn Gabirol

Ibn Gabirol also runs north through the city from the Ha-Bimah Theater. To the right of Ibn Gabirol on Sha'ul

ha-Melekh Street, a rival cultural complex, the **Tel Aviv Museum of Art** Ⓦ (Mon, Wed Sat 10am–6pm, Tue, Thur 10am–9pm, Fri 10–2pm, closed Sun ; tel: 03-607 7020; www.tamuseum. org.il; charge), has four central galleries, an auditorium that often features film retrospectives, numerous other halls, a sculpture garden, a cafeteria, and a shop. There are exhibitions of 17th-century Dutch and Flemish masters, 18th-century Italian paintings, Impressionists, post-Impressionists, and a good selection of 20th-century art from the US and Europe, in addition to modern Israeli work.

Next to the museum, the **Tel Aviv Center for Performing Arts** was inaugurated in the 1990s. This attractive new building includes the New Israel Opera as well as both a theater and an auditorium.

Architectural contrasts

At the corner of Sha'ul ha-Melekh and Weizmann are several of the more striking modern edifices in the city, the most unusual being **Asia House**, created by architect Mordechai

Ben-Horin in gleaming white to resemble a horizontal series of giant rolling waves. Its entrance hall holds a permanent exhibit of sculpture under a pastel-colored mosaic ceiling. The **IBM Building** next door towers above, a three-sided cylinder supported on a mushroom-like shaft. Designed by Israeli architects Yasky, Gil & Silvan, it creates a handsome profile for the city skyline. Across the street, the red slated roofs of the **German Templar Colony** (1870–1939) provide yet another architectural style in a city of contrasts.

On the other side of the Kirya, the IDF's headquarters, is the **Azrieli Center**: three towers – one round, one square, and one triangular joined together on the lower floors by a large shopping mall. For several years these towers were the tallest buildings in Israel, although they have since been surpassed by Aviv Tower in Ramat Gan. Travel up to the 49th-floor observatory of the round tower for one of the best views in Israel, although it is marred by heat haze in the summer (Sun–Thur 10am–8pm, Fri 10am–6pm,

Outside the Museum of Art.

Tel Aviv Center for Performing Arts.

Sat 10am–8pm; tel: 03-608 1179; charge). The Azrieli Center has direct access to the Ha-Shalom train station.

Yitzhak Rabin Square

Moving back westward to Ibn Gabirol, the road leads northward to the central square of the city, next to the headquarters of the municipality. It was here, when it was then known as Kikar Malchei Yisrael (the Square of the Kings of Israel), on November 4, 1995, that Prime Minister Yitzhak Rabin was assassinated after a huge demonstration in support of the peace process. The square was immediately renamed **Yitzhak Rabin Square** (**Kikar Yitzhak Rabin**) **X**, and there is an unusual memorial close to the spot where he fell, at the northern end of the square, just behind the steps to the City Hall. Portraits, paintings, and graffiti cover the area as the people's memorial to a man respected by many of differing convictions.

East along Jabotinski is **Kikar Ha-Medina**, where the road makes a huge circle and contains many of the country's most expensive clothes stores. Farther east, a dense forest of high-rise buildings suddenly looms on the horizon. Technically speaking, the Diamond Exchange district is in adjoining Ramat Gan rather than Tel Aviv itself. The gleaming office blocks contain not only the diamond traders, who handle some US$20 billion-worth of the precious stones each year, but also many of the country's most successful high-tech enterprises.

The **Diamond Exchange** **Y** has a museum (Sun–Thur 10am–4pm, Fri 8am–noon; tel: 03-576 0219; charge), which tells the story of diamonds. The complex is also the site of Israel's tallest building, the 69-floor Aviv Tower.

Farther to the east, **Ramat Gan**, with a population of 160,000, is home to Bar Ilan University, Sheba Medical Center, Israel's largest hospital, and a **safari park** where lions, elephants, hippopotami, and other Asian and African animals entertain the occupants of passing cars (Sat–Thur 9am–4pm, winter 2.30pm), Fri 9am–2pm; tel: 03-630 5305; www.safari.co.il; charge).

The Yitzhak Rabin Square eco-pool and Holocaust memorial after renovation.

Nightlife

Tel Aviv's energy feeds through into its nightlife, and it's a family affair: pedestrians of all ages jam the streets until the early hours.

In the late 1980s an advertising campaign for Tel Aviv's nightlife revolved around the slogan "The City That Never Stops." The label has stuck. Tel Avivians are proud of their energy and stamina, working hard by day and playing hard at night. Nightlife in Tel Aviv, as throughout Israel, starts late. The restaurants don't get busy until after 10pm, and the bars, cafes, and nightclubs start filling up from midnight onward.

But if night birds start late in terms of time, they start early age-wise. Parents will often take small children to bars and cafes at midnight, while unaccompanied 14-year-olds roam the streets well into the early hours. Israeli parents take the relaxed attitude that there is nothing youngsters can do at three in the morning that they couldn't do at three in the afternoon.

In any event, Tel Aviv's streets are jammed with pedestrians of all ages, as well as cars, well into the early hours of the morning, especially at the weekends (remember that the weekend days off are Friday and Saturday).

At night tourists might do well to stick to the seafront. Tel Aviv's Mediterranean coast stretches from the fashionable restaurants of Tel Aviv Port and Little Old Tel Aviv in the north, through the male gay pick-up venue in Independence Gardens (Gan Ha'atsma'ut), to the cafes popular with teenagers to the south of the hotel district, and the sleazy red-light district behind the Opera Tower.

Farther south are the restaurants of the Yemenite Quarter and then Yafo, with its nightclubs and fish restaurants. Perhaps the latter are the most delightful night-time experiences. Taboun is the pick of these. Enjoying a meal with the sound of the sea lapping against the shore is not only romantic but can also be a delicious relief from the city's stifling humidity.

But, humidity aside, those who want to search inland for the core of Tel Aviv nightlife are also not starved of choice. Those looking for culture tend to hang out in the vicinity of the Ha-Bimah Theater/Mann Auditorium complex at the beginning of Dizengoff. Farther north on Dizengoff, near the junction with Gordon, Israelis like to stroll around at night popping into art galleries and sipping coffee at nearby cafes. Gallery crawling is also the done thing in Old Yafo.

Sheinkin versus Florentin

Dizengoff, however, is no longer the main after-dark attraction. The trendiest neighborhood is Sheinkin, a narrow street to the north of the financial district which runs eastward from the Yemenite Quarter. Sheinkin offers an abundant choice of small restaurants, cafes, and bars. Sheinkin is trendy for the middle-aged but Florentin to the south (northeast of Yafo) is the pulsating, hip place for the young, whether bohemian, artsy, affluent, or anyone just looking for a good time.

Remember that the essence of Tel Aviv nightlife is outdoors. As elsewhere in the Mediterranean there is a fine dividing line between a cafe and a bar, and it is acceptable just to have a drink in a cafe, or go to a pub for a meal or a soft drink or coffee. Nothing is nicer than to find an outdoor table and watch the world go by. The night crowds can be noisy and lively, but drunkenness is very rare. Indeed, Israelis are infamous for spending long hours in bars nursing one beer.

Be it in the cafes or the clubs, age is no barrier to enjoying the nightlife in "the city that never stops."

Beit Guvrin's bell-shaped caves.

THE INLAND PLAINS

Don't rush through the plains between Tel Aviv and
Jerusalem or you'll miss the monasteries, caves,
and splendid views of the Judean foothills.

I t is not the most acclaimed tourist area in the Holy Land, nor is
it the most famous for its ruins,
and many visitors pass through
Israel's inland plains, from Tel Aviv to
Jerusalem and back, never venturing
from the main roads. Yet the consistent flow of conquerors, immigrants,
wayfarers, and settlers has left its mark
on the landscape, and the area – still
the central crossroads of the nation –
is rich in history.

Rising from the flat coastal plain
into the gently rolling Judean foothills, this area has always been one
of the most densely populated in the
country. Some of the first modern
Jewish settlements in the 1880s and
1890s were established here. Today,
several of these villages have grown
into cities; while others, with their
lush vegetation and smell of cow
dung, convey an air of tranquility at
odds with the hectic pace of so much
of modern Israel.

Groundbreaking research

Start your journey at **Rekhovot ❶**,
about 20km (12 miles) southeast
of Tel Aviv. This is the home of the
Weizmann Institute of Science
(www.weizmann.ac.il), the R&D center
named after Chaim Weizmann, the
country's first president, and situated near the northern entrance to

the city on Highway 412. Weizmann
was also an organic chemist of international renown and for many years
the leader of the Zionist movement.
He invented a new method of producing acetone, which assisted the
British war effort during World War
I, and he was instrumental in secur-
ing the Balfour Declaration. Founded
in 1934, the Weizmann Institute
originally concentrated on agriculture and medicine, but has become a
world-class research institute. Today
it has 2,600 researchers and graduate

Main Attractions
Rekhovot
Ramla
Lod
Modi'im
Latrun
Abu Ghosh
Motsa
Sorek Cave
Beit Guvrin

*Professor Zvi Livneh at the Weizmann Institute
of Science.*

The Vaulted Pool in Ramla.

students, and more than 400 research projects in such fields as cancer cures, hormones, immunology, aging, cell structure, atomic particles, and astrophysics. The Institute has produced three Nobel prize winners in recent years. Children will enjoy the hands-on **Clore Garden of Science** (Sun–Thur 9am–5pm, Fri 9am–6pm; tel: 08-934 4401).

The center's moving spirit in its early years was Meyer Weisgal, an American showbiz impresario who, in addition to raising millions of dollars for the institute, used to pace the grounds picking up discarded cartons and even matchsticks. The institute is still one of the tidiest places in Israel. There are daily guided tours of the grounds. The view from the top of the futuristic atomic particle accelerator is good, and Weizmann's house, designed by Erich Mendelsohn in 1936–7, is worth seeing.

Opposite the Weizmann Institute is another prestigious academic campus: the **Hebrew University's Faculty of Agriculture**, one of the world's leading research centers in this discipline,

which has played an important role in the development of the country's leading-edge farming capability.

Slightly north of Rekhovot on Highway 40 from the southern entrance to the city lies Ramla and Lod (Lydda). They were originally Arab towns, but many of their inhabitants left during the War of Independence in 1948. Today they are two of the few mixed Jewish-Arab communities in Israel.

Three important mosques are to be found in **Ramla** ❷: the 8th-century **White Mosque**; the **Mosque of the Forty**, built by the Mamelukes in 1318; and the **Great Mosque** (Sun–Thur 8–11am; charge), situated west of the bus station near the market and built on the site of the Crusader Cathedral of St John. The **Vaulted Pool**, an underground cistern in the town's center, dates from the 9th century. The **British War Cemetery**, 2km (1.25 miles) east of Ramla, has become a place of pilgrimage for Israeli children who seek the grave of Corporal Harry Potter, a hitherto unsung 19-year old soldier killed in action in Hebron in 1939.

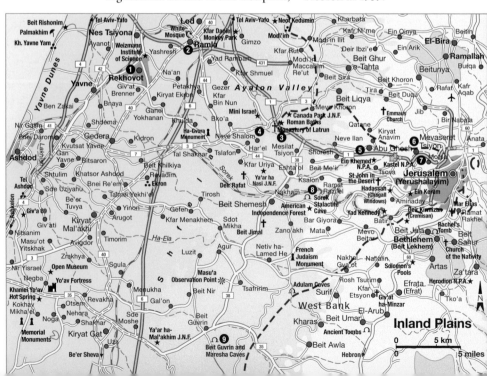

North of **Lod** is **Ben Gurion International Airport**, named after Israel's first prime minister. Now lying in the shadow of soaring jetliners, Lod was an important town during the biblical and Second Temple periods. Visit the ancient **Sheikh's Tomb**, in the center of the derelict Old Town, built over the ruins of a 12th-century Crusader church, in the basement of which is allegedly the **Tomb of St George**. The fact that the church is not open to visitors suggests that the patron saint of England and legendary slayer of dragons is not really buried here.

The Judean foothills

East of Ramla, in the Jerusalem foothills (take Highway 443), is the site of **Modi'im**, the birthplace of the Hasmonean family, leaders of the 2nd-century BC revolt against the Syrian-Greek empire which then controlled Judea. The revolt began in Modi'im when an official ordered the people to sacrifice a cockerel on a pagan altar, in accordance with the imperial policy of fostering Hellenization and repressing Judaism. Mattitiahu, a local priest, and his five sons killed the official and his military escort, triggering the conflict. The revolt, led by Judas Maccabeus, the third son, expanded all over Judea, resulting in the recapture of the Temple and the restoration of Jewish worship in Jerusalem.

Not much remains of ancient **Modi'im**, but an attractive park has been laid out, with a model of a village of the period of the revolt. Visitors can bake pitta bread in the ancient-style ovens, handle replicas of ancient agricultural implements, and spin yarn. At Hanukkah, the festival commemorating the revolt, a torch is lit at Modi'im and carried in relays to Jerusalem to light candles at the Western Wall. Next to Modi'im is **Neot Kedumim** (Sun–Thur 8.30am–sunset, Fri 8.30am–1pm; tel: 08-977 0777; www.n-k.org.il; charge), a biblical landscape reserve, which presents

the plants and agricultural lifestyle of biblical times. Children will also enjoy the nearby **Kfar Daniel Monkey Park** (Sun–Thur 10am–5pm, Fri 9am–2pm, Sat 10am–3pm; tel: 08-928 5888; charge). Farther along Highway 443 looms the new town of Modi'in, which has grown into a city of 75,000 and offers young Israeli couples a high quality of life midway between Jerusalem and Tel Aviv.

Return to the main road to Jerusalem, and travel the 15km (9 miles) southeast on Highway 1 to the French Trappist **Monastery of Latrun ❸** (just across the old border with Jordan). The monks make and sell wine, which complements the locally produced cheeses. The remains of a 12th-century Crusader fortress called **Le Toron des Chevaliers**, and an almost perfectly preserved Roman villa and bathhouse, are also located nearby.

Mini Israel

A kilometer back north on Highway 424 is **Mini Israel**, with miniature models of the country's principal sites (see page 260).

TIP

You can pick up the train at Beit Shemesh station for the scenic ride through the hillsides to Jerusalem.

The Monastery of Latrun.

DRINK

Many wineries in the Valley of Elah welcome visitors. Try the visitors' center at Kibbutz Tsova, west of Beit Shemesh (Sun–Fri 10am–1pm; tel: 02-990 8261).

A little to the north on Highway 3 is **Canada Park**, a recreation center with vineyards, almond orchards, ancient fig trees, and adventure playgrounds. In the park are the ruins of a village thought to be the Emmaus of the New Testament, where according to St Luke's Gospel the risen Jesus was seen. Emmaus was also the site of one of the Hasmoneans' greatest victories.

If you take Highway 3 southwest from Latrun you will shortly come to **Neve Shalom** ❹, a heartening experiment in Jewish-Arab coexistence. The only settlement founded specifically for people of the two groups to live together, it runs special courses where Jewish and Arab schoolchildren learn about each other's cultures, and has a Jewish-Arab kindergarten and elementary school.

Back toward Jerusalem, Highway 1 enters the gorge of **Shaar Hagai**, west of Latrun, then climbs steeply through the wooded hills. They weren't always so green; when the first Jewish pioneers arrived, they saw a hilly desert stripped of trees by centuries of abuse. The early forests were

made up almost entirely of indigenous Jerusalem pine, which still dominates, but foresters are diversifying for both ecological and aesthetic reasons, planting cypress, acacia, eucalyptus, pistachio, carob, and varieties of the local scrub oak.

Climbing the hill, the nearby villages of Shoresh, Neve Ilan, Yad Hashmona, Kiryat Anavim, and Ma'ale ha-Khamisha offer guesthouses with stunning views of the Judean Hills and swimming pools.

A little farther along are three Arab villages, each of them with features of interest. The largest, **Abu Ghosh** ❺, has two fine churches and a French Benedictine monastery. A sacred spring, where Jesus is said to have drunk, is situated in a garden of towering pines and old palm trees. Some great local Arab restaurants offer tasty spiced pitta bread, *houmous*, and *tahina*.

Nearby **Ein Naquba** is the only Arab village built by the State of Israel from scratch; it was constructed for villagers whose homes were taken over by new immigrants after they fled from their village of Beit Naquba in the 1948 war.

Although most of its fruit trees and vegetable plots are watered by modern methods, neighboring **Ein Rafa** has an irrigation system that dates back to biblical times. Some 4 hectares (10 acres) of land are watered by a natural spring, which flows into the individual plots according to a traditional, stringently observed eight-day rota system.

Between the two villages and the main road, right by the exit from Highway 1 at the Khemed interchange, is **Ein Khemed** (or Aqua Bella; daily 8am–4pm, until 5pm Apr–Sept; tel: 02-534 2741; charge), a landscaped camping site and nature reserve with a stream flowing through it, and a restored Crusader farm. Up the hill is the Jerusalem outer suburb of **Mevaseret Tsiyon** ❻, built beneath **Kastel** (daily 8am–4pm, until 5pm Apr–Sept; tel: 02-533 0476; charge),

An ancient olive press has survived in the Maresha Caves.

an important Arab fortress (the name derives from castle) and site of a key battle for Jerusalem in 1948. The fortress has been preserved as a memorial to those who died, and some of the bunkers and pillboxes restored. There are magnificent views of the surrounding Judean Hills and the gleaming expanse of Jerusalem.

Continuing in the direction of Jerusalem, you will come to the village of **Motsa** ❼, and the stump of **Herzl's Cypress**. Planted by the founder of modern Zionism on his visit to the Holy Land in 1898, the tree became a place of pilgrimage, and was later cut down as an anti-Zionist gesture. A glass case has been built around the stump, and it is traditional for presidents of Israel to plant a tree in the surrounding garden as a symbol of the continuing growth of Zionism. On the curve of Highway 1 at the bottom of the hill is a restored 19th-century synagogue with remains of a Byzantine synagogue in the basement; a recently opened visitors' center sits behind it.

The Jerusalem corridor

From Kastel, take Highway 3965 south to the junction of 395. Here is **Sataf**, where there are clearly visible remains of a 4000 BC Chalcolithic village with some of the oldest agricultural traces in the region, as well as the remains of a pre-1948 Arab village. Two springs, Ein Sataf and Ein Bikura, flow into the Sorek river bed below, and the terraces have been converted to show how they would have been farmed in biblical times.

Take Highway 395 westward. **Kibbutz Tsova** has the ruins of a Crusader castle called Belmont and a hotel of the same name. Travel down the road to Beit Shemesh and back eastward along 3855 and 3866 to the spectacular **Sorek Stalactite Cave** ❽ (Sun–Thur, Sat 8am–4pm, until 5pm Apr–Sept, Fri 8am–3pm; tel: 02-991 1117; charge), which extends across some 6 hectares (15 acres) of the

Avshalom Nature Reserve. Discovered by chance during routine quarrying, it is by far the largest cave in Israel and contains stalactites and stalagmites of breathtaking beauty. After viewing a film about the formations, visitors walk down a path in the cave, which can take about 45 minutes.

Just to the south, back along Highway 38, is the **Valley of Elah**, where David killed Goliath, the Philistine from Gath. The battle is described in I Samuel 17. The actual site of the encounter is not marked; today a kibbutz and a TV satellite receiving station stand in the valley.

South of here, farther along 38 and right onto 35 on the road to Kiryat Gat, is the ancient site of **Beit Guvrin** ❾, opposite a modern kibbutz of the same name. There are many Crusader ruins here, but it is the **Maresha Caves** (daily 8am–4pm, until 5pm Apr–Sept; charge; tel: 08-681 1020) that are of special note. There are hundreds of these bell-shaped caves caused by ancient Roman quarrying, although some date right back to Greek and even Phoenician times.

The church at Abu Ghosh.

Stalactites in Sorek Cave.

MINI ISRAEL

Mini Israel provides a polyurethane panorama of the entire country, from the traffic-clogged streets of Tel Aviv to the ski lifts of Mount Hermon.

Israel may be a small country, but it is still impossible to take in all of its major sites in a single visit. One solution is a trip to Mini Israel, where 350 model buildings, the snow on Mount Hermon, Red Sea fish, and much more can all be seen on a 5-hectare (13-acre) site. With good disabled access, it's either an ideal introduction to Israel or a final summing up.

Located midway between Tel Aviv and Jerusalem, Mini Israel is just a 20-minute drive from Ben Gurion International Airport. The largest of the world's 45 miniature model parks, it was built by private investors with assistance from Madurodam in Holland and opened in 2001. Its Star of David layout overcomes several problems. Firstly, Israel's long, thin shape would make the park impossible to walk around without backtracking. Secondly, the country has no consensus borders anyway. Most models are on a 1:25 scale, and are a delight of detail.

The miniature figures at the Western Wall sway in prayer. Beh the wall is a scale model of Jerusalem's Dome of the Rock.

The players move in grooves and the crowd waves in Jerusalem's Teddy Stadium.

Where to find it

Mini Israel is located on Highway 424, 1km (0.6 miles) north of Latrun – just off Highway 1. Buses leave for it from major hotels in Tel Aviv, Jerusalem, Netanya, and Herzliya (check with your hotel). Fri 10am–2pm, Sat–Thur Nov–Mar 10am–6pm, Apr–May and Sept–Oct until 7pm, June until 8pm, July–Aug until 10pm. Food: self-service restaurant and snack bars. Recommended tour time: 2–3 hours. Tel: 1-700-559-559 Email: info@minisrael.co.il www.minisrael.co.il

A statue of Mordechai Anilewitz, leader of the Warsaw Ghetto Uprising in 1943.

e animals enter two by to in this model of the Biblical Zoo, usalem.

n Gurion International Airport, in reality just a few minutes ay, in carbon-friendly form.

Just some of Jerusalem's more notable buildings, including the Montefiore Windmill and the majestic King David Hotel.

THE BIG EFFORT TO THINK SMALL

Mini Israel's 30,000 mini-residents include every type of Israeli imaginable, as well as the distinct clothing of dozens of Christian sects. The miniature Jews by the Western Wall sway, while Muslims on the Temple Mount kneel down.

This realism at Mini Israel extends to nature as well. The park has 50,000 plants, including 20,000 miniature trees such as olives, palms, cypresses, and pomegranates. All this greenery is fed by 25km (15 miles) of irrigation pipes.

Most of the models were created by new immigrant artists from the former Soviet Union, many of whom were then asked to undertake the models for Turkey's miniature park Miniaturk, which opened in 2003.

From March to September the best time to visit Mini Israel is in the early evening. Visitors not only avoid the oppressive daytime heat, but as twilight approaches more than 2,000 light bulbs are turned on to illuminate the models and enable them to be seen from an enchanting new angle.

You don't have to visit the original site of the Sermon on the Mount, in the Galilee, to see the Church of the Beatitudes.

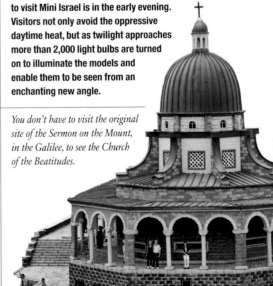

Hiking in the Judean desert.

THE WEST BANK

This remains a contentious area, but its
holy sites, biblical lands, and ancient
cities still draw pilgrims and tourists.

Hamas flags.

Lying at the heart of the Holy Land, the West Bank
is also at the heart of the Israeli-Palestinian conflict. Since 1994, the area has been divided with
the Palestinian Authority ruling the major cities like
Bethlehem and Nablus from Ramallah, and Israel controlling most of the area through a military administration
seen as an occupation even by its allies.

For centuries, Jews, Christians, and Muslims have paid
homage here, and today pilgrims still flock to its shrines. Scattered
throughout the region, these places are often claimed by more than one
religion, and such spots lend a physical immediacy to age-
old conflicts. More than a millennium has not erased the
tension in this contested land.

After the end of the British Mandate in 1948 the West
Bank, including East Jerusalem, was occupied by Jordan. In
1967 it was captured by Israel, making 300,000 Palestinians
into first-time refugees; another 150,000 picked up their
belongings for the second time. Many moved to Jordan
proper. In the mid-1970s Yitzhak Rabin's Labor government began setting up Jewish settlements in the West Bank,
exploiting the messianic spirit of right-wing extremists, for
what they saw would subsequently be a bargaining chip
in future peace negotiations with the Arabs. But the bluff
came back to haunt the Israeli left. When the right-wing
Likud came to power for the first time in 1977, the pace of
Jewish settlement became rapid, the West Bank was officially renamed
Judea and Samaria, and the declared policy was the eventual annexation
of all of the Land of Israel.

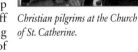

*Christian pilgrims at the Church
of St. Catherine.*

Rabin was returned to power in 1992, and in 1994 he took the first
tentative steps to restore the Occupied Territories to the Palestinian people, with all the major cities becoming part of the Palestinian Authority.
Ehud Barak proposed giving almost all the West Bank, including much
of East Jerusalem, to the Palestinians, but the offer was not enough. In
2005, for the first time, Jewish settlements were abandoned in Northern
Samaria within the framework of Ariel Sharon's disengagement policy.
Today much of the West Bank is separated from Israel by a harsh concrete
Security Wall, and the area should be approached with caution regarding
the security situation.

The Church of the Nativity,
Bethlehem.

LANDS OF THE BIBLE

Bethlehem is the high spot for many visitors to the West Bank, but the pastoral landscapes of the Bible also have many other interesting sites to explore.

I sraelis call the northern part of the West Bank by its biblical name, Samaria (Shomron in Hebrew), while south of Jerusalem is known as Judea (Yehuda). The road running through the heart of the West Bank, along the ridge of the mountain chain 800–1,000 meters (2,625–3,280ft) high, is known historically as the King's Highway and was an alternative trading route to the Via Maris (Mediterranean coastal road) linking Mesopotamia to Egypt 5,000 years ago. These mountain ridges, with a cooler, less humid climate, attracted much of the region's population, and the King's Highway passes through the major West Bank cities under autonomous Palestinian rule, as well as Jerusalem.

Known by Israel as Route 60, the highway is a worthwhile trip for the adventurous, passing through stunning countryside and pastoral biblical landscapes as well as the Palestinian urban enclaves. Clearly, when the security situation is tense it is impracticable to travel this route, and it may be necessary to change taxis at Israeli/ Palestinian roadblocks.

Highway 60, which comes down from the Galilee, enters the West Bank through the Jezreel Valley about 14km (8 miles) south of Afula. The most northerly of the Palestinian autonomous zones is **Jenin**, the

focus of the bitterest fighting in the second Intifada. To the south is the picturesque Dotan Valley, dropping dramatically to the west. It was here, so the story goes, that Joseph was sold to Egyptian traders by his jealous brothers. It is in this region that Israel abandoned three Jewish settlements – the first ever to be given up in the West Bank – in 2005.

Omri's stately capital

A little over 10km (6 miles) northwest of Nablus and 30km (18 miles) south

Main Attractions
Sebastya
Nablus
Shilo
Ramallah
Rachel's Tomb
Bethlehem
Herodion
Hebron
Wadi Kelt
Jericho

A terraced hillside in Samaria.

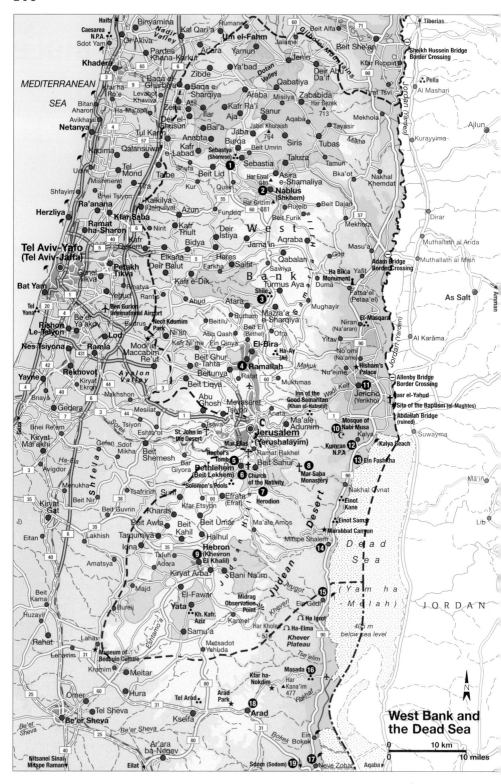

West Bank and
the Dead Sea

0   10 km

0   10 miles

of Jenin is the site of one of the most impressive ruins in the Holy Land: **Sebastya** ❶ (Shomron National Park; 8am–4pm; charge). Once called Samaria, it was the capital of the northern Kingdom of Israel upon King Omri's accession to power in 887 BC. He and his son, the ill-tempered Ahab, built magnificent palaces and temples inside a circular protective wall. Ahab incurred the wrath of the Lord by adding temples to Baal and Astarte, cult figures favored by his wife, Jezebel.

The remains of **Ahab's Palace** adjoin the impressive steps, which led to Herod's **Temple of Augustus**, constructed c.30 BC. Herod's grandiose style is not lost in the rubble, and parts of many of his massive constructions still stand. In addition to Herod's work, Sebastya's ruins include an enormous hippodrome, the acropolis, a basilica, and many remains of Israelite and Hellenistic walls. The colonnade-lined street is a majestic reminder of Sebastya's opulence.

In the village of Sebastia, just outside the Roman wall, lie the ruins of a Crusader cathedral. It is reputed to stand over the tombs of the prophets Elisha and Obadiah and of John the Baptist. This site is included in the **Mosque of Nabi Yaya**, in which a small chamber is believed to hold the head of John the Baptist.

Some 10km (6 miles) farther south is **Nablus** ❷ (Shkhem in Hebrew), which is many things to many people. One of the largest cities in the West Bank, with an estimated population of over 400,000 in the metropolitan area, it is chock-full of sites with biblical resonances. From a distance, Nablus looks like a *pointilliste* painting: innumerable blue doors dot houses neatly spread across a hillside. Within earshot there's a cacophony of sounds: honking car horns, the majestic *muezzin* calling the Muslim faithful to prayer, and the ululations of Arab women.

Rich in history, the area just outside today's city center is mentioned in Genesis as the place where Jacob pitched his tents. **Jacob's Well**, located here, is still in use by Nablus residents. According to St John's

TIP

Before venturing into the West Bank, check on the prevailing political climate. Modest dress (no shorts) is recommended. Several companies offer group tours, though these invariably have a Jewish nationalistic theme.

Banksy grafitti on a wall in Bethlehem.

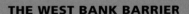

THE WEST BANK BARRIER

It was conceived in the tradition of the Great Wall of China – to keep out the barbarians – but it has attracted the opprobrium of the Berlin Wall. Its 670km (420-mile) length varies from a 5-meter (16ft) high wire-and-mesh fence-like structure set in a concrete base to an 8-meter (26ft) high solid concrete wall incorporating watchtowers. With a deep ditch on one side, the barrier seems to many to symbolize the gulf between Israelis and Palestinians.

The Israeli government, announcing the plan in 2002, said the purpose was to exclude Palestinian suicide bombers. Some opponents within Israel feared it might be interpreted as the future border with a Palestinian state. But the wall, estimated to cost US$2 million a kilometer, didn't simply follow Israel's pre-1967 boundaries. It embraced significant chunks of the West Bank containing Israeli settlements, thus enabling Palestinians to condemn it as a blatant land grab.

The effects on many Palestinians were more than symbolic. According to one United Nations report, the wall separated more than 200,000 Palestinians from their hospitals, schools, and workplaces. Farmers claimed their livelihoods were threatened when the wall separated their homes from their land. The only consolation is that few expect it to have the longevity of the Great Wall of China.

TIP

There are many Israeli army checkpoints in the West Bank where overseas tourists are required to show their passports.

Gospel (4:25–6), Jesus stopped here for refreshment, weary from his travels. He spoke to a Samaritan woman who drew water from the well. "I know that the Messiah cometh, which is called Christ," she told him, whereupon Jesus responded, "I that speak unto thee am he." Adjoining this structure is a Greek Orthodox convent built on the remains of a Crusader church.

Nearby, the **Tomb of Joseph** is a shrine reputed to hold the great man's bones "in a parcel of ground which Jacob bought of the sons of Hamor the father of Shkhem" (Joshua 24:32). (Defying scripture, there is another cenotaph for Joseph at the Tomb of the Patriarchs in Hebron.)

During the time of the Judges, Abimelech, the son of Gideon, had himself proclaimed king here; some 200 years later, in 928 BC, the 10 northern tribes called on Jeroboam to be king, and for several years Shkhem served as the capital of the new northern kingdom of Israel. Going farther back into biblical history, Abraham probably stopped in Shkhem just after he

arrived in Canaan, and some believe that here he was given the covenant between God and man.

The Samaritans

Standing like gateposts at the southeastern entrance to Nablus are two historic peaks, **Har Eival** and **Har Grizim**, named by Moses as the mountains of cursing and blessing. After the conquest, Joshua built an altar on Har Eival. The Samaritan ceremony of the Paschal sacrifice on Har Grizim is a colorful tourist attraction – but not for the squeamish, as lambs are slaughtered.

Har Grizim is the center of the Samaritan religion. The sect's origins date back to 720 BC, when Assyria swept through the northern kingdom. Returning from exile in 538 BC, the Jews shunned the Samaritans for their intermarriage with the conquerors, although the Samaritans claimed strict adherence to the Mosaic Law. Today, about half the 800 remaining Samaritans (they were tens of thousands strong during the Middle Ages) celebrate the Passover holiday.

Members of the Samaritan sect pray to mark the Shavuot Feast on Mount Gerizim.

In biblical times the city of **Shilo** (Siloah) ❸ stood equidistant between Nablus and Bethel. According to the Bible, it was at Siloah that the main division of the Promised Land among the 12 tribes was made and where the cities were allocated. In the 11th century BC it was the religious center for the Israelite tribes, and for over 200 years, the sacred ground for the Ark of the Covenant. It was here that the great prophet Samuel's mother Hannah prayed for his birth. In time, the Philistines defeated the Israelites, captured the ark, and burned Siloah to the ground. Today the *tel* of Siloah spans less than 3 hectares (8 acres), although archeologists have unearthed remnants of civilizations dating to the Bronze Age (1600 BC). There is also a large modern Jewish settlement nearby.

As you travel south of Nablus en route to Ramallah, limestone terraces climb up and down the hills, retaining all the mineral-rich soil they can. Knotty olive trees edged with flora grace the landscape. These olives are harvested by the local farmers, who transport them to the villages for pressing. Twelve kilometers (7 miles) northwest of Ramallah, **Bir Zeit** is the oldest and most prestigious Palestinian university, founded as a school in 1924 and becoming a university in 1975.

Just north of Ramallah, two towns atop nearby hills serve as natural landmarks: **Bethel** and **Ai**. Bethel is prominent in early biblical narratives as the site where Jacob dreamed of a ladder ascending to heaven. At this spot he made an altar and called it Beit El, or House of God. This is also where the Ark of the Law remained until the time of the Judges. Ai was one of the earliest cities captured by Joshua and the Israelites during their military conquest of Canaan.

Ramallah

The Palestinian town of **Ramallah** ❹ sees itself as the capital of the West Bank. Much smaller than Nablus, and without the historical significance of Jerusalem, Ramallah is most remarkable for its affluence. Streets and streets of large, luxurious villas testify to the town's wealth. While adjoining El Bira is predominantly Muslim, Ramallah itself is mainly Christian, and almost every Ramallah family has immediate relatives living in the US. Ramallah provides much of the intellectual fervor and financial fuel for the Palestinian national movement. The town's status was further enhanced by the fact that Yasser Arafat's widow Suha is a Christian from Ramallah (she converted to Islam before marrying the Palestinian leader), although she now lives in Paris. Ramallah's importance was consolidated when Arafat spent his last years virtually imprisoned by the IDF in the Mukatar government complex north of the city. He is also buried here, although in a "mobile" grave that the Palestinians plan moving to Jerusalem "when the time comes".

Demographically speaking, Ramallah is in effect part of the Jerusalem

Tenacious flora.

Downtown Ramallah.

An acacia tree thriving in the wilderness.

Bethlehem at night.

conurbation, as the southern suburbs of Kalandia lead into the northern neighborhoods of Israel's capital – Atarot (which has Jerusalem's airport as well as a large industrial zone), the affluent suburb of Beit Ha'nina, and the Shu'afat refugee camp.

Bethlehem is in the same manner also part of the Jerusalem metropolitan area. The southern Jerusalem neighborhood of Gilo almost touches the town of Christ's birth, while somewhere within Jerusalem's city limits, Samaria becomes Judea.

The Jewish settlements in this region, such as Adam, Ofra, Psagot, and Bet El, can be reached via a bypass road to the east of the Ramallah road, going through the northern Jerusalem suburb of Pisgat Ze'ev.

Judea

There is no clear boundary marking the transition of the hills of Samaria to those of Judea, as both are part of the same central range of high ground, reaching from above Ramallah in the north through the Judean cities of Bethlehem and Hebron. Yet the **Judean Hills** have sustained a body of legend as a wellspring of the Old and New Testaments. To the east, marking the descent of the range into the Jordan Rift Valley, lies the **Judean Desert**, which over the centuries served as a place of refuge for prophets, monks, and kings. Judea is as elusive as it is revered; all around, the arid rolling hills remind you of biblical times and belie the tensions below the surface.

The approach to Bethlehem, just south of the border within the Palestinian autonomous zone, holds **Rachel's Tomb ❺** (still inside Israeli-held territory), where the wife of the Patriarch Jacob and mother of Joseph and Benjamin is said to be buried. The shrine is one of the holiest in Israel, a place of worship for Jews and Muslims. The dome over the site was rebuilt by British philanthropist Sir Moses Montefiore in 1841, at the place where, it is said, "Jacob set a pillar upon her grave."

Shrines of Bethlehem

Centuries after Rachel, Boaz married Ruth after she gleaned his fields. (Their great-grandson David became the poet-king of Israel.) On the eastern edge of **Bethlehem ❻** lies the **Field of Ruth**. It is near the Arab village of **Beit Sahur** (House of the Shepherd), and is believed to be the field where the angel appeared to the shepherds to announce the birth of Jesus.

On **Manger Street**, which leads directly into the hub of the town, up a flight of stairs, you'll find three huge water cisterns hewn out of rock, said to be **David's Well**. When he was battling the Philistines in their garrison here, thirst prompted David to cry, "Oh that one would give me water to drink of the well of Bethlehem, which is by the gate." But, offered the water drawn from the well of his enemies, he refused to drink.

Today, music, bells, and churches grace the town. The area teems with pilgrims during the holidays, and

the festivities don't stop after Christmas and Easter. The pomp, ornate decor, and beautiful displays continue year-round.

Christ was born in Bethlehem. The exact routes taken by the Nazarene in life remain unknown, and the Gospels do not even agree on chronology, but over the ages there has been a broadening consensus on the exact site of his birth. Following the road into Manger Square, you come to the **Church of the Nativity** (daily dawn–dusk), entered by stooping through a small entrance, reduced to such a size by the Crusaders for defense purposes. The original basilica was built in 325 by Emperor Constantine the Great. The foundation for it is the cave revered in Christian tradition as the place where Jesus was born, which is mentioned in the writings of St Justin Martyr just 100 years after Christ.

Beyond the vestibule is the nave; much of this interior, including the towering wooden beams, dates from Emperor Justinian's rebuilding in the 6th century. At the front of the church, downstairs, is the **Grotto of the Nativity**, where the altar features a barely discernible 12th-century mosaic. But the eye is riveted to a gleaming star on the floor of this small space, inscribed in Latin *Hic de virgine Maria Jesus Christus natus est* (Here Jesus Christ was born of the Virgin Mary). Next to the ornate and gilded grotto is the **Chapel of the Manger**, where Mary placed the newborn child.

The Church of the Nativity adjoins several churches of varying Christian denominations. The most celebrated on Christmas Eve is **St Catherine's**, from which Bethlehem's annual midnight mass is broadcast worldwide.

A few minutes' walk down Milk Grotto Street will take you to the **Milk Grotto Church**. Its milky white color gives it the name; the legend is that while Mary was feeding the newborn Jesus, some of her milk splashed to the stone floor and permanently whitened it. Today stone scrapings are sold to pilgrims to improve breastfeeding.

Outside the churches and shrines, countless self-appointed tour guides promise to show you all you wish to

FACT

The Crimean War in 1854 began as a result of an ownership dispute between the Catholic and Greek Orthodox Churches over a corner of the Church of the Nativity. The Ottoman Turks sided with the Catholics while the Russian Orthodox Church rushed to defend their Greek brothers.

Armenian Orthodox christians worship at the Church of the Nativity.

The Mar Saba area is inhabited by Bedouin, who claim to descend from the monastery's ancient caretakers, who came here from Byzantium.

see. They often know some interesting tidbits about the history of the town, but you must pay for this "freely" offered information or be hounded around Manger Square and its environs. All over town, but particularly in the square, vendors offer a wide array of religious articles and artifacts. They are freshly minted but traditionally inspired, often of olive wood, ceramics, or Jerusalem stone. If you are persistent but not too pushy, you can bargain and take care of all your Christmas shopping in one go.

As you look north, steeples rise from the hillside maze of houses, proclaiming the city's sanctity to the 12,000 Arab Christians who live here (controversially, the city of 25,000 now has a Muslim majority). Among the various religious institutions is an Arabic-language university directed by the Catholic Order of the Brothers of Christian Schools and known as **Bethlehem University**.

Castles in the wilderness

Some 8km (5 miles) southeast of here is the desert citadel of **Herodion** ❼

On the streets of Hebron.

(daily 8am–4pm; charge tel: 050 623 5821) – take Route 356 in southern Jerusalem past Har Homa and toward Nokdim and Tekoa. This is one of the most outstanding of Herod the Great's architectural conceits. A monstrous circular protective wall struck with four watchposts guarded Herod's living space; included in the layout were hot baths, arcades, a synagogue, and numerous other luxuries. The banqueting hall of the palace is as immense as a football stadium. In 2007 a Hebrew University professor discovered the tomb of Herod, 100 meters (110yds) from the site.

Even more remote, dug into the canyon walls overlooking the Kidron River to the northeast, is the blue-domed **Mar Saba Monastery** ❽ – it is so out of the way that you should not attempt to reach this location without a guide. St Saba used this serene niche in the desert as a retreat for study and worship, and in AD 492 he established the monastery named after him. In the 7th century, Persians and Arabs ruined the monastery and murdered the monks; it was rebuilt, however, and early in the 8th century John of Damascus came to the site. The writing he completed here made an important contribution to Christianity and is representative of Christian/Islamic differences at the time. Today the most prominent feature of the hermitage is the huge protective wall surrounding the complex. Among the finds displayed inside are the robed remains of St Saba himself, returned here in 1965 from Venice, where they had been preserved for more than 700 years. Also on view are the skulls of the hundreds of monks killed by the Persians in 614. Women are not allowed to enter the monastery.

Along the path to Mar Saba is the church of **St Theodosius**, where the three wise men are said to have rested after they worshiped the infant Jesus, and where St Theodosius died in 529 at the age of 105.

Roughly 8km (5 miles) from Bethlehem, as you head south toward Hebron, lie the dark-green cisterns known as **Solomon's Pools**. Tradition attributes them to the great Jewish king in the 10th century BC; archeology suggests they date from Roman times. In either case, an aqueduct carried water from here to the population of Jerusalem, and today the cisterns still serve as a source of water for the city.

Passionate Hebron

Close to 25km (15 miles) south of Bethlehem is the ancient city of **Hebron** ❾. The city represents layers of history, but its agricultural and urban community is progressive. Farmers, goat-keepers, shepherds, and food packers have made great strides in production by mechanizing their tasks.

The town also has a major **Islamic University**, which enrols nearly 2,000 Arab students. In existence since 1971, this institution is noted for promoting Palestinian culture and nationalism, much to the chagrin of the Israeli authorities, who close the facility every so often, citing anti-Israel activity.

Meander through the crisscross of alleyways in the Hebron *kasbah*. Here you will find a variety of artisans crafting pottery, compressing and sculpting olive wood, and blowing the colorful glass for which Hebron is widely known. Fresh fruits can be bought along the road sides and in the souk. Hebron-grown peaches, pale and sweet, are in demand all over the Middle East, and Hebron's produce, including dried and fresh fruits as well as many types of vegetables, is transported (with Israeli agreement) to Arab countries by way of the Allenby Bridge.

The Jewish presence in Hebron dates back to when God gave Abraham his son Isaac as well as Ishmael. Abraham chose this airy hill as the burial ground for his family, and today the **Tomb of the Patriarchs** (daily dawn to dusk) dominates the city and is visited by both Jews and Muslims. According to Genesis, Abraham bought the Cave of Machpelah from Ephron the Hittite as the burial site for his wife Sarah.

Here all three Patriarchs and their wives are believed to be buried, and

Mar Saba Monastery.

HEBRON KNOW-HOW

Hebron is definitely not the place to flaunt your knowledge of Hebrew (unless you find yourself in the small Jewish settlements in the city center), but any attempt to speak a few words of Arabic will be appreciated by the local people. The chances are that you'll be beckoned into a web of merchants' stalls or to a private home to enjoy a cup of tea. Turning down such an invitation will offend, but if you do go along steer clear of controversy. Debating the merits of Israel's presence on the West Bank, for example, is an ill-advised topic, especially since this is the last Arab town, under the Oslo Agreements, from which Israel has not fully retreated. Hebron is a place that remains volatile, with a Jewish enclave in the southeastern part of the city.

their cenotaphs form the center of the edifice: Abraham and Sarah in the center, Jacob and Leah on the outer side of the enclosure, and on the other side, within the mosque area, Isaac and Rebecca. More expansive folklore further contends the site holds the graves of Adam, Eve, Esau, and all 12 sons of Jacob as well.

Just outside the structure is **Joseph's Tomb**, at least in name – according to the Book of Joshua (24:32), Joseph's bones were laid to rest instead at Shkhem (Nablus) after their transport from Egypt.

The entire rectangular building gives the impression of a massive fortress, and was built with typical architectural confidence by Herod the Great. The Arabs later made a mosque of it, and the Crusaders made it a church during their stay, adding the rooftop crenellations. In 1188 it was taken by Saladin and again turned into a mosque.

Eight hundred years after Abraham, David was crowned King of Israel in Hebron, and later made it his capital. With David's capture of Jerusalem

from the Jebusites in around 1000 BC, the capital was shifted, although Hebron remained one of the four holy cities of Israel, along with Jerusalem, Tiberias, and Safed. The city's Jewish community survived the destruction of both Temples and remained until the year 1100, when they were expelled by the Crusaders. The population increased and dwindled alternately over the centuries. In 1929, and again in 1936, the community was wiped out in anti-Jewish riots, and after that it was not until 1967 that Jews re-entered Hebron. In 1968 a group of Jewish settlers gained *de facto* rights to settle in the area, although not in Hebron's Arab center. The result is a suburb called **Kiryat Arba** (Hebron's name in biblical times), overlooking the city from a nearby hill.

Today's tensions

Both Jews and Muslims claim descent from Abraham, and the Hebron area (particularly the Tomb of the Patriarchs) is a center of separate worship and mutual confrontation. Adding to the friction is the fact that a mosque

The old part of Hebron includes the Kasbah and Tomb of the Patriarchs.

covers part of the site, which had at one time been a synagogue.

The situation in Hebron has been tense ever since the 1967 war, and Israeli soldiers are on constant patrol in the area. Violent clashes between Jews and Arabs have riddled the town. Due to sporadic unrest here, it is best to consult the Israeli Government Tourist Office in Jerusalem before traveling to Hebron. Be sure you plan your return trip in advance, however – Hebron is the one place in the West Bank where you should not spend the night.

Leaving Hebron

On the outskirts of Hebron stands the gnarled but living **Oak of Abraham**, believed to be 600 years old. It is reputed to be on the site where Abraham was visited by three angels who told him of Isaac's impending birth. It is owned by Russian monks, who have a small monastery here. This place's ancient name is Mamre; Abraham supposedly built an altar and a well here, and Herod's structure on the site was where Bar Kochba's defeated troops were sold into slavery.

North of Hebron, along the road to Bethlehem, lies the **Etsyon Bloc**, where the agricultural-religious community of Kibbutz Ha-Dati was founded in 1926. It was abandoned in the Arab riots of 1929, and in 1948 its new settlers were wiped out in the War of Independence. The Etsyon Bloc and the surrounding Hebron Hills were retaken by the Israeli Army in June 1967, and several months later **Kibbutz Kfar Etsyon** was resettled by children of the original kibbutznikim. The Jewish city of Efrat now dominates the hillside.

From Kfar Etsyon the highway leads directly back to Jerusalem, some 14km (8 miles) away, through a newly constructed series of tunnels and bridges that bypasses Bethlehem. Just off the highway is the kibbutz of Ramat Rakhel, which offers an inspiring view of the desert, and nearby to the south

is the 11th-century Crusader monastery **Mar Elias**. Elijah supposedly slept here when fleeing from Jezebel. Close by, Israeli archeologists recently uncovered a Byzantine church. It has attractively preserved mosaics, and, more importantly, the Greek Orthodox Church recently proclaimed that the large flat stone in the 4th-century complex is to be called "The Mary Stone." The belief is that the pregnant Mary rested on this rock on her way south to Bethlehem.

To reach Jericho, travel the highway down from French Hill to Ma'ale Adumim, or through the new tunnel under Mount Scopus past the Hebrew University. After **Ma'ale Adumim**, the largest Jewish city in the West Bank, follow the highway down through the billowing stone hills of the Judean Desert to the lowest point on earth: the Dead Sea.

Hidden hermitage

On the road northeast of Jerusalem to Wadi Kelt, reached from Highway 1 down to the Dead Sea, turn right near Mitzpe Yericho. Here, the silence is so

Mountain bearing the ruins of the ancient fortress of Sartaba, northern Jordan Valley.

pure that it creates a ringing in your ears. For 1,600 years, since the age of the Patriarchs, monks have inhabited this surreal place, where the **Wadi Kelt River** meanders through a dramatic gorge in the canyon between Jericho and Jerusalem. This 35km (22-mile) stretch includes ruins on top of ruins, monasteries, eerie hermits' caves, and surprising watering holes. Honeycombing the rock face are hollowed-out niches which serve as cells for monks, who live off the fruit of the land. The **Greek Orthodox Monastery of St George** (Mon–Sat 8am–5pm) is just over a century old, but its community long precedes it. Hasmonean, Herodian, and Roman remains line this circuitous course.

South of Jericho, off the Jerusalem–Jericho highway, is the astounding **Mosque of Nabi Musa** ❿. It appears out of nowhere in the middle of nowhere. Here Muslims worship at the Tomb of Moses. The Mamelukes constructed the mosque in the 13th century, providing a high cenotaph for Moses. It is open during the times of Muslim prayer, and all day Friday.

Visiting the Monastery of St George.

Only Muslims are admitted in April, when thousands make their pilgrimage. The Muslim route to Nabi Musa intersects the procession of Christians making their Easter pilgrimages to al-Maghtes on the Jordan River, and clashes have resulted.

The walls of Jericho

The northern border between Israeli-held land and the Palestinian autonomous zone of Jericho is marked not by an international frontier but the **Oasis Casino**. The casino, a huge investment by an Austrian leisure chain, opened in 1998 just inside Palestinian territory past the checkpoint but was closed in 2000 following the start of the Second Intifada. Highway 90, going north to the Galilee along the Jordan Valley, once went through the city of Jericho itself but now bypasses it to the east.

Jericho must have been a prime spot for the earliest city-dwellers on earth some 10,000 years ago. Widely considered to have sprouted the first agricultural community, the town today is once more centered on agriculture. It is ensconced in an oasis in the midst of barren land; its greenery is nurtured by underground springs, the secret of the town's endurance. It was the first Arab town in the West Bank to be handed over to the Palestinian Authority (both in 1994 and 2005).

In times past, rulers used this spot as a warm-weather retreat. One such was Hisham, the 10th Umayyid caliph, who built the fabulous **Hisham's Palace**, about 3km (2 miles) from the city, in the 8th century. An enormous aqueduct supplied water from the nearby Ein Dug Springs to a cistern, which then doled it out to the palace as needed. The carvings and monumental pillars are awesome, and the palace floors contain examples of the finest Islamic mosaics.

A few kilometers south of the palace is **Elisha's Spring**, a fountain that the Jews believe was purified by the prophet after the populace claimed

it was harmful to crops: it is referred to by Arabs today as Ein-es-Sultan. Nearby is the preserved floor of a 6th-century synagogue, featuring a mosaic menorah in its center, within the walls of a Jericho home.

Ancient **Jericho** ⓫, which lies under Tel es-Sultan, is where the walls came tumbling down on the seventh day after they were encircled by Joshua and the Children of Israel. Archeological excavations confirm that settlements here date to 8000 BC, when hunters and gatherers completed the transition to sedentary life to become the earliest practitioners of agriculture and animal husbandry.

Jericho today is a sleepy town of 7,000 people, with most of the activity confined to its center. Here, men and women gather to sit on rattan stools, talk, sip coffee, or play backgammon. The markets are ablaze with fruit and vegetables, and huge bunches of dates and bananas swing from their beams. The cafes offer authentic Middle Eastern foods and refreshment.

In the stark wilderness outside this small town, Jesus was tempted by the devil on a peak the Bible calls the **Mount of Temptation** (also called Qarantal). Hinged to the rock face here is the **Greek Orthodox Monastery of the Temptation**, constructed in front of the grotto where Jesus was said to have fasted for 40 days and nights. A cable car takes visitors up to the monastery.

Along the River Jordan

Some 10km (6 miles) east of Jericho, at a ford north of the Dead Sea known as **al-Maghtes**, Jesus is said to have been baptized, "and it came to pass in those days, that Jesus came from Nazareth of Galilee, and was baptised by John in Jordan" (Mark 1:6–9). Not surprisingly, this **Site of the Baptism** is one of the places favored today by Christians as an authentic location.

Mark Twain described the Jordan River as "so crooked that a man does not know which side of it he is on

half the time. In going 90 miles it does not get over more than 50 miles of ground. It is not any wider than Broadway in New York." It is true that the symbolism attached to this stream – its muddy waters barely flowing in winter – far exceeds its actual size.

The **Allenby Bridge** (Sun–Thur 9am–2pm, Fri and Sat 7am–noon) is the river crossing from the West Bank to Jordan. During the 1967 war it was reduced to scaffolding and jammed with Palestinians fleeing to Jordan. It has been rebuilt, and its traffic is strictly monitored by Israeli security. It is the gateway for West Bank produce into the marketplaces of the Arab world. Visits are exchanged by families and friends on both sides of the Jordan, and many West Bank residents go to Amman for banking and commercial links. Although Israel and Jordan are officially at peace, the Palestinian community living between the two still constitutes a security threat in the eyes of Israelis. The strict security surrounding the bridge is a potent reminder that peace is not at hand.

Looking east from Jericho to Jordan.

Salt deposits in the Dead Sea.

THE DEAD SEA

Float in the salt water and bathe in the therapeutic mud at the lowest spot on earth, then visit Masada, Israel's most spectacular archeological site.

Christian pilgrims traveling here over the centuries were aghast at the lifelessness they encountered, and gave the **Dead Sea** (**Yam ha-Melah**) its name. It's an apt one, for the most saline body of water on the face of the earth contains no life of any sort, and for most of its history there has been little life around it either. Yet today it is a source of both life and health: the potash contained in its bitter waters is an invaluable fertilizer, exported all over the world, while the lake and the springs that feed it are said to have cured everything from arthritis to psoriasis, since ancient times. Sun-worshipers from Scandinavia and health fanatics from Germany fill its spas and hotels, seeking remedies and relaxation. International and Israeli tourists come here to breathe in the abundant oxygen, float on the water's salty surface, and marvel at the rugged panoramas.

Situated some 405 meters (1,300ft) below sea level in a geological fault that extends all the way to East Africa, the Dead Sea is the lowest point on the face of the globe, and is surrounded by the starkest scenery the world has to offer. Steep cliffs of reddish flint rise sharply to the west, contrasting with beige limestone bluffs and the blinding white salt flats of the plain. Across the shimmering gold surface of the water to the east, the mauve

The mud is said to keep skin young and fresh.

and purple mountains of the biblical Moab and Edom are almost indistinguishable in the morning, gaining visibility throughout the day. In late afternoon their wadis and canyons are heavily shadowed, forming a spectacular backdrop of ragged earth.

Mild and pleasant in winter, the Dead Sea Basin is an oven in summer. The hot air seems to have an almost solid presence, and the glare from the sun is ferocious.

The Dead Sea is drying up as a result of the use of the waters of the River

Main Attractions
Kalya
Kumran
Ein Fashkha
Ein Gedi
Masada
Arad

Fun in the mud.

One way of storing a bicycle.

Jordan by both Israel and Jordan, and the mining of minerals. Indeed, the sea has already separated into two lakes, although it will be many thousands of years yet until the Dead Sea completely disappears. On the Israeli side, dykes built for the potash plant form a network of artificial lakes designed for the extraction of chemicals; they are also used by bathers.

The Judean Desert

The **Judean Desert**, the area between the hills of Judea and the Dead Sea, was a region of hermits, prophets, and rebels. David hid here from Saul. The Hasmoneans, who raised the banner of Jewish independence from the Syrian-Greek Empire in the 2nd century BC, regrouped here after their initial defeat. Jesus retired to the desert to meditate, and the Essenes established a community in its desolate wastes. The Jewish War against Rome of AD 66–73 started with the capture of the Judean desert fortress of Masada.

Israel's pre-1967 border with Jordan ran just north of Ein Gedi, about halfway up the western shore of the Dead Sea, so only the southern half of the Judean desert was in Israel. Some of the sites described here became accessible to Israelis only after the Six Day War, and may revert back to Arab administration. However, the highway down from Jerusalem and along the western shore of the Dead Sea runs through desert and is under the complete control of the Israeli authorities, making it safe to travel at all times.

On descending from Jerusalem, the first available opportunity to "float" in the Dead Sea is at **Kalya Beach** (daily 8am–sunset; tel: 02-994 2391; charge) on the northwest shore, shortly after the main road turns southwards at a 90 degree right turn. It is clearly signposted. Bathing here is a unique experience: the swimmer bobs around like a cork, and it's possible to read a newspaper while sitting on the surface. The salinity of the water – 10 times that of the oceans – can make it painful if you have a cut or scratch. Emperor Vespasian threw manacled slaves into the sea to test its buoyancy. Most modern bathers go in voluntarily. Non-swimmers can float easily, but must be careful to maintain their balance. The bitter taste of even a drop can linger all day, and a mouthful of Dead Sea water should be avoided.

The scrolls of Kumran

On the northwest shore of the Dead Sea is the Essene settlement of **Kumran ⑫** (daily 8am–4pm, until 5pm Apr–Sept; tel: 02-994 2235; charge), where the Dead Sea Scrolls were found. The Essenes, an ascetic Jewish sect of the Second Temple period, deliberately built their community in this inaccessible spot. It was destroyed by the Romans in AD 68.

In the early summer of 1947 a Bedouin shepherd stumbled across the most exciting archeological discovery of the century: scrolls, dating from the first centuries before and after Christ, preserved in earthenware jars. Some of these documents were acquired by Israel in rather dramatic

circumstances. Eleazar Sukenik, Professor of Archeology at the Hebrew University, was offered by an Armenian dealer the chance of buying a collection of ancient scrolls. He was shown a fragment briefly and was impressed by its antiquity – but, to see the collection, he had to travel to Bethlehem. It was the period just prior to the establishment of the State of Israel, and Jerusalem was a war zone; Bethlehem was in the Arab-controlled area, and dangerous for Jews. Sukenik approached his son Yigael Yadin for advice. Yadin, an archeologist himself, and at that time chief of operations of the new Israel Defense Forces, replied, "as an archeologist, I urge you to go; as your son, I beg that you do not go; as chief of operations of the army, I forbid you to go." Sukenik did go to Bethlehem, at considerable personal risk, and managed to buy three scrolls. He could not complete the purchase of the other four, which were eventually taken to the US and later repurchased for Israel by Yadin.

Subsequent searches of the caves unearthed other scrolls and thousands of fragments, most of which are now on display in Israel, either in the Shrine of the Book at the Israel Museum in Jerusalem or in the Rockefeller Museum. They have revolutionized scholarship of the Second Temple period and thrown new light on the origins of Christianity, indicating that Jesus may have been an Essene, or at least was strongly influenced by the sect. The scrolls have revealed the mood of messianic fatalism among the Jews of that time, explaining both the emergence of Christianity and the fervor of the Jewish rebels in their hopeless war against Rome. The scrolls have also disclosed much about the nature of the Essene way of life and their beliefs, ritual and worship.

The partly reconstructed buildings of Kumran are on a plateau some 100 meters (330ft) above the shore and are well worth a visit. Numerous caves, including those where the scrolls were found, are visible in the nearby cliffs, but are not accessible to the tourist. Near the caves is a tourist center, run by the neighboring **Kibbutz Kalya**, which also offers accommodations

TIP

Take care: people do drown in the buoyant Dead Sea each year. They are usually elderly people who, after lying on their backs in the water, don't have stomach muscles strong enough to help them stand up. They panic, flip over, and drown floating face down.

The dream-like landscape of the Judean Desert.

Birdwatching in the desert.

Kibbutz Ein Gedi benefits from a lush setting.

and runs the aforementioned beach and water park.

Salt baths

The oasis of **Ein Fashkha (Enot Tsukim)** ⓭ (daily 8am–4pm, until 5pm Mar–Sept; charge tel: 02-994 2355), where the Essenes grew their food, is 3km (2 miles) to the south. Today it is a popular bathing site, although only in the freshwater pools. The Dead Sea's alarming evaporation means that there is no longer access to the sea itself, which is surrounded by mud and quicksand.

Some 14km (9 miles) south of Kumran is the kibbutz of **Mitspe Shalem** ⓮. The original site, on a cliff overlooking the sea, has been converted into a field school, **Metsukei Dragot**, which offers desert safaris in jeeps, rock climbing, and rappelling. Past the school there is access to the steep-sided **Murabbat Canyon**, which contains caves where other 1st- and 2nd-century scrolls were discovered. The canyon descends to the Dead Sea, but at that point it is sheer and un-scalable. A walk down the canyon from the field school is a memorable experience, but not to be undertaken alone. Would-be hikers are advised to go in a group from the school, with expert guides.

Also found in the Murabbat caves were fragments relating to a later revolt against Rome in AD 32–5 led by Simon Bar Kochba. They include a letter written by Bar Kochba himself to one of his commanders. The nearby Mineral Beach (daily 9am–5pm; tel: 02-9944888; charge) is preferable to the public beaches at Ein Gedi in terms of cleanliness and tidiness.

Ein Gedi

Less than 15km (8 miles) farther south is the lush oasis of **Ein Gedi** ⓯, site of a kibbutz, a nature reserve, and another field school, a particularly beautiful spot, with the greenery creeping up the steep cliffs beside the springs. Ein Gedi Nature Reserve (daily 8am–4pm, until 5pm Apr–Sept; tel: 08-658 4285; charge), founded in 1972, is the home of a large variety of birds and animals, including gazelles, ibex, hyrax, oryx, foxes, jackals, and even a few leopards.

The most popular site for hiking and bathing is **David's Spring**, which leads up to a beautiful waterfall, fringed in ferns, where tradition says David hid from King Saul, when he was the victim of one of the king's rages. "Then Saul took three thousand chosen men out of all Israel, and went to seek David and his men upon the rocks of the wild goats" (I Samuel 24:2). According to the biblical account, David crept up on Saul as he slept and cut off a piece of the king's robe, proving he could have killed him but desisted. A tearful reconciliation followed.

On most days, summer and winter, the area around David's Spring is thronged with visitors, so the more energetic may prefer to hike along the course of **Nakhal Arugot**, 1km (0.6 miles) south. This canyon is full of wildlife and has deep pools for bathing.

Kibbutz Ein Gedi runs a guesthouse, a youth hostel, and a spa for bathing in the Dead Sea water and nearby sulphur springs and mud baths. A camping site, and an additional youth hostel and restaurant, are situated on the shore below the kibbutz near the Ein Gedi spa.

A little farther south is the canyon of **Nakhal Khever**. Of particular interest here are two caves: the **Cave of Horror**, where 40 skeletons dating from the time of the Bar Kochba revolt were discovered; and the nearby **Cave of Letters**, in which 15 letters written by Bar Kochba to his commanders were found. As with Murabbat, visitors are not advised to climb to the caves alone.

Masada

About 20km (12 miles) south of Ein Gedi, towering almost 300 meters (1,000ft) above the Dead Sea shore, is the rock of **Masada** ⑯ (daily 9am–4pm; tel: 03-539 6700; www.masada.org.il; entrance charge and cable car charge), otherwise known as the most spectacular archeological site in Israel. Part of the line of cliffs that rises up to the Judean Desert Plateau, Masada is cut off from the surrounding area by steep wadis to the north, south and west.

It was on this desolate mesa, in 43 BC, that Herod the Great seized an

> **FACT**
>
> In Hebrew the Dead Sea is called the Salt Sea and in Arabic the Stinking Sea. Both names are apt.

A full moon illuminates Masada.

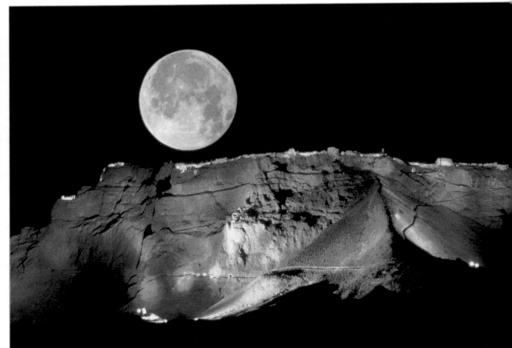

existing fortress and used it as a retreat from his potentially rebellious subjects. Visitors to the site can wander through the magnificent three-tiered palace that extends down the northern cliff; the Roman bathhouse, with its ingenious heating system; the vast storehouses; the western palace with its fine mosaics; and the huge water cisterns hewn in the rock. They can appreciate the view of the remarkable desert landscape from the summit, which can be climbed easily from the west via the Roman ramp, ascended by cable car from the east or, more energetically, climbed via the **Snake Path**, also from the east.

These features alone make the fortress worth a visit, but what has made Masada a place of pilgrimage second only to the Western Wall is the story of the epic siege of the fortress: in AD 66 a group of Jewish rebels known as Zealots, and also called the Sicarii – named after the *sica* (dagger), their favorite weapon – seized Masada from its Roman garrison, an event that triggered the Jewish War against Rome (see box).

Touring the sights at Masada.

The account in *The Jewish War* by Flavius Josephus has become one of the legends of modern Israel. In recognition of the symbolic importance of the site, young soldiers being inducted into the armed forces today swear their oath of allegiance atop the fortress and vow: "Masada shall not fall again."

The excavations by Yigael Yadin in the 1960s uncovered the magnificence of Herod's fortress and palaces, but the most moving finds were of the Zealots' living quarters in the casement wall, their synagogue and ritual baths, the remains of a fire, and fragments of their final meal. The skeletons of a man, woman, and child were uncovered in the northern palace; more were found in a nearby cave, where they had apparently been thrown by the Romans.

The country caught its collective breath when the discovery was announced of a set of inscribed pottery sherds, which may have been the lots cast by the defenders to decide who would kill the others. One of them was inscribed "Ben Yair."

MASADA AND THE JEWISH WAR

In AD 66, having seized Masada from its Roman garrison and secured their base there, the Sicarii proceeded to Jerusalem, where they took over the leadership of the revolt. In bitter infighting between the rebel groups their leader was killed, and they returned to Masada to regroup.

The new Sicarii leader, Elazar Ben-Yair, waited out the war at Masada and was still in possession after the fall of Jerusalem in AD 70. Three years later the Roman 10th Legion arrived to put an end to this last Jewish stronghold. The legion numbered more than 15,000, while defending Masada were fewer than 1,000 Jewish men, women, and children. The Romans destroyed the aqueduct feeding the cisterns from dams in the wadi, but the cisterns had enough water for a prolonged period and were accessible from the summit.

The legion constructed a wall around the rock, which blocked the main possible escape routes, and then built a ramp that pointed like a dagger at the perimeter wall of the fortress. The final defenses were set on fire. When the blaze died down the Romans entered Masada to discover the bodies of the defenders laid out in rows. Repudiating defeat and refusing slavery, the men had first killed their own families and then themselves, drawing lots for a final 10 to carry out the act, one last electee killing the other nine before committing suicide.

Sodom's soothing spas

Ensconced along the shore just north of biblical Sodom, the resorts of **Ein Bokek** and **Neve Zohar** ⑰ attract health-seekers from across the globe, with a wide range of accommodations based around the mineral springs. Famous since the 1st century AD, the healing waters are believed to cure a spectrum of ailments, from skin disease to lumbago, arthritis, and rheumatism (see page 291). The clinics, run by medical staff, offer sulfur baths, mineral baths, salt baths, mud baths, massage, and exercise programs. The prices range from reasonable to expensive, the latter in five-star hotels where the spas are actually on the premises.

Don't miss the mud if you do stay: Cleopatra is said to have sent slaves here to fetch it for her, and today Dead Sea mud has once more become a sought-after export as a natural moisturizer.

Arad, old and new

Between the spas and the chemical plant a road (Highway 31) wends its way westward into the mountains, climbing over 1,000 meters (3,300ft) in less than 25km (15 miles), to **Arad** ⑱, Israel's first planned town.

Arad has a history of human habitation going back 5,000 years, but while the modern town is constructed on an elevation near the Dead Sea to ensure a mild climate, the historic settlement is set in farming land 8km (5 miles) farther west (take Highway 31 and then turn north onto 2808). The ancient mound of **Tel Arad** (daily 8am–4pm, until 5pm Apr–Sept; tel: 057-776 2170; charge) has been excavated and partly reconstructed. Sections of a Canaanite town of the 3rd millennium BC have been found, with pottery from the First Dynasty in Egypt, indicating trade between the two nations at that time.

A 10th-century BC fortress from the time of King Solomon was the next settlement. Far smaller than the original Canaanite city, the enclosure contained a sanctuary modeled on the Temple in Jerusalem, with a courtyard, an outer chamber, and a Holy of Holies, the only one of its kind ever to have been discovered.

TIP

The Dead Sea's unique atmosphere filters out most of the sun's harmful UV rays so that despite the heat, the danger of sunburn and skin cancer is greatly reduced.

Ascending to Masada and King Herod's ancient fortress.

Mount Sedom.

Archeologists found the remains of a burned substance on two smaller altars inside the Holy of Holies. Analysis showed it to be traces of animal fat, indicating sacrifices. This is consistent with the denunciations of the prophets, recorded in the Bible, of continuing sacrifices on the "high places." King Hezekiah, who ruled Judah from 720 to 692 BC, heeded the advice and "removed the high places and broke the images."

Modern Arad, founded in 1961, was the most ambitious new town project of its time. It was meant to provide housing, health services, and tourism facilities, plus regional industries. It was well placed to utilize the natural resources and mineral spas at the Dead Sea, and offered dry desert air, suitable for asthma treatment. Architecturally, it was conceived as a fortress against the desert: the buildings were grouped around squares; the paved walkways were shaded by houses; greenery was planted in small concentrations that did not require too much water. The six basic neighborhoods and the town center were compact: less than a mile across. Arad is an interesting example

of theory being changed by practice. It was initially assumed that the inhabitants would wish to cluster together in the desert environment, but this did not prove to be the case, and the planners were forced to modify their designs to meet demand for more space.

Arad is the epitome of planned pioneering: the rational creation of a town, adapted to the desert and utilizing its resources. King Uzziah, the Bible records, "built towers in the wilderness." Constructed only a few miles from where the king's buildings stood, Arad's apartment blocks are Israel's new towers in the desert, a symbol of today's Israel: a modern community arising where an ancient one used to exist.

Sodom, "city of sin"

From Arad, take the road back to Neve Zohar, then south to **Sodom** (Sdom) . There is a peaceful atmosphere about modern Sodom which, despite its oppressive heat, makes it an unexpectedly calm place to swim, stroll or sunbathe. This is in stark contrast with the "cities of sin," Sodom and Gomorrah, which were destroyed with fire and brimstone for the decadence and sexual perversion of their inhabitants. The Bible is rather coy regarding the exact nature of these sins, but homosexuality and buggery are implied (originating the term "sodomite").

According to the story, God allowed Lot, Abraham's nephew, to escape with his family, but his wife, disobeying instructions, looked back, and was turned into a pillar of salt. On the Dead Sea shore there is a cave with a hollow tower. Called **Lot's Wife**, the pillar is said to be the remains of that unhappy lady. Take a walk inside, lick your finger, and taste the salt.

Farther south, the conveyor belts, funnels, and ovens of the **Dead Sea Mineral Works** grind and roar day and night. Articulated trucks move ponderously out of the yard, hauling the potash, magnesium, and salt down the Arava to Eilat, or up the ridge to the railway and Ashdod ports.

ISRAEL'S FOUR SEAS

The Med, the Red, and the Dead – and, of course, the Sea of Galilee: Israel's four seas offer a wide variety of pleasures and experiences.

According to the map, Israel has four seas, but in reality there are only two. The Sea of Galilee and the Dead Sea are actually lakes, relatively small bodies of water linked by the River Jordan.

Also known as Lake Tiberias, the Sea of Galilee is a mere 230 sq km (88 sq miles) in size. Surrounded by the hills of the Galilee and the Golan, the lake is edged by artificial beaches. Although only some 100km (60 miles) farther south, the Dead Sea lies amid a barren sweep of rocky desert. Set at the lowest point on earth, 400 meters (1,300ft) below sea level, it has a unique mineral composition, including a 30 percent salt content which makes bathers float. The sea has now split into two as a result of evaporation and excessive mining of potassium and bromides.

The Red Sea, another 200km (125 miles) to the south, a northern finger of the Indian Ocean, is the closest that tropical waters come to Europe. At the Coral World Underwater Observatory Marine Park, a submarine – yellow, of course – takes visitors on underwater trips to see fish of all shapes, sizes, and colors, and the exquisite coral.

Sandy beaches dominate the 200km (125-mile) Mediterranean coastline from Rosh ha-Nikra to Ashkelon – beautiful, but often very crowded at weekends with Israelis escaping the city heat.

Stoney shoreline at the Sea of Galilee.

The port of Caesarea.

The Red Sea offers a wide range of water sports, so swimmers should be alert.

Sunbathing on the Dead Sea shore.

MUD, MUD, GLORIOUS MUD

Despite its slimy, salty nature, the Dead Sea is extremely therapeutic. The fashionable and fun way to let the sea's minerals work wonders on your body is by covering yourself in Dead Sea mud. Among the minerals found in the water are bromine, which soothes the nerves, and iodine and magnesium, which ease arthritis, rheumatism, psoriasis and skin problems, as well as respiratory complaints. The mud can be applied professionally by medical staff in the region's hotels within the framework of comprehensive treatment, or simply slapped on beside the sea.

There are also sulfur baths available at Ein Gedi and Ein Bokek. Other health advantages to the Dead Sea region include the high level of oxygen in the low-altitude air, and evaporating gases, which rise from the sea and create a filter that takes out the sun's harmful ultraviolet rays. Thus the cancerous risks of sunbathing are reduced, despite searing summer temperatures of 40°C (104°F). The winter average is a delightful 21°C (70°F).

ithin a natural environment, observe, play, and swim with lphins at Dolphin reef, Eilat.

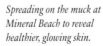

The shore near Ein Bokek.

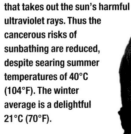

Spreading on the muck at Mineral Beach to reveal healthier, glowing skin.

The Visitors' Center at Mitspe Ramon.

THE NEGEV

King Solomon's Mines and the market at Be'er Sheva are
not the only sights in the Negev – there are magnificent
craters, nature reserves, and a high-tech university.

he very name "Negev" conjures
up an image of the rugged outdoors, jeeps, camels, frontiers-
men – an unforgiving expanse of bleak
wastes, sunlight, and sharp, dry air. It
is every bit as vast and intimidating
as it sounds, containing 60 percent of
Israel's land area but less than 10 percent of its population. Yet the Negev is
far from barren: it supports successful
agricultural communities, a sprawling
"capital", a complex desert ecosystem,
and – since Israel relinquished the Sinai
in 1982 – a variety of defense activities.

The Hebrew word means "parched",
and the Negev is indeed parched, with
rainfall varying from an annual average of 30cm (12in) in the north to
almost zero in Eilat. But don't expect
white sand and palm trees. The northern and western Negev is a dusty plain
slashed with wadis: dried-up riverbeds,
which froth with occasional winter
flash floods. To the south are the bleak
flint, limestone, chalk, dolomite, and
granite mountains, with the Arava Valley to the east dividing them from biblical Edom, today part of Jordan.

History

The Negev is saturated with history.
In Abraham's time, around 2000 BC,
the area was inhabited by nomadic
tribes. When the Children of Israel
left Egypt (around 1280 BC) the war-
like Amalekites blocked their path to

the Promised Land. Joshua eventually
conquered Canaan and awarded the
Negev to the tribe of Simeon, but only
the northern part was settled. King
David extended Israelite rule over the
Negev in the 10th century BC, and his
son Solomon built a string of forts.
Solomon also developed the copper
mines at Timna, and the port of Etzion Geber (Eilat). After the division of
the kingdom into Israel and Judah, the
area was occupied by the Edomites,
who were expelled by the Nabateans
in the 1st century BC.

Main Attractions

Be'er Sheva
Nabatean Settlements
Large and Small Craters
Sde Boker
Mitspe Ramon
Khai Bar Nature Reserve
Timna

Rare blooms.

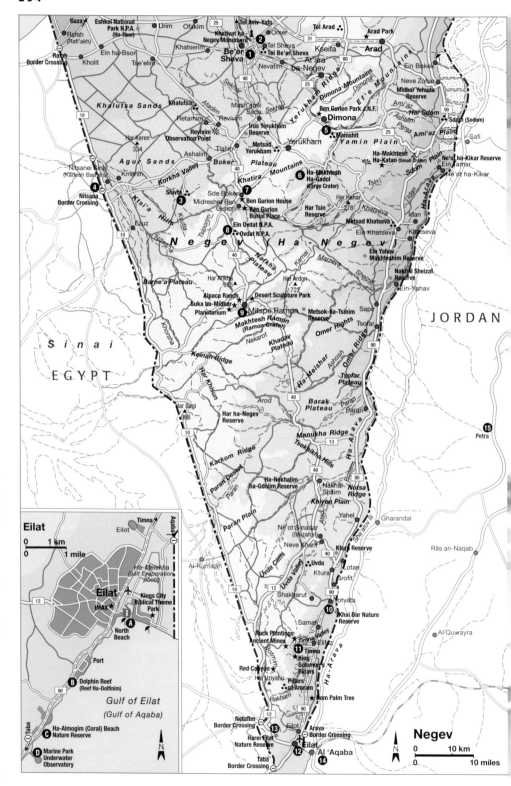

Negev

0   10 km

0   10 miles

In the Middle Ages the Negev was an important Byzantine center. In subsequent centuries it remained the domain of nomadic Bedouins until the start of Zionist immigration in the 1880s. But it was not until 1939 that the first successful kibbutz, **Negba**, northwest of Be'er Sheva, was established. Three other outposts in the western Negev were created in 1943, and a further 11 were thrown up on a single day in 1946.

The Jews fought hard for the inclusion of the Negev in the new State of Israel, and the UN partition plan awarded most of it to the Jewish state. The rest was won in the War of Independence of 1948, when the Egyptian and Transjordanian armies were expelled.

David Ben Gurion, Israel's first prime minister, believed passionately in the development of the Negev. When he retired he went to live in what was then a tiny isolated kibbutz, Sde Boker, where he is also buried.

Capital of the Negev

Be'er Sheva ❶ still has something of its old frontier atmosphere: brash, bustling, and bursting with energy. You don't see too many suits or ties here.

The municipal center is reached directly from the northern entrance to the city center but the Old City, farther east, remains the heart of the town. Here, in Ha'atzmaut Street, the **Negev Museum of Art** (Mon–Tue, Thur 10am–4pm, Wed noon–7pm, Fri–Sat 10am–2pm; closed Sun tel: 08-699 3535; www.negev-museum.org.il) is in the former building of the Turkish Governor. The unusual rectangular formation of its streets was the work of a German engineer who served with the Turkish Army in the years before World War I.

Today, with a population of 210,000, a flourishing industrial base, a university, hospital, medical school, music conservatory, dance school, an orchestra, and arts center, Be'er Sheva is Israel's fourth city. If it's a mess, it's a

triumphant mess. Be'er Sheva is the capital of the Negev, providing services for the surrounding population. The regional offices of the companies extracting potash, phosphates, bromide, magnesium, salt, and lime are all here, alongside new factories for everything from ceramics to pesticides. Be'er Sheva has got in on the high-tech act, too, with an advanced technology park in **Omer**, 10km (6 miles) north of the city, near the affluent suburb of the same name.

The town accommodates people from more than 70 countries, the earlier immigrants from Romania and Morocco rubbing shoulders with more recent arrivals from Argentina, the former Soviet Union, and Ethiopia. An Arab town until 1948, it is now a predominantly Jewish community, but several hundred Bedouin have moved here from the surrounding area and form an important part of the population.

City sights

Every Thursday morning there is a **Bedouin market** on the southern edge of town, for which a special

TIP

A fast rail link to Be'er Sheva was opened in 2012, cutting journey time from Tel Aviv to 50 minutes. There are stations at the university and city center.

A Bedouin trader at the weekly market.

TIP

To learn more about Bedouin culture, travel to the Joe Alon Museum of Bedouin Culture – 24km (15 miles) north on Highway 40 and east along 325 to Lahav (Sun–Thur 8am–4pm; tel: 08-991 3322; www.joealon.org.il; charge).

The futuristic library at Be'er Sheva's Ben Gurion University.

structure has been built. The Bedouin still trade their camels, sheep, and goats here, but in recent years the market has become a tourist attraction, providing opportunities to buy all kinds of arts and crafts.

The name Be'er Sheva means "well of the covenant", in memory of the covenant between the patriarch Abraham and a local ruler, Abimelech, in which Abraham secured the use of a well to water his flocks. There is a dispute as to the location of the actual **Well of the Covenant**. The traditional site is at the bottom of the main street in the Old Town, but more recently archeologists have suggested that it is the 40-meter (130ft) well excavated at the site of Tel Be'er Sheva, some 6km (4 miles) east of the modern city.

Ben Gurion University of the Negev (www.bgu.ac.il) is one of Israel's largest universities, with 19,000 students. The university has transformed the town from a desert backwater into a modern community, with its own sinfonietta orchestra and light opera group. The university is doing much to aid understanding of the desert environment, with major projects on water resource management and the ecology of arid regions.

About a mile to the northeast, overlooking the city (near Omer on Highway 60), is the **Khativat ha-Negev** Monument to the Palmach, which captured Be'er Sheva in the War of Independence. Designed by sculptor Dani Karavan, who spent five years on the project, its trenches, bunkers, pillboxes, and tower (through which visitors are encouraged to climb and crawl) create a claustrophobic atmosphere evocative of a siege. The sinuous concrete edifice is a worthy commemoration of the bitter battle for the Negev between the Egyptian Army and the fledgling Israeli forces backing the kibbutz outposts during the 1948 war.

South of the monument is an animal hospital, attached to the life sciences department of Ben Gurion University. It includes a camel clinic.

The Negev Bedouin

Southeast of the hospital, next to ancient Tel Be'er Sheva, is **Tel Sheva** ❷, a modern village built for the local Bedouin. It is the first of five Bedouin villages in the Negev replacing some of the traditional tented camps of the nomads, which, as a rule, are spread out over a large area. High-walled courtyards separate the houses, in an attempt to preserve as much privacy as possible.

The concept was developed by an Arab architect, and its logic seemed unassailable. But in fact the Bedouin were not keen on Tel Sheva and some have steadfastly refused to move either there or into similar new towns proposed by the government. Subsequent developments are encouraging the former nomads to build their own homes (see box).

Ancient Tel

Several kilometers before Tel Sheva is **Tel Be'er Sheva National Park** (daily 8am–4pm, until 5pm Apr–Sept; tel: 08-646 7286; charge). Tel Be'er Sheva was recognized in 2005 as a Unesco World Heritage Site, along with Tel Megiddo and Tel Hatzor in the north. This tel sits near the confluence of the Be'er Sheva and Hebron Rivers, where settled land meets the desert. Archeologists working at Tel Be'er Sheva have uncovered two-thirds of a settlement from the early Israelite period (10th century BC), when a fortified administrative city was built on the tel. The site has unparalleled importance for the study of biblical-period urban planning.

The meticulously planned water-works are evidence of tremendous engineering expertise. The centerpiece of the water system is a huge rectangular shaft dug 15 meters (50ft) into the ground. The walls of the shaft are tiled with pieces of stone. The shaft descends into a large reservoir, fed by the floodwater that flowed through the Hebron River. A 70-meter (230ft) well, Israel's deepest, was also discovered on the site. Large parts of the ancient buildings have been reconstructed, using mud blocks. Visitors will want to see the well, the city streets, the storehouses, the public buildings and private homes, the city wall and gates, and the reservoir. Especially interesting is the reconstructed horned altar, parts of which were found on the site. There is also an observation tower.

The western Negev

Immediately west of Be'er Sheva along Highway 2357 is **Kibbutz Khatserim,** where modern drip irrigation was invented. Just past the kibbutz is the **Khatserim Air Force Museum** (Sun–Thur 8am–4.30pm, Fri 8am–11.30am; tel: 08-990 6853; charge), which records the history of the Israel Air Force and exhibits the aircraft that enabled the country to consolidate its presence in the region.

West from Be'er Sheva along Highway 25, the Negev is flat and dull, more suitable for settlement than for tourism. It is an area of cotton and potatoes as well as extensive wheat fields, irrigated by the run-off from the National Water Carrier, which ends in this area.

The first Negev kibbutzim were built in this region in the 1940s, and,

The Khatserim Air Force Museum holds a significant collection of ex-Israel Air Force airplanes and helicopters, as well as some civil aviation aircraft.

Bedouin men in the desert.

NEW BEDOUIN VILLAGES

Israel's Bedouin claim large tracts of the desert over which they formerly grazed their herds, but the lands were never registered, and this has led to disputes with the government. In some cases the Bedouin have been given title to the land around their camps. Where the land has been appropriated by the government, as with Nevatim Airforce Base east of Be'er Sheva, monetary compensation has been awarded. But at present 85,000 Bedouin, about half of the Negev Bedouin, are fighting for government recognition of some 39 "unrecognized" villages. Although the campaign is bearing fruit, with the government recognizing Bedouin ownership of the land in many villages, the Negev tribesmen must then continue fighting to be connected to basic utilities like water, sanitation, and electricity.

FACT

The soil in the Eshkol region is called *loess* – a type of very fertile sand that is great for growing winter crops like tomatoes and cucumbers, as well as melons and peppers.

after the peace treaty with Egypt, some of Israel's northern Sinai settlements were moved to Pithat Shalom (the Peace Region) next to the international border in 1982. East of these communities along Route 241 lies the **Eshkol National Park** (Ha-Bsor; daily 8am–4pm, until 5pm Apr–Sept; tel: 08-998 5110; charge), 3,300 hectares (750 acres) of trees, lawns, and playing fields with an amphitheater, a swimming pool, and a natural pond, surrounded by cat-tails and cane and stocked with fish.

The Western Negev road, which goes south from this region, is designated as a military area as it is right on the Egyptian border, and travelers using it have to fill in forms provided by the military. Since the peace treaty with Egypt in 1978 it is not regarded as dangerous, but the army wants to know who is using it so that travelers are not stranded there after dark. The southern sector of the road winds attractively through the **Negev mountains**, providing some spectacular views of Sinai to the west and the Negev to the east.

The ancient site of Mamshit.

Shivta

There is a road (number 222) from Eshkol to the junction at Mash'abei Sade, just past the Revivim Observation Point. This road passes the former Nabatean settlement of **Khalutsa**. From Mash'abei Sade, follow the road toward the Egyptian border and you will come to **Shivta** ❸, to the south in the Korkha Valley, a Nabatean city later rebuilt by the Byzantines in the 5th century. An Arab tribe, the Nabateans dominated the Negev and Edom in the first centuries BC and AD. Although less accessible than Ovdat, Shivta is still relatively well preserved, with three churches, a wine press, and several public areas still intact. There is also a direct route here from Be'er Sheva. Shivta, together with the region's other three Nabatean settlements – Ovdat, Mamshit, and Khalutsa – were also named a Unesco World Heritage Site in 2005, called the incense or spice route.

Nitsana ❹, 25km (16 miles) farther west at the intersection of the western highway, is one of two active border crossings to Egypt (Sun–Thur

8am–4pm). The village also located at Nitsana – a desert outpost that now has a thriving school for new young immigrants and a seminar center for desert science – was founded in 1987 and lies just next to the border.

To reach Eilat from Nitsana, you can continue down the road, which hugs the Sinai border, but there are two other main routes to the pleasure resort on the Red Sea. From Be'er Sheva the main highway leads down the eastern side of the Negev, through the **Ha-Arava**, and that is the one to take if your aim is simply reaching the sunny beaches. Alternatively, a narrow, beautiful, scenic road goes right through the middle of the desert. The traveler may well feel that the Negev between Be'er Sheva and Eilat is a mythical badland dividing Israel from the Red Sea paradise to the south, but there is plenty to see on both routes.

Nuclear Negev

The eastern route takes you past the moshav of **Nevatim**, settled in the early 1950s by Jews from Cochin in southern India. Even within the kaleidoscope of the Israeli population these beautiful, dark-skinned people stand out as "more different" than others. In the past few years they have become famous for growing winter flowers, exported by air to Europe. This industry, which takes advantage of the mild desert climate, has been taken up by others and become a major Israeli export.

Farther east, the development towns of **Yerukham** and **Dimona**, built in the mid-1950s, were settled primarily by immigrants from North Africa. Yerukham has a park, 10km (6 miles) south of the road, which is a rare green patch in the arid gray-brown wasteland, but so far the dust tends to dominate the man-high trees. Nearby is an artificial lake, created by a dammed wadi, fed by the winter rains. A huge variety of birds migrate across the Mediterranean coast from Africa to Europe in the spring and return in the autumn; Israel is one of their favorite way-stations.

Dimona is home to the fierce, harsh desert climate that many thought would prove too much for people to live and work in. The few original

Geological strata in Mitspe Ramon.

LARGE AND SMALL CRATERS

Ha-Makhtesh Ha-Gadol (Large Crater) and **Ha-Makhtesh Ha-Katan** (Small Crater) are natural geological faults near Dimona and southeast of Yerukham that form **part** of a trio of impressive geological formations, together with **Mitspe Ramon,** sometimes known as the Great Crater. The Large Crater is 14km by 6km (8.5 by 3.5 miles) across and 410 meters (1,345ft) deep, and resembles a moonscape. It is best viewed from Mount Avnon, which is 700 meters (2,300ft) high. The Small Crater is 8km by 7km (5 by 4.5 miles) across and 400 meters (1,312ft) deep. Although less extensive, it is more beautiful and accessible, with geological layers in some locations exposed like a rainbow cake: the stone and sand range in color from silver, brown, and yellow to red, purple, and white.

The origin of the craters is unknown. One theory ascribes the Negev craters to volcanic activity, while another theory put forward (discounted by most scientists) suggests the fall of large meteors in the distant past.

To reach the Small Crater, travel on Highway 25 east of Dimona for about 40km (25 miles). A minor road leading south to the Small Crater is marked; the road is located 5km (3 miles) west of the junction with Highway 90.

FACT

Nitsanei Sinai (Kadesh Barne'a), on the Sinai border, was the only one of Solomon's fortresses to be rebuilt.

settlers have now blossomed into a town of 38,000. Although it's called the "Flower of the Desert," Dimona is known more for its nuclear plant, Black Hebrew community, and not least its most famous son, soccer star Yossi Benayoun, than for its flora. A small Indian-Jewish community also resides here, and their delicatessens supply great Indian spices and poppadums.

Southeast of Dimona, on Highway 25, the dome of Israel's infamous **Nuclear Research Station** looms on the plain behind its numerous protective barbed-wire fences.

Nearby is the site of **Mamshit ❺** (daily 8am–4pm, until 5pm Apr–Sept; tel: 08-655 6478; charge), called Kurnab by the Arabs. A fine example of a Nabataean site of the 1st century AD, it contains the remains of two beautiful Byzantine churches and a network of ancient dams. The settlement was also famous for breeding Arabian horses. Nearby is the **Camel Farm** of Mamshit, home to the original ships of the desert. It is still worth a visit even if this alternative mode of travel is not to your taste. Safaris,

4-wheel-drive tours, rappelling and hiking are among the other options.

South of the road is **Ha-Makhtesh Ha-Gadol** (The Large Crater) ❻, a spectacular geological fault (take 206 to the south and then 225). Farther east is **Ha-Makhtesh Ha-Katan** (The Small Crater; see box).

A spectacular road

The old road south – today a dirt track – cuts through the desert south of the small crater, connecting with the Arava Valley via **Scorpions' Pass**. The most spectacular road in the southern desert, it plunges down a series of dizzying loops that follow each other with frightening suddenness. To the right are the heights of the Negev, great slabs of primeval rock, slammed together. Below are the purple-gray lunar formations of the **Tsin Valley**, with the square-shaped hillock of **Ha-har** rising up from the valley floor. Be warned: the rusty metal drums that line the road have been unable to prevent accidents.

The main road from Mamshit (Highway 25) reaches the Arava Valley south of the Dead Sea, at the Arava Junction, near the moshav farming village of **Neot ha-Kikar**. Situated in the salt marshes and utilizing brackish water, it has become one of the most successful settlements in Israel, exporting a variety of winter vegetables to Europe. In the 1960s Neot ha-Kikar was settled by an eccentric group of desert lovers, who established a private company. As initial attempts at farming the area proved less than successful, they set up a desert touring company for trips by camel and jeep to the less accessible locations of the Negev. Those initial settlers eventually abandoned the village, but their company (still called Neot ha-Kikar) continues to thrive, with offices in Tel Aviv and Eilat.

The road through the Arava is bordered by the flint and limestone ridges of the Negev to the west; 19km (12 miles) to the east tower the

The fields of Kibbutz Sde Boker.

magnificent mountains of **Edom** in Jordan, which are capped with snow in winter. These mountains change color during the day from pale mauve in the morning, to pink, red, and deep purple in the evening, their canyons and gulleys etched in gray.

To the south lies the **Paran Plain**, the most spectacular of the Negev wadis, which runs into the Arava. The road twists through the timeless desert scenery before joining the southern stretch of the Arava road on its way to Eilat. You can continue on this route, taking in the Khai Bar Nature Reserve and Timna (see page 303), but return to Be'er Sheva and take the central desert road through the Negev Plateau.

The Negev Plateau

The most interesting route south is also the oldest and least convenient, but it passes a number of interesting sites, the first of which is **Sde Boker ⑦**, some 50km (30 miles) south of Be'er Sheva. Either take Highway 40 south directly from Be'er Sheva or Highway 204 from Dimona and Yerukham. The kibbutz was the final home of David Ben Gurion, Israel's first prime minister, and his wife, Paula. Their simple, cream-colored tombstones, which overlook the Wilderness of Tsin, several kilometres to the south, form a place of pilgrimage for Israeli youth movements and foreign admirers. The old man is said to have selected his burial place, with its view of beige and mustard limestone hills, the flint rocks beyond, and the delicate mauve of Edom in the hazy distance.

Midreshet Ben Gurion (Sde Boker), is a college south of the kibbutz and overlooking Ben Gurion's grave, is divided into three sections: Ben Gurion University's Institute for Arid Zone Research coordinates desert biology, agriculture, and architecture; the Ben Gurion Institute houses the prime minister's papers and records; and the Center of the Environment runs a field school and a high school with an emphasis on environmental studies.

South of the college is **Ein Ovdat**, (daily 8am–4pm, until 5pm Apr–Sept; tel: 08-653 2016; charge) a steep-sided canyon with freshwater pools fringed with lush vegetation. Rock badgers, gazelles, and a wide variety of birds inhabit this oasis, where the water is remarkably cold even in the heat of summer. A swim can be refreshing, but the water is deep and sometimes it is difficult to climb out onto the slippery rocks. Lone hikers should not take the risk, and parties of visitors should take it in turns, leaving some out of the water to haul out their companions. There are paths up the sides of the cliffs, with iron rungs and railings.

Reconstruction at Ovdat

A few kilometers farther south is **Ovdat ⑧** (daily 8am–4pm, until 5pm Apr–Sept; tel: 08-655 1511; charge) the site of the Negev's main Nabatean city, built in the 2nd century BC. Situated on a limestone hill above the surrounding desert, Ovdat was not only excavated but also partly reconstructed

TIP

If you are going into the Tsin Valley as an independent traveler, remember that it should be negotiated very slowly in a 4-wheel-drive vehicle, or else on foot.

An ostrich, one of the biblical animals at the Khai Bar Nature Reserve.

in the early 1950s. With its impressive buildings, burial caves, a kiln, workshop, and two Byzantine churches, it is one of the most rewarding sites in the country; what makes it fascinating, though, is the reconstruction of Nabatean and Byzantine agriculture.

With their capital at Petra (today in Jordan), the Nabateans' achievements in farming the desert are unsurpassed. Their technique was based on the run-off systems of irrigation. Little rain falls in this part of the desert, but when it does, it is not absorbed by the local loess soil; it cuts gulleys and wadis, running in torrents to the Mediterranean in the west and the Dead Sea and the Arava in the east.

A botanist, Michael Evenari, working with archeologists and engineers, has reconstructed Ovdat and two other farms, growing a variety of crops without the help of piped water: fodder, wheat, onions, carrots, asparagus, artichokes, apricots, grapes, peaches, almonds, peanuts, and pistachios are among them.

The giant Mushroom Rock.

What started as research into ancient agriculture has proved to be relevant to the modern era, as the system could provide valuable food crops in arid countries of the developing world using only existing desert resources, thus preserving the delicate ecological balances. Indeed, although the ancient Nabateans managed to grow grape vines here 2,000 years ago, they didn't irrigate them with salt water. New scientific research using saline water has begun to reap rewards in the form of Cabernet Sauvignon and Sauvignon Blanc.

Mitspe Ramon

A half-hour south of Ovdat is the town of **Mitspe Ramon** ⑨, perched at an elevation of 1,000 meters (3,300ft) along the northern edge of the **Makhtesh Ramon**, the largest of the three craters in the Negev (40km/25 miles long and 12km/7 miles wide). Despite its vast size, the crater comes into view quite suddenly – and it's an awesome sight. Among the finds have been fossilized plants and preserved dinosaur footprints dating back 200 million years to the Triassic and Jurassic periods. Mitspe Ramon has an observatory,

DESERT PRECAUTIONS

Although the Negev and Judean Desert comprise most of Israel, the land expanse is negligible compared with North Africa, North America, and other parts of the world. The nearest gas station is never going to be more than 30km (18.5 miles) away. Even so, never let the tank get too low, and remember there are a few remote areas without cellular coverage, or where your phone may flip over to the Jordanian network.

Always have plenty of spare water for both the car and yourself. If you go hiking in the desert, make sure you drink plenty of water, keep yourself well covered from the sun, and be aware of what time the sun sets.

Other dangers include flash flooding between October and April. Make sure you listen to the weather forecasts, and if floods are expected, stay clear of dry wadi beds when hiking and heed warning signs on low points on the road. In winter, the desert remains hot during the day but will reach freezing cold temperatures at night.

Note also that much of the desert is an army firing zone, although restricted areas are well signposted.

Poisonous snakes and scorpions are relatively rare, but don't go looking for them under rocks.

connected with Tel Aviv University, which takes full advantage of the dry desert air. In the Makhtesh Ramon a geological trail displays the melting-pot of minerals present in the area, evident from the patches of yellow, ocher, purple, and green that tint the landscape.

Start off at the **Mitspe Ramon Visitors' Center** (Sun–Thur 8am–4pm, Apr–Sept until 5pm, Fri 8am–4pm; tel 08-658 8691; charge) at the edge of town, which not only explains about the crater's unique geological formations but also offers a splendid view. The center was expanded in 2013 to include a memorial museum to Israel's only astronaut – Ilan Ramon, killed in 2003 on the fatal Columbia space mission.

From here the road snakes south, joining with the eastern route near the Jordanian border just before Ktura. The next stop is at **Kibbutz Yotvata**, 50km (30 miles) north of Eilat, with the fascinating **Khai Bar Nature Reserve ⑩** (Sun–Thur 8.30am–5pm, Fri–Sat 8.30am–4pm; tel: 08-637 6018; buy tickets at the Visitors' Center). At this unusual game park, conservationists have imported and bred a variety of animals mentioned in the Bible which had become extinct locally: wild asses, ostriches, and numerous varieties of gazelle. A holiday village, with modest but comfortable accommodation, swimming pools, and a mini-market, is on-site, as is the **Arava Visitors' Center,** with a museum and audiovisual display of the desert. **Ktura**, a kibbutz 16km (10 miles) to the north, offers horse riding.

There is an alpaca farm near Mitspe Ramon. Although imported from Latin America and not indigenous to this region, the alpaca is actually the closest cousin to the camel.

Timna

Timna ⑪, 24km (15 miles) farther south (Sat–Thur 8am–4pm, Fri 8am–1pm; July–Aug Mon–Thur, Sat 8am–8.30pm, Fri, Sun 8am–1pm; tel: 08-631 6756; www.timna-park.co.il; charge) is the site of **King Solomon's Mines**, a little to the south of the modern copper mine. The ancient circular stone ovens for roasting the copper ore look simple enough, with stone channels to the collection vessels for the metal, but the air channels were skilfully angled to catch the prevailing north wind, which comes down the Arava. The late archeologist Nelson Glueck, who excavated the mines, called the ventilation system "an ancient example of automation."

The area surrounding the mines has been developed as a privately owned park, with an artificial lake and a fine scenic route in the northeast of the park to facilitate touring. Highlights include **King Solomon's Pillars**, a natural formation of Nubian sandstone, and the redoubtable **Mushroom Rock**, a granite rock shaped like a mushroom. The time-worn remains of a settlement, a fortress, and two Egyptian sanctuaries used by the ancient mine-workers can also be seen. From here, it's just 30km (18 miles) to Eilat and the Red Sea.

King Solomon's Pillars in Timna Valley National Park.

The mountains of Jordan, a
backdrop to Eilat.

EILAT

Eilat is a hedonistic playground, a birdwatcher's
delight, and a jumping-off point for visits to
Jordan to see the great Nabataean city of Petra,
or to the Sinai in Egypt.

emote from the rest of Israel, Eilat ⑫ is searingly hot and parched dry. But, with guaranteed year-round sunshine – average January temperatures of 21°C (70°F) – the closest tropical waters to Europe, with remarkable marine life and coral formations, and the unique flora and fauna of the only land link between Africa and Europe/Asia, Eilat has a lot to offer.

Consequently it is one of Israel's most popular tourist resorts. Vacationers migrate instinctively, like the billion birds that fly overhead twice each year journeying back and forth between Africa and Europe/Asia.

Eilat is Israel's southernmost community, with easy access to Egypt and Jordan. It is the state's flipper-hold on the Red Sea. It is also a mecca (if such a word can be used in Israel) for snorkelers, scuba-divers, windsurfers, water-skiers, swimmers, sailors, sandcastle builders, sun-worshipers, tropical-fish fanatics, and birdwatchers.

Eilat's single significant industry lies in assisting visitors to do nothing productive. It is a sensual city, which caters for people who like magnificent natural beauty, lazy afternoons, spicy food, and cold beer. To help keep prices down, the Israeli government has made Eilat a free-trade zone, which means it has no sales tax (VAT) and many items are cheaper than

elsewhere in the country – although overseas visitors are anyway exempt from this tax for expensive goods and services paid for with foreign currency. If you rent a car, make sure to fill up with gasoline in Eilat only, as VAT (18 percent) is charged outside of the city.

First City

Eilatis whimsically call their town Israel's "First City" because it was the first piece of land in what is now Israel to be occupied by the Children

Main Attractions

Harei Eilat Nature Reserve
North Beach
Dolphin Reef
Coral Beach Nature Reserve
Underwater Observatory
  Marine Park
Birdwatching
Petra
Sinai

Dolphin Reef, Eilat.

Built in the style of a palace and spread over three levels, Eilat's Kings City is an indoor theme park with a biblical theme.

In the foreground, the turrets of Kings City.

of Israel after the Exodus from Egypt (Deuteronomy 2:8). But Moses was only a tourist; he moved north to find milk and honey soon afterward.

A few centuries later King Solomon built a port here and called it Etzion Geber. With the help of his friend King Hiram of Phoenicia, he sent a fleet of ships east to the land of Ophir, "and fetched from thence gold, four hundred and twenty talents, and brought it to King Solomon" (I Kings 9:26). Since there were about 3,000 shekels to the talent, and about a half-ounce to the shekel, the sailors must have lugged some 20 tonnes of gold back to Jerusalem.

Eilat changed hands many times during the following centuries. The Edomites grabbed it for a while, and then King Uzziah took it back for the Israelites. The Syrians later wrested it away from him. A succession of conquerors marched through – Nabateans, Greeks, Romans, Mamelukes, Crusaders, Ottoman Turks, and others. The Crusaders left behind their 12th-century fortress at Coral Island, just south of Taba. The celebrated

Colonel T.E. Lawrence, popularly known under the moniker Lawrence of Arabia, trekked through these parts after his conquest of Aqaba across the bay, which is believed to be the biblical Etzion Geber.

The most recent army to conquer Eilat was the Israel Defense Forces, which swooped down on this exotic pearl during Operation Uvda in March 1949 and scared the daylights out of several sleepy lizards and a tortoise living in the ruins of Umm Rashrash – an otherwise uninhabited mud-brick "police station," which stood all alone in what is now the center of the town. Although the United Nations had allocated Eilat to Israel in its partition plan, the capture of this corner of the Promised Land in the War of Independence was so hastily organized that Israeli troops arrived without a flag to proclaim it as part of their new state. So, a soldier with artistic talent was issued a bed sheet and a bottle of blue ink with which to produce an Israeli flag of appropriate dimension and design.

Development town

The new flag didn't fly over very much, but the Israeli authorities knew that Eilat was located in a highly strategic position, and rapid steps were taken to create a town. It was strategic because it provided Israel's only access to the Indian Ocean, and trade with Asia, East Africa, Australia, and Oceania, including the vehicles and other manufactured goods on offer from Japan, Korea, and China. Holding on to Eilat also meant a break in land continuity between Egypt and Jordan, thus offering a military advantage to the defense forces.

In the rush to create a city on the Red Sea, Eilat's builders, as throughout Israel, didn't invest much in fine architecture. Instead, they went for fast, simple, sturdy construction of apartments to house immigrants trickling in after the horrors of Nazi-occupied Europe, and the expulsions by Arab states such as Iraq and Yemen. Visitors to Eilat can see some of the older 1950s apartment buildings still standing like concrete bastions on the hillside. They're still quite serviceable, and are occupied by Eilati families who have affectionate nicknames for them, such as "Sing Sing," and "La Bastille."

Crisis and boom

Egypt's President Gamal Abdel Nasser also realized the strategic value of Eilat and its potential as a multimillion-dollar tourist playground. In May 1967 he imposed a blockade on Eilat and shut down its shipping, including the then vital oil supplies from Iran, by closing off the Strait of Tiran at the tip of the Sinai peninsula. Next, he ordered the UN peace-keeping forces out of Sinai and moved his own army into the mountains northwest of Eilat, within clear view of Jordan. With one quick push, the fear was, he could have cut off Eilat, linked up with the Jordanian Arab Legion and created a solid, integrated southern front against Israel. Eilat was in an extremely vulnerable position until the Israeli pre-emptive strike against Egyptian airfields deprived Nasser of the vital air cover his troops would need. The

FACT

Attractions in Eilat include the Kings City Biblical Theme Park near the North Beach, the What's Up Observatory on the North Beach Promenade, which explains the desert sky, and the IMAX Theater, a 3-D cinema located in a blue pyramid opposite the airport, with a screen eight stories high.

A celebration in Eilat's hotel district.

A bridge leading to some of Eilat's many major hotels, which are testament to the city's high ranking in the tourism stakes.

Camping out at Taba.

following six days witnessed Israel's lightning conquest of Sinai, and the removal of military threats against Eilat.

Even after 1967, Eilat didn't really take off as a tourist destination. For most Israelis it was a stop-off point en route to Sinai, where the desert was more dramatic and the diving and marine life even more remarkable. The return of Sinai to Egypt in 1982 and growing affluence in Israel enabled Eilat to begin to grow. And grow it has. Today the city has about 12,000 rooms in 75 hotels, including many of the major international chains.

Most of the tourists are Israelis, who drive the four-hour trans-desert trek from Jerusalem and Tel Aviv for their vacations and can withstand average summer temperatures above 40°C (104°F). But many others, especially in winter, are foreigners who take charter flights from Europe directly to Eilat. Arkia, Israel's domestic airline, also operates several flights a day from here to other cities in Israel.

Plenty of rocks

An adage grew up among Eilatis, "If we could export rocks, we'd all be millionaires." The key to Eilat's tourism has been to twist the adage to bring the foreigners to the rocks. Nearly all of these rocks are pre-Cambrian, formed by the forces of the earth in the epochs before the beginning of life on the planet. Aeons ago they covered the land facing the north, where the ancient Tethys Sea flowed over what is now the State of Israel.

To the south extended the primordial megacontinent of Gondwanaland, which eventually drifted apart to form India, Africa, South America, Australia and Antarctica, and the bed of the Tethys Sea was pushed up to form the bedrock of Israel. Geologists are forever pottering about the Eilat mountains, picking at chunks of granite, gneiss, quartz-porphyry and diabase. In some places they are after an attractive bluish-green malachite, which merchants in town call Eilat Stone, a type of copper ore that can be shaped and given a high polish. In fact, this stone has been used in jewelry-making in the region for thousands of years, and is still very evident in many Eilat tourist shops.

For those who like to see their rocks in the rough, there are the Eilat mountains, spectacular ascents of colorful stone. In some areas it appears as if their volcanic genesis was fast-frozen, and their flowing magmas interrupted in full flood. Erosion here has taken some bizarre and incredibly beautiful courses. In places it is possible to walk through narrow canyons with walls towering hundreds of meters vertically, but just a meter or two apart. The harsh desert wind has carved monumental pillars among the mountains, particularly in the sandstone regions, such as the **Pillars of Amram** (named after the father of Moses), some 9km (5 miles) north of Eilat and 3km (2 miles) west of the main highway. The site is laced with

lovely ravines and clusters of imposing natural columns.

About 4km (2.5 miles) south of Eilat, along the coastal highway leading to Sinai, is the entry to **Solomon's Canyon**, a popular hiking area. A dusty granite quarry at the mouth of the canyon tends to obscure the formations lying beyond, but those following the path markers in the **Harei Eilat (Eilat Mountains) Nature Reserve** ⓭ will be treated to an exotic geological adventure. As you enter the canyon, **Ha-Metsuda** (The Stronghold) rises to the left. This great rock was vital to Eilat's defenses against invasion from the Sinai coast. The path then leads another 16km (10 miles) up into the mountains, twisting and turning along the route of the canyon. Hikers pass first beneath **Har Yehoshafat**, then **Har Shlomo**, and then **Har Uziya**, each of which towers more than 700 meters (2,300ft) overhead.

Eventually the trail crosses the paved **Moon Valley Highway,** which leads into central Sinai. Across the highway, the trail continues on to the spectacular cliffs and oasis at **Ein Netafim** (The Spring of the Drops), which trickles across a barren rock into a picturesque pool at the foot of an imposing cliff. Farther along is **Red Canyon**, another impressive natural wonder of erosion-sculpted sandstone.

Seaside sojourning

Beaches are a year-round attraction in Eilat. Even in the summer, when temperatures can range well above baking at 40°C (104°F), the waters of the Red Sea are cool and soothing. Midwinter swimming, however, is usually left to the Europeans and Americans, while native Eilatis stare from the shore, bundled up in parkas to dispel the wintry gusts, which usually hover at around 18°C (roughly 64°F).

Eilat has a number of distinct and attractive beaches, stretching 11km (7 miles), ranging from fine sand to gravel. **North Beach** Ⓐ, close to the center of

the town and to the west of the marina and lagoon, is the local hangout for sun-worshipers. The bay is protected, the swimming is easy, and dozens of hotels line the shore. The eastern end of North Beach also has inexpensive bungalows and even camping facilities for those on a tight budget.

Farther south is **Dolphin Reef** Ⓑ (Sun–Thur 9am–5pm, Fri–Sat until 4.30pm; tel: 08-630 0111; www. dolphinreef.co.il; charge), a private beach where you can swim with the dolphins. If you have a license you can hire diving equipment and dive with them too. There are qualified guides to accompany divers. The dolphins are very friendly – so much so that they are sometimes used in therapeutic programs for children with disabilities.

A little farther down the coast, past the navy station, port facilities, and vast lots containing tens of thousands of imported cars from Japan and Korea, many of which are transported to Europe, is Coral Beach opposite a small cluster of hotels. There is the free beach where diving

Geological field trip.

TIP

You can learn to dive while in Eilat: several schools advertize prominently in the town.

gear can be hired, or a little further south is the **Coral Beach Nature Reserve** ◉ (daily 9am–5pm; tel: 08-637 6829; charge). This reserve includes a fine sandy beach and a truly spectacular coral reef. Here visitors can rent diving masks, snorkels, and flippers from the reserve's office and swim along any of three marked routes, which lead over different parts of the coral reef. Special markers set into the reef itself identify different types of coral and plants growing there, as well as some of the more common fish.

The reserve also has changing rooms, showers, snack and souvenir stands, and other tourist amenities. But tourist-friendly though it may be, this is a monitored nature reserve. Swimmers must be very careful not to bruise any of the coral. Removal of any pieces of coral is taken very seriously indeed and will result in the culprit paying a visit to the local judge.

Conservationists recently won a major victory near here, when the courts ordered fish farmers to remove their undersea fish cages because the fish feces were damaging the surrounding coral reefs.

Observing fish

Farther south is the **Underwater Observatory Marine Park** ◉ (daily 8.30am–4pm; tel: 08-636 4200; www. coralworld.com; charge), an unusual commercial aquarium and undersea observatory. Here the visitor walks out on a long pier to the observatory building, which is set into the reef itself. Descending the spiral staircase within the observatory, one emerges into a circular room with windows facing out into the coral reef at a depth of 5 meters (16ft). All sorts of fish swim freely about outside the window, and the many colors and shapes of the living reef are astonishing sights that should not be missed.

There is also a museum, which exhibits the marine life and coral on a comprehensive A–Z basis, a shark tank, and, for an extra charge, a yellow submarine, the *Jacqueline*, which will take you on one-hour underwater trips. Nothing quite as lovely has been seen since Jules Verne's Captain

Coral Beach Nature Reserve.

Nemo retired the *Nautilus*. Also, for an additional charge, the Oceanarium offers a 3-D cinema show with a screen surrounding the viewer, while even the seats move.

Those who abjure actually going into the water might be more inclined to ride on it instead. A large marina and lagoon at North Beach is the mooring for many boats and yachts, from expensive charter schooners to more affordable windsurfing craft. There are also several glass-bottomed boats for reef-viewing, and a number of water-skiing speedboats available for charter. Licensed diving clubs, which will rent diving equipment and offer diving courses, include Lucky Divers, Red Sea Divers, and Eilat Aqua Sport.

Observing birds

Birdwatching, too, is a year-round attraction in Eilat, and several dozen species of resident bird can be found in the mountains and deserts, by the seashore, and among the fields of neighboring **Kibbutz Eilot**. The spring migration season, however, is particularly dazzling and is the best time to be here. Millions upon millions of migratory birds fly across the Eilat region on their northward journeys from warm wintering havens in Africa to their breeding grounds scattered across Eurasia. Great waves of eagles and falcons fill the sky, and highly respected ornithologists keep producing reports giving strangely precise figures, such as 19,288 steppe eagles, 26,770 black kites, and 225,952 honey buzzards in the course of a single migration season.

Sharp-eyed birdwatchers will also pick out booted eagles, snake eagles, lesser spotted eagles, imperial eagles, marsh harriers, sparrowhawks, and osprey. And then come the pelicans and storks in their tens of thousands. There is a ringing and birdwatching center north of North Beach near the salt flats, where many of the migrating birds stop off for a nibble after traveling across the sea and/or desert. Numbers of migrating birds observed have been down in recent years, but no obvious explanation has yet been found. The best time of day to visit

Underwater Observatory Marine Park.

Fun with the dolphins.

is dawn and the best time of year is the Eilat Birds Festival Week in mid-March (www.eilatbirdsfestival.com).

For those looking for a leisurely vacation there are scores of restaurants here, ranging from inexpensive pizza parlors and *falafel* stands, through reasonably priced places selling very good seafood, to high-priced haute cuisine in the Eilat Center, the New Tourist Center, and the Hotel District. Most of the larger hotels also have nightclubs, discos, and other entertainments. The **Red Sea Jazz Festival** each August has become an annual summer fixture, drawing thousands of jazz fans to several nights of live entertainment by local acts and international stars.

Aqaba and Petra

In the wake of the Middle East peace process, Eilat has become a popular base for visits to Sinai in Egypt and Petra in Jordan. The region is marketed as a Middle Eastern French Riviera, and its tourist industry is flourishing.

The **Arava Crossing** to Jordan, northeast of Eilat, has offered access

Idol of the goddess Hayyan in the Petra Museum.

to the Hashemite Kingdom since the peace accord was signed between Israel and Jordan in 1994. The frontier can be reached along a road running eastward off the main Arava highway several kilometers north of Eilat, not far from Kibbutz Eilot. The Arava Checkpoint is open Sun–Thur 6.30am–8pm and Fri–Sat 8am–8pm. It is closed on Yom Kippur and Id el Fitr. Passport holders can enter Jordan without a visa if they pay a US$10 charge. It is not yet possible to take vehicles from Israel into Jordan, but bus 16 leaves Eilat Central Bus Station once an hour for the border crossing.

The town of **Al Aqaba** ⓮ is unexceptional. Sitting alongside Eilat on the northern shore of the Red Sea, Aqaba is Jordan's only outlet to the sea and therefore a busy port. The tourist infrastructure here is much less significant than in Eilat, making the beaches quieter. The name Aqaba was given to the town in the 14th century by the Mamelukes, and it was the first town captured from the Turks in 1917 by the Arab forces led by T.E. Lawrence (Lawrence of Arabia).

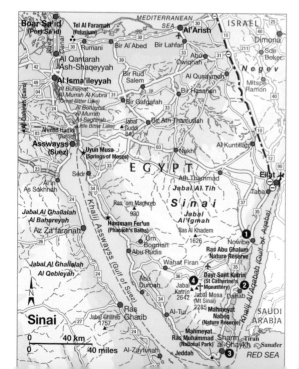

By far the most popular excursion into Jordan involves traveling northward some 120km (75 miles) to the fabulous Nabatean city of **Petra** ⑮ (see box). Reached through a narrow canyon, Petra is best known for the dramatic tomb and temple facades carved into the Nubian sandstone mountains. The pink, red, and purple-hued mountain walls would be exquisite enough, but in addition you get the romance and history of a location that lay forgotten for nearly 2,000 years until "discovered" by the Swiss explorer Ludwig Burckhardt in 1812.

Visiting the Sinai

The Sinai was captured by Israeli forces in 1967 and returned to Egypt in 1982 under the Camp David peace treaty. It remains a popular playground for Israelis, who built up a tourist infrastructure along the Red Sea coast during the years when they held the territory. Since then the Egyptians have greatly expanded the region's tourist facilities, but vast stretches of the Sinai remain gloriously isolated. It is more rugged and spectacular than the Negev, and everything here is on a grander scale.

The Sinai can be reached from the **Taba Border Crossing** (tel: 08-636 0999), 10km (6 miles) south of Eilat. The Taba enclave itself, which has a number of hotels with casinos, is technically in Egyptian territory, but is open to all who can produce valid passports. The crossing into the Sinai is open 24 hours a day, seven days a week, closing only for the Jewish festival of Yom Kippur and the Muslim festival of Id el Fitr. Visas for a two-week stay in the Sinai peninsula only are given at the frontier itself for a small charge, but people wishing to visit the rest of Egypt must obtain a full visa from an Egyptian Consulate in Eilat or elsewhere. Bus number 15 will take you to the border, and there are buses and taxis on the Egyptian side running through Sinai and on to Cairo. Passenger cars can be taken into the Sinai for a modest charge.

Note that there have been security incidents in Sinai since the political upheavals in Egypt in February 2011, and it is advisable to check the latest

The King Solomon Hotel.

The Treasury (El Khazneh), Petra, Jordan.

PETRA

Petra is far and away Jordan's most spectacular touristic site, offering a powerful and always invigorating combination of Nabatean antiquities and sensational natural scenery. From sunrise to sunset, its footpaths bustle with tourists, yet an uncanny otherworldliness prevails. In the very midst of what was obviously a thriving city, the Nabateans built a host of elaborate funerary monuments. These, combined with the intense glow of the rock and prolific references to gods, animals, and mythological beings, create an almost supernatural aura. The city was all but abandoned by the late 8th century, yet the details of the monuments appear amazingly fresh. A full week is required to see every important part of the Petra Basin, which in its entirety comprises nearly 100 sq km (38 sq miles).

TIP

In the Sinai and Negev, take heed when Bedouin warn of flash floods in the winter. The skies may be clear, but heavy rains can sweep down through dry canyons and river beds. The Bedouin, smelling the rainwater in the air, know what's coming.

security situation before entering the peninsula.

Sharm al-Shaykh

There are three major resorts along the Sinai's Red Sea coast: **Nowibe ❶**, 60km (38 miles) south of Eilat, **Dahab ❷**, 135km (85 miles) south of Eilat, and **Sharm al-Shaykh ❸**, 225km (140 miles) south of Eilat. You can stop en route to eat fresh fish in one of the coastal villages. Desert safaris to nearby wadis and oases are offered from all these locations, but an even bigger attraction than the stunning desert landscapes is the marine life, and the coral reefs especially.

The Sinai is considered one of the world's premier locations for divers. Generally speaking, the coral formations are more remarkable to the south, with Sharm al-Shaykh being the favorite choice of seasoned divers. Conservationists are increasingly concerned about the harm caused to coral at Ras Muhammad National Park; this is mainly due to over-harvesting and damage from ships' anchors, but also to illicit souvenir-hunting.

St Catherine's and the Chapel of the Burning Bush

The other major attraction of Sinai is **St Catherine's Monastery ❹** (daily 9.30am–noon; closed public holidays), reached from a road running southwest for 35km (21 miles) from a point located midway between Nuwayba and Dahab. Built by funding from the Byzantine ruler Justinian in the 6th century on a site where some believe the burning bush spoke to Moses, the monastery is today home to Greek Orthodox monks. It has a magnificent basilica and a splendid fresco depicting the transfiguration of Christ. The tiny Chapel of the Burning Bush stands on the spot where the biblical event is said to have taken place.

The nearby summit at an altitude of 2,642 meters (8,660ft) offers a breath-taking view of the desert.

All-inclusive tours to both the Sinai and Petra involving overnight stays are available from the many travel agents in Eilat. As the price and content of these tours vary a lot, it is worth shopping around for the best value.

Mount Sinai just before the break of dawn.

Diving in Eilat

Beautiful coral reefs, clear waters and swarms of tropical fish, coupled with a reputation for safety, have made Eilat a top diving destination.

Eilat is one of the world's top destinations for warm-water diving. What makes its marine environment especially magical are the exquisite coral reefs, the colorful and remarkable array of tropical fish, and the clarity of the water, with average underwater visibility of 30 meters (100ft). An extra incentive to visit Eilat, should one be needed, is the excellent 350 days of sunshine a year.

Expert divers consider diving in the Sinai in Egypt to the south of Eilat to be much better, but the tourist infrastructure there is less well developed. Moreover, Eilat's lack of currents, due to its location in a sheltered bay at the northern end of the Red Sea, combined with the shallowness of the reefs, greatly reduces the dangers associated with diving. It also means that Eilat is nicknamed the "underwater classroom" because of the large numbers of budding divers who flock to the resort to learn the skills of scuba-diving.

The safety factor is also enhanced by the fact that diving in Israel is strictly regulated by Knesset legislation. It is a criminal offense for any of the several dozen diving equipment businesses in the city to rent out equipment to a person who can't present a valid diving license issued by an internationally recognized organization such as PADI (Professional Association of Diving Instructors).

Most of the diving clubs are located near Coral Beach, several miles south of the city center. If you do not have a license, then a typical diving course for beginners comprises five full days of instruction, from classroom theory through to pool training and ultimately the real thing.

Diving alternatives

The less adventurous need not be denied the fantastic spectacle of Eilat's underwater world. Snorkeling is simple to do. Simply buy or rent a snorkel, wade in and stick your head under water. Alternatively, many of the diving clubs have snorkeling tours – a bit like a nature hike with a professional guide.

There are dozens of other ways to enjoy the Red Sea from above the water. The bay's strong breezes are ideal for windsurfing, and for those who prefer to travel faster there is no lack of water-skiing (including jet skis, tube skis and bob skis for the initiated). If you don't want to get your feet wet, then you can hire a kayak, canoe, rowing boat, or speedboat, while a glass-bottomed boat is ideal for appreciating the marine life.

There is also the yellow submarine, located inside the Underwater Observatory Marine Park (see page 310). The Marine Park itself is probably the best place for non-divers to enjoy Eilat's incredible underwater seascapes.

Practical information

For renting diving equipment or taking courses it is best to head for Coral Beach:

Aqua-Sport: P.O. Box 300, Eilat; tel: 08-633 4404; www.aqua-sport.com; email: info@aqua-sport.com.

Red Sea Lucky Divers: P.O. Box 4191, Eilat; tel: 08-632 3466; www.luckydivers.com; email: lucky sue@luckydivers.com.

The lack of currents and the shallowness of the coral reef make diving relatively safe.

People walk down a narrow alley in Jerusalem's Old City.

INSIGHT GUIDES TRAVEL TIPS
ISRAEL

TRANSPORTATION

GETTING THERE AND GETTING AROUND

GETTING THERE

The website of the Israel Airports Authority has information in English about all Israel's airports and land border crossings: www.iaa.gov.il

Travel security

For decades before 2001's terrorist attacks on America – in fact, since aircraft hijacking began in the late 1960s – Israel's border and aviation security has been rigorous. Since 9/11, international travel and aviation authorities have adopted the security norms tried and tested by Israel over the decades (often in consultation with Israeli experts). For example, as a matter of procedure since the 1970s, the door to the pilot's cockpit has been locked at all times, and Israeli fighter aircraft are scrambled to escort any plane that doesn't respond to air traffic control routine calls as it approaches Israeli airspace. Passengers taking flights to and from Israel should get to the airport two to three hours before take-off.

Israel's security philosophy has always been to focus on people rather than their baggage, and travelers should brace themselves for intrusive personal questions as well as searches. For example, you may be asked about the nature of your relationship with the person you are traveling with or visiting in Israel.

By air

Ben Gurion International Airport
The main hub for international air traffic is Ben Gurion International Airport, which is located in Lod

(Lydda), near the Mediterranean coast, 15km (9 miles) southeast of Tel Aviv, 50km (30 miles) west of Jerusalem and 110km (68 miles) southeast of Haifa. Eleven million passengers passed through the airport in 2008.

Terminal 3: International passengers arrive and depart from Terminal 3, a new, spacious facility.

Terminal 2: This is a relatively small terminal near the eastern entrance to the airport used for domestic flights.

Terminal 1: This old terminal has been refurbished and is used for low-cost airlines such as easyJet.

There is a free shuttle bus service between Terminals 3 and 1.

About 25 percent of international flights in and out of Ben Gurion International Airport are operated by El Al Israel Airlines, the country's national carrier, which was privatized in 2005. El Al carries nearly 4 million passengers a year. Most major airlines from North America and Europe have regular flights to Israel, as well as many charter companies.

The airport has ATMs, banks, and a post office, which is open 24 hours a day (except Friday night/Saturday). Ben Gurion International Airport: (03) 975 5555 or *6663.

Flight arrival, departure, and other information at Ben Gurion International Airport: (03) 972 3332

Airport car rental

All the major car rental companies operating in Israel have offices at the airport:

Avis: tel: (03) 977 3200. www.avis.co.il
Best: tel: 1-800-22-015. www.best-car.co.il
Eldan: tel: (03) 977 3400/1/7. www.eldan.co.il

Europe: tel: (03) 622 2240. www.europcar.co.il
Hertz: tel: 1-700-507-555. www.hertz.co.il
Budget: tel: (03) 971 1504. www.budget.co.il
Shlomo SIXT: tel: 1-700-501-502. www.sixt.co.il
Thrifty: tel: (03) 605 8000. www.thrifty.co.il

To and from Ben Gurion International Airport

Train: There is a rail link from Terminal 3. Details about times of trains and fares are available on the internet: www.rail.co.il; or tel: *5770 or 077 232 4000. There is no train service on the Jewish Sabbath from Friday sunset to Saturday evening or on public holidays. There are no trains after midnight and before 3am. There is a regular service to Tel Aviv and from there to most major cities in Israel. For Tel Aviv's hotel district, take the train to Tel Aviv Merkaz (Central) and catch a taxi from there.

Taxis: Taxis to Jerusalem cost about US$50–60 and to Tel Aviv about US$30–35.

Shared Taxis: This service to Jerusalem costs about US$16 per person. For booking a shared taxi from your hotel or any other address in Jerusalem back to the airport, telephone Nesher: (02) 625 7227 or 1-599-500-205; www.neshertours. co.il. This service to Haifa costs about US$30 – for booking back to the airport phone Amal: (04) 866 2324.

Taxis are notorious for ripping off tourists, especially to and from the airport, and you are encouraged to contact the airport's Taxi Supervision Unit if you have a complaint about pricing or the behavior of drivers: tel: (03) 975 2383.

Israel's transportation facilities are mostly ultra-modern.

VIP Services: The following companies provide limousine and minibus transportation to and from the airport, and personal guided tours.

Tal Limousine
Minibus transportation services, only by telephone booking in advance. Tel: (03) 975 4044.

Tour Bus Ltd
Transportation services to and from the airport, 24 hours a day, by telephone booking in advance. Location of the company's counters is at the parking lot opposite the front of Terminal 3. Tel: (03) 975 4200.

Shashir
Transportation services to and from the airport, 24 hours a day, by telephone booking in advance. Location of the company's counters is at the parking lot opposite the front of Terminal 3. Tel: (03) 975 4033.

Super B
Guided tours, transportation, and VIP accompaniment in limousines. Location of the company's counters – the parking lot opposite the front of Terminal 3. Tel: (03) 973 1780.
Buses: Timetables available on www.egged.co.il or tel: (03) 694 8888 or *2800.
Bus stops are located by the three-

Other airports

Apart from Eilat Airport and Uvda Airport in the Negev, which take in a limited number of international flights bound for Eilat, all Israel's other airports are for domestic traffic only.
(Sde) Dov Hoz (Tel Aviv) Airport: (03) 698 4500
Haifa Airport: (04) 847 6100
Eilat: 1-700-705-022
Rosh Pina (North): (06) 693 6478
Uvda: 1-700-705-022
Herzliya: (09) 971 9555

story bridge on the second floor next to Gates 21 and 23.
Egged bus line 5 is an internal bus service taking passengers to Airport City nearby to link up with bus lines traveling throughout the country. Passengers using just this service must pay, but those linking up with inter-city services receive their ticket free of charge.
From Airport City: Egged bus lines 930, 943, 947, and 950 travel to Jerusalem in one direction and Haifa in the other.
Egged bus lines 423 and 475 travel to Tel Aviv.
Metropoline runs a bus service to Be'er Sheva (tel: *5900).

Hotels
There are no hotels next to the airport, but Tel Aviv is only 20 minutes away and offers a wide choice of hotels.

Private planes
Pilots interested in flying their own planes to Israel should provide the Israel Airports Authority with all mandatory information at least 48 hours in advance of the estimated time of arrival and await clearance before commencing the flight. For further information contact: Israel Airport Authority, P.O. Box 7, Ben Gurion International Airport, 70100 Israel, tel: (03) 977 4500.
Chim Nir Flight Services Ltd rents and services private aircraft and helicopters.
Tel: (09) 952 0520.

By sea
The main ports are Haifa (tel: (04) 851 8518) and Ashdod (tel: (08) 851 7604). Several shipping lines offer regular services from Greece and Cyprus to Haifa and Ashdod ports, and many Mediterranean cruises include Israel in their itineraries. Official ports of entry for foreign

yachts and boats, in addition to these, include the marinas at:
Akko: Tel: (04) 991 9287
Ashdod: Tel: (08) 855 7246. Email: bmarina@netvision.net.il
Ashkelon: Tel: (08) 673 3780. www.ashkelon-marina.co.il
Eilat: Tel: (08) 637 6761.
Haifa (Kishon): Tel: (04) 842 2106
Herzliya: Tel: (09) 956 5591. www.herzliya-marina.co.il
Tel Aviv: Tel: (03) 527 2596. www.telaviv-marina.co.il
Yafo: Tel: (03) 683 2255
Contact the marina of your choice and reserve berthing several weeks in advance, providing full details of your vessel. When 80km (50 miles) off the Israeli coast, report (IMOT) to Haifa Radio 4xo and to the Israeli Navy. Stand by VHF channel 16.

Landing for the day
If you visit Israel on a cruise ship or yacht, you will be given a Landing for the Day card, which permits you to remain in the country for as long as your ship is in port, and you need not apply for a visitor's visa. This applies only to people wishing to enter Israel for tourism purposes.

By Road

From Jordan
Bringing your car into Israel is not recommended. It can be brought in by land from Jordan or Egypt, but this is fraught with bureaucratic problems – not least from Israeli excise officials.
Israel now recognizes Jordanian stamps in passports and visas, and vice versa. Visitors can cross on foot at several border crossings: the Allenby Bridge (easiest for travel between Amman and Jerusalem/Tel Aviv), the Jordan River Crossing (near Beit She'an), and the Arava Checkpoint (between Eilat and Aqaba).
Allenby Bridge (near Jericho), some 40km (25 miles) from Jerusalem, is the main crossing-point. Closed Yom Kippur and Id el Fitr; for information tel: (02) 548 2600. (Israelis are not allowed to use this crossing point.)
The visa requirements are the same as those at any other point of entry into Israel (it is not possible to get an Israeli visa upon arrival at the bridge or in Jordan). The bridge is open Sun–Thur 8am–8pm and Fri–Sat 8am–3pm. At Allenby Bridge, a Tourist Information Office is open at the same time as the bridge. Other facilities are: currency exchange, post office, public telephones, cafeteria, toilets, porters, and sherut

(service) taxis to Jerusalem, Jericho, Bethlehem, Hebron, Ramallah, and Gaza. For opening hours and restrictions at points of entry between Jordan and Israel, check details with Israel's Ministry of Tourism, or contact the border.

Jordan River (near Beit She'an): Sun–Thur 6.30am–9pm and Fri–Sat 8am–8pm, closed Yom Kippur and Id el Fitr; tel: (04) 609 3400.

Yitzhak Rabin (Arava) Checkpoint (near Eilat): Sun–Thur 6.30am–8pm and Fri–Sat 8am– 8pm. Hourly bus service (route 16) from Eilat. Checkpoint closed on Yom Kippur and Muslim New Year. Tel: (08) 630 0555.

From Egypt

Points of entry open between Israel and Egypt are Nitsana and Taba. **Nitsana**, the main point of entry, is about 60km (37 miles) southwest of Be'er Sheva and is open Sun–Thur between 8.30am and 4.30pm, closed Fri, Sat, and Jewish and Muslim festivals; tel: (08) 656 4666. It is served by Egged bus 44 from Be'er Sheva.

Taba, just south of Eilat, is open 24 hours a day, tel: (08) 636 0999. Take bus 15 to Eilat.

Rav-Kav multi-ride discount electronic card

www.dan.co.il
This electronic card can be purchased at central bus stations and main railway stations. It offers discounts and convenience and is interchangeable between bus companies, Israel Railways, and the Jerusalem Light Rail. In cities, Rav-Kav holders can take a second follow-on journey within 90 minutes of their first journey.

GETTING AROUND

Buses

Buses are the most common means of public transport for both urban and inter-urban services (although the railways are making a rapid resurgence). Services are regular and the fares are reasonable, though the prices have risen in recent years due to the withdrawal of government subsidies.

Egged and Dan (Tel Aviv) are the dominant bus companies, and there are a growing number of smaller companies. Services are punctual and, if anything, impatient drivers tend to leave half a minute before time. If traveling to Eilat, it is

advisable to reserve seats several days in advance.

Egged runs the urban routes in Jerusalem, Haifa, and Eilat. Egged information, tel: (03) 694 8888. Route details and timetables are available in English at www.egged.co.il. The site offers updated information about discounted and multi-ride tickets for various periods and in various cities, discounts for children and students, bus maps, etc.

Bus 99 – US$16 per adult and US$13 per child – allows you to travel around 25 major tourist points in Jerusalem on a double-decker, London-style bus, alighting and getting back on again when you feel like it.

Lost Property: Tel Aviv, tel: (03) 638 3924; Jerusalem, tel: (02) 568 5670.

Dan Bus information, that is for city buses in the Greater Tel Aviv region, can be had by calling (03) 639 4444; www.dan.co.il/english/

Other companies: Superbus (Modiin, Beit Shemesh, Jerusalem), tel: (08) 920 5005; Kavim (Greater Tel Aviv), tel: *8787 or (072) 2588787; Metropoline (Hasharon, Beersheva and south), tel; *5900 or (073) 210 0422

Times: Buses do not run from Friday before sundown until Saturday after sundown. Inter-urban bus services start around 6am and finish in the early evening except for the Tel Aviv–Jerusalem and Tel Aviv–Haifa lines, which continue until midnight. Urban services run from 5am to just after midnight.

Locations: The Jerusalem Central Bus Station is in Yafo, at the western entrance to the city. The Tel Aviv Central Bus Station is a vast shopping mall complex on Levinski in the south of the city (connected to Haganah train station). Haifa has two bus stations: Hof Hacarmel (connected to the train station of the same name) at the city's southern entrance and Checkpost at the northern entrance to the city.

There are no bus services on the Sabbath, or on Jewish holidays except within Haifa, Eilat, and Arab cities.

Trains

Israel Railways have undergone major expansion in the past 20 years and reach most major cities (except Eilat and Tiberias); tickets are slightly more expensive than for comparable rides on buses. Note the old Jerusalem train station is no longer used but there is a station at Jerusalem Malkah serving the scenic route to Tel Aviv via

Metro

Israel's only subway operates in Haifa and is called the Carmelit. This recently renovated system is in fact an underground cable car. It is also the quickest way of getting about Haifa. The train runs from Central Mount Carmel to downtown Haifa every 10 minutes and makes six stops. The trip takes 9 minutes. It operates Sun–Thur 6am–midnight, Fri 6am–3pm, and Sat from sunset to midnight (tel: (04) 837 6861; www.carmelithaifa.com).

Beit Shemesh. A new suburban line running south of Tel Aviv to Holon, Bat Yam, and West Rishon Lezion opened in 2011 with an extension to Yavne, Ashdod, Ashkelon, and Sderot was completed in 2013.. A new fast line between Tel Aviv and Jerusalem is under construction, but will not be completed until at least 2017.

For information, tel: (03) 577 4000; www.rail.co.il
There is a map of the Israel Railway network at http://www.rail.co.il/EN/Stations/Map/Pages/RouteMap.aspx
There is no train service on the Sabbath, or on Jewish holidays.

Jerusalem Light Rail

A tram system operating from Pisgat Ze'ev in northern Jerusalem via the city center along Jaffa Road to Herzl Boulevard and Yad Vashem in the southwest. Flat fare tickets can be bought online at www.citypass.co.il or at automatic ticket machines at each of the 22 stops.

Taxis

Taxis offer a quick and convenient mode of travel in Israel. You can phone for a taxi in any major city, or hail one in the street. All urban taxis have meters, whose operation is compulsory. If the driver wants to turn off the meter he may be trying to take you for a ride in more ways than one – in fact taxis are notorious for overcharging tourists (see page 318). Tipping is not compulsory, but is appreciated. Prices are fixed between cities, and the driver will tell you your fare in advance, or show you the official price list if you ask for it.

Driving

Israelis drive on the right and with Mediterranean creativity. In cities, traffic is chaotic, with a great deal

Tipping taxi drivers isn't compulsory but is appreciated.

of horn honking, overtaking on the inside, and general improvisation; in rural areas life on the road is much quieter. With well over 2 million vehicles on the roads, Israel has one of the world's most densely populated road systems.

There are around 450 fatalities each year from road accidents, which is comparable with death rates on Western European roads. Drinking and driving offenses are relatively rare but drinking and driving laws are strictly enforced with frequent routine breathalysing. All cars are legally bound to have air conditioning.

Strict law enforcement

Laws are strictly enforced, and it is necessary to wear seat belts at all times (both front and back) and strap children under four into appropriate seats. Speed limits are 90–120kph (55–68mph) on highways and 50–70kph (30–40mph) in urban areas. There are many speed traps and cameras on major highways, with fines of up to US$170 for exceeding the speed limit by more than 10 percent. Police tend to be lenient with tourists but can take you straight in front of a judge if they wish to. Keep your passport, driver's license, and other papers to hand at all times (you will

also need them for the many security checkpoints you will pass through).

Talking or texting on a cellular/mobile phone that is not in a hands-free installation is also an offence, which police penalize with a fine of US$280. There are speed cameras on many highways, and there are also cameras at many traffic light intersections primed to photograph cars crossing the lights one second after the lights have turned red. Note: Israelis tend to move off very quickly at traffic lights the moment they turn green, making it especially dangerous to shoot a red light even before the one-second grace that the police give drivers before issuing a ticket.

Fuel: All cars manufactured in the past decade (all vehicles are imported) take unleaded gasoline or diesel called benzine and solar in Hebrew respectively. Leaded fuel is no longer available at most gas stations. Fuel is about the same price as Western Europe, but more expensive than in America. In Eilat, a VAT-free zone, you do not pay the usual 18 percent VAT charge (sales tax) on fuel.

Parking

Parking is very difficult in the major city centers, and it is best to look for

a parking lot. These can cost US$3 an hour in Jerusalem, and up to US$5 per hour in parts of Tel Aviv. If a curbside is marked in blue and white, you need a ticket, which you can purchase from stores or from streetside machines or in some cases there are parking meters. It costs about $2 per hour in most cities.

Parking is usually free after 7/8pm and before 8pm, though it is prohibited in many residential areas. In Jerusalem most blue and white curbsides have parking meters or nearby machines to dispense tickets. If you fail to display a ticket, or the ticket has expired, you are liable for a US$30 fine, though this need not be paid for several months.

Do not ignore red and white marked curbsides or No Parking signs. If you park here you may be clamped with a "Denver boot" or even towed away. In either instance it will cost you US$125 (or more) and a lot of wasted time in redeeming your car.

Highway Six

Highway Six is Israel's first toll highway, running a length of 140km (87.5 miles) from north to south parallel to the Mediterranean about 15–25km (9–15 miles) inland. The 35km (22-mile) southern stretch from the Sorek Interchange is free. Extensions stretching farther south and north are under construction. The highway is especially useful when traveling from Jerusalem to Haifa and the north because it misses out the heavily congested Tel Aviv region, and during morning and evening rush hours it can reduce by one hour what would otherwise be a three-hour trip between Jerusalem and points north.

The toll is collected electronically. The highway was built on a BOT basis by a private consortium. The speed limit on the highway is 120kph (75mph). Cameras photograph vehicles' number plates and send the bill by mail to the owners several months later. A one-way journey of about 70km (44 miles) costs US$7, and subscriptions are available. Note: Car-hire firms take an additional handling fee on using Highway Six.

Carmel Tunnels (Haifa)

The Carmel Tunnels bypass the city by running east to west from the southern entrance of Haifa to the Checkpost Interchange. The tunnel breaks in the middle, enabling vehicles to exit to the city at Neve Shaanan on Mount Carmel. This is a toll tunnel costing US$2.20 for

Shared taxis: sherut

The sherut is Israel's own indigenous mode of transport, operating in and between main cities every day but Shabbat; some private companies or owners operate on Shabbat as well. Individuals share a minibus or cab, which can take up to 10 people at a fixed price, usually equivalent to the bus fare for the same route.

In Jerusalem sheruts between cities leave from near the Central Bus Station, and from near Kikar

Tsiyon (Zion Square) in the city center. In Tel Aviv the sheruts leave from near the Central Bus Station for Jerusalem, Haifa and most other cities. Local sheruts follow the main bus routes, making similar stops in quicker time and charging the same fare. In all Israeli cities, taxi drivers will often follow bus routes charging a similar fare; but beware – they can become opportunistic about the price when faced with a tourist.

each section and US$4.30 for the full 6.5km (4 miles). Unlike Israel's other toll roads, payment is by cash at toll booths.

Tel Aviv Fast Lane

The world's first dynamic toll lane runs along Highway 1 from 13km (8 miles) east of the city near Ben Gurion Airport. The toll costs a minimum of US$2 up to US$30, depending on how badly jammed the highway is, but there is an extra handling fee of US$8 rising to US$20 for vehicles that have not registered in advance. The toll level is clearly marked at the entrance to the lane. Vehicles with four passengers including the driver travel free, but you must register with an inspector halfway along. It is also possible to pay the toll to the inspector and avoid handling fees, especially with a rented car. Unregistered cars can also register for free with the inspector.There is also a free park and ride service 7km (4.5 miles) into the lane, with buses to the Azrieli Center in Tel Aviv and Diamond Exchange in Ramat Gan. Cars using the park and ride service do not pay the toll.

Hiring a car

Car-hire companies require drivers to be over 21 and to have held a full license for at least one year. Drivers must present an international driving license, or national license if written in English or French, plus a passport and international credit card.

Many of the world's principal car-hire companies have outlets here. Israel's largest car-hire company, Eldan, also has offices overseas. These companies can supply you with a car at the airport and allow you to leave it there on departure. They have a network of offices around the country.

Car rental costs around US$180 a week for a small saloon or US$300 a week for a medium-sized car. Shop around, as prices vary considerably. Traffic is heavy and parking difficult in Israel's big cities. Hiring a car, though convenient, is not necessarily vital for the center of the country, which has good bus, rail, and taxi services. It is not possible to cross the border from Israel into neighboring countries in a rental car.

However, hiring a car can be the best way of touring the Galilee or the Negev, and it can be cheaper off-season (Oct–Apr) or if you do a deal with one of the many local, smaller companies. But in general it is much cheaper to book a car in advance as part of a package deal (flight, hotel,

car) with a travel agent overseas.

As with everywhere in the world, carefully check that there is no damage to the car, that the spare wheel, jack, and other equipment are in place, and that oil and water are sufficient before accepting a car. Note that car-hire companies will deduct parking and police fines from your credit card. They will also take the toll charges from Highway Six and the Tel Aviv Fast Lane – some companies take a handling fee of US$11 for paying tolls, others charge double the actual toll.

Payments in foreign currency are exempt from VAT (18 percent), and rates usually include just theft insurance. Commercial vehicles cannot be hired with VAT exemption.

Car rental

(See Ben Gurion Airport section pages for details about car-hire offices there.)

Avis: (www.avis.co.il)
22 David ha-Melekh, Jerusalem. Tel: (02) 624 9001/2. Email: celine@avis.co.il
113 Ha-Yarkon, Tel Aviv. Tel: (03) 688 4242.

Budget: (www.budget.co.il)
22 David ha-Melekh, Jerusalem. Tel: (02) 624 8991. Email: info@budget.co.il
99 Ha-Yarkon, Tel Aviv. Tel: (03) 524 5233.

Hertz: (www.hertz.co.il)
18 David ha-Melekh, Jerusalem. Tel: (02) 623 1351.
Central reservations, tel: 1-700-507-555.Email: hertzjerusalem@hertz.co.il
144 Ha-Yarkon, Tel Aviv. Tel: (03) 522 3332.

SIXT: (www.sixt.co.il)
14 David ha-Melekh, Jerusalem. Tel: (02) 624 8204/5.
112 Ha-Yarkon, Tel Aviv. Tel: (03) 524 9764.
Central reservations, tel: 1-700-501-502.

Best-Car: (www.best-car.co.il)
159 Yaffo, Jerusalem. Tel: (02) 538 9226.
3 Arlozorov, Tel Aviv. Tel: (03) 524 4122.

Eldan: (www.eldan.co.il)
24 David ha-Melekh, Jerusalem. Tel: (02) 625 2151.
114 Ha-Yarkon Tel Aviv. Tel: (03) 527 1166.
Eldan USA: 1114 Quentin Road, 2nd Floor, Brooklyn, New York 11229, USA. Toll free: 1-800-938-5000. Local: 1-718-998-5500.
Eldan UK: 136B Burnt Oak Broadway, Edgware, Middlesex HA8 0BB. Tel: 020-8951 5727.

Europcar: (www.europcar.co.il)
76 Ha-Yarkon, Tel Aviv (03) 541 7676

Specialist tours

So much history gets missed without an expert guide to explain the significance of each site, so it is well worth joining an organized tour. Major tour bus companies include:
Egged Tours
Tel: 1-700-70-75-77; www.egged.co.il
United Tours
Tel: (02) 625 2187 or (03) 616 2656; www.inisrael.com
Diesenhaus Unitours/Galilee Tours
Tel: (03) 565 1313; www.diesenhaus.com

Pedestrians

Drivers cannot be relied upon to stop at pedestrian crossings. And pedestrians can't always be relied on not to wander casually into the road. The safest place to cross is at traffic lights. Beware at right-turn filters where the pedestrian light is green but traffic may still pass. In Jerusalem and other cities, police hand out fines to pedestrians who cross at red pedestrian lights.

Hitchhiking

This is a highly acceptable form of getting around, within and between cities. Hitchhiking stations, looking rather like bus stops complete with shelters, are provided at major junctions. In recent years the competition has become less fierce as soldiers are now prohibited from hitchhiking. Women should of course beware of predatory males.

Cycling

Drivers, as in many places worldwide, are very inconsiderate of cyclists' needs and the dangers they face. Although not legally required, helmets are a good idea. Jerusalem and Haifa are hilly cities, adding to the difficulties challenging cyclists, but cycling can be a good way of getting around in the Greater Tel Aviv area, which has 100km (62 miles) of cycle tracks (see page 340).
For rentals:
Tel-O-Fun, 197 Ben Yehuda Street, tel: (03) 544 2292 (see page 249)
The Bike Center, 100 Menachem Begin, tel: (03) 562 2584.
Ein Elli, 115 Hachashmonaim Street, tel: (03) 561 2520.

ACCOMMODATIONS

HOTELS, YOUTH HOSTELS, BED AND BREAKFASTS

CHOOSING ACCOMMODATIONS

There is a wide choice of accommodations in Israel, from deluxe suites in high-class hotels to budget hotels, bed and breakfasts, and youth hostels. But there is a lack of charm about Israeli hotels, many of which were built in recent decades, offering modern comfort and convenience without much character. Unique Israeli forms of accommodations include kibbutz guesthouses (relatively expensive rural retreats) and Christian hospices (more luxurious than they sound and not to be confused with hospitals for the terminally ill). Both these offer an unusual taste of Israel.

In the past decade bed-and-breakfasting has become increasingly popular in Israel, while the zimmerim (taken from the German) are popular in northern Israel. Ideally this is some sort of country lodge, chalet, or log cabin, in a rural retreat, though often it is a less romantic prefabricated structure. Youth hostels range from hole-in-the-wall downtown joints to the facilities of the Israel Youth Hostel Association, which are usually well appointed, and of three-star hotel quality (with prices to match).

HOTELS

Until the late 1990s, the Ministry of Tourism graded hotels from one to five stars according to size, service, and facilities. The system was discontinued, making it trickier to monitor quality.

Hotels require guests to check out by midday, but on Saturday and holidays guests can pre-arrange to retain their rooms until the Sabbath

or holiday finishes in the evening. Check-in is usually after 3pm.

Prices can be more expensive during the high season, which is Easter/ Passover, July to August, Jewish New Year and Christmas. But prices cater for every pocket down to the cheapest youth hostels, which charge about US$10–15 a night. Hotel rates are generally quoted in dollars and include a 15 percent service charge. If you pay in foreign currency you are exempt from 16 percent VAT. Eilat is VAT-free.

Major hotel chains

Fattal Hotels: Israel's largest chain, with 29 hotels including the Herods, Leonardo, U and Magic brands. Tel: (03) 511 0050; www.fattal.co.il.
Dan Hotels: Israel's largest luxury chain of 14 hotels includes the flagship King David. Tel: (03) 740 8966, toll free from North America 1-800-223-7773/4; Europe 00-800-326-46835; www.danhotels.com.
Prima Hotels: Eleven four-star hotels around the country, some of which have more character than their five-star counterparts. Tel: (03) 552 2220 or *9995; www.prima.co.il.
Isrotel: Specializes in Eilat, where it has nine hotels, and has eight other hotels around the country. Tel: (08) 638 7799; www.isrotel.co.il.
Rimonim Hotel: Eleven hotels with a lot of character, in particular the Ruth Rimonim Safed, and Rimonim Galei Kinnereth Tiberias. Tel: (03) 675 4591; www.rimonim.com

KIBBUTZ GUESTHOUSES

Visitors wanting a truly Israeli experience should try a kibbutz

guesthouse. They usually offer all the facilities of a luxury hotel plus the chance to get acquainted with kibbutz life at first hand. Though many of these guesthouses are in isolated rural areas, especially in the northern Galilee, others are located in the countryside but just 20 minutes or so by bus or car from Jerusalem or Tel Aviv. Many kibbutzim have opened country lodges (zimmerim). These are fairly inexpensive and guests can benefit from kibbutz facilities such as swimming pools, sport and fitness amenities, and good-value meals in the dining hall.
For further information, contact:
Kibbutz Hotels Chain
90 Ben Yehuda, Tel Aviv 61031
Tel: (03) 560 8118.
www.kibbutz.co.il
For kibbutz reservations in the US:
Israel Tourism Center
Tel: 888-669-5700, 201-556-9669.

CHRISTIAN HOSPICES

Another fascinating Holy Land experience is the broad array of Christian hospices. Originally designed principally for pilgrims, and owned by churches, these hospices cater for all-comers, including many Israeli Jews on vacation, who enjoy the old-world European charm of these establishments. Because these locations are often subsidized by the church that owns them, they offer excellent value.

The term hospice is misleading. Some resemble luxury hotels. Others reflect the ethnic origins of their founders. For a full list of hospices in Israel, contact the Ministry of Tourism, Pilgrimage Promotion Dept., POB 1018, Jerusalem.

TRANSPORTATION

ACCOMMODATIONS

EATING OUT

ACTIVITIES

A – Z

LANGUAGE

JERUSALEM

Addar
53 Nablus Road, Jerusalem
Tel: (02) 626 3111
www.addar-hotel.com
A relatively new and comfortable Arab hotel in an old building opposite St George's Cathedral. **$$**

American Colony
Nablus Road, Jerusalem
Tel: (02) 627 9777
www.americancolony.com
Jerusalem's oldest hotel has much character and charm, and is favored by the foreign press corps on account of its location between West and East Jerusalem. **$$$**

Arthur Hotel
13 Dorot Rishonim Street, Jerusalem
Tel: (02) 623 9999
Stylish boutique hotel in the center of Downtown Jerusalem's pedestrian precinct. **$$$**

Austrian Hospice
37 Via Dolorosa, POB 19600, Jerusalem 91194
Tel: (02) 626 5800
Grand and ornate 19th-century building on the Via Dolorosa that served as a hospital for many years but was renovated in the late 1980s. **$$**

Caesar Hotel
208 Yafo, Jerusalem
Tel: (02) 500 5656
Modern and nondescript, but right by the Central Bus Station, this hotel is ideal for itinerant tourists. **$**

Christmas
Ali Ibn Abi Taleb Street, East Jerusalem
Tel: (02) 628 2588
www.christmas-hotel.com
Attractive, small Arab hotel in the heart of East Jerusalem, with a delightful garden. **$**

Dan Jerusalem
32 Lekhi, Mount Scopus, Jerusalem
Tel: (02) 533 1234

Formerly the Regency, stylish interior. Commands a splendid view of the Old City. **$$**

David's Citadel
7 David ha-Melekh, Jerusalem
Tel: (02) 621 1111
www.thedavidcitadel.com
Formerly the Hilton, this attractively designed and well-appointed hotel is near the Jaffa Gate and downtown Jerusalem. **$$$**

Holiday Inn Crowne Plaza
Givat Ram, Jerusalem
Tel: (02) 658 8888
www.afi-hotels.com
Landmark high-rise building at the entrance to the city, opposite the Central Bus Station, this hotel offers luxury accommodation for modest prices. **$$**

Holyland Hotel
Bayit va-Gan, Jerusalem
Tel: (02) 643 7777
Email: holyland@isracom.co.il
Away from town in an attractive 1950s building, with a laid-back ambience and great view of West Jerusalem. **$$**

Inbal
3 Jabotinski, Jerusalem
Tel: (02) 675 6666
www.inbal-hotel.co.il
Formerly the Laromme, overlooking the Liberty Bell Garden, this delightfully designed hotel has attracted some world leaders away from the King David. **$$$**

King David Hotel
23 David ha-Melekh, Jerusalem
Tel: (02) 620 8888
www.danhotels.com
Israel's premier hotel, where political leaders and the rich and famous stay. It has style and an old-world ambience, but in terms of quality of service its newer rivals try harder. Has beautiful gardens overlooking the Old

City. **$$$**

Little House in Baka
80 Hebron Road, Jerusalem
Tel: (02) 673 7944
Cross between a boutique hotel and guesthouse in large, stylish 1920s home in Jerusalem's trendy Baka neighborhood. **$$**

Mamilla Hotel
11 King Solomon Street, Jerusalem
Tel: (02) 548 2222
Jerusalem's newest hotel is also one of the city's most luxurious and inevitably most expensive. Best of all, the hotel is above the newly opened Mamila shopping mall and adjacent to the Old City walls, with breathtaking views. **$$$**

Mount Zion
17 Hebron Road, Jerusalem
Tel: (02) 568 9555
www.mountzion.co.il
Originally an ophthalmology hospital, built over a century ago, this building was converted into a luxury hotel overlooking the Old City walls in the 1980s. **$$**

Notre Dame
POB 20531, Jerusalem (opposite the New Gate)
Tel: (02) 627 9111
Superbly appointed hospice opposite the Old City walls offering luxurious accommodations, splendid 19th-century architecture, and one of Jerusalem's best (non-kosher) restaurants. Vatican-owned, it has been extensively renovated. **$$**

Our Sisters of Zion
Ein Kerem
Tel: (02) 641 5738
Delightful Provençal-style pension in Ein Kerem. Spacious gardens filled with olive trees and grape vines. Comfortable accommodations. **$$**

Palatin Hotel
4 Agripas Street, Jerusalem
Tel: (02) 623 1141
Email: info@palatinhotel.com
A clean and comfortable hotel, with a central location in West Jerusalem and close to the Mahane Yehuda market. **$**

Prima Palace
6 Pines Street, Jerusalem
Tel: (02) 538 1111
www.prima.co.il
Colorful ultra-Orthodox establishment in the heart of West Jerusalem. **$$**

Ramat Rachel Hotel and Spa
Kibbutz Ramat Rachel, M.P. North Judea, Jerusalem 90900
Tel: (02) 670 2555
www.ramatrachel.co.il

Spring is an attractive time of year on a kibbutz.

Although within the city limits, the kibbutz grounds offer a stirring view of the Judean Desert. The kibbutz is adjacent to an unusual olive garden. $$$

Reich Hotel
1 Hagai Street, Beit ha-Kerem, Jerusalem
Tel: (02) 652 3121
Email: reichhtl@zahav.net.il
Located in the leafy suburbs of Beit ha-Kerem, the hotel is not far from the city and the bus station. $$

Seven Arches
Mount of Olives
Tel: (02) 626 7777
Email: svnarch@trendline.co.il
Built on a desecrated Jewish graveyard, making it un-kosher for religious Jews, but offers classic view of the Old City. $$

St Andrew's Scots Memorial Hospice
1 David Remez Street, POB 8619, Jerusalem 91086
Tel: (02) 673 2401
Intimate guesthouse atmosphere in central location. No kippers, but there is sometimes haggis. $

Waldorf Astoria
26-28 Agron Street, Jerusalem 9419008
Tel: (02) 542 3333
Run by the Hilton chain, this newly opened high-end luxury hotel is opposite the Mamilla mall and used the facade of the Ottoman built Palace Hotel. $$$

YMCA
26 David Ha-Melekh, POB 294, Jerusalem 91002
Tel: (02) 569 2652

Stylish 1930s building opposite the King David Hotel, designed by the same architect who planned the Empire State Building. $$

Jerusalem Hills

Kibbutz Tsuba Belmont Hotel
Kibbutz Tsuba (near Jerusalem)
Tel: (02) 534 7090
Inexpensive apartments near Crusader fortress on a hilltop. $$

Kibuutz Kiryat Anavim Cramim Resort & Spa
Kibbutz Kiryat Anavim, Judean Hills (near Jerusalem)
Tel: (02) 548 9800
Newly opened hilltop resort and spa hotel in the Jerusalem hills on the airport and Tel Aviv side of the city. Managed by the Isrotel chain. $$$

GALILEE AND THE GOLAN

Nazareth is the country's largest Israeli-Arab city.

Galilee and Golan Heights

Kfar Blum Guesthouse
Kibbutz Kfar Blum (Upper Galilee)
Tel: (04) 683 6611
www.kfarblum-hotel.co.il
Idyllic location along the banks of the River Jordan in the Upper Galilee. The kibbutz hosts a classical music festival each August. $$

Moshav Keshet
Ramat Hagolan 12140
Tel: (04) 696 2505
Email: keshetyo@netvision.net.il
Ideal base for Mount Hermon on the Golan Heights. $

Metula

Arazim
Tel: (04) 699 7143
Hotel in charming Swiss-style village high in the mountains on the Lebanese border. $

Nazareth

Casa Nova Franciscan Hospice
Casa Nova Street, POB 198, Nazareth
Tel: (04) 645 6660
Opposite the Basilica of the Annunciation. The Franciscan brothers lend the hospice an Italian atmosphere with Italian cuisine to go with it. $

Fauzi Azar Inn
Near the Basilica of the Anunciation
Tel: (04) 602 0469
Very special converted Ottoman-style Arab mansion in the heart of Old Nazareth. $$

Golden Crown
2015 Mount of the Precipice, Nazareth 16000
Tel: (04) 650 8000
www.goldencrown.co.il
Large hotel on the edge of the city. $$

Rimonim Hotel (Mary's Well)
Paulus IV Road, Mary's Well Square

Tel: (04) 650 0000
www.rimonim.com
Large hotel in the city. $$
Up the hill from the basilica, with excellent views of the city and a less religious atmosphere than the Catholic hospices. $

Safed

Ron
Hativat Yiftah Street, Safed
Tel: (04) 697 2590
Small hotel in the heart of the Old Town. $

Ruth Rimon Inn
Artists' Quarter, Safed
Tel: (04) 699 94666
www.rimonim.com
Best hotel in the city, with relaxing hillside views. $$$

Tiberias

Aviv
66 Hagalil, Tiberias
Tel: (04) 671 2272
Conveniently located next to the Old City of Tiberias. $

Rimonim Mineral Tiberias
Habanim Street, Tiberias
Tel: (04) 672 8555
www.rimonim.com
This hotel benefits from a great view of the Sea of Galilee and offers free

PRICE CATEGORIES

These prices are for double rooms per night and usually include breakfast.
$ = under $100
$$ = $100–160
$$$ = more than $160

entrance to the nearby Tiberia Hot Springs. $$$
Nof Ginosar Hotel
Kibbutz Ginosar (near Tiberias)
Tel: (04) 670 0300
www.ginosar.co.il
On the shores of the Sea of Galilee,

close to the sacred Christian sites of Ein Tabgha and Capernaum. $$
Leonardo Hotel
Gdud Barak St., Tiberias 14101
Tel: (04) 670 0800
www.fattal-hotels.com
Overlooking the Sea of Galilee and

right in the heart of town. $$$
Scots Hotel
Downtown Tiberias
Tel (04) 671 0710
Elegant 19th century building with stylish rooms overlooking the Sea of galilee and the Golan Heights. $$

HAIFA AND THE NORTH COAST

Akko
Palm Beach
Sea Shore, POB 2192, Akko 24101
Tel: (04) 987 7777
Email: palmbeach@netvision.net.il
The hotel has its own private beach and is a 20-minute walk from Akko's Old City. $$

Haifa
Carmel Forest Spa Resort
Carmel Forest, Haifa
Tel: (04) 830 7888
www.isrotel.co.il
Located out of the city in the Carmel forest: ideal for nature lovers, with a splendid view of the Mediterranean and lots of massages and spa treatments. Renovated after devastating fire in 2010. $$$
Carmelite Pilgrim Center "Stella Maris"
POB 9047, Haifa 31090

Tel: (04) 833 2084
Hospice on the slopes of Mount Carmel with good views of the bay.
$
Crowne Plaza
111 Yefe Nof Street, Haifa 34454
Tel: 180 945 3716
Business hotel on the Carmel next to the Bahai Gardens with splendid view of the bay. $$$
Dan Carmel
85–87 Hanasi Boulevard, Haifa
Tel: (04) 830 6306
www.danhotels.com
The city's most stylish hotel, located on Mount Carmel, with a breathtaking panorama of Haifa Bay and the azure-colored Mediterranean. $$$
Eden
8 Shmariyahu Levin Street,
Tel: (04) 866 4816
Compact and convenient in the center of town. $

Kibbutz Nahsholim Guest House
M.P. Hof Carmel 30815 (Haifa)
Tel: (04) 639 9533
www.nahsholim.co.il
Great location on the coast south of Haifa. $$
Leonardo
10 David Elazar Street, Haifa
Tel: (04) 850 8888
www.fattal-hotels-israel.co.il
Very large hotel located right on the beach at the southern entrance to the city, near the train and bus stations. $$$

Nahariya
Sol Marine
Ha'alyah Street,
Nahariya
Tel: (04) 995 0555
Seafront hotel in Israel's northernmost Mediterranean beach resort. $$

CENTRAL AND SOUTH COAST

Ashkelon
Dan Gardens
56 Rehov Hatayasim, Ashkelon Beach Front
Tel: (08) 671 1261
www.danhotels.com
Excellent value in what is probably Israel's quietest Mediterranean resort. Indoor and outdoor themed areas keep the kids entertained. $$
Samson's Gardens Hotel
38 Hatamar Street, Ashkelon, 78450
Tel: (08) 673 4666
Email: shimsho@zahav.net.il
Good value near the beach front. $

Herzliya
Dan Accadia
Derekh Hayam, Herzliya
Tel: (09) 959 7070
One of Israel's oldest and most elegant luxury hotels, this is the pick of the accommodations in this upscale resort to the north of Tel Aviv. $$$
The Ritz Carlton
4 Hashunit Street, Herzliya 46555

Tel: (09) 373 5555
www.ritzcarlton.com
Newly opened and overlooking the marina, this offers the last word in opulence. $$$
Eshel
3 Ramot Yam Street, Herzliya 46748
Tel: (09) 956 8208
Small 36-room hotel on the seafront. $

Sharon
5 Ramot Yam Street, Herzliya 46748
Tel: (09) 952 5777
Email: Sharon@sharon.co.il www.sharon.co.il
Good location on the seafront and good value. $$
Shfayim Guesthouse
Kibbutz Shfayim (near Tel Aviv/Herzliya)
Tel: (09) 959 5595
www.h-shefayim.co.il

Floating those cares away at Le Méridien Dead Sea Resort and Spa Hotel.

TRANSPORTATION

Close to the Mediterranean coast and a short bus ride away from Tel Aviv. **$**

Netanya

Grand Yahalom Hotel
15 Gad Machness, Netanya
Tel: (09) 8624888
Located in Netanya's hotel district

opposite the sea; makes a pleasant base for touring the country. **$**
King Solomon
18 Hma'apilim, Netanya
Tel: (09) 833 8444
Pick of the budget-price hotels in Netanya. Near the beach and center of town. **$$**

The Seasons
Nice Boulevard
Tel: (09) 860 1555
www.seasons.co.il
On the cliffs overlooking the sea, the city's smartest hotel, offering a wide choice of rooms, from studios to large suites and super-suites. **$$$**

TEL AVIV

Cinema
2 Zamenhoff, Dizengoff Circle, Tel Aviv
Tel: (03) 520 7100
www.cinemahotel.com
In the heart of Tel Aviv's cafe district (not near the beach), this 80-room hotel is in a converted cinema and one of the city's finest examples of Bauhaus architecture. **$$**
City
9 Mapu Street, Tel Aviv
Tel: (03) 524 6253
www.atlashotels.co.il
Near the beach and center of town, this clean and comfortable hotel puts a roof over your head. **$**
Crowne Plaza Hotel Tel Aviv City Center
132 Menachem Begin Road, Azrieli Center, Tel Aviv 63453
Tel: (03) 777 4000
One of the city's newest hotels is on the upper floors of the iconic Azrieli Center. Offers splendid views of the city but is far from the beach. **$$$**
Dan Tel Aviv
99 Ha-Yarkon, Tel Aviv 63432
Tel: (03) 520 2525
www.danhotels.com

The city's veteran luxury hotel offers excellent sea views and is renowned for comfort, style, and convenience. **$$$**
Dan Panorama
10 Kaufmann, Charles Clore Park, Tel Aviv
Tel: 03-519 0190
www.danhotels.com
Away from the main hotel district, the Dan Panorama is conveniently close to Yafo and offers good value for a luxury hotel. **$$$**
David InterContinental
12 Kaufman Street, Tel Aviv
Tel: (03) 795 1111
www.interconti.com
Adjacent to the Dan Panorama near Old Yafo, this is the city's largest hotel and is often favored by the business community due to its proximity to the financial district. **$$$**
Howard Johnson Express Shalom
216 Ha-Yarkon, Tel Aviv 62405
Tel: (03) 524 3277
www.hojo.com
Well located for Tel Aviv Port and the beach. **$$**
Leonardo Boutique
17 Harbarzel Street, Tel Aviv
Tel: (03) 5110066

Convenient for the Ramat Hahayal high-tech business district and the nearby Ramat Gan soccer stadium. **$$**
Leonardo City Tower
14 Zisman Street, Ramat Gan
Tel: (03) 754 4444
Technically this hotel, formerly the Sheraton, is in Ramat Gan and not Tel Aviv, and is ideal for the Diamond Exchange and central train station, though far from the beach. **$$$**
Rothschild Hotel
96 Rothschild Boulevard, Tel Aviv 65224
Tel: (03) 957 8888
www.rothschild-hotel.co.il
A delightful boutique hotel in an elegant building from the 1920s that has been impressively renovated. Has a gourmet fish restaurant. **$$$**
Tel Aviv Hilton
Independence Gardens, Tel Aviv
Tel: (03) 520 2222
www.hilton.co.uk/telaviv
Generally accepted as the city's most luxurious hotel and very fashionable with Tel Aviv high society, with prices to match. One minute from the beach thanks to its clifftop location, but with a saltwater pool, too. **$$$**

THE DEAD SEA AND THE NEGEV

Arad

Nof Arad
Rehov Moav, Arad
Tel: (08) 995 7056
Great views of the desert and Masada from the western approach. **$$**

Be'er Sheva

Leonardo Negev
4 Henrietta Szold, Be'er Sheva 84102
Tel: (08) 640 5444
www.fattal-hotels-israel.com
Unexceptional accommodations, but a convenient stop-over if you want to get to the Bedouin market early. **$$**

The Dead Sea

All hotels in the Dead Sea region offer medically supervised facilities.

The sea's unique mineral content is beneficial for a range of ailments, including psoriasis, rheumatism, and respiratory problems. Many European health services send patients to the Dead Sea for treatment.
Ein Gedi Guest House
Kibbutz Ein Gedi (Dead Sea)
M.P. Dead Sea 85525
Tel: (08) 659 4222
www.eingedi.co.il
Overlooking the remarkable Dead Sea and Judean Desert, close to the spa, and the kibbutz has a rare tropical garden. **$$**
Herods Dead Sea Hotel
Ein Bokek, Dead Sea
Tel: (08) 659 1591
www.nirvana.co.il

Set away from the main hotel district for those who prefer isolation in this most isolated of locations. **$$**
Hod Hotel
Ein Bokek, Dead Sea
Tel: (08) 668 8222
www.hodhotel.co.il
Cheap and comfortable, and near the Dead Sea in the main hotel district. **$**
David Dead Sea Resort & Spa
Ein Bokek, Dead Sea

PRICE CATEGORIES

These prices are for double rooms per night and usually include breakfast.
$ = under $100
$$ = $100–160
$$$ = more than $160

Tel: (08) 659 1234
www.fattal-hotels-israel.com
This large hotel, formerly the
Hyatt Regency, offers therapeutic
treatment based on the Dead
Sea's minerals and has a range of

recreational facilities.
$$$
Leonardo Inn Dead Sea
Ein Bokek Dead Sea
Tel: (08) 668 4666
www.fattal-hotels-israel.com

Very popular with English-speaking
tourists and has its own Dead
Sea spa alongside the regular
swimming pool – as well as tennis,
handball, and a mini soccer pitch.
$$$

EILAT

Dan Eilat
North Beach, Eilat
Tel: (08) 636 2222
www.danhotels.com
The flagship hotel of Israel's leading
chain. Good service and good value.
$$$
Eilot Hotel
M.P. Eilot 88805
Tel: (08) 635 8816
Closest kibbutz to Eilat, several kilo-
meters north of the Red Sea resort.
$$
Etzion
1 Sderot Hatamarim, Eilat
Tel: (08) 637 0003
www.hoteletzion.co.il
Far from the beach, but in the town
and near the Central Bus Station.
$
Isrotel King Solomon's Palace
North Beach
Tel: (08) 636 3444
www.isrotel.co.il
Elegantly designed hotel overlooking
the marina with an excellent choice of
restaurants, and consistently rated by
guests as the city's best-value hotel,
far from the most expensive at any
rate. $$
Isrotel Lagoona
North Beach, Eilat
Tel: (08) 636 6666
www.isrotel.co.il
Tranquil location north of the city, on
the lagoon, with a good view of the
Red Sea. $$
Magic Palace
North Beach, Eilat
Tel: (08) 636 9999

Eilat's hospitality.

www.fattal-hotels-israel.com
Built for a family holiday with small
children; grown-ups without offspring
should steer clear. $$
Magic Sunrise Club Hotel
Tel: (08) 630 5333
www.fattal-hotels-israel.com
Located slightly inland with a shuttle
to the beach, the hotel has excellent
sports club facilities. $$
Orchid Hotel
Coral Beach, Eilat
Tel: (08) 636 0360
Email: orchid@netvision.net.il
Set on the hillside above Coral
Beach south of the city, the hotel is
comprised of separate cabins built
like a Thai village. $$
Prima Music Hotel
Opposite Coral Beach

Tel: (03) 552 2220 *9995
Modest hotel opposite the more
secluded Coral Beach with tasteful
music them decor. $$
Princess Hotel
near Taba border crossing, POB 2323 Eilat
Tel: (08) 636 5555
Email: princess@isdn.net.il
Well away from the town and near
the Egyptian border, this hotel is a
self-contained complex of swimming
pools and restaurants. $$$
Red Sea Sports Club
Coral Beach
Tel: (08) 638 2222
www.redseasports.co.il
Compact and comfortable: this is
the place to be if you enjoy diving.
The hotel also offers courses for
beginners. $

PALESTINIAN TERRITORIES

A range of luxury and basic hotels
exists in the West Bank and Gaza,
offering high-quality accommodations
and very good value prices, far
cheaper than in Israel; see www.
palestinehotels.com

Jacir Palace InterContinental
Jerusalem–Hebron Road
Tel: (180) 945 3716
Located in a delightful 19th-century

Ottoman building.

Grand Palace Hotel
Al Rasheed Street
Tel: (08) 2849498
Comfortable, with glorious view of
Gaza's white sandy Mediterranean
beaches.

InterContinental Jericho Hotel

Jericho–Jerusalem Road
Tel: (02) 2311 200
An oasis of luxury and good value in
this oasis city.

Movenpick Hotel
Emil Habibi St
Tel: (970) 22 985 888
Ramallah's only five-star hotel was
opened in 2008 and is part of the
international chain.

OTHER

Bed and breakfast

With the exception of the Galilee, there is a very limited amount of B&B accommodation in Israel, partly because Israelis live in relatively small apartments, so rarely have rooms to offer. For a list of B&Bs in Jerusalem see: www.bnb.co.il

Country lodges (Zimmerim)

Located mainly in the rural north, the Galilee and the Golan, these include:
Noga Country Lodging
Maale Gamla, Golan Heights
Tel: (04) 673 2430
Great view of the Sea of Galilee. $
Beit Alfa
M.P. Gilboa
Tel: (04) 6533026.
Email: bb-ba@betalfa.org.il
In the Lower Galilee opposite the Gilboa mountains. $

Vacation apartments

For a longer stay in one place, it can be very economical to rent an apartment with its own kitchen, etc. For families it can mean a cheap way of accommodating the children; for couples, individuals, or groups, it can be a more natural experience of the country, living as the locals do.
As with vacation accommodations, options range from the economical to the luxurious. A few recommended places are:
Rivka's Holiday Apartments
52 Azza St, Jerusalem
Tel: (02) 643 6211
Sea Tower Apartment Hotel
1 Trumpledor St, Tel Aviv 63433
Tel: (03) 795 3434
The Home Apartment Hotel
106 Ha-Yarkon, Tel Aviv
Tel: (03) 522 2695
Email: thehome@internet-zahav.net

Campgrounds

Israel is a good place for camping, with campsites providing excellent touring bases for each region. They offer full sanitary facilities, electric current, a restaurant and/or store, telephone, first-aid facilities, shaded picnic and campfire areas, and day and night watchmen. They can be reached by bus, but all are open to cars and caravans. Most have tents and cabins, as well as a wide range of equipment for hire. All sites have swimming facilities on the site or within easy reach.

Camping sites
Beit Zait (near Jerusalem)
Tel: (02) 534 6217

Ein Gedi (by Dead Sea)
Tel: (08) 658 4342
Eilot (near Eilat)
Tel: (08) 637 4362
Neve Yam (near Haifa)
Tel: (04) 884 4827
Kibbutz Ma'ayan Baruch (Upper Galilee)
Tel: (04) 695 4601

Youth hostels

There are 25 youth hostels throughout the country, operated by the Israel Youth Hostel Association (IYHA), which is affiliated to the international YHA. They offer dormitory accommodations or private double rooms, and most of them provide meals and self-service kitchen facilities. There is no age limit. Some hostels also provide family accommodations. Individual reservations should be made directly with the hostel.

Useful addresses
Head Office – IYHA
POB 6001, Jerusalem 91060
Tel: (02) 655 8400
Email: iyha@iyha.org.il
www.iyha.org.il
Agron, Jerusalem
2 Agron, 94266 Jerusalem
Tel: (02) 621 7555
Email: agron@iyha.org.il
Carmel, Haifa
18 Rehov Tzvia Veitzhak, Haifa
Tel: (04) 853 1944
Email: haifa@iyha.org.il
Eilat
POB 152, Eilat 88101
Tel: (08) 637 0088
Email: eilat@iyha.org.il
Ein Gedi, Dead Sea
D.N. Dead Sea 86980
Tel: (08) 658 4165
Email: eingedi@iyha.og.il
Karei Deshe, Sea of Galilee
M.P. Korazim 12365, Kare Deshe
Tel: (04) 672 0601
Fax: (08) 672 4818
Email: kdeshe@iyha.org.il
Masada
M.P. Dead Sea, Masada 86901
Tel: (08) 995 3222
Email: masada2@iyha.org.il
Meyouchas, Tiberias
2 Jordan Street, POB 81, Tiberias 14100
Tel: (04) 672 1775
Email: tiberias@iyha.org.il
Mitspe Ramon
POB 2, Mitspe Ramon 80600
Tel: (08) 658 8443
Email: mitzpe@iyha.org.il
Poriah, nr Tiberias
POB 232, Tiberias 14101

Mount Tabor in springtime.

Tel: (04) 675 0050
Email: poria@iyha.org.il
Tel Aviv
36 Bnei Dan, POB 22078, Tel Aviv 62260
Tel: (03) 544 1748
Email: telaviv@iyha.org.il
Tel Aviv (Jaffa)
Shderot Yerushalayim cnr Ben Tzvi, Jaffa
Tel: (03) 682 7700
Email: r-daniel@iyha.org.il
Tel Hai
POB 9001, M.P. Upper Galilee 12100, Tel Hai
Tel: (04) 694 0043
Email: telhai@iyha.org.il
Yitzhak Rabin, Jerusalem
1 Nachman Avigad Street (near Israel Museum), POB 39100, Jerusalem 91390
Tel: (02) 678 0101
Email: rabin@iyha.org.il
The Society For the Protection of Nature in Israel (SPNI) has a nationwide chain of nine field schools, most of them in the Galilee and Golan Heights. A room for two costs US$90 a night. www.aspni.org/aspni_field_schools.html
Other Private Youth Hostels
Gesher
10 Hamelekh David, Jerusalem
Tel: (02) 624 1015
www.gesher.co.il
Gordon Hostel
2 Gordon St cnr. Ha Yarkon, Tel Aviv
Tel: (03) 523 8239
St George
Nablus Road, Jerusalem
Tel: (02) 628 2573

PRICE CATEGORIES

These prices are for double rooms per night and usually include breakfast.
$ = under $100
$$ = $100–160
$$$ = more than $160

EATING OUT

BEST RESTAURANTS, CAFÉS, AND BARS

WHAT TO EAT

Eating is a national pastime in Israel, one engaged in as much and as often as possible. On the street, at the beach, in every public place and in every home, day and night – you'll find Israelis tucking into food.

The biblical residents of the Land of Canaan were nourished by the fertility and abundance of a land "flowing with milk and honey." But the milk was mainly from sheep and goats, and the honey from dates, figs, and carobs. Much depended on the sun, the rains, and the seasons. Food was simple; feast followed famine. Times have changed – at least in the culinary sense.

Just as Israel is a blend of cultures from all over the world, so its cuisine is a weave of flavors and textures, contrasts and similarities. There is no definitive Israeli fare, just as there is no definitive Israeli. Rather, there is a rare merging of East and West, and the results are a profusion of culinary delights, enhanced in recent years by growing affluence while also dulled by the import of junk food. The predominant food style reflects the country's geographical location – somewhere between the Middle East and the Mediterranean.

When dining out, note that "Oriental" refers to the Middle East, rather than the Far East. "Oriental" Jews are those of Sephardic (Spanish or Arab) heritage. Each Jewish ethnic group, whether Moroccan, Libyan, Tunisian, Yemenite, Iraqi, or native (sabra) Israeli, has its own special dish and its own holiday fare. Their foods are similar yet quite distinct

from each other. Basic herbs and spices include cumin, fresh and dried coriander, mint, garlic, onion, turmeric, black pepper, and sometimes cardamom and fresh green chilli. Dark, fruity olive oil adds further fragrance.

Arab food is considered "Oriental," and both Arab and Jewish meals begin the same way: with a variety of savory salads. Houmous – ground chickpea seasoned with *tahina* (sesame paste), lemon juice, garlic, and cumin – is probably the most popular dip, spread and salad rolled into one. You'll also find the most astounding variety of aubergine salads you've ever seen: aubergine in *tahina*, fried sliced aubergine, chopped aubergine with vegetables, chopped liver-flavoured aubergine, and more. Assorted pickled vegetables are considered salads as well.

While the waiters may show some signs of disappointment, you can order a selection of these salads as a meal in themselves. Or you can follow them with kebab (grilled ground spiced meat), *shishlik* (grilled sliced lamb or beef with lamb fat), *seniya* (beef or lamb in *tahina* sauce), stuffed chicken or pigeon, chops, or fish.

Don't expect pork in either a kosher or a traditional Muslim restaurant; both religions prohibit its consumption. Seafood, while forbidden by Jewish law and permissible by Muslim, is widely available. Shrimps and calamari are the predominant varieties.

Try the fish, particularly in the seaside areas of Tiberias, Tel Aviv, Yafo, and Eilat (there are no fish in the Dead Sea). Trout, gray and red mullet, sea bass, and St Peter's fish

are generally served fried or grilled, sometimes with a piquant sauce.

Since Israelis are major-league eaters, snacks play a starring role in the day. Favorites include bagel-shaped sesame-sprinkled breads (served with za'atar), nuts, and sunflower seeds. But the ultimate sabra snack has to be falafel (fried chickpea balls served in pitta bread with a variety of vegetables). Along the sidewalks of major streets you can usually find several adjoining falafel stands where you're free to stuff your pitta with salads for as long as the bread holds out. Tel Aviv's Betsal'el Souk is probably the most famous of the falafel centers.

Eating kosher

The laws of *kashrut* are extremely complex, but in practical terms they mean that many animals, most notably the pig, cannot be eaten at all. Furthermore, kosher animals such as the cow and chicken must be killed in a specific way (by having their throats cut), otherwise the meat is not considered kosher.

The blood must also be drained out of kosher meat, often making a steak, for example, somewhat desiccated and lacking in flavor.

In addition, while most fish are permissible, all seafood (prawns, lobsters, octopus, etc) is considered unclean. Finally, meat and milk cannot be consumed together.

This said, many secular Jews disregard dietary laws, and most restaurants, especially those outside Jerusalem, are not kosher. Outside of hotels, all kosher restaurants are closed on the Jewish festivals and the Sabbath from sunset on Friday to sunset on Saturday.

EILAT

Wonderful baked goods in Tel Aviv.

Restaurants

Denise Kingdom
Fish Hatchery, Laguna
Tel: (08) 637 9898
This kosher restaurant specializes in the denise fish (bream) and sea bass raised by kibbutz Eilot – adjacent to the restaurant is a fish farm and visitors' center, which explains about the fish. Diners know that they are getting fresh fish straight from the farm, and the salads are excellent too. The restaurant is open Sun–Thur noon–11pm, Fri closes before sunset and reopens Sat night. **$$**

Eddie's Hideaway
68 Almogim Street
Tel: (057) 944 4190
Perhaps the best restaurant in the city. Because of its out-of-the-way location, the restaurant will take your taxi fare from the hotel off your bill on presentation of a receipt. Eddie specializes in a range of creative meat and fish dishes. Open Mon–Sat 6pm–midnight. **$$**

Ginger Asian Kitchen
12 Yotam Street
Tel: (08) 637 2517
One of the city's newer restaurants, offering sushi and Asian fusion food – trendy but informal. You will taste spices from many Asian cultures including Chinese, Japanese, Thai, Malaysian, Vietnamese and Indonesian. It can be advisable to book in advance. Open daily noon–3am. **$$**

La Barracuda
4 Durban Street, Eilat
Tel: (08) 631 7176
The place to come if you want to know what those peculiar-looking Red Sea fish really taste like. Also offers meat. Most of the food is chargrilled, giving it a distinctive smokey flavor. Open daily 11am–11pm. **$$**

Shipudei Eilat
10 Ha'Oman Street,
Industrial Zone
Tel: (08) 633 2343
The industrial zone, albeit with a different ambience from the rest of the Red Sea resort, offers good-value kosher meat eateries, including Shipudei Eilat. One of the few non-hotel kosher restaurants. Open Sun–Thur noon–11pm, Fri 11am–3pm, Sat sunset–11pm. **$**

Tandoori
King's Wharf (by the Laguna Hotel)
Tel: (08) 633 3879
Excellent Indian restaurant, part of an Israeli chain set up by an Indian-Jewish family. Specialties include a ginger marinade and coconut milk sauce. Has delightful Indian decor and artefacts. Open daily noon–3pm 6pm–midnight. **$$$**

Bars and pubs

The Three Monkeys
Promenade by the Royal Beach Hotel
Tel: (08) 636 8989
The city's most popular English-style pub, featuring live music on Thursday, Friday and Saturday nights and a full menu to go with the drinks. Open daily 9pm–3am.

Yussuf's Bedouin Tent
Coral Beach
Tel: (050) 550 3826
Authentic Bedouin tent with all the relaxed hospitality and delicious Arab mezze salads with pita bread, confectionery, and coffee one would expect, with a narghila to smoke if required. Open daily 9am–midnight.

HAIFA

Tempting pistachios.

Restaurants

Dolphin
13 Bat Galim Avenue
Tel: (04) 852 3837
Inland from the Bat Galim Promenade just south of the city center, the restaurant offers some of Israel's best seafood. Open daily noon–4pm, 7pm–midnight. **$$**

Douzan
35 Ben Gurion Boulevard
Tel: (04) 852 5444
An unusual fusion of Oriental and Western food, but with eastern ambience, in the delightful German Colony in an historic German Templar building. The Arab-owned restaurant's diverse cuisine echoes the relative ethnic tolerance of the city. Open daily 11pm–midnight. **$$**

Fattoush
38 Ben Gurion Boulevard
Tel: (04) 852 4930
Named for an Arab bread, this offers a delightful selection of salads, fish and meat in either a relaxing garden environment or surrounded by traditional Arab decor. Open daily 9am–2am. **$$**

PRICE CATEGORIES

Restaurant prices are given in shekels:
$ = under NIS 80 a person.
$$ = NIS 80–250
$$$ = more than NIS 250

Shawarma Ahim Sabah
37 Allenby
Tel: (04) 855 2188
Located in midtown Hadar;
specializes in meat cut from the spit
and eaten in pitta with a wide range
of salads and relishes. Open daily
11am–midnight. $

Cafés

Eva's
51 Ha'atzmaut
Tel: (04) 866 3113
Located near the port, Eva reputedly
serves the best coffee in Haifa.
Open Sun–Thur 7am–5pm, Fri
7am–1.30pm.

Bars and pubs

Bear Pub
135 Ha-Nassi Boulevard
Tel: (04) 838 1703
On the Central Carmel in a nightlife
hotspot. Open Sun–Fri 11am–4am,
Sat 6pm–4am.

JERUSALEM

Restaurants

Abu Shukri
63 Al Wad Road (Via Dolorosa)
Tel: (02) 627 1538
Arab restaurant in the Old City
legendary for offering the best
houmous. Also try the falafel, baba
ghanoush, tehina, and labane
cheese. Plain, unassuming decor but
located on the historic Via Dolorosa.
Open daily 8am–4.30pm, later in
summer and Sat. $

Al Dente
50 Ussishkin Street
Tel: (02) 625 1479
Small neighborhood restaurant in
Rehavia offers its own unique Tuscany
cuisine at modest prices. Kosher non-
meat menu. Usually full so best to
book. Start with focaccia or antipasti
and move on to a wide range of
pastas and vegetable sauces. Sun–
Thur noon–11pm, Fri 11am–4pm,
Sat 8pm–midnight. $$

Anna Ticho House
Off Ha-Rav Kook, Jerusalem
Tel: (02) 624 4186
Dairy food in a garden restaurant
which forms part of a museum. The
house special is onion soup served
in a round loaf of brown bread.The
apple strudel is also recommended.
Open Sun–Thur 11am–midnight, Fri
11am–3pm, Sat night. $$

Arabesque/American Colony Hotel
Nablus Road, Jerusalem
Tel: (02) 627 9777
A la carte menu and a beautiful

courtyard in which to dine or or
enjoy the gracious Middle Eastern
interior. Offers Arab favourites and
international gourmet cuisine. Open
daily 6.30am–midnight. $$$

Cafe Kadosh
6 Shlomtsiyon Hamalka St.
Tel: (073) 758 1573
A restaurant despite its name. Run
by the Kadosh family, this is one of
Jerusalem-native Yotam Ottolenghi's
favourite restaurants. Kosher dairy
menu with fresh pasta and lasagna
dishes, fish and smoked fish. Open
Sun–Thur 7am–midnight, Fri 7–
shabbat, Sat after sunset. $$

Darna
3 Horkenos Street
Tel: (02) 624 5406
North African food and Moroccan
atmosphere including authentic
implements and ceremonial service.
Kosher. Open Sun–Thur 7–11pm,
Sat after sunset. $$$

Kohinor
Holiday Inn Crowne Plaza, Givat Ram,
Jerusalem
Tel: (02) 658 8888
The only kosher restaurant in this
chain of Indian restaurants serving
delicious foods, including a choice of
meat and vegetarian dishes. Open
Sun–Thur noon–midnight, Fri lunch
and Sat night. $$$

La Regence
23 Ha Melekh David, King David Hotel
Tel: (02) 620 8888
Considered the city's finest kosher

restaurant in the city's best known
hotel. Nouvelle cuisine and traditional
French cooking with a stirring view of
the Old City. Open Sun–Thur 6.30–
10.30pm and Sat after sunset. $$$

Notre Dame
8 Shivtei Yisra'el Street
Tel: (02) 628 8018
Situated in the magnificent Notre
Dame hospice complex, this is one
of the city's finest restaurants and
offers good-value fare. Open daily
7–11pm. $$

Shipudei Hagefen
74 Agripas, Jerusalem
Tel: (02) 625 3267
The pick of the Middle Eastern
restaurants; near Makhane Yehuda
market. Open Sat–Thur noon–11pm,
Fri noon–4pm, Sat night. $$

Simas
78 Agripas, Jerusalem
Tel: (02) 423 3002
Speedy service and good-value food
in the cheapest steakhouse in town.
Try the Jerusalem mixed grill, which
is a famous meat dish throughout
Israel. Open Sun–Thur noon–11pm,
Fri noon–4pm, Sat night. $

Taverna
2 Naomi Street, Abu Tor
Tel: (02) 671 9796
Located by the Abu Tor Promenade,
the Taverna commands great views
of Jerusalem and the Judean Desert.
Interesting selection of cheeses and
salads. Open Sun–Thur noon–11pm,
Sat after sunset. $

Cafés

Aroma
Mamila Pedestrian Mall
Tel: (02) 624 1304
This new branch of a national chain
of quality coffee houses provides
uplifting views of the Old City walls.
Long lines to get in on weekend

At the American Colony Hotel.

PRICE CATEGORIES

Restaurant prices are given in
shekels:
$ = under NIS 80 a person.
$$ = NIS 80–250
$$$ = more than NIS 250

evenings can be offputting. Open Sun–Thur 8am–midnight, Fri 8am–4pm, Sat 8pm–midnight.
Rimon Cafe
4 Lunz
Tel: (02) 625 2772
A popular hangout by the Ben Yehuda Street Mall, with a choice of light meals and cakes. Open Sun–Thur

8am–midnight, Fri 8am–3pm, Sat night.

Dublin
2 Shammai Street
Tel: (02) 622 3612
A piece of Ireland in Jerusalem, allowing for the fact that late at night

the emphasis is more on disco. Open daily 11am–3am.
Mike's Place
37 Yafo Street, near Zion Square
Tel: (02) 267 0965
English-style pub with live music, live TV soccer, and a wide choice of draft beers and pub grub. Open daily 11am–3am.

TEL AVIV

Israeli breakfast spread.

Restaurants

Abulafia
4 Yefet Street, Yafo
Tel: (03) 682 8544
Tel Aviv's best-known Middle Eastern fast food restaurant – great for schwarma, falafel, houmous, etc. Also good for a wide range of fresh flat breads like pita, and lafa. Open daily 11am–3am. **$**
Boya
Old Tel Aviv Port
Tel: (03) 544 6166
One of Israel's leading seafood restaurants, where you can also savor the atmosphere of Tel Aviv's recent reinvention of its Old Port as a leisure complex. Open daily 9am–1am. **$$**
Chinese Wall
26 Mikve Israel
Tel: (03) 560 3974
This Chinese restaurant is one of the city's few top-quality kosher restaurants outside of the hotels. Open Sun–Thur 11am–11pm, Fri 11am–4pm, Sat night. **$$$**
Elimelech
35 Wolfson
Tel: (03) 681 3459
Excellent place for those who like traditional Eastern European (but not kosher) food. Located south of the business district. Open daily 9am–2am. **$$**
Lev Harachav ("Wide Heart")
Rabbi Akiva, Carmel Market
A no-nonsense, tasty, and cheap authentic Israeli restaurant with excellent houmous. Open Sun–Fri

noon–6pm. **$**
Rachmo Hagadol
98 Menachem Begin Road
Tel: (03) 562 1022
The pick of the falafel eateries near the old Central Bus Station. Excellent, clean, and astonishingly cheap. Open Sun–Fri 11am–6pm. **$**
Raphael
87 Ha-Yarkon
Tel: (03) 522 6464
Owner and chef Rafi Cohen, still only in his early 30s, is considered the country's leading chef. Cohen built his reputation in Jerusalem's King David Hotel, where he adapted the cooking of his Moroccan mother. Open daily 6pm–midnight. **$$$**
Taboon
Old Yafo Port
Tel: (03) 681 6011
In a pleasant spot in Yafo's old port; specializes in oven-cooked Mediterranean fish. Open daily 12.30pm–midnight. **$$**
The Old Man and the Sea
1 Hangar, Old Yafo Port
Tel; (053) 809 4346
An impressive array of mezze Arab salads followed by a tasty choice of fish and meats, if you still have room. Eat outside on the quayside of Jaffa's ancient port. Open daily 11am–midnight. **$$**
Yin Yang
64 Rothschild Boulevard
Tel: (03) 560 6833
A Chinese restaurant run by Israeli Aharoni, the country's best-known

celebrity chef. Open daily noon–midnight. **$$$**
Zion
4 Peduim
Tel: (03) 517 8714
The pick of the meat restaurants in the city's famous Yemenite Quarter (Kerem ha-Teimanim) by the Carmel market. Open Sun–Thur noon–midnight, Fri noon–4pm, Sat night. **$$**

Cafés
Café Nordau
145 Ben Yehuda Street
Tel: (03) 524 0134
One of the city's best-known gay spots. Open daily 11am–1am.
Ilan's Coffee Shop
90 Ibn Gvirol Street
Tel: (03) 523 5334
Excellent espresso. Open Sun–Fri 7.30am–7pm.
Orna and Ella
33 Sheinkin Street
Tel: (03) 620 4753
One of the best-known cafes in the trendy Sheinkin area. Open daily 9am–1am.

Bars and pubs
Bugsy's
26 Florentin, cnr Washington Street
Tel: (03) 681 3138
One of the trendiest bars in the heart of the city's trendiest district, Florentin, with an interesting menu for vegetarians. Open daily 11–3am.
Hashoftim
39 Ibn Gvirol Street, cnr Hashoftim Street
Tel: (03) 695 1153
One of the city's oldest and best-known pubs. Open daily 6pm–2am.
M.A.S.H.
275 Dizengoff Street
Tel: (03) 605 1007
The closest thing to an English pub, with darts and live soccer. Open daily 11am–3am.
Molly Bloom's Traditional Irish Pub
2 Mendele Street
Tel: (02) 522 1558
The name says it all. One of many Irish pubs near the seafront. Open daily 6pm–2am.

ACTIVITIES

FESTIVALS, THE ARTS, NIGHTLIFE, SHOPPING, AND SPORTS

FESTIVALS

The Israel Festival of Music and Drama takes place in May of each year, with the participation of the country's leading talent and world-famous visiting companies and artists. The festival centers on Jerusalem.
The Abu Ghosh Vocal Music Festival – June.
Israel Festival – the country's premier international theater festival, every June.
The Jerusalem International Film Festival – July.
The Haifa International Film Festival – September/October.
The Karmiel Dance Festival – July.
Jerusalem International Arts and Crafts Fair – Sultan's Pool Jerusalem, August.
Jerusalem International Puppet Festival – Jerusalem's Liberty Bell Park, August.
Klezmer Hasidic Jewish Music Festival – Safed, August.
The Red Sea Jazz Festival (Eilat) – August.
The Akko Fringe Theater Festival – September/October during Sukkot (Tabernacles).
In addition, the **Jerusalem International Book Fair** is held every two years (those ending in odd numbers) in March. An international Harp Contest takes place every three years, drawing young musicians from all over the world. The **Zimriya**, an international choir festival, is another well-established triennial event.
Spring in Jerusalem and **Spring in Tel Aviv** annual festivals include music, drama, and dance, and the **Rubinstein Piano Competition** brings talented young artists from around the world to Israel.

Events in Haifa include the **International Flower Show** (Floris), when hundreds of thousands of flowers from all over the world, typical of their countries of origin, adorn the city.

Religious festivals

Jewish: Public holidays fall on the Jewish festivals listed below. On Rosh Hashana (New Year), Yom Kippur (Day of Atonement), the first and last day of Succot (Tabernacles), the first and last day of Pesach (Passover) and Shavuot, all shops and offices are closed and there is no public transport. Independence Day is also a public holiday. On Holocaust Day, Memorial Day, and Tisha B'Av, all places of entertainment and restaurants are closed.

Israel observes a solar–lunar year in accordance with Jewish religious tradition, the New Year occurring in September/October with the festival of Rosh Hashana. But the standard Gregorian system is also in daily use everywhere.

The working week runs from Sunday to Thursday, and most businesses are also open on Friday mornings. From sunset on Friday to sunset on Saturday, however, everything shuts down in observance of the Jewish Sabbath, or Shabbat. This includes all banks and public services, including buses and other forms of transportation. In Tel Aviv and Haifa, however, small minibuses run along the main bus routes and inter-city sheruts (communal taxis) also run some services. On Saturday evening, most of the transport and other public services are resumed.

The Hebrew calendar is a lunar calendar, with a leap month added every two to three years to ensure

that the year is also a solar one. Jewish holy days, therefore, fall on different dates in the general calendar each year, so exact dates cannot be given. Therefore, the months only are indicated in the following list.
Christian: While the Catholic Churches use the Gregorian calendar, the Orthodox Churches still use the Julian calendar, therefore Christmas and sometimes Easter are celebrated on different dates from the Western Churches.
Muslim: The Muslim calendar is completely lunar with festivals falling throughout the year in relation to the solar calendar – so, for example, Ramadan rotates backward through the seasons – and generally Muslim festivals cannot be attributed to any single Gregorian month.

January/February

Christmas – January 6 for most Orthodox Churches (Greek, Russian, etc); **January 13** for Armenian Orthodox Christmas.
Tu B'Shvat – 15th of the Hebrew month of Shvat, Jewish New Year for trees – mid-January to mid-February. Tree-planting ceremonies around the country and activities by "greens."

March/April

Purim – 15th of the Hebrew month of Adar, or Adar Shani during a leap year. This one-day festival recalls the biblical story of Esther. Set in Persia, the Jews are saved from extermination after Queen Esther appeals to her husband King Ahasuerus. The festival is celebrated in walled cities like Jerusalem a day later than the rest of the country. Traditionally Jews go around in fancy dress, there are many carnival-style dresses, and religious Jews are urged

to get drunk (unless they're driving).
Pesach (Passover) – 15th–21st of
Nisan. Celebrating the Jewish Exodus
from Egypt, the festival lasts seven
days, of which the first and last are
public holidays. During this period,
Jews abstain from bread and eat
matzot – unleavened bread, similar
to crackers.
Easter – The Crucifixion and
Resurrection of Christ are celebrated
(usually) the weekend after Passover.
One of the central events is the
Good Friday procession along the Via
Dolorosa in Jerusalem.

May/June
Holocaust Day – 24th Nisan.
Memorial day for the 6 million Jews
killed in the Holocaust. All places of
entertainment are closed.
Memorial Day – 4th Iyar. Memorial
day for members of the security forces
killed in action, and victims of terror.
All places of entertainment are closed.
Independence Day – 5th Iyar. Marks
Israel's Declaration of Independence
in 1948. A public holiday, but public
transport operates and shops are
open. Sometimes falls in the last days
of April.
Lag B'Omer – 18th Iyar. A Jewish
bonfire night marks various favorable
Jewish historical events down the
centuries.

Religious etiquette

Of obvious sensitivity is religious
etiquette. When visiting holy
sites, women should dress
conservatively (no bare legs or
shoulders), and men should
wear shirts and long trousers.
When visiting Jewish shrines or
memorials, it's also standard
for men to cover their heads; if
you don't have a *kepah* or hat,
a cardboard substitute is often
provided. In some religious
neighborhoods, especially in
Jerusalem, these conservative
rules of dress apply as general
practice. While not all Israelis are
observant, you should be aware
that religious Jews see the Sabbath
as a holy day, and smoking, using
a camera or mobile phone, or
other informal behavior can be
considered offensive. Some streets
in Orthodox neighborhoods are
blocked to traffic on the Sabbath.
When visiting mosques it is
customary to remove shoes before
entering, although in recent years
some mosques have barred entry
to non-Muslims.

Shavuot (Pentecost) – 6th Sivan.
Fifty days after Passover this festival,
which is a public holiday, marks the
giving of the Torah to Moses on Mount
Sinai. It is also a harvest festival.

July/August
Tisha B'Av – 9th Av. A fast day to
commemorate the destruction of both
Temples. All places of entertainment
are closed.

September/October
Rosh Hashana – 1st–2nd Tishrei.
Jewish New Year.
Yom Kippur – 10th Tishrei. The most
solemn day in the Jewish calendar, as
an individual's fate is sealed for the
year to come. Fast day. Public holiday,
and no vehicles travel on the roads.
Sukkot (Tabernacles) – 15th–22nd
Tishrei. Jews build tabernacles to
remind themselves of their 40 years
in the desert after leaving Egypt. The
first and last days are a public holiday.
The last day – Simchat Torah – marks
the beginning and end of the annual
Torah reading cycle.

November/December
Hanukkah (25th Kislev to 3rd Tevet).
The festival of lights recalls the Jewish
victory over the Greeks.
Christmas – Catholic, Protestant,
and other Western Churches
celebrate the birth of Christ.

Muslim Festivals

Friday is a holy day for Muslims,
and places of worship are closed to
visitors during prayers on that day, as
they are on all holy days. The most
important Muslim holidays are:
Id el Adha, Sacrificial Festival (four
days).
New Year.
Mohammed's Birthday.
Feast of Ramadan (one month of
fasting from sunrise to sunset).
Id el Fitr, Conclusion of Ramadan
(three days).
BoxText Header: Religious Etiquette

Religious services

Jews and Muslims will have no
problems finding synagogues and
mosques, which are on virtually every
street corner in some neighborhoods.

Jewish
Jerusalem Great Synagogue
56 Ha-Melekh George
Tel: (02) 624 7112
Chabad Synagogue
16 Yirmiyahu, Jerusalem
Tel: (02) 581 4755

Center for Conservative Judaism
4 Agron, Jerusalem
Tel: (02) 622 3539
Union for Progressive Judaism
13 David ha-Melekh, Jerusalem
Tel: (02) 623 2444
Tel Aviv Great Synagogue
110 Allenby
Tel: (03) 560 4905
Beit Yisrael
Independence Square, Netanya
Tel: (09) 862 4345
Haifa Central Synagogue
Rabbi Herzog Street
Tel: (04) 866 0599

Muslim
The best-known mosques in Israel
are the El-Aqsa Mosque (tel: 02-628
1248) on Jerusalem's Temple Mount,
the El-Jazzar Mosque in Akko, and
the White Mosque in Ramla. There
are also many mosques in Arab
towns and villages throughout Israel.
Mohammed is said to have prayed
in the El-Aqsa Mosque during his
lifetime, and the Dome of the Rock
is a shrine built on the rock where
the Prophet is said to have risen to
heaven after his death in Medina.

Christian
While Israel has much to offer every
tourist, for the Christian pilgrim a
trip to Israel is more than just a
journey, because here he or she has
the unique opportunity of tracing
the footsteps of Jesus and the early
Christians and visiting sites significant
to the life and teaching of Jesus:
Bethlehem, his birthplace; Nazareth,
the town of his boyhood; the Sea of
Galilee, scene of miracles and his
ministerial teaching; Mount Tabor, site
of the Transfiguration; the Garden of
Gethsemane and Jerusalem, where
he spent his last hours of prayer
and agony; and Latrun, the site of a
Trappist monastery, near the biblical
Emmaus, where Jesus is said to have
appeared after the Resurrection.

Jerusalem
Armenian Cathedral of St James
Tel: (02) 628 4549
Mon–Fri 3am–3.30pm, Sat and Sun
2.30am–3.15pm.
Baptist House Center
Tel: (02) 625 5942
Prayer meetings Sun 10.45am and
5.30pm, Wed 1.30pm.
Christ Church (Anglican)
Tel: (02) 627 7727
Sun services 9.30am, 4.30pm,
6.30pm, Tue 6.15pm.
Church of God (Seventh Day
Adventists)
Tel: (02) 673 1347

Service Sat 7pm.
Church of God Pentecostal (Mount of Olives near Commodore Hotel)
Tel: (02) 627 3899
Services Sun 10.30am.
Church of the Dormition
Tel: (02) 565 5300
Sun services 9am, weekdays 7.15am except Thur 5.45pm.
Church of the Holy Sepulcher (Old City)
Tel: (02) 627 7000
For more details about services for various denominations, contact the Christian Information Center, tel: (02) 627 2692.
Coenaculum Franciscan Chapel
Tel: (02) 627 2692
7am–noon, 3pm–sundown. Ring bell.
Ein Kerem: Visitation
Tel: (02) 641 7291
9am–noon, 3–6pm. Services daily 6.30am.
Flagellation
Tel: (02) 628 2936
6am–noon, 2–6pm, winter 2–5.30pm.
Garden Tomb
Tel: (02) 627 2745
8am–1pm, 3–5pm, winter 8am–12.30pm and 2.30–4.30pm. Sun closed.
Lithostrotos-Ecce Homo
Tel: (02) 628 2445
8.30am–4.30pm, Sun closed, winter 8.30am–4pm.
Lutheran Church of the Redeemer
Tel: (02) 626 6800
9am–1pm, 2–5pm, Fri 9am–1pm, Sun for services only.
St Andrew's Scottish Church (1 David Remez Street)
Tel: (02) 673 2401
Services in English Sun 10am, in Dutch Sun 4.30pm.
St George's Cathedral (20 Nablus Road)
Tel: (02) 627 2133
6.45am–6.30pm, services Sun 8am, 11am, 6pm.

Outside Jerusalem

Abu Ghosh Crusader Church
Tel: (02) 534 2798
8.30–11am, 2.30–5pm.
Bethlehem, Church of the Nativity
6am–6pm.
Capernaum: "City of Jesus"
Tel: (06) 672 1059
8.30am–4.30pm.
Church of Scotland, Tiberias
Tel (04) 672 3769
Church of the Multiplication (Tabgha)
Tel: (04) 667 8100
8.30am–5pm daily.
Emmaus: Qubeibeh
Tel: (04) 995 2495 ext: 4
6.30–11.30am, 2–6pm.

Latrun Monastery
Tel: (08) 922 0065
7.30–11.30am, 2.30–5pm.
Mount Carmel: Stella Maris
Tel: (04) 833 7758
6am–noon, 3–6pm, winter 3–5pm.
Mount of Beatitudes
Tel: (04) 679 0978
8am–noon, 2–4pm.
Nazareth: Basilica of the Annunciation and St Joseph's
Tel: (04) 657 2501
8.30–11.45am, 2–6pm, Sun 2–6pm; winter 2–5pm.
Tabor Transfiguration
Tel: (06) 656 7489
8am–noon, 3–5pm.
The **Christian Information Center**, inside the Old City's Jaffa Gate, opposite the Citadel (tel: (02) 627 2692; Mon–Fri 8.30am–5.30pm, Sat 8.30am-12.30pm, Sun closed), offers information on all churches, monasteries, and other Christian shrines. The office also issues certificates of Christian pilgrimage.

Baptismal sites

An organized baptismal site has been erected at Yardenit at the mouth of the River Jordan, 8km (5 miles) south of Tiberias (tel: (04) 675 9111). Descent is by steps or wheelchair-accessible ramp. There is ample space for groups. The site is open during daylight hours. Al-Maghtes, near Jericho, also claims to be the site of Christ's baptism, and is accessible to pilgrims.

Direct line

Jerusalem has a fax number for sending your messages direct to heaven: c/o The Western Wall, fax: (02) 561 2222. The telephone company places your fax in the cracks of the wall. The Aish Hatorah Yeshiva in Jerusalem offers a free service enabling people to email the wall. Emails are printed out and placed in the wall – www.thewall.org

THE ARTS

Israel has a wealth of cultural and artistic entertainments. Ticket agencies in each city or town sell tickets for concerts, plays, and other events (try Le'An, 101 Dizengoff Street, Tel Aviv, tel: (03) 524 7373; and Bimot, 8 Shamai Street, Jerusalem, tel: (02) 623 7000). Tel Aviv Annual festivals of all art, cultural, and musical events are booked up well in advance. Calendars of events are available at the tourist information offices.

Music

There are several orchestras, of which the most famous is the Israel Philharmonic, playing under the baton of the great conductors of the world (Zubin Mehta since 1991) and featuring distinguished guest artists. The Jerusalem Symphony Orchestra gives a weekly concert in Jerusalem in the winter season.
There are frequent performances by the Haifa Symphony Orchestra, the Rishon Le-Tsiyon Symphony Orchestra, and the New Israel Opera.
Mann Auditorium (for Israel Symphony Orchestra), 1 Huberman, Tel Aviv. Tel: (03) 621 1777. www.hatarbut.co.il
Israel Opera Israel Opera House, Sha'ul ha-Melekh Boulevard. Tel: (03) 692 7777. www.israel-opera.co.il
Henry Crown Hall (for Jerusalem Symphony Orchestra), Marcus, Jerusalem. Tel: 1-700-70-4000. www.jso.co.il
Israel Northern Symphony Haifa
Tel: (04) 836 3131
Israel Kibbutz Orchestra
Tel: (09) 960 4757
Israel Andalusian Orchestra
Tel: 1-800-693-693

Dance

Professional dance companies include the Israel Classical Ballet, the Batsheva Dance Company, the Bat-Dor Dance Company, Kol Hademana, and the Kibbutz Dance Company. Batsheva and Bat-Dor are both modern dance groups. All perform regularly in the three main cities, as well as in other towns and kibbutzim.
Suzan Dalal Center, 6 Yekhi'el, Neve Tsedek, Tel Aviv. Tel: (03) 517 1471. For Batsheva and Inbal Dance Troupes:
Batsheva
Tel: (03) 516 0231
Inbal
Tel: (03) 517 3711
Israel Ballet
Tel: (03) 696 6610
Kibbutz Contemporary Dance Co.
Tel: (03) 692 5278
Jerusalem Dance Theater
Tel: (02) 679 5626

Theater

The theater is very popular in Israel, and there are many companies performing a wide range of classical and contemporary plays in Hebrew, including original works by Israelis. The best known are the Ha-Bima and Carmeri Theaters in Tel Aviv and the Haifa Municipal Theater,

TRANSPORTATION

which take their productions all over the country. In Jerusalem, the Center for Performing Arts includes the Jerusalem Theater, the Henry Crown Auditorium, and the Rebecca Crown Theater. Also Sultan's Pool Ampitheater, located beneath the walls of the Old City, is a must for a concert. Smaller companies offer stage productions in English, Yiddish, and other languages. One such theater, Gesher (meaning bridge), founded in Tel Aviv in 1991, is the first Russian-speaking theater in Israel.

Jerusalem Theater, Marcus, Jerusalem, tel: (02) 561 0011, 561 0293.

Khan Theater, David Remez, Jerusalem, tel: (02) 671 8281.

Ha-Bima Theater, Tarsith Boulevard, Tel Aviv, tel: (03) 526 6666.

Carmeri Theater, 101 Dizengoff, Tel Aviv, tel: (03) 523 3335.

Beit Lessin Theater, 34 Weizmann, Tel Aviv, tel: (03) 695 6222.

There are cinemas in all the big towns; most have three showings a day, one at about 4pm and two in the evening.

For about US$12 (US$17 if the film is in 3D) you can see the latest Hollywood offerings. You'll also find the latest movies from France, Germany, Italy, Hungary, Russia, the Arab world, Japan, and elsewhere. These films usually have English subtitles, but ask at the box office first if unsure.

Israel itself produces a dozen or so films a year, and these offer an insight into the local culture. These, too, have English subtitles. The local cinematheques show golden oldies as well the more recent films.

Jerusalem Cinematheque, Derekh Hevron, tel: (02) 565 4333. www.jer-cin.org.il

Tel Aviv Cinematheque, 2 Sprintzach, tel: (03) 693 8111.

Haifa Cinematheque, Hanassi 142, tel: (04) 838 3424.

Museums

Israel has more than 100 museums. The most important are:

Jerusalem

Israel Museum, reached from the Knesset along Kaplan to Derekh Ruppin (Sat–Mon, Wed–Thur 10am–5pm, Tue 4–9pm, Fri 10am–2pm; charge; tel: (02) 670 8811; www.imj.org.il) is Israel's national museum and a leading showcase for the country's art, archaeology, and Judaica. The Museum's most famous exhibit is the **Shrine of the Book**, which displays

the Dead Sea Scrolls. These scraps of tattered parchment represent the oldest known copy of the Old Testament. The **Second Temple Model of Jerusalem** in AD 66 is now in the Museum compound.

Bible Lands Museum (opposite the Israel Museum; Sun– Thur 9.30am–5.30pm, Wed 9.30am–9.30pm, Fri, Sat 10am–2pm; charge; tel: (02) 561 1066; www.blmj.org) in Avraham Granot displays artifacts dating from biblical times.

Along Ruppin northeast is the hands-on **Bloomfield Science Museum**, near Israel Museum; Mon– Thur 10am–6pm, Fri 10am–2pm, Sat 10am–3pm; charge; tel: (02) 654 4888; www.mada.org.il), which is imaginative and popular with children.

Yad Vashem Holocaust History Museum (Sun–Wed 9am–5pm, Thur 9am–8pm, Fri 9am–2pm; free; tel: (02) 644 3802; www.yadvashem.org) is a striking memorial to the 6 million Jews massacred by Nazi Germany. Daring in its design, the museum is housed in a linear, triangular structure (basically, in the shape of a Toblerone container), which stretches for 160 meters (525ft) beneath the Jerusalem hillside. Only the apex of the structure is above ground, forming a skylight. The gray concrete walls intensify the harshness of the structure, which gashes brutally through the Jerusalem hillside. The new Yad Vashem uses the latest multimedia means to recount the dreadful history from 1933 to 1945. It typifies Israeli daring, and in this alone it is an eloquent and optimistic postscript to Europe's darkest hour.

Tower of David Museum of the History of Jerusalem (Fri-Sat 9am–2pm, Sun–Thur 9am–4pm, in

Easy navigation.

summer until 5pm and 10pm on Sun, Tue, and Thur; charge; tel: (02) 626 5333; www.towerofdavid.org.il), inside the body of the Citadel, contains displays describing the tumultuous history of the city, figurines of Jerusalem characters, a 19th-century model of the Old City, and the multi-layered ruins of the structure itself. A multimedia show with a separate entrance describes the various moods of Jerusalem via numerous slide projectors.

Tel Aviv

Museum of the Jewish Diaspora (Bet Hatefusoth) (Sun–Tue 10am–4pm, Wed–Thur 10am–7pm, Fri 9am–1pm; charge; tel: (03) 745 7808; www.bh.org.il) on the university campus. Founded in 1979, it was, when set up, in concept and methodology a radical departure from the accepted notion of a museum. Apart from a few sacramental objects, Bet Hatefusoth contains no preserved artifacts. Its principal aim is reconstruction. The body of the main exhibit is handled thematically, focusing on general themes of Jewish life in the Diaspora: family life, community, religion, culture, and the return to Zion. Its striking displays include a collection of beautifully intricate models of synagogue buildings from across the globe.

Eretz Israel Museum (Sun–Wed 10am–4pm, Thur 10am–8pm, Fri 10am–2pm, Sat 10am–3pm; charge; tel: (03) 641 5244; www.eretzmuseum. org.il). The museum comprises the most comprehensive storehouse of archaeological, anthropological, and historical findings in the region. Its spiritual backbone is **Tel Kasila**, an excavation site in which 12 distinct layers of civilization have been uncovered, with finds including an ancient Philistine temple and Hebrew inscriptions from 800 BC. The complex consists of 11 pavilions, including exhibits of glassware, ceramics, copper, coins, folklore, and ethnography, and a planetarium.

Tel Aviv Museum of Art (Mon, Wed, Sat 10am–6pm, Tue, Thur 10am–9pm, Fri 10am–2pm, ; charge; tel: (03) 607 7020; www. tamuseum.co.il), has four central galleries, an auditorium which often features film retrospectives, numerous other halls, a sculpture garden, a cafeteria, and a shop. There are exhibitions of 17th-century Dutch and Flemish masters, 18th-century Italian paintings, Impressionists, post-Impressionists, and a good selection of 20th-century art from the United

ACCOMMODATIONS EATING OUT ACTIVITIES A – Z LANGUAGE

States and Europe, in addition to modern Israeli work.

NIGHTLIFE

Nightlife starts late in Israel and is very vibrant. From 11pm onward, Israelis are out on the streets of Tel Aviv, and also in Jerusalem and virtually every Israeli city. Street-side cafes and restaurants are busy until well after midnight, and bars and nightclubs have a brisk trade right through the night. Because Friday and Saturday constitute the weekend, Thursday night is a big night out.

Tel Aviv seafront and other hotspots are crowded right through the night, and it is remarkable to see the traffic jams along the seafront promenade at 3am. Nightclubs abound in the main cities and resort towns. Many have regular floor shows, while others offer more informal entertainment. Rock, jazz, folk, and pop music are the usual fare. Jerusalem and Tel Aviv are the hotspots. Bohemian Florentin is another popular nightspot in Tel Aviv, as well as the newly renovated Tel Aviv Port and Old Yafo Port.

Tel Aviv

Abraxas
40 Lilienblum Street
Tel: (03) 510 4435
The Dome
30 Hatzfira Street
Tel: (03) 561 1022
Minerva
98 Allenby Street
Tel: (03) 560 3801
Popular gay club.
Nanuchka
28 Lilienblum Street
Tel: (03) 516 2254

Jewelry for sale in a Jerusalem market.

Jerusalem

Although lower-profile than that of Tel Aviv, Jerusalem's nightlife is certainly vibrant. This is especially true between April and October, when it is warm enough to stroll through the streets and sit outside at cafes and restaurants. The city's nightlife, as elsewhere in Israel, gets going after 10pm and the streets remain packed until well after midnight.

The Ben Yehuda Street Mall and adjacent pedestrian precincts at the bottom end of the street are especially busy. After 1am the focus moves over to the pubs and bars in the Russian Compound, on the north side of Yafo. The Talpiyot Industrial Zone is where most nightclubs and discos are located, but if you're over 30, you may feel out of place. More mature revelers should stick to the clubs and bars in the large hotels.
Mike's Place
Courtyard off 39 Yafo (Jaffa) Road, also accessible from Yoel Salomon Street
Tel: (02) 267 0753
Popular pub with labyrinth of different bars and outside seating. Also shows live soccer.
Yellow Submarine
13 Harekhevim Street
Tel: (02) 679 4040
Popular bar, disco, and live music venue in the Talpiyot Industrial Zone.
The Lab
28 Hebron Road
Tel: (02) 629 2000
Trendy disco on the renovated compound of the old train station also doubles as a small theater.

SHOPPING

Shops tend to open long hours, usually 9am–9pm, and even later on Saturday night. Shops are closed

Art galleries

The area around Gordon Street in Tel Aviv between Ben Yehuda and Dizengoff Streets is full of art galleries. Trendy Tel Aviv culture vultures will walk around the galleries at night as if they were public museums. This is acceptable behavior, and casual visitors will not be approached by eager sales staff. Another popular area with many art galleries is in Old Yafo near the Franciscan church.

Friday afternoons and Saturday during the day.

A strange thing has happened in Israel in recent years. If once consumer goods were far more expensive than in the US and Western Europe, this is no longer necessarily the case. Imported branded household items do still tend to be considerably more expensive than overseas, but many items, especially clothing, are comparable to prices of goods in Western Europe (though not usually North America), although the strengthening of the Israeli shekel in recent years has eroded this advantage. In any event, it is worth looking through major clothes stores when in shopping malls, including Castro, Golf, and Fox.

Otherwise, shoppers will be hunting for items that were always good value in Israel, such as exclusive jewelry and diamonds; Oriental carpets and antiques; fashionable women's wear and elegant furs; leather goods; paintings and sculptures; ceramics; silverware and copperware; embroidery and batiks, and of course religious requisites, particularly Judaica. Several hundred shops are approved by the Ministry of Tourism. These shops display a sign stating "Listed by the Ministry of Tourism" and the ministry's emblem (two scouts carrying a bunch of grapes on a pole between them), which is the symbol of quality merchandise. Try the G.R.A.S. chain for good-value arts and crafts gifts.

In addition, colorful Oriental markets and bazaars are found in the narrow alleyways of the old cities of Jerusalem, Bethlehem, Akko, Nazareth, and Hebron, and in Druze villages like Daliyat el-Karmel near Haifa. These sell handmade arts and crafts – including olive wood, mother-of-pearl, leather and bamboo items, hand-blown glass – and clothing, vegetables, and fruit.

Duty-free shops are located at Ben Gurion and Eilat Airports and at most of the leading hotels. Foreign-made articles such as watches, cameras, perfumes, tobaccos, and liquors, as well as many fine Israeli products, may be purchased with foreign currency for delivery to the plane or ship prior to departure.

Judaica
Besides these items, Israel has a unique variety of traditional crafts and Judaica for sale, ranging from religious articles like menorahs, mezuzot, and spice boxes to wall hangings and statuary. They range from loving reproductions to stark minimalism.

Centers for buying fine crafts include several locations in Jerusalem, among them the House of Quality, Khutsot ha-Yoster (Arts and Crafts Lane), Yochanan Migush Halav, and the Me'a She'arim area, the last for the best bargains while King David Street has the exclusive, upscale antique and Judaica stores.

Shopping areas

In the Old City of Jerusalem and other Arab marketplaces, bargaining is standard practice. Usually you can buy an item at 25 percent off by starting to haggle at half the quoted price. Avoid haggling if you are not really interested in buying or if an item is cheap. Brassware, carvings, and fabrics are among the more popular buys. The center of downtown Jerusalem is also full of souvenir and Judaica stores.

Other popular shopping places include the weekly Bedouin market in Be'er Sheva on Thursday mornings, the Druze markets in the north, such as Daliyat el-Karmel, and Nakhalat Binyamin in Tel Aviv, where artisans trade their wares on Tuesday and Friday, and of course Jaffa's flea market.

In the market of the Old City of Jerusalem, the Bedouin market and sometimes in smaller stores when buying jewelry or Judaica, bargaining is the name of the game. The storekeeper inflates the price and the shopper needs to bluff that the purchase is not very important and offer a far lower price. Poker players will do well here. It is always worth walking away in the hope that the storekeeper will call you back with a lower price. If he doesn't, then remember that the item you seek is probably available in other stores and you have had a useful first-round exercise in scouting out the price of the sought item. Bargaining is best done by those with patience.

Shopping malls
Malkha Shopping Mall, Malkha, Jerusalem, tel: (02) 679 3261.
Mamila Shopping Mall, Mamila, Jerusalem, tel: (02) 621 1111.
Azrieli Shopping Center, 132 Petach Tivah Road, Tel Aviv (by Hashalom Railway Station), tel: (03) 608 1199.
Dizengoff Center, cnr Dizengoff Street and King George Street, Tel Aviv, tel: (03) 525 1249.

Export of antiquities

It is forbidden to export antiquities from Israel unless a written export permit has been obtained from the Department of Antiquities and Museums of the Ministry of Education and Culture, Jerusalem. This applies also to antiquities that accompany tourists who are leaving the country. Antiquities proved to have been imported to Israel after 1900 are exempted. Antiquities are defined as objects fashioned by man before the year 1700. A 10 percent export fee is payable on the purchase price of every item approved for export.

The articles must be dispatched by post, with an accompanying cheque for the appropriate amount, or taken in person to: **The Department of Antiquities and Museums**, Rockefeller Museum, opposite Herod's Gate, POB 586, Jerusalem. It is advisable to telephone (02) 627 8627 for an appointment first.

VAT (sales tax)

After your passport has been stamped by customs, apply to Bank Leumi in the exit hall. A refund of VAT (value-added tax) of 16 percent is made at the point of your departure. However, you must make sure that:
The total net sum (after the 16 percent reduction) on one invoice is not less than US$50. The following items are not included in this scheme: tobacco products, electrical appliances and accessories, cameras, film and photographic equipment. The purchased items are packed in a plastic bag with at least one transparent side; the original invoice (white) is placed inside the bag in such a manner that the entries on it can be read; the bag is sealed or glued shut; the bag remains sealed during your entire stay in Israel.

When arriving at the departure hall on leaving the country, you must present the sealed bag with the purchased goods to customs for approval of refund.

After checking and placing the stamp of approval on the invoice, the customs official will direct you to the bank counter where the refund will be made in US dollars.

Note that Eilat is a VAT-free zone, and these regulations do not apply to goods purchased there.

Also, many hotels and stores will exempt you from VAT if you pay in foreign currency.

How to complain

Be persistent in arguing with shopkeepers if you have a complaint. You cannot expect a shopkeeper to respond to your problem if you do not articulate your grievance, and they are not accustomed to people accepting inferior goods or services without complaint. Be polite, but vocal. If all else fails, contact: **the Ministry of Industry, Trade and Labor's Consumer Protection Service**, 76 Maze Street, Tel Aviv, tel: (03) 560 4611.

SPORTS

Participant sports

Israel is an ideal place for sports enthusiasts. Here they will find excellent facilities and an opportunity to combine interests such as skin and scuba-diving, riding, tennis, golf, swimming, and skiing with a general tour of the country. The Mediterranean climate guarantees most outdoor sports year-round (the exception being snow-skiing, which is available only in winter).

Fishing equipment, both for angling and underwater, can be hired along the Mediterranean and the Red Sea, though the latter is now a protected area, with fishing permitted only in certain places.

Tennis and squash courts are available at a number of hotels.

There is a fine 18-hole **golf course** at Caesarea and a 9-hole course north of Herzliya at Gaash. You can find **horseback-riding** clubs throughout the country. During the winter, there is skiing on the slopes of Mount Hermon. Marches, races, and swimming competitions are organized by the Ha-Po'el and Maccabi sports organizations. The highlight of the year is the annual Jerusalem March, a highly organized event in which thousands of Israelis from all over the country, as well as overseas visitors, both individually and in groups, make a colorful and high-spirited pilgrimage to the capital. This event is usually held in April.

Sea safety

The Mediterranean shoreline, the Sea of Galilee, and the Red Sea are ideal for water sports: swimming, surfing, sailing, and water-skiing. Having said that, it is advisable to swim on beaches with lifeguards (most beaches have lifeguards from sunrise to sunset between April and October) and obey instructions. Beware the seemingly calm Mediterranean, which has a strong undercurrent and results in more than 100 drowning deaths each year. All the large hotels have swimming pools, and there are municipal or private pools all over the country.

July is jellyfish season, and while the stings are very painful they are not life-threatening. The pain from the stings is best soothed by rinsing with vinegar, although sea water also helps.

Biking

Bicycles can be rented in most cities, and cycling tours of the country can be arranged. Biking is especially popular in Tel Aviv, which has 120km (75 miles) of cycle tracks, including one along the length of the Mediterranean Promenade. There are 120 municipal biking stations, where it is possible to rent bikes using credit cards. Bicycles can be used free for up to 30 minutes after paying a small registration fee.. For queries or problems, tel: *6070 or go to www.tel-o-fun.co.il for maps of tracks and stations.

Golf
Caesarea Golf Club
Tel: (04) 610 9600
Gaash Golf Club
Tel: (09) 951 5111

Skiing
Mount Hermon Ski Site
Tel: (04) 698 1337

Sport for the disabled
Etgarim – Israel Outdoor Sports and Recreation Association for the Disabled.
Tel: (03) 561 3585
Israel Sports Center for the Disabled
Tel: (03) 575 4444

Water sports
The marinas in Tel Aviv, Herzliya, Eilat, Ashkelon, Ashdod, Haifa, and Akko offer yachting as well as sailing, while skin and aqualung diving are especially popular along the Gulf

of Eilat; centers at Eilat will rent equipment (to those with a valid international license) and provide instruction for those without.

Israel is truly a diver's paradise. Its mild climate ensures year-round diving in the crystal-clear waters of both the Mediterranean and Red Seas, where hundreds of miles of easily accessible coral reefs and spectacular seascapes await the diving enthusiast. A variety of diving experiences includes underwater photography, archaeological diving, grotto and cave diving. It should be noted that, unless divers have a two-star license, they must take a special diving course, though diving without a license can be done if you are accompanied by instructors.

Skin and scuba-diving courses
The courses for beginners last about five days and cover the theory of diving, lifesaving, physiology, physics, and underwater safety. The only qualifications necessary are the ability to swim, a certificate from a doctor confirming fitness to learn diving, and a chest X-ray. Beginners can also go out on individual introductory dives, lasting from 1–1.5 hours, accompanied throughout by an instructor.

It is possible to rent all the necessary skin and scuba-diving equipment at the following centers:
Eilat
For renting diving equipment or taking courses it is best to head for Coral Beach:
Aqua-Sport
POB 300, Eilat
Tel: (08) 633 4404
www.aqua-sport.com
Red Sea Lucky Divers
POB 4191, Eilat
Tel: (08) 632 3466
www.luckydivers.com
Tel Aviv
Octopus Diving Center
Tel Aviv Marina
Tel: (03) 527 1440
www.octopus.co.il

Spectator sports

Soccer is the number one spectator sport, with several matches every week. Israeli teams participate in the major European competitions. Basketball is also very popular, and Israelis are especially proud of the Maccabi Tel Aviv basketball team, which has won the European championship twice. There are many international matches during the winter season at stadiums in the Tel Aviv area.

Stadiums
The Ramat Gan National Soccer Stadium
POB 3591 Ramat Gan
Tel: (03) 570 9239
Nokia Arena Basketball Stadium
Yad Eliahu, Tel Aviv
Tel: (03) 527 2112

CHILDREN'S ACTIVITIES

Places of Special Interest for Children

The Israel Museum in Jerusalem (Sat–Mon and Wed–Thur 10am–5pm, Tue 4–9pm, Fri 10am–2pm; tel: (02) 670 8811) has a children's wing.
Bloomfield Science Museum (Mon– Thur 10am–6pm, Fri 10am–2pm, Sat 10am–4pm; tel: (02) 654 4888) is designed with children in mind.
Jerusalem Biblical Zoo is a must (Sun–Thur 9am–7pm, Fri 9am–4.30pm, Sat 10am–6pm; tel: (02) 6750 111).
Ramat Gan Safari Park: you can tour in your own car or take a guided tour (Sat–Thur 9am–4pm, Fri 9am–2pm; tel: (03) 630 5326).
Monkey Park at Ben Shemen Forest, near Ben Gurion International Airport (Sun–Thur 10am–5pm, Fri 9am–2pm, Sat 10am–3pm; tel: (08) 928 5888).
Tzapari, bird park in Tel Aviv's Yarkon Park, 80 Rokach Boulevard (Sun– Thur 10am–4pm, 5pm in summer, Fri 9am–3pm, Sat 10am–6pm; tel: (02) 642 2888).
The **Israel Opera** in Tel Aviv holds special weekly opera performances for children (tel: (03) 692 7777).
Mini Israel: Kids love the world's largest miniature model park (Sat– Thur 10am–6pm Nov–Mar, until 7pm Apr–May, Sept–Oct, until 8pm June, until 10pm July–Aug; Fri 10am–2pm; tel: 1-700-559-559).
Underwater Observatory Marine Park, Eilat – an absolute must to let kids see the wondrous marine life of the Red Sea (Sat–Thur 8.30am–5pm, Fri 8.30am–4pm; tel: (08) 636 4200).
There are two major funfairs in Israel: **Superland**, 5 Maryland Avenue, Rishon Lezion (Sat 10am–8pm and during school vacations; tel: (03) 642 7080), and **Luna Park**, Gan Yehoshua, Rokach Boulevard, Tel Aviv (Sat 10am–9pm and school vacations including July and Aug; tel: (03) 961 9065).
And of course the **beaches** (almost all of them free) are especially popular with children.

A – Z

A HANDY SUMMARY
OF PRACTICAL INFORMATION

A

Admission charges

The major museums are relatively inexpensive, charging an entrance fee of about US$8–9, with half price for children and senior citizens and reductions for students. The Israel Museum charges half price for repeat visits. The Yad Vashem Holocaust Museum is free. The Israel National Parks Authority, which runs the major archeological sites, charges US$6 admission fee, half price for children and senior citizens. It is well worth buying a ticket for the entire country's national parks for US$45. Tel: (02) 500 6261, or *3639 from within Israel. Most beaches are free.

B

Budgeting for your trip

Israel can be very expensive or quite cheap, depending on how you live. Modest accommodations start at US$50 a night and a luxury hotel might charge US$150 or even more. But you can find a youth hostel for just US$25 a night. Good negotiating skills can bring down prices considerably in all situations. A cheap meal in a restaurant is likely to cost US$8 or US$9, and a good meal with wine no more than US$30. Best value is a falafel in pitta bread and as much salad and chips as you want for just US$5. A flat-fare bus ticket in a city costs US$2.50, and the bus or train between Tel Aviv and Jerusalem is about US$6. The taxi between the two cities would cost US$35. A cinema ticket is US$12 (US$17 for a 3-D film).

C

Children

Israelis love children, who are expected to be seen and heard, and people should not feel threatened by the forward behavior of strangers in the street or on the next restaurant table. They are likely to engage in conversation with your child and offer all types of candies.
Eating: Restaurants, hotels, and cafes are very flexible in meeting children's fussy food needs, but tend not to have a formal child's menu. McDonald's, Burger King, Kentucky Fried Chicken, Sbarro, and Pizza Hut are always near at hand for kids who like familiar junk food.
Accommodations: Many hotels operate babysitting services and are very flexible in adding beds in the parents' room for a minimal rate for an additional child. Here, too, good negotiating skills and persistence can help.
Transportation: Children under 5 travel free on buses but thereafter pay full fare unless a multi-ride ticket is acquired. On the trains children under 5 go free and get a 20 percent discount between the ages of 5 and 10. Children under 4 must be harnessed into special seats when traveling in cars (except taxis).
Dangers to avoid: The Mediterranean Sea is deceptively calm. There is a strong undercurrent and more than 100 people are drowned each year, many of them tourists. Be sure to bathe when lifeguards are on duty (see page 340). Children are especially susceptible to the sun, particularly if they are fair-skinned. A high-factor

sunscreen can help, but it's prudent to keep children out of the sun and, while in the sun, in clothes that cover as much of the skin as possible. Dehydration is a major problem, and children should be encouraged to drink substantial amounts of water.

Climate

For a small country Israel has very diverse climate zones. Israeli summers are long (lasting from April to October), hot and virtually rainless. During these months Tel Aviv and the coast are humid (average 70 percent), while the atmosphere in hill towns such as Jerusalem is drier and cooler (average 30 percent). Because Jerusalem is in the hills, summer evenings can be pleasantly cool. The winter season (from November to March) is generally mild, but quite cold in hilly areas (close to freezing at nights). Spells of rain are interspersed with brilliant sunshine. During the

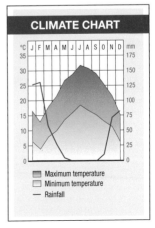

CLIMATE CHART

°C J F M A M J J A S O N D mm

■ Maximum temperature
□ Minimum temperature
— Rainfall

winter the Tiberias area on the Sea of Galilee, the Dead Sea, and Eilat (all searingly hot in summer) have ideal warm, sunny weather.

The weather allows for year-round bathing: from April to October along the Mediterranean coast and around the Sea of Galilee; and throughout the year, though especially enjoyable in winter, along the Dead Sea shore and the Gulf of Eilat.

When to visit

The best time to visit is early spring, when the hillsides are ablaze with flowers and the weather is still mild. Late autumn (November) is also very pleasant, while Eilat and the Dead Sea are best appreciated in the winter. The hot summers are strictly for those who enjoy high temperatures and know how to handle the heat (ie drink lots of liquid, use sunscreen, move slowly, and stay in the shade).

Annual rainfall

Jerusalem and Tel Aviv: 550mm (22 inches).
Galilee: 650mm (26 inches).
Eilat: 20mm (0.79 inches).

All rain falls between October and April, with most of it concentrated in December, January, and February.

What to wear

Dress in Israel is informal by Western standards. Few people wear jackets and ties in the summer, except for business occasions. However, even in the summer, Jerusalem can get quite cool in the evenings. Be sure to bring some conservative clothes for visiting religious sites. It is anyway recommended to keep arms, legs, and shoulders covered to prevent sunburn. Also, wear a hat for sun protection.

Suggested packing lists might include the following:
Summer (April to October): slacks, shorts, and open-necked shirts for men; plenty of light cotton daytime dresses and a slightly smarter dress for more formal occasions for women; light shoes, sandals and more solid shoes for touring; sunglasses, broad-brimmed hat, swimsuit, and beachwear; a light coat, jacket, or sweater for cool evenings in the hills.
Winter (November to March): warm coat, sweaters, raincoat and hat, walking shoes, overshoes; shirts, slacks, sports jacket; woolen or heavy suit, blouses, skirts, and slacks, long dress or evening skirt for women; lighter clothing and swimsuit for Eilat and the Dead Sea coast.

Crime and safety

Israel has a high rate of non-violent crimes (theft from homes, cars, other property, pickpocketing, etc), but relatively little violent crime (mugging, murder, and rape). Do not leave valuables in hotel rooms, or cars, or leave wallets sticking out of pockets. Take all the usual precautions.

In terms of violent crime the security situation is the most pressing problem, but incidents are few and far between. Under no circumstances leave unattended baggage lying around in a public place – police sappers will blow it up within a few minutes. You should report all suspicious packages.

Before taking trips to the West Bank or Gaza, you should ask about the prevailing security situation there. Phone **100** – Police

Drug Offenses: Hashish/marijuana is illegal, but prosecutions are rarely brought. Because neighboring Lebanon supplies much of the world's hashish, the drug is widely available in Israel, with peddlers frequenting bars. The use of heroin, also grown in Lebanon, is regarded much more seriously by the Israeli authorities, as are chemical drugs.

Customs and entry

The red–green customs clearance system is in operation at Ben Gurion Airport. Tourists with nothing to declare or bringing in the goods mentioned below may choose the Green Channel and leave the airport. Tourists bringing in other goods, even if they are exempt from duty, must use the Red Channel.

Green Channel

Every adult tourist may bring into the country, without payment of duty, the following articles, provided that they are for personal use: eau de Cologne or perfume not exceeding 0.2 liters (0.44 pint), wine up to 2 liters, and other alcoholic drinks not exceeding 1 liter; tobacco or cigars not exceeding 250 grams or 250 cigarettes; gifts up to US$200 in value, including assorted foodstuffs not exceeding 3 kg (6.5lb), on condition that no single type of food exceeds 1 kg (2.25lb).

Red Channel

Israel's customs authorities are having trouble keeping up with the proliferation of new technology, gadgets, and apps, so that according to official orders cellular phones

should be declared. In practise, anything from an iPhone and a laptop to a video camera that are clearly being used by the traveler can be taken through the Green Channel. However, if such items are not being used by the traveler and are meant as gifts to somebody in Israel, then they should be declared in the Red Channel and are subject to import duties and VAT.

Israeli customs also specify that portable work tools and diving equipment should be declared and are subject to import duties and VAT and/or guarantees.

Pets, plants and seeds, and of course weapons and large quantities of prescription drugs must also be declared and special approval is needed to take these items into Israel.

Note that gift parcels sent unaccompanied by post are also liable to VAT and import duties.

Customs deposits

The customs authorities are entitled to demand deposits or guarantees on any article brought in by a tourist or sent separately. This is usually enforced only for very expensive professional equipment or other costly items. The guarantees or deposits are returned to tourists when they leave the country and take the articles out with them. Since the formalities take some time, it is advisable to make all arrangements a day or two before departure, and preferably at the port of entry of the goods, so that the return of the guarantee can be carried out more conveniently.

For further information, contact: **The Department of Customs and Excise**, 32 Agron, POB 320, 91000 Jerusalem, tel: (02) 670 3333.

D

Disabled travelers

For a list of tourist services for the disabled, contact Yad Sarah: Yad Sarah House – Kiryat Weinberg, 124 Herzl Boulevard, Jerusalem 96187; tel: (02) 644 4444; www.yadsarah.org. This website lists those museums and other places that are accessible for those in wheelchairs.

There have been major efforts in Israel to make the country accessible for the disabled but, while intentions are good, they are not always put into practice. The country has very progressive legislation, and by law all municipalities must make all junction crossings (ramps on sidewalks) and public buildings accessible for the disabled. To help the blind, pedestrian crossings at traffic lights make a loud flicking noise when the light is green and pedestrians may cross. For information about disabled rights in Israel, see www.bizchut.org.il.

Public transport: For the most part inter-urban buses do not have access for the disabled, but urban buses do. In the past decade Israel Railways have bought rolling stock with low entry platforms for the disabled, but then built several new stations that have no access for the disabled.

Public buildings: Most museums and many public buildings in Jerusalem and Tel Aviv have wheelchair access but often spoil matters by having the odd stair requiring the disabled to request assistance.

E

Electricity

Standard voltage in Israel is 220 volts AC (single phase 50 cycles). Most plugs are three-pin, but in some instances can be two-pin. Adapters and transformers can be purchased throughout Israel.

Embassies and consulates

Jerusalem

UK Consulate General
19 Nashabibi, Sheikh Jarah
Tel: (02) 628 2545

Emergencies

In case of a serious accident or emergency, telephone for an ambulance **101** and/or police **100**. The Fire Service is **102**, and **103** is the emergency number for the electricity company. In such situations people are very helpful. Hotel receptionists or taxi drivers are obvious people to ask for help, but don't be afraid to stop passers-by in the street.

By dialing ***3888** from any phone, tourists can receive immediate answers and assistance regarding tourist services as well as assistance from the Israel Police, Ministry of Interior services, Airport Authority and more.

For emergencies, tel: (02) 541 4100.
Bet Ha'Omot Building
101 Hebron Road, 1st Floor, West Jerusalem.
Tel: (02) 671 7724
US Consulate
16 Agron
Tel: (02) 622 7200,
West Jerusalem.
27 Derekh Shkem
Tel: (02) 628 2452,
East Jerusalem.

Tel Aviv

Australian Embassy
37 Shderot Sha'ul ha-Melekh
Tel: (03) 695 0451
www.australianembassy.org.il
Canadian Embassy
3 Nirim Street, 63405
Tel: (03) 636 3300
Visa section, 7 Khavakuk ha-Navi
Tel: (03) 544 2878
www.canadainternational.gc.ca
Embassy of the Republic of South Africa
Dizengoff 50 (Dizengoff Tower)
Tel: (03) 525 2566
www.safis.co.il
Ireland
Tel: (03) 696 4166
UK Embassy
192 Ha-Yarkon, Tel Aviv 63405
Tel: (03) 527 8574
Consular Section, 1 Ben Yehuda
Tel: (03) 510 0166
For emergencies, tel: (03) 725 1222.
www.britemb.org.il
US Embassy
71 Ha-Yarkon,Tel Aviv 63903
Tel: (03) 519 7575
http://usembassy-israel.org.il

Etiquette

Israelis are very informal and do not take offense if people are curt. Dress code is very confusing in Israel. In Tel Aviv little is left to the imagination as everyone flaunts the maximum amount of flesh (not advisable for fair-skinned foreigners out in the sun). In Jerusalem and Arab locations it is advisable to dress very modestly. Arabs and Sephardi Jews are fussy about footwear. Shoes must be removed before entering mosques, and it is rude to put your feet up on tables or chairs. (See page 335.)

G

Gay and lesbian travelers

Homosexuality between consenting adults (aged 18 and over) became

legal in Israel in 1988, when the Law of Equal Rights in the Workplace was also amended to ban discrimination against gay people. Tel Aviv has a Community Center housing support and study groups, a library, and art gallery. Gay clubs abound in the city. The Hilton Beach is popular with the LGBT community as is Gaash Beach north of Herzliya. Jerusalem also has a gay scene, albeit smaller.

Useful Addresses

LGBTQ Center
Meir Park, Tel Aviv
Tel: (03) 525 2896/7
Jerusalem Open House
2 Hasoreg Street, Jerusalem Tel: (02) 625 0502
www.joh.org.il

Government

Israel is a democracy with a 120-member single-chamber Knesset (parliament) elected every four years by all citizens aged 18 and over. Seats are allocated by proportional representation. The president, elected every five years by a secret ballot of Knesset members, is a titular head of state, rather like the British monarch. After elections the president asks the leader of the largest party to become prime minister and form a government. Israel has no formal constitution, but the Supreme Court has the power to interpret Knesset legislation.

H

Health and medical care

There are no vaccination requirements for tourists entering Israel except if they are arriving from infected areas.

Israel has advanced healthcare services, with all Israeli citizens guaranteed medical attention by law. Visitors are advised to have medical insurance, as even the shortest stay in hospital and elementary surgery is likely to cost thousands of dollars.

With more than 30,000 physicians for a population of 7.9 million, the country easily has the highest per capita number of doctors in the world. Lists of doctors, dentists, and duty pharmacies are available from hotel receptions. A private consultation with a doctor is likely to cost US$30. If in pain, Israelis tend to be expressive. So if you are sitting in the emergency room of a hospital with an appendix that is about to burst, go ahead and yell. If you stoically play the strong silent type, then staff will tend to assume you are not really in pain and others will be treated before you.

By far the biggest health problem affecting visitors stems from a lack of respect for the sun. Sunburn and sunstroke afflict bathers, while dehydration plagues those who over-exert themselves sightseeing.

The first symptoms of dehydration are tiredness, headache, and lack of appetite. Advanced dehydration can express itself in unpleasant symptoms, from migraines and fever to diarrhoea and vomiting. Medication will not help. Recovery will come about through rest and sipping water, possibly with some salt added, though it is probably best to consult a doctor to ensure that the problem really is dehydration.

Upset stomachs are also common. Here, too, rest and a diet simply of water are the best medicine. Tap water is as drinkable as anywhere in the developed world, though mineral waters are available everywhere.

Aids: The number of cases of Aids in Israel is considerably lower than in the countries of Western Europe, but is nevertheless on the increase. The usual precautions should be taken. The Ministry of the Interior requires all visitors seeking to extend their stay beyond three months to take an Aids test.

Useful details

Phone **101** – Ambulance
To hire medical equipment contact Yad Sarah: Yad Sarah House – Kiryat Weinberg, 124 Herzl Boulevard, Jerusalem 96187; tel: (02) 644 4444; www.yadsarah.org

L

Left luggage

There are few left luggage facilities in Israel because of the security situation. One such 24-hour service is at Ben Gurion International Airport, tel: (03) 975 4436.

Lost property

Ben Gurion Airport, tel: (03) 975 4436.
El Al, tel: (03) 977 1111
Israel Railways, tel: (03) 693 7555
Egged Buses, tel: (03) 638 8924 or (02) 568 5670.
Otherwise phone the police: **100.**

M

Media

Television stations

The Israel Broadcasting Authority (IBA) has a 10-minute news bulletin in English (currently at 4.50pm) www.iba.org.il. Channels 2 and 10 are commercial stations, and then there is cable and digital television offered by two companies, Yes and Hot. These companies offer subscribers packages of up to 60 channels including Sky, BBC, Fox, and CNN.

Radio stations

The government-run Israel Broadcasting Authority (IBA), modeled on the BBC, has a comprehensive radio service broadcasting on six networks. On the foreign-language service there are English-language news bulletins several times a day, online at www.iba.org.il. Listen to the news on the REKA network at 6.30am, 12.30pm, and 8.30pm (local time) in the AM band on 954 kHz in the center and south of the country, and 1575 in the north; and on the FM band: Jerusalem 101.3 and 88.2; Tel Aviv 101.2; Be'er Sheva 107.3; Haifa 93.7; Upper Galilee 94.4. At 10pm, English news may additionally be heard on 88.2 FM in Jerusalem and parts of Central Israel. A recording of the latest news can be heard on the internet at www.israelradio.org.

Other Israeli stations include the BBC World Service (1323 KHz), Voice of America (1262 KHz), and Jordan's English-language radio station.

Print

Israelis are prolific newspaper readers. With several dozen daily newspapers and countless weekly and monthly magazines, they read more newspapers per head of the population than almost any other country in the world. Most of these newspapers are in Hebrew, the three largest being the afternoon journals *Yediot Ahronot*, *Ma'ariv*, and the *Yisrael Hayom* freesheet, which each sell over 600,000 copies of their Friday (weekend) edition. This is a very high number when you consider that there are only 8 million Israelis.

The *International Herald Tribune* is published daily in Tel Aviv, together with an English translation of the Hebrew daily *Ha'Aretz* (www.haaretz.

com), which has a left-of-center editorial line. This is Israel's best-quality newspaper.

The right-wing *Jerusalem Post* (www.jpost.com) is published in English six days a week (except Saturday). The Friday paper has an English listing of what's going on in the arts, music, theater, television, and radio. The paper also carries useful information about medical services, religious services, etc.

The *Jerusalem Report* (www.jrep.com) is an English-language magazine appearing every two weeks. It gives comprehensive news and features insights into Israeli life.

Dedicated news websites include www.timesofisrael.com and www.globes.co.il/serveen for business and technology news.

There is also a dynamic Arab press with more than 20 publications, including six dailies and six weeklies.

Money

Israel has no currency controls and tourists can bring in and take out as much money as they want.

Israel's currency is the New Israeli Shekel (NIS), which officially succeeded the old Israeli shekel in 1985. The shekel is divided into 100 agorot. Bills are issued in four denominations: 20 NIS (green with a portrait of former prime minister Moshe Sharett), 50 NIS (purple with a portrait of Nobel Prize-winner Shmuel Agnon or green with portrait of Shaul Tchernikovsky), 100 NIS (gray with a portrait of former president Yitzhak Ben Zvi) and 200 NIS (reddish-brown with a portrait of former president Zalman Shazar). Change comes in the bronze coins of 5 agorot, 10 agorot, 0.5 shekel, and silver coins 1 shekel, 2 shekels, 5 shekels, and 10 shekels (silver and gold).

A series of new notes is being issued over the next few years and the current notes are being phased out but remain legal tender. A green NIS 50 was issued in September 2014 with others to follow. www.newbanknotes.org.il/en/

Banks and **bureaux de change** are everywhere, and it is usually more convenient in terms of queues and bureaucracy to change money at one of them rather than elsewhere. Exchange rates are the same in all banks and bureaux de change. The NIS is stable and floats freely against the world's major currencies, with a revised exchange rate each day.

ATMs are everywhere. In the event of losing your card contact: Visa, tel: (03) 617 8800. MasterCard/Eurocard and Diners Club, tel: (03) 572 3666. American Express, tel: 1-800-877-877.

VAT on purchases of more than US$50 can be claimed back at Ben Gurion International Airport on presentation of a tax receipt.

Tipping

In restaurants, if a service charge is not included, then 10–15 percent is expected. Israelis do not tip taxi drivers, but drivers will expect a small tip from tourists. Hotel staff such as porters (bell hops) will be happy with a few shekels for each item of baggage. Hairdressers also expect a small tip.

O

Opening hours

Generally places are open Sun–Thur daytime and close Friday lunchtime through to Saturday night. Stores are open long hours, usually 9am–9pm Sun–Thur, but close at 2pm on Fridays and are closed Saturdays. Banks are open Sun–Thur 8.30am–1pm. Some branches stay open until 3pm and some are open in the late afternoon, 4–6pm on Mondays and Thursdays. Some branches open Friday morning, and all banks are closed on Saturday and some banks are closed Sunday. Places of entertainment are open until late. Bars are usually open until 3am. Restaurants usually stay open until at least midnight.

P

Postal services

Post offices have many branches and can be identified by a logo of a white stag leaping across a red background. Postboxes are red. Letters take 5–9 days to reach Europe and America. Express service

Time zone

Israel is at Coordinated Universal Time UTC (GMT) +2 – in other words 2 hours ahead of GMT in winter, and 1 hour in summer. Israel is 7 hours ahead of New York in winter, and 6 in summer.

takes half the time, and Super Express (which is very expensive) about one-third of the time.

Post office hours are 8am–12.30pm and 3.30–6pm. Major post offices are open all day. On Friday afternoon, Saturday, and holidays, post offices are closed all day.

Postcodes (zip codes)

Israeli addresses include a zip code of five numbers after the city and before Israel (if sent from abroad). Use of the zip code is not compulsory, but mail will arrive more swiftly if it is used.

Public holidays

The following Jewish festivals are also public holidays:
March/April: first and last days of Passover (Pesach).
May/June: Independence Day, Shavuot.
Sept/Oct: Jewish New Year (Rosh Hashanah); Yom Kippur, first and last days of Succot.
Note: The eve of a festival is like Friday, with most businesses, banks, post offices, etc closing at lunchtime.

T

Telephones

Israel's country code is **972** when phoning from abroad.

There are still some public phones in Israel, many of which accept pre-paid cards bought in post offices, or in some instances credit cards.

Within Israel

02- Jerusalem
03- Tel Aviv
04- Northern Israel
08- Southern Israel
09- Herzliya and Netanya
These are the dial codes for the landlines of Bezeq, the Israel Telecom Corporation, which is in the process of losing its monopoly on domestic calls. It should be stressed that national flat-rates are charged between area codes, and it is no more expensive to phone the north or south from Jerusalem than to phone within Jerusalem.

Telephone numbers made up of only a few digits preceded by an asterisk (for example Ben Gurion International Airport, tel: *6663) are shortcuts which can be dialled on cellphones from within Israel.

Six companies provide VOIP domestic calls: the recent

introduction of number portability for both landline and mobile phones means there is not necessarily any correlation between the number prefix and the company.
072 – Smile
073 – Netvision
074 – Orange
077 – Hot

Overseas calls

Some country codes:
11 US and Canada
44 UK
61 Australia
64 New Zealand
353 Ireland
27 South Africa
When phoning abroad use the following codes of international call providers, then the country code.
012 – Golden Lines/Smile
013 – Barak/Netvision
014 – Bezeq International
016 – Golan Telecom
017 - Hot
018 – Xfone
019 - Telzar
For details of tariffs, which should be no more than 6 or 7 cents a minute to Western Europe and North America, phone 1-800-012-012 for Golden Lines, 1-800-013-013 for Barak, etc. For collect calls, phone 1828 (Golden Lines), 1838 (Barak), and so on.

Phone books are available only in Hebrew, but call 144 for directory enquiries, or www.b144.co.il (businesses only, in English).

Other useful numbers

100 – Police
101 – Ambulance
102 – Fire Brigade
103 – Electricity
166 – Telephone repairs
199 – Telephone company information
Israel's four mobile/cellular phone providers claim to have 8.5million subscribers in a country of 8million.
050 – Pelephone
052 – Cellcom
053/057 - Hot
054 – Orange
055 22 – Home
055 66 – Rami Levy
055 88 - YouPhone
058 – Golan Telecom
059 – Jawwal (Palestinian)
Overseas cellular phones work in Israel provided you have made appropriate arrangements with your provider, and phones can be hired in Israel for about US$5 a day. Along the Jordanian border phones often flip over to the Jordanian mobile provider.

TRANSPORTATION
ACCOMMODATIONS
EATING OUT
ACTIVITIES
A – Z
LANGUAGE

Tourist offices

Outside of Israel
US
Tourism Commissioner for North America
Tel: 00-1-212-499-5650
Information center (general public):
Tel: 00-1-888-77-ISRAEL
Travel industry: 00-1-800-514-1188
www.goisrael.com
Los Angeles
Israel Government Tourist Office,
6380 Wilshire Blvd #1718
Los Angeles, CA 90048
Tel: (323) 658 7463
New York
Israel Government Tourist Office,
800 Second Avenue, New York,
10017
Tel: (212) 499-5650
Canada
Israel Government Tourist Office,
180 Bloor Street West,
Suite #700,
Toronto, Ontario M5S 2V6
Tel: (416) 964 3784/800-669-2369.
UK
180 Oxford Street,
London W1D 1NN
Tel: (020) 7299 1111

In Israel
Arad, Paz Gas Station
Tel: (08) 995 4160
Ben Gurion Airport
Tel: (03) 975 4260
Eilat, 8 Beit Hagesher Street
Tel: (08) 630 9111
Haifa, 48 Ben Gurion Street
Tel: 1-800-305090
Jerusalem, Jaffa Gate
Tel: (02) 628 0403
Nazareth, Casa Nova Street
Tel: (04) 675 0555
Netanya, 12 Ha'atzmaut Square
Tel: (09) 882 7286
Tel Aviv, Municipal Building,
Ibn Gbriol
Tel: (03) 521 8500
46 Herbert Samuel Street
Tel: (03) 516 6188
Tiberias, 23 Habanim Street
Tel: (04) 672 5666
All these offices are open Sun–Thur
8.30am–5pm, Fri 8.30am–noon.

Tour operators in Israel

Egged Tours
Tel: (03) 920 3992
Eshet Tours
Tel: (03) 608 6222
United Tours
Tel: (03) 617 3333

Travel agents

EMCO Travel, Jewish Travel
Tel: 00-1-877 466 2934 (toll free)
www.jewishtravelagency.com
Longwood Holidays
Tel: 00-44-20 8418 2522
www.longwoodholidays.co.uk

V

Visas and passports

Tourists are required to hold passports valid for Israel, which are valid for at least six months from the date of arrival. Stateless persons require a valid travel document with a return visa to the country of issue. Citizens of the USA, Canada, the European Union, Australia, and New Zealand do not need a visa to enter Israel, only a valid passport. For citizens of these countries, there are no special health requirements.

Financial restrictions
Unlimited amounts of money can be brought into and out of the country and freely converted to and from New Israeli Shekels (NIS). But sums of more than NIS80,000 (about US$20,000), which are converted or deposited in a bank, must be reported to the Bank of Israel within the framework of international regulations to prevent money laundering. Banks will provide appropriate forms.

Visa extensions
Those entering Israel on holiday can only stay for three months and are not allowed to work for money. Anyone wishing to enter the country for work, study, or permanent settlement must apply for the appropriate visa at an Israeli Diplomatic or Consular Mission before leaving their own country. Due to a rise in illegal workers in Israel, even visitors from North America and Western Europe may be refused entry if they do not have return tickets, sufficient funds for their stay, or an Israeli citizen prepared to vouch for them.

Entry and exit formalities
All visitors to Israel, including diplomats, are required to fill in an entry form, AL-17, upon arrival. This form should be supplied on the flight to Israel.
Visitors who intend continuing to Arab or Muslim countries (except Egypt and Jordan) after their visit to Israel should ask the frontier control officer to put the entry stamp on this form instead of in their passports, as they may subsequently be refused entry into countries hostile toward Israel if an Israeli stamp appears on the passport itself.

Extensions of stay
Tourists who wish to stay in the country for longer than three months must obtain an extension of stay. This applies also to citizens of those countries that are exempt from entry visas, and generally requires the stamping of your passport. The extension may be obtained through any district office of the Ministry of Interior – an appointment for this purpose must be made ahead of time.
The main offices are located at:
Jerusalem: General Building, 1 Shlomtsion ha-Malka, tel: (02) 629 0239 (Sun–Thur 10am–2pm).
Tel Aviv: Shalom Meyer Tower, Visa Department, 9 Akhad Ha'am, tel: (03) 763 2534 (Sun–Thur 8am–3pm).
Haifa: Government Building (opposite Municipality), 11 Hassan Shukri, tel: (04) 863 3349 or 863 3353 (Sun–Thur 1.30–3.30pm).

W

Websites

www.goisrael.com – official Israel Ministry of Tourism website.
www.goisrael.co.il – private company giving information about Israel.
www.aboutisrael.co.il – inspiring aerial photos of Israel.
www.parks.org.il – Israel's national parks website.
www.jerusalem.muni.il – Jerusalem municipality website.
www.timesofisrael.com – English language news
www.jpost.co.il – Jerusalem Post newspaper site.
www.haaretz.com – Ha'Aretz newspaper site.
www.tel-aviv.gov.il – Tel Aviv municipality site.
www.maven.co.il – Jewish web directory with comprehensive Israel section.
www.mfa.gov.il – Israel's Foreign Ministry.
www.cbs.gov.il – Israel's Central Bureau of Statistics.
www.globes.co.il/serveen – Israel's financial news in English.

רה ומלקוש ואספת דגנך ותיר שך ויצהר ך ונתתי
עשב בשדך לבהמתך ואכלת ושבעת השמרו לכם
פן יפתה לבבכם וסרתם ועבדתם אלהים אחרים
והשתחויתם להם וחרה אף יהוה בכם ועצר את

LANGUAGE

UNDERSTANDING THE LANGUAGE

HISTORY

Hebrew is the ancient language of the Old Testament, and is now spoken by the overwhelming majority of Israelis. Hebrew script is descended from Phoenician, which also gave rise to the Greek and ultimately the Roman and Cyrillic alphabets. With a lot of patience and persistence, it is just possible to make out the similarities with English letters. Even the names of Hebrew letters derive from their original pictorial meanings: alef and bet (which gave us the word "alphabet," via Greek) are, respectively, a bull's head and a house. The Hebrew language developed throughout biblical and early times but remained fixed thereafter until the late 19th century.

During the intervening period, Hebrew was used solely for ritual and scholarly purposes, and played no part in ordinary daily life. Hebrew is thus the only language of antiquity to have been truly resurrected after lying dormant for many centuries.

MODERN HEBREW

The modern language has uniform rules of grammar and pronunciation, though its vocabulary is eclectic and draws on the Bible, on the medieval languages of the Mediterranean, and on modern international scientific terminology. There is relatively little in the way of regional dialect, but Hebrew-speakers or their ancestors may have brought with them from other countries special words for cultural specialties, such as food, dress, and social customs.

Speakers of Hebrew from a Middle Eastern background tend to stress the guttural sound of some letters more than those of European descent. The Middle Eastern pronunciation is supposed to be the authentic ancient pronunciation.

Hebrew has a masculine and feminine form of "you" – which means that the sentence changes slightly depending on whether you are talking to a man or a woman. These differences are indicated as m/f in the vocabulary section below.

SPELLING

There is currently no standardized spelling of Israeli place names. Thus one has: "Acre," "Akko," and "Acco;" "Nathanya," "Natanya," and "Netanya;" "Elat," "Elath" and "Eilat;" "Ashqelon" and "Ashkelon;" "S'fat," "Zefat," "Tzfat," and "Safed," etc. As if to confuse the visitor deliberately, all such variations are used freely. This guide has attempted to standardize spellings, but do not be surprised if you come across many different versions of place names on maps and road signs.

USEFUL WORDS AND PHRASES

It is a good idea to know some basic Hebrew words and phrases before coming to the country. Deciphering the written language requires serious study, so we have provided simplified phonetic transcriptions, with emphases indicated in bold type.

Essential expressions

Yes *ken*
No *lo*
Okay *beseder*

Please *bevakasha*
Thank you *toda*
good *tov*
bad *ra*
and/or *ve/o-*

Greetings

(all-purpose) *shalom*
Good morning *boker tov*
Good evening *erev tov*
Goodnight *loyla tov*
Goodbye *lehitra-ot*
Sorry! *slikha*
Don't mention it *eyn be-ad ma*
Happy birthday *yom huledet same-akh*
Congratulations! *mazal tov*
Best wishes! *meytav ha-ikhulim*

Communication difficulties

Do you speak English? [m]: *ata medaber anglit* [f:] *at medaberet anglit*
I don't speak much Hebrew [m]: *ani lo medaber harbe ivrit* [f]: *ani lo medaberet harbe ivrit*
Could you speak more slowly? [m]: *tukhal ledaber yoter le-at* [f]: *tukhli ledaber yoter le-at*
Please write it down [m]: *bevakasha ktov et ze* [f]: *bevakasha kitvi et ze*
Can you translate this for me? [m]: *tukhal letargem et ze bishvli* [f]: *tukhli letargem et ze bishvli*
What does this mean? *ma zot omeret*
I understand *ani mevin* [f]: *mevina*
I don't understand [m]: *ani lo mevin* [f]: *mevina*
Do you understand? [m]: *ata mevin* [f:] *at mevina*

Emergencies

Help! *hatzilu*

Go away! *lekh mipo*
Leave me alone! *azov oti*
Stop thief! *ganav*
Call the police! *haz-ek-mishtara*
Get a doctor! *kra lerofe*
Fire! *srefa*
I'm ill *ani khole*
I'm lost *ta-iti baderekh*
Can you help me? *tukhal la-azor li*

Exclamations

At last! *sof sof*
Go on [m]: *tamshikh* [f]: *tamshikhi*
Nonsense! *shtuyot*
That's true *ze nakhon*
No way! *beshum ofen lo*
How are things? *eykh ha-inyanim*
Fine *tov*
Not bad *lo ra*
Not good *lo tov*
Terrible *nora*
You look great! *ata nir-e nifla*
Why's that? *madu-a ze*
Why not? *madu-a lo*

Everyday purchases

stamps *bulim*
envelopes *ma-atafot*
writing paper *neyar ktiva*
map *mapa*
book *sefer*
newspaper *iton*
magazine *magazin*
chocolate bar *tavlat shokolad*
matches *gafrurim*
pen *et*
how much? *kama?*

Sights

Old Town *ha-ir ha-atika*
ruins *ha-khoravot*
museum *ha-muze-on*
art gallery *galeriyat ha-omanut*
theater *ha-te-atron*
historic site *ha-atar ha-histori*
park *ha-park*

Eating out

Can you recommend a good restaurant? *tukhal lehamlitz al mis-ada tova*
inexpensive *zola*
cafe *beyt kafe*
restaurant *mis-ada*
Middle Eastern *mizrakhit*
Italian *italkit*
Chinese *sinit*
vegetarian *tzimkhonit*
pizzeria *pitzeriya*
steakhouse *mis-adat stekim*
soup *marak*
St Peter's fish *amnun*
cod *bakala*
trout *shemekh*

Problems with accommodations

I have a reservation *yesh li hazmana*
May I see the room? *efshar lir-ot et hakheder*
The air conditioning doesn't work *ha mizug avir lo po-el*
There is no hot water/toilet paper *eyn mayim khamim/neyar to-alet*
My room has not been made up *lo sidru et hakheder sheli*
There are insects in our room *yesh kharakim bakheder shelanu*
I've locked myself out of my room *sagarti et atzmi mikhutz lakheder*
I'd like to move to another room *ani rotze la-avor lekheder akher*
I'd like to speak to the manager *ani rotze ledaber im hamenahel*
Are there any messages for me? *yesh hoda-ot bishvili*

Payments

May I have my bill, please? *efshar lekabel et hakheshbon bevakasha*
I think there's a mistake in this bill *ani kkoshev sheyesh ta-ut bakheshbon*
Could I have a receipt, please? *efshar latet li kabala bevakasha*

salmon *iltit*
shrimp/prawns *khasilonim*
omelet *khavita*
eggs *beytzim*
beef *bakar*
chicken *of*
duck *barvaz*
lamb *tale*
liver *kaved*
kidneys *klayot*
carrots *gezer*
cabbage *kruv*
green beans *she-u-it yeruka*
peas *afuna*
mushrooms *pitriyot*
rice/pasta *orez/itriyot*
potatoes/fries *tapudim/chips*
fruit juice *mitz perot*
milk *khalav*
bread *lekhem*
butter *khem-a*
rolls *lakhmaniyot*
toast *tost*
honey *dvash*
jam *riba*
marmalade *ribat tapuzim*
lemon *limom*
mustard *khardal*
salt/pepper *melakh/pilpel*
sugar *sukar*
ketchup *ketchup*
mayonnaise *mayonez*
knife/fork *sakin/mazleg*
spoon *kaf*
plate *tzalakhat*
cup/glass *sefel/kos*
napkin *mapit*
Where are the restrooms? *eyfo hasherutim*
The bill, please *kheshbon bevakasha*

Drinks

beer *bira*
wine *yayin*
red/white *adom/lavan*
dry/sweet *yavesh/matok*
mineral water *mayim mineraliyim*
sparkling/still *toses/lo toses*

Travel

airport *nemal hate-ufa*
taxi *monit*
train *rakevet*
bus *otobus*
station/bus stop *takhanat*
one-way ticket *bekivun ekhad*
round trip *halokh vashov*
where is? *eyfo?*
right *yemin*
left *smol*
straight *yashar*

Colors

white *lavan*
black *shakhor*
red *adom*
pink *varod*
blue *kakhol*
yellow *tzahov*
green *yarok*

Numbers

zero *efes*
one *ekhad*
two *shnayim*
three *shlosha*
four *arba-a*
five *khamisha*
six *shisha*
seven *shiv-a*
eight *shmona*
nine *tish-a*
ten *asara*
hundred *me-a*
thousand *elef*
million *milyon*

Days

Sunday *yom rishon*
Monday *yom sheni*
Tuesday *yom shlishi*
Wednesday *yom revi-i*
Thursday *yom khamishi*
Friday *yom shishi*
Saturday *shabat*

FURTHER READING

BOOKS

Altneuland – Theodor Herzl. The Zionist visionary's dream of what a Jewish homeland might be like.

Beaufort – Ron Leshem. Graphic story about the horrific reality of war for young Israelis.

The Bible – This is where it all happened.

The Butcher's Theater – Jonathan Kellerman. A detective story set in Jerusalem.

The Case for Israel – Alan Dershowitz, America's leading defense lawyer, defends Israel's right to exist.

The Diary of Anne Frank – Helps the reader understand what makes Israelis tick.

Durable Peace – Benjamin Netanyahu, a different vision of the future of the Middle East.

Encyclopaedia Judaica – offers the most comprehensive information about Judaism and Israel.

Exodus – Leon Uris's novel that became an epic movie.

Fathers and Sons – Amos Eilon. Entertaining account of the Zionist founding fathers.

From Beirut to Jerusalem – Thomas L. Friedman's account of his time as a New York Times correspondent in Lebanon and then Israel.

Homecoming – Eshkol Nevo. Surprisingly good first novel by a young Israeli, which focuses on personal matters more than the Israel–Palestinian conflict. His second novel **World Cup Wishes** is even better.

The Little Drummer Girl – John Le Carré's Middle East novel.

Missing Kissinger – Etgar Keret, one of four collections of very short stories by a unique writer.

Murder on a Kibbutz – A Communal Case – Batya Gur. Part of a series of Israeli detective novels that also give a fascinating insight into the country's complex society.

My Michael – Amos Oz, Israel's leading contemporary novelist. Oz's other novels include **To Know a Woman, Elsewhere Perhaps**, and the autobiographical **A Tale of Love and Darkness**.

The New Middle East – Shimon Peres, the former Israeli prime minister's vision (often derided by the Right) of a peaceful Middle East.

O Jerusalem – Larry Collins. The history of Jerusalem brought alive through personal stories.

The Reluctant Bride – A.B. Yehoshua, Israel's leading contemporary writer.

The Source – James Michener, basing his story on an archeological site, Khatsor ha-Glilit, creates fictional accounts of what might have happened in a Canaanite/Israelite/Palestinian village down the centuries.

To Jerusalem and Back – Saul Bellow. About the late Nobel Prize winner's visit to Israel.

Warrior, An Autobiography – Ariel Sharon, the former prime minister who was transformed from warlord to peace maker.

The Wedding Canopy – Shai Agnon, the only Israeli winner of the Nobel Prize for literature.

The Yellow Wind – David Grossman, about Israel's occupation of the Palestinians. His latest novel **To the End of the Land** is a fictional story based on the death of his son in the Second Lebanon War in 2006.

FILMS

Ajami. Award-winning Israeli movie about Arabs and Jews in Jaffa which was nominated for an Oscar.

Beaufort. The movie of Ron Leshem's aforementioned book about Israel's occupation of Lebanon, also nominated for an Oscar.

Cast a Giant Shadow. Kirk Douglas wins independence for Israel in Melville Shavelson's 1966 movie.

Exodus. Paul Newman wins independence for Israel – Otto Preminger's 1960 filming of the Leon Uris novel.

Jesus Christ Superstar. Norman Jewison's poor 1973 version of the Tim Rice and Andrew Lloyd Webber musical was filmed by the Dead Sea and in the Judean Desert.

Lebanon. Director Samuel Maoz's film about his own experiences in the 1982 war won the Golden Lion award in Venice in 2009.

The Little Drummer Girl. George Roy Hill's 1984 version of John le Carré's novel had Diane Keaton being recruited by Mossad.

Raid on Entebbe. Yet more Israeli heroics in 1977 TV movie, with Peter Finch as Yitzhak Rabin.

Waltz With Bashir. Animated documentary about Israel's 1982 war in Lebanon, nominated for an Oscar for best foreign film in 2009.

CREDITS

Photo Credits

123RF 99, 157, 270, 293
Alamy 224B
Amos Gil 243B
AP/Press Association Images 220
AWL Images 280
Axiom 202MR
Bigstock 162, 191
Central Zionist Archives 39, 40, 42, 45, 47
Corbis 22, 38, 49, 93BR, 158/159T
Getty Images 8/9, 10/11, 12/13, 14, 20, 23, 24/25, 28, 30, 31, 36/37, 41, 46, 48, 53, 56, 57, 66, 68, 76, 79, 83, 85, 88, 94, 97, 98, 107, 116, 118, 119, 146/147, 228, 233, 253, 255, 262/263, 266
IDF 54
Israel Tourism 112/113, 198, 199T, 200, 205, 206, 207, 218T, 277, 278, 279, 297T, 299, 307, 311B
Isreali Government Press Office 51, 52
iStock 1, 2/3, 4M, 6B, 27B, 35, 55, 65, 71L, 73, 74, 75, 77, 78, 80, 81, 82, 86, 87, 89, 93BL, 95, 109, 111, 114, 115, 132/133B, 140, 141T, 144, 153, 154, 158BR, 158BL, 159BR, 159BL, 166, 167, 168, 169, 170T, 174, 182B, 183, 185, 188B,

194, 196/197, 201, 202/203T, 202BL, 203B, 204, 208, 209T, 209B, 215B, 219, 226, 227, 230B, 235, 237, 250T, 254, 256, 257, 259B, 265T, 265B, 269, 271B, 272T, 272B, 273, 274, 275, 276, 283, 290/291T, 297B, 306B, 310, 313T, 314, 315, 316, 331TL, 347, 349
Leonardo 165, 332
Library of Congress 44
Mini Israel 260BR, 261ML, 261TR
Nowitz Photography/Apa Publications 4BR, 4ML, 4BL, 5B, 5TR, 5ML, 5TL, 5ML, 5MR, 6T, 7TL, 7ML, 7B, 15T, 15B, 16T, 16B, 17, 18, 19, 21R, 21L, 26, 27T, 33, 34, 50, 58/59, 60, 61, 62R, 62L, 63, 64, 67, 69, 70, 71R, 72, 84, 90R, 90L, 92/93T, 92BR, 92BL, 93ML, 93TR, 96, 100, 101, 102, 103, 104, 105, 108, 110, 117L, 117R, 120/121, 122/123, 124/125, 126, 127T, 127B, 130, 131, 132T, 134, 135, 136, 137, 139, 142T, 142B, 143, 145T, 145B, 146T, 146B, 148, 149B, 149T, 150, 151, 152, 155, 156B, 156T, 163, 159TR, 170B, 171, 172, 173T, 173B, 175, 176, 177, 180, 181, 182T, 184, 188T,

189, 190, 192, 193, 195B, 195T, 199B, 202BR, 203ML, 203TR, 210, 211, 212, 213, 215T, 216T, 216B, 217, 221, 223T, 224T, 225, 230T, 231, 232, 234, 238, 239, 240, 241, 242, 243T, 244, 245T, 245B, 246, 247, 248B, 249, 250B, 251T, 258, 260BL, 260/261T, 261BR, 261BL, 264, 267, 271T, 281, 282B, 282T, 284T, 284B, 285, 286, 287, 288, 289, 290BL, 290BR, 291ML, 291BR, 291BL, 291TR, 292, 295, 296, 298, 300, 301, 302, 303, 304, 305, 306T, 308T, 308B, 309, 311T, 312, 318, 319, 321, 323, 324, 325, 326, 328, 329, 330, 331BL, 333, 334, 337, 338, 341
P. Lavon Institute for Labor Research 43
Pictures Colour Library 159ML
PikiWiki 251B
Public domain 29, 32, 106
Robert Harding 164/165
Ron Henzel 252
SuperStock 91, 186/187, 218B, 229
Talmoryair 223B, 248T
Xinhua/Photoshot 141B
Yadid Levy/Apa Publications 313B

Cover Credits

Front cover: Old City of Jerusalem *Corbis*
Back cover: (top) Tel Aviv beach *Nowitz Photography/Apa Publications*; (middle) shepherd *iStock*

Front flap: (from top) Eilat *iStock*; man in Mea Shearim *iStock*; Caesarea, *iStock*; tourists enter Church of St. Catherine *iStock*
Back flap: men praying *iStock*
Spine: shekel *123RF*

Insight Guide Credits

Distribution
UK
Dorling Kindersley Ltd
A Penguin Group company
80 Strand, London, WC2R 0RL
sales@uk.dk.com

United States
Ingram Publisher Services
1 Ingram Boulevard, PO Box 3006,
La Vergne, TN 37086-1986
ips@ingramcontent.com

Australia and New Zealand
Woodslane
10 Apollo St, Warriewood,
NSW 2102, Australia
info@woodslane.com.au

Worldwide
Apa Publications GmbH & Co. Verlag
KG (Singapore branch)
7030 Ang Mo Kio Avenue 5
08-65 Northstar @ AMK
Singapore 569880
apasin@singnet.com.sg

Printing
CTPS-China
© 2015 Apa Publications (UK) Ltd
All Rights Reserved

First Edition 1992
Eighth Edition 2015

www.insightguides.com
Project Editor
Sarah Clark
Author
Simon Griver
Picture Editor
Tom Smyth
Map Production
Original cartography Colourmap Scanning Ltd, updated by Carte Warsaw
Production
Rebeka Davies

Legend

City maps

Regional maps

Contributors

This new edition of Insight Guide Israel was commissioned by **Tom Stainer** and edited by **Sarah Clark**. The book has been comprehensively revised by **Simon Griver**, British-born but resident in Israel since 1978. His authoritative journalism is much in demand in the UK and the US. Even after so long in the country, he still values "the year-round sunshine, the exotic desert landscapes, and the informality of the people".

Israel's recent turbulent history meant that Griver needed to rewrite sections of the book, but significant portions of text remain from the specialist writers whose in-depth knowledge made past editions of the book so valuable to readers. They include **Geoffrey Wigoder, Walter Jacob, William Recant, Helen Davis, Barbara Gingold, Mordechai Beck, Asher Weill, Nancy Miller, Matthew Nevisky, Michal Yudelman, Daniel Gavron, Muriel Moulton, Leora Frucht, Bill Clark**, and **Amy Kaslow**.

Most of the stunning images are by photographer-cum-filmmaker **Daniella Nowitz**, a part-time Israeli resident, and her father **Richard Nowitz**.

About Insight Guides

Insight Guides have more than 40 years' experience of publishing high-quality, visual travel guides. We produce 400 full-colour titles, in both print and digital form, covering more than 200 destinations across the globe, in a variety of formats to meet your different needs.

Insight Guides are written by local authors who use their on-the-ground experience to provide the very latest information; their local expertise is evident in the extensive historical and cultural background features. All the reviews in **Insight Guides** are independent; we strive to maintain an impartial view. Our reviews are carefully selected to guide you to the best places to stay and eat, so you can be confident that when we say a restaurant or hotel is special, we really mean it.

INDEX

Main references are in bold type

Travel guides, ebooks, apps and online
www.insightguides.com

INSIGHT GUIDES

INSPIRING YOUR NEXT ADVENTURE

Insight Guides offers you a range of travel guides to match your needs. Whether you are looking for inspiration for planning a trip, cultural information, walks and tours, great listings, or practical advice, we have a product to suit you.

www.insightguides.com

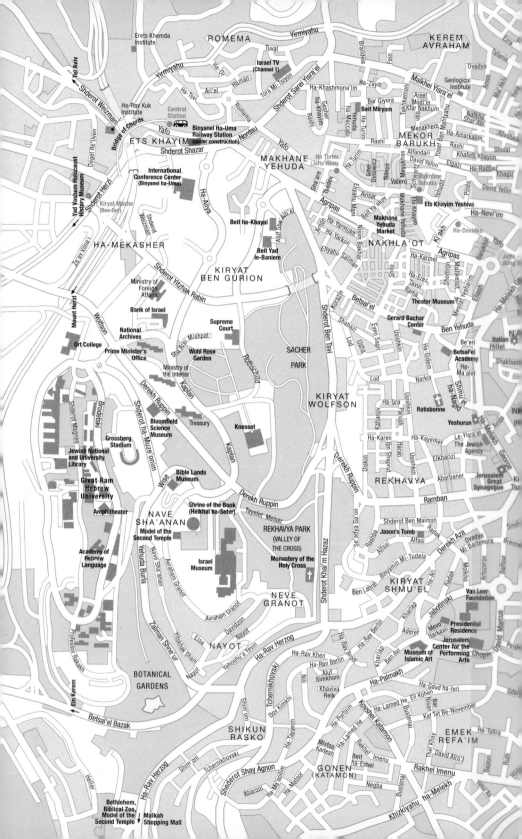